T0326565

The Emergence of Developmental States
from a New Institutionalist Perspective

Emerging Markets Studies

Edited by Joachim Ahrens, Alexander Ebner, Herman W. Hoen,
Bernhard Seliger and Ralph Michael Wrobel

Vol. 2

PETER LANG

Frankfurt am Main · Berlin · Bern · Bruxelles · New York · Oxford · Wien

Manuel Stark

The Emergence of Developmental States from a New Institutionalist Perspective

A Comparative Analysis
of East Asia and Central Asia

PETER LANG
Internationaler Verlag der Wissenschaften

Bibliographic Information published by the Deutsche Nationalbibliothek
The Deutsche Nationalbibliothek lists this publication in the Deutsche Nationalbibliografie; detailed bibliographic data is available in the internet at http://dnb.d-nb.de.

Zugl.: EBS Universität für Wirtschaft und Recht, Univ., Diss., 2012

Cover Design:
Olaf Gloeckler, Atelier Platen, Friedberg

D 1540
ISSN 2190-099X
ISBN 978-3-631-63882-8
© Peter Lang GmbH
Internationaler Verlag der Wissenschaften
Frankfurt am Main 2012
All rights reserved.

www.peterlang.de

Acknowledgement

Writing this dissertation has been one of the most interesting and most challenging tasks of my life and I want to thank several persons who have supported me over the last years. First and foremost, my thanks go to my Doktorvater Prof. Dr. Joachim Ahrens, who has contributed to my work in innumerable ways. Prof. Ahrens gave me the freedom to pursue my own ideas whenever possible and provided me with guidelines to achieve my objectives whenever necessary. Furthermore, I would like to thank my second supervisor, Prof. Dr. Florian Täube, for sharing his insight and advice, in particular on methodological issues, with me.

The dissertation has benefitted extensively from two research projects that I was involved in. Beginning in 2007, I worked as a researcher in the project *Emerging Market Economies in Central Asia*, funded by the Volkswagen-Stiftung. Through this project, I was able to travel several times to Central Asia in order to conduct some of the interviews that serve as the analytical base for the empirical part of this dissertation. However, most of the interviews were conducted by my colleagues Roman Vakulchuk, Farrukh Irnazarov, Zafar Salmanov, and Gerhard Töws, whom I thank for their contribution. On the other hand, I was involved in beginning in 2010 in the project *Institutions and Institutional Change in Post-socialist Countries*, funded by the Bundesministerium für Forschung und Entwicklung. Apart from granting me financial support, this project enabled me to meet young researchers from other disciplines, which was a major benefit for my work.

In addition to my supervisors, I want to thank Prof. Martin Spechler from Indiana University, Prof. Richard Pomfret from the University of Adelaide, Prof. Alexander Libman from the Frankfurt School of Finance, and Manuela Troschke from the Osteuropa Institut for their important contributions the project *Emerging Market Economies in Central Asia* and to my research. Furthermore, I want to thank several organizations in Central Asia that supported this research project, namely the GIZ and the Chamber of Commerce in Uzbekistan and the KIMEP in Kazakhstan. In particular, I want to thank Sevilya Muradova and Shameer Khanal from the GIZ and Prof. Dixon from the KIMEP for their cooperation and help.

Finally, I want to thank my family, my girlfriend Katia, and my friends who shared both happy and difficult moments over the last years and where a tremendous source of encouragement and motivation. I dedicate this book to them.

Manuel Stark   Marburg, 15 July 2012

Foreword

Economists, political scientists, and development practitioners have offered numerous convincing explanations of why development projects often fail or policy and institutional reforms are implemented only half-heartedly and do not materialize as expected. In fact, empirical research confirms that the vast majority of less or least developed countries experienced a slow or highly volatile economic growth performance over the last sixty years. Only a few countries managed to sustainably grow over a long period of time with only minor or short recessions, but with social progress and significant reductions in poverty. Almost all of these high-performing economies are located in East Asia.

This book is dedicated to these so-called developmental states. The study addresses the question why and how successful economic catching-up processes could be realized. The author applies Chalmers Johnson's developmental-state approach and improves its theoretical foundation so that it gains explanatory power and becomes applicable to a greater variety of research questions. This approach, located at the interface of economics and politics, is being theoretically founded by linking it to Douglass C. North's theory of institutional change. Thereby, the author is able to explain success and failure of economic reform and catching-up processes by accounting for the importance of political, economic, and social institutions, formal as well as informal ones, in political settings in which governments assume an active role in shaping and conducting economic policies.

Confronting the reader with detailed, comprehensive case studies of developmental states in Asia, Manuel Stark persuasively argues that the state has been always an important part of the solution for problems of economic backwardness and underdevelopment. Sometimes, the state has even proven to be the driving force. Since this book identifies the institutional conditions under which states can effectively assume more active roles, its theoretical framework can be applied to a great variety of less developed countries and emerging market economies. This is being done exemplarily for Kazakhstan and Uzbekistan, the two most important Central Asian transition countries, which, in a non-democratic setting, have performed economically well over the last decade.

This book is a differentiated, critical, theoretically well-founded analysis of developmental states in Asia. Economists, political scientists, and sociologists as well as actors in the policy-making community will greatly benefit from reading the book and learning about its case studies. The work considerably improves our understanding of the importance of institutional constraints for economic development and how to politically shape them in order to make economic growth and social progress a viable policy choice. Most important new insights relate to the research into comparative economic systems and the historical and comparative analysis of institutions.

Joachim Ahrens (editor)   Göttingen, 12 June 2012

Table of contents

List of Abbreviations

BOT	Board of Trade (Japan)
CEPD	Council for Economic Planning and Development (Taiwan)
CIS	Commonwealth of Independent States
EBRD	European Bank for Reconstruction and Development
EDB	Economic Development Board (Singapore)
ENRC	Eurasian Natural Resource Company (Kazakhstan)
EPB	Economic Planning Board (South Korea)
ESB	Economic Stabilization Board (Japan)
FIC	Foreign Investor's Council (Kazakhstan)
GATT	General Agreement of Tariffs and Trade
GLC	Government-linked Company
HCIA	Historical and Comparative Institutional Analysis
HICOM	Heavy Industries Corporation of Malaysia
HPAEs	High-performing Asian Economies
IDB	Industrial Development Board (Taiwan)
KMT	Kuomintang
LDP	Liberal Democratic Party of Japan
MCI	Ministry of Commerce and Industry (Japan)
MITI	Ministry of International Trade and Industry (Japan)
NIE	New Institutional Economics
NJPPCC	National Joint Public and Private Sector Consultative Committee (Thailand)

NPE	New Political Economy
OECD	Organization for Economic Cooperation and Development
PAP	People's Action Party (Singapore)
QCA	Qualitative Content Analysis
SCAP	Supreme Commander for the Allied Powers
UMNO	United Malays National Organization

List of Tables

List of Figures

1 Introduction

1.1 Research scope

1.1.1 Central Asia after 20 years of transition

In the scientific literature on the political and economic development of Central Asia, there are few historical events that are referred to as frequently as the "Great Game". This term stands for the rivalry over the control of the region between the British and Russian Empires that started at the beginning of the 19th century and lasted for approximately 100 years. In earlier centuries, Central Asia had been among the scientifically, culturally and economically most advanced regions in the world. However, the khanates that ruled over the Central Asians at the beginning of this Great Game were far from being on par with the European powers regarding economic, technological or military aspects. Central Asia was not an active player in the Great Game, it was its target.

For those that inhabit the five countries of Central Asia—Kazakhstan, Uzbekistan, Turkmenistan, Kyrgyzstan and Tajikistan—the Great Game ended with Russian and later Soviet domination. The following decades of foreign rule had a profound impact on the region's economy and culture. Today, more than two decades after the collapse of the Soviet Union, both scholars and political journalists have started to write about a new great game in Central Asia with different contenders, in particular China and the United States (see Edwards, 2003; Klevemann, 2003; Menon, 2003; and the articles in the collective volume of Laruelle, Huchet, Peyrouse, & Balci, 2010). Yet, maybe the biggest difference between the current power struggle and the situation in the 19th century is not that more or different powers have joined the contest, but that the Central Asian republics themselves have become active participants and are able to choose their path of development within certain constraints.

Since the region has always been at the intersection of various cultural and political influences, it is extremely difficult to foresee which path its development might take. Russia, bordering Central Asia to the north, still maintains close relations with the former Soviet Republics. Russia remains influential, especially in northern Kazakhstan and Kyrgyzstan, which are home to large Russian minorities. With its southern neighbors—Iran, Afghanistan and Pakistan—Central Asia shares a common cultural, religious and historical heritage that predates Russian influence. To the east, Kazakhstan, Kyrgyzstan and Tajikistan have a common border with China, whose thriving economy has made it more influential over the last years. To the west, the region is delimited by the Caspian Sea with its rich oil reserves. Furthermore, the region is geographically close to Turkey, whose language is closely related to the languages of four of the five Central Asian countries,[1] and Eastern Europe, which shares the challenge of post-communist transition with Central Asia.

As the most recent transition indicators of the European Bank for Reconstruction and Development show, the market-oriented reforms undertaken by the Central Asian governments since the dissolution of the Soviet Union have not led to the emergence of a full-fledged market economy in any of the republics (EBRD, 2011). Whereas the transition from a command economy to a market economy has progressed well in Eastern Europe, Central Asia is lagging behind. It is reasonable to argue that this outcome is at least partly due to different historical and geopolitical conditions that the Central Asian republics faced when they became independent. When Russia and the former communist countries of Central and Eastern Europe began the transition, it was apparent that the Western market economies would serve as the main reference model for the reform process. For the smaller European countries, which had the prospect of becoming members of the European Union, both the reform path and its objective were clearly defined through the *acquis communautaire*, which assured the commitment of the political decision makers to the reforms (Ahrens, 2002, pp. 306–318). Russia also started the transition by implementing political and economic reforms that were largely consistent with the Western model of a liberal capitalist democracy (Ahrens, 1994, pp. 74–96), even though in recent years Russia has distanced itself more and more from the West.

The conditions for transition in Central Asia differed significantly from Eastern Europe and Russia in the 1990s and they continue to differ even today. The five republics were among the poorest and least industrialized parts of the USSR (Pomfret, 2003, p. 34), and had the task of supplying agricultural goods and raw materials to the Soviet economic system. In contrast to most other countries of the former Eastern Bloc, the transition in Central Asia takes place under non-European and non-democratic conditions. Political reforms that preceded the transition toward market economies in Eastern Europe are unlikely to take place soon in most of the Central Asian countries.[2] The region is both geographically and culturally more distant from the West than Eastern Europe and

---

1   Uzbek, Kazakh, Kyrgyz and Turkmen are Turkic languages, whereas Tajik is a variety of the Persian language.

2   Kyrgyzstan is the notable exception. In 2010, President Kurmanbek Bakiyev, who had come to power after the Tulip Revolution in 2005, was overthrown after domestic unrest. Democratic elections took place in early 2011, which resulted in the victory of the pro-Russian political leader Almasbek Atambajew (Bidder, 2011).

Russia. These factors not only lead to different constraints and incentives for political decision makers in Central Asia, but also result in more difficulties in accessing the European market. The fact that all Central Asian republics are landlocked additionally inhibits the access to potential export markets. Recommendations and reform approaches that served as the basis for the economic transition in other former communist countries may not be valid under the current conditions in Central Asia. Therefore, there is no apparent reference model for Central Asia, yet it is reasonable to take a broader perspective and to analyze not only the institutional settings of the liberal democracies of Western Europe and North America, but also the institutions of other successful economies.

1.1.2 The East Asian miracle and its relevance for Central Asia

There are extremely few examples of non-Western economies that were able to achieve sustainable economic growth over a long period of time. When looking for countries beyond Western Europe and North America that could serve as reference models for successful industrialization, the leading example is clearly East Asia, where most of the remarkable economic success stories have taken place.

The first country to be mentioned in this context is Japan. At the height of imperialism in the 19th century, Japan was at the verge of being colonized by Western powers (Kohli, 1999, p. 100). Partly triggered by this imminent danger, drastic political changes took place in the course of the Meiji Restoration in 1868. Over the following decades, rapid modernization and industrialization was successfully pursued under the slogan "rich country, strong military" (Johnson, 1982, p. 20). After the devastating defeat of the Second World War, the economy in the after-war period showed another impressive growth performance, known as the Japanese miracle. By the second half of the 20th century, Japan had surpassed most Western countries to become the world's second largest economy behind the United States.

In the 1960s, Japan was joined by other East Asian economies in the process of catching up with the most advanced economies. The four *East Asian Tigers*, South Korea, Taiwan, Singapore, and Hong Kong, began a process of rapid industrialization and economic growth. This process was sustained over decades, resulting in a drastic increase of their societies' standard of living. During the 1980s and early 1990s, yet another group of East Asian economies—Malaysia, Thailand, and Indonesia—had begun to follow a similarly successful path of development. All eight countries, collectively referred to as the *high-performing*

Asian economies (HPAEs), received unprecedented attention in economic research. The notion of an East Asian economic miracle had become widespread, as is apparent from publications such as the World Bank's "The East Asian Miracle: Economic Growth and Public Policy" (1993) or "The Key to the East Asian Miracle: Making Shared Growth Credible" by Campos and Root (1996).

In light of Japan's drastic economic slowdown in the 1990s and the East Asian economic crisis of 1997 and 1998, economists and other analysts have become more critical of the accomplishments of the HPAEs. Already in his 1994 "Myth of the Asian Miracle," Nobel laureate Paul Krugman noted that forecasts assuming that the HPAEs impressive economic growth would continue indefinitely were naïve: "Rapid Asian growth is less of a model for the West than many writers claim, and the future prospects for that growth are more limited than almost anyone now imagines" (p. 64). He based this assertion on the observation that most of the economic growth in East Asia could be explained by an astonishing mobilization of productive factors, which would not continue indefinitely (Krugman, 1994, pp. 69–75; see also Young, 1995, pp. 671–675). When the Asian Crisis of the late 1990s seemed to show that the East Asian miracle was indeed over, the attention of both the public and academia began to shift toward other emerging economies. The People's Republic of China immediately became the center of attention, along with other countries such as India and Brazil. Due to the dynamic economic development of these countries and their large populations, they seem to pose a more serious threat to the Western economic domination.

However, this shift of attention of public and scholarly perspectives on the HPAEs is only partly justified. As Table 1 shows, six of the ten fastest growing economies of the second half of the 20th century belong to the group that the World Bank subsumed as HPAEs in 1993 (World Bank, 1993, p. I).[3] This period includes Japan's *lost decade* of the 1990s as well as the break-down of economic growth that several newly industrializing economies suffered from in 1998. The central accomplishments of the most successful among the high-performing Asian economies lie both in the achievement of high rates of economic growth and in the ability to sustain high growth rates over a long period of time. Japan's GDP per capita in purchasing power parity has risen from a fifth of the American value in 1950 to more than 73% in 2008 (it amounted to more than 80% in 1990 before growth began to slow).[4] South Korea and Taiwan

---

3   The HPAEs that do not appear on the list, Malaysia and Indonesia, rank 20th and 28th, respectively.
4   Own calculations based on Maddison (2010).

raised their per capita GDP in purchasing power parity from less than 11% (South Korea) and 12% (Taiwan) of the American value to more than 60% in 2008; Singapore and Hong Kong have achieved a similarly impressive catch up.[4] As a result, South Korea and Taiwan have shifted from the status of developing countries to that of advanced economies within 40 years. While Krugman's statement that the rapid growth of these East Asian economies does not represent a model for the economically advanced Western countries may be true, this does clearly not mean that there are no lessons to be learned from East Asia for developing and emerging economies.

Table 1: Ranking of countries by real GDP per capita growth (PPP) 1950–2000

Rank	Country	Compound annual real growth rate 1950–2000 [%]	Cumulated real growth 1950–2000 [%]
1	Taiwan	6.00	1742.4
2	South Korea	5.81	1583.4
3	Equatorial Guinea	5.45	1322.2
4	Botswana	5.05	1071.9
5	Oman	4.99	1041.5
6	Japan	4.87	979.7
7	Hong Kong	4.82	951.7
8	Singapore	4.74	914.8
9	Thailand	4.20	683.0
10	China	4.15	663.5

Source: Own calculation based on Maddison (2010. Data available for 172 countries and political entities.

The virtually unprecedented economic success of the HPAEs did not go unnoticed by the political leaders that came to power in the newly independent Central Asian republics in the 1990s. When President Nursultan Nazarbayev announced the *Strategy 2030* in his "Message of the President of the country to the people of Kazakhstan" in 1997, he made the importance of the East Asian success for Kazakhstan explicit:

> Many of you know that some of the poorest countries in Asia extricated themselves of poverty within some thirty years to turn into prosperous industrial states. Korea, Taiwan and Singapore were pioneers, so say, followed by Malaysia, Indonesia and Thailand. (….)

> Forty years ago when Singapore gained its independence, it was one of the poorest countries in the world with an annual per capita income less than $200. Today the per capita income of Singaporeans exceeds $20,000. Malaysia, a country similar to

ours with respect to the population, ethnic composition and many other parameters, gained a 10-fold rise in living standards of its citizens within less than twenty years. Such staggering achievements made these countries world famous assigning them the name of Asian Tigers. Are there any obstacles which might prevent Kazakhstan availing of fine opportunities from scoring the same success? None whatsoever. (....)

I, for my part, am sure that by the year of 2030 Kazakhstan would have become a Central-Asian Snow Leopard and would serve a fine example to be followed by other developing countries. (Nazarbayev, 1997, Section 2, para. 1–3)

The title of Nazarbayev's address itself was possibly inspired by Malaysia's *Vision 2020*, which had been announced by the Prime Minister Mahathir bin Mohamad in 1991.

Although the announcements of politicians may not necessarily influence a country's actual path of development, there are several conditions that increase the relevance of the East Asian experience for the countries of Central Asia. As one of the leading experts on Central Asia, economist Martin Spechler notes important similarities between the colonial heritage left behind by Japan in South Korea and Taiwan and that of the Soviet Union in Uzbekistan in "Hunting for the Central Asian Tiger" (Spechler, 2000a, pp. 101–102). These historical factors apply to a similar degree to the other Central Asian republics. Specifically, both Soviet and Japanese dominance resulted in massive investments in the physical infrastructure and human capital in their dependencies.

In addition, the development of countries such as South Korea, Taiwan and Singapore may have a particular relevance for Central Asia because the economic catch-up of these countries largely took place in a non-democratic setting. Both South Korea and Taiwan were governed by authoritarian regimes until the late 1980s, and the regimes of Singapore and other Southeast Asian economies are still not fully democratic.[5] Although Japan has been a democratic country since it regained its independence after the Second World War, the rule of a single party, the Liberal Democratic Party of Japan (LDP), has been virtually uninterrupted. In Central Asia, the two most populous countries, Kazakhstan and Uzbekistan, have been ruled by Nursultan Nazarbayev and Islam Karimov respectively since their independence in 1991. In 2011, Freedom House considered none of the Central Asian republics to be a free country. While the Kyrgyz Republic was evaluated as being "partly free", the other four republics were categorized as "not free" (Freedom House, 2011).

---

5   According to Freedom House (2011) indices, South Korea shifted from being "partly free" to "free" in 1988, and Taiwan achieved this change in status in 1996. In 2011, Singapore, Malaysia and Thailand are still considered to be only "partly free".

For economists, the explanation for the conditions under which East Asian economies achieved fast and sustainable growth is also a theoretical issue. Explanations for the remarkable East Asian performance have varied over time, but there is a central theoretical concept that has gained wide recognition in the literature: the notion of a *developmental state*. The term was coined in 1982 by the political scientist Chalmers Johnson, who argued in his seminal book "MITI and the Japanese Miracle" that the key to the economic performance of Japan was the leadership of the state during industrialization and the rational manner with which the Japanese state filled this role (Johnson, 1982, pp. 17–20).

Soon thereafter, economists began to argue that the governments in the newly industrializing economies of South Korea and Taiwan were taking on a similar role as in Japan. Johnson himself had already extended his concept to cover South Korea and Taiwan (Johnson, 1986), and other publications followed (White & Wade 1988, Wade 1988, Luedde-Neurath, 1988). Two seminal books that provide extensive and detailed analyses of state intervention gained particular attention in the scientific discourse: "Asia's Next Giant" by Alice Amsden (1989) on South Korea and "Governing the Market" by Robert Wade (1990/2004) on Taiwan. In addition, Singapore is commonly acknowledged to be a developmental state (Doner, Ritchie and Slater, 2005, p. 328; Huff 1995). Whether the emerging Southeast Asian economies of Malaysia, Thailand and Indonesia should be considered developmental states has been a subject of controversy. Even though it is generally acknowledged that they share some of the attributes that are considered characteristic for such states, they differ in several ways from the more advanced economies in Northeast Asia and Singapore (for diverging perspectives on this issue see Akyüz, Chang & Kozul-Wright, 1998; Doner et al., 2005; Jomo, 2004; Leftwich, 1995; Vu, 2007). The most successful East Asian economy of recent times, the People's Republic of China, was not included in the World Bank's study on the East Asian miracle (1993) and is generally not included in the literature on the developmental state. Due to China's large size and distinct conditions, it probably represents a model of its own.[6]

The concept of the developmental state and the discussion it initiated among economists and other scholars directly relates to a question that has been a key issue of economics since its beginnings: What is the role of the state in the economy and what influence does it have on economic success? This is not only a theoretical question but also a practical question with immediate importance

---

6   For an analysis of the institutions, economic policy, and reform process of the People's Republic of China see Ahrens, 2002, chap. VI.; Shirk, 1993; Quian & Weingast, 1997.

for political decision makers, especially in transition countries such as the Central Asian republics. Scholars such as Johnson, Amsden, and Wade were motivated to write their respective studies on Japan, South Korea, and Taiwan in order to object to the prevailing recommendation that a state should not intervene in the economy and instead limit itself to assuming a purely regulatory role. However, while their work represented a challenge to the applicability of neoclassical reasoning to the reality of economic policy, it did not constitute a new theoretical framework of comparative scope and depth itself. In order to evaluate the relevance of the East Asian experience for Central Asia, it is necessary to examine the role of the state and the concept of the developmental state based on a broader theoretical perspective which takes into account the varying institutions that govern economic exchange in different countries.

1.1.3 Research questions and the relevant unit of analysis

The main research objective of this dissertation is to analyze whether institutions that were characteristic for developmental states in East Asia are present or emerging in Central Asia. The text focuses on the two most important economies of the region, Kazakhstan and Uzbekistan. Institutions in this context are defined in accordance with Nobel laureate Douglass North as "the humanly devised constraints that shape human interaction" (North, 1990, p. 3). Since both economic and political processes are relevant to the concept of the developmental state, this dissertation takes an interdisciplinary perspective at the intersection of economics and political science. The *units of analysis* of the dissertation are consequently the characteristic institutions of developmental states.

However, there is at least one preliminary research question that has to be addressed in order to answer the final research question specified above: What are the characteristic institutions of developmental states and under which circumstances did they emerge in East Asia? While the literature on the developmental state has expanded since the publication of "MITI and the Japanese miracle" in 1982, research varies widely in its focus. In most cases, studies on the developmental state lack an explicit theoretical framework, and do not put the concept into the broader perspective of economic theory. As a consequence, it has to be noted that there is no commonly recognized model which provides a clear, feasible and theory-based definition of what a developmental state actually is, even though there is widespread agreement on some key aspects of a possible model. As suggested by Kang (1995, p. 587), I will attempt to close this still existing gap by analyzing the developmental state in the context of the New Institutional Economics (NIE).

The objectives of this study can therefore be outlined as follows:

(I) to contribute to the literature on the developmental state by providing a new approach to this concept from the dynamic perspective of the NIE and

(II) to contribute to the literature on Central Asia by comparing the state of research in current literature with results from an empirical study based on interviews in Kazakhstan and Uzbekistan and analyzing to which degree institutions that are relevant for the emergence of successful developmental states are present in Central Asia.

1.2 Theoretical Framework

Since institutions are the basic unit of analysis, this study is grounded in the extensive stream of research that is collectively known as the New Institutional Economics (NIE). However, it should be noted that the NIE is not a single and coherent theory held together by universal assumptions and research objectives. Instead, it is common to distinguish between three different schools of thought within the NIE that differ in their assumptions and consequently in their respective methods of inquiry and conclusions. These schools of thought are usually referred to as *rational-choice institutionalism, historical institutionalism* and *sociological institutionalism* (see for a comprehensive summary on the three institutionalisms Hall & Taylor, 1996; furthermore DiMaggio 1998; Thelen 1999).[7]

For the purposes of this study, Douglass North's seminal book "Institutions, Institutional Change and Economic Performance" and some elaboration on North's research in Ahrens (2002, in particular pp. 38–113) will serve as the theoretical basis of the analysis. Even though North is one of the main exponents of rational-choice institutionalism, his later work (including North 1990) is conceptually close to the historical institutionalist school of thought in several aspects, as Thelen (1999, pp. 379–380) notes. One of these aspects is the importance of culture and the relevance of cultural factors for the path of institutional development (Thelen, 1999, p. 376), an interrelationship that is particularly relevant for the issues discussed in this study.

While the NIE is a deductive approach that rests on explicitly stated assumptions that are confirmed using historical examples, most literature on the

---

7　DiMaggio instead distinguishes between rational-action institutionalism, mediated-conflict institutionalism and social-constructionist institutionalism (DiMaggio, 1998, pp. 696-697).

developmental state derives conclusions in an inductive way without specifying assumptions. Through a qualitative analysis of the existing research on these topics, I attempt to provide conclusions with implications for economic theory. In contrast, the section on Central Asia takes an essentially exploratory case-study approach. Desk research will be complemented by expert interviews with members of international organizations, major domestic and foreign companies, members of the bureaucracy and academics in the respective regions.

1.3 Ontological and methodological considerations

This study is conceptually close to a stream of research that Stanford economist Avner Greif has called *historical and comparative institutional analysis* (HCIA) in an article published in the Papers and Proceedings issue of the American Economic Review (Greif, 1998). According to Greif, the essence of HCIA is "the examination of the factors determining the relevant rules of the game, the forces that make these rules self-enforcing, and the self-enforcing constraints on behavior that emerge within these rules" (1998, p. 80). An essential difference between the study presented here and most of the research that Greif considers to be within the field of HCIA is that formal game-theoretical models will be neither applied nor developed. Instead, a comparative institutional approach that is explicitly and intentionally qualitative is presented. Even though research in economics has become increasingly focused on mathematical models for theory development and econometric analysis for theory testing over the last decades, these methods are not suitable for all issues that economic research should cover. The emergence of developmental states in East Asia and the institutional environment in Central Asia today are examples of such issues for various reasons.

The most important of these reasons is the complexity of the relevant systems and mechanisms in the process of institutional change. Furthermore, the problem of institutional equivalence, the impossibility to observe crucial decision-making processes, the large time frame of the case studies and the lack of reliable data—in particular for Central Asia today and for East Asia during the emergence of developmental states—make an analysis based on formal and quantitative methods infeasible. Similar to the contribution of North and Weingast on the institutions of seventeenth-century England (North & Weingast, 1989), I follow a qualitative, but explicitly theory-based case study approach to historical and comparative institutional analysis.

A key criticism of qualitative approaches that accounts for the relative decline of these methods in several social sciences over the last few decades is their comparative lack of analytical rigor and, in consequence, a presumed lack of generalizability as well as reliable findings. Qualitative research does have some inevitable shortcomings concerning these issues. However, several scholars have suggested approaches to tackle these shortcomings without having to relinquish the fundamental advantages of qualitative analysis, in particular its ability to deal with complex social phenomena and its applicability to environments that are characterized by a lack of reliable data.

The approach to qualitative research used in this study was developed by Alexander George and Andrew Bennett (George, 1979; George & Bennett, 2005; Bennett, 2008) and is known as the method of *structured focused comparison.*[8] *Structured* in this context means that a set of general questions which reflect the previously defined research objective are devised and then asked of each case—i.e. of each country within the scope of the present study—in order to make a systematic comparison and cumulation of the conclusions possible (George & Bennett, 2005, p. 67). *Focused* means that only specific aspects of the analyzed cases are examined (George & Bennett 2005, p. 67). In the context of the present study, these specific aspects are the relevant institutions for the developmental state as well as factors that influence the emergence of these institutions.

While both the theoretical framework of the NIE and the structured focused comparison method will be applied to all cases in this study, there are major differences between the East Asian and the Central Asian cases concerning the methodology for data collection and the questions asked. These differences are a direct result of the research objectives specified above and the diverging time frames of the case studies. The examination of institutions and institutional development in several economically successful East Asian countries has the objective of identifying the essential characteristics of a developmental state. Thus, it takes an explanatory approach based on a synthesis of the extensive literature on the developmental state and the historical development of these economies during the relevant period, which reaches back till the 19th century in the case of Japan. In contrast, the analysis of Central Asia evaluates whether developmental states are currently emerging in this region. As a result, it is rather exploratory in nature and hardly deals with developments dating back further than the dissolution of the Soviet Union. The analysis is based on conclusions from the preceding sections of this study, insights of economic research on the region and inter-

---

8   This methodology was strongly advocated for qualitative research in the social sciences (in particular in the field of international business) by Lorraine Eden, editor in chief of the Journal of Business Studies in a presentation at the 46th Annual International Studies Association Convention (Eden, Herman, & Li, 2005).

views conducted in Kazakhstan and Uzbekistan. Since the economic research on Central Asia is comparatively limited and the reliability of available data often subject to doubt, these interviews represent a particularly valuable source of information for the purposes of this study.

1.4 Outline of the study

The study is divided into three main parts subsequent to this introduction. The first part establishes the theoretical and analytical framework for the country studies in two stages. The first stage summarizes and interprets the relevant literature on the role of the state in the economy from a theoretical perspective, focusing mainly on the *Northian* New Institutional Economics and related concepts such as the New Political Economy. The second stage summarizes the extensive literature on the East Asian economic miracle and on the concept of the developmental state, focusing on the different questions asked by researchers, the diverging definitions of the concept and its placement within the economic schools of thought.

The second major part of this study is dedicated to East Asia. After specifying the methodology and the set of research questions for the historical case studies, the institutional development of several countries that are commonly considered developmental states is analyzed along chronological and conceptual lines. The focus is on the most prominent examples of developmental states. The analysis starts with Japan, the archetype of the East Asian developmental states, and continues with its two closest followers in terms of economic success and development strategy, South Korea and Taiwan. In addition, the developmental city-state of Singapore is analyzed, before discussing Malaysia, Thailand, and Indonesia more briefly in Section 5.5. This analysis of developmental states addresses the political sphere, the private sector and the international environment that these countries faced during their fast growth. Because of the limited scope of the present study and the reasons given above, the institutional development of People's Republic of China is not discussed here.

The third and final part of the study focuses on Central Asia, especially on the implications of preceding findings for Kazakhstan and Uzbekistan. After summarizing the current state of research on the issues relevant for the purposes of this study, the objectives and methodology of the empirical study based on interviews carried out within the region are explained. After the methodology is explained, the results and conclusions from these interviews are presented. In the final section, the study evaluates whether or not developmental states are currently emerging in Central Asia or could emerge in this region in the future.

PART I:

SETTING THE FRAMEWORK

2 The state from the perspective of economic theory

2.1 NPE and NIE as extensions of neoclassical economics

In economics and political science, the dominating view on the adequate role of the state in the economy has dramatically changed over the last few decades. In the 1950s and 60s, it was common that research in the field of economic policy focused on market failures and ways to correct them through state action, without paying much attention to the possibility of state failure (Krueger, 1993, p. 49). The presumed prevalence of market failures lead to an emphasis on infant-industry promotion and the support of physical capital accumulation, whereas possible gains from trade were deemed less important (Rodrik, 1996, p. 12). However, neoclassical economics, which introduced a radically different perspective on the state, became more dominant in both research and economic policy over the following decades.

In contrast to their classical predecessors such as Adam Smith, early neoclassical economists, like William Stanley Jevons or León Walras, developed their economic theories while assuming an essentially institution-free environment (Alesina, 2007, p. 2). Other important contributions to the neoclassical framework follow the same path. Nevertheless, economic policy and, consequently, the role of the state have always been a major topic for some economists from both the Neoclassical/Monetarist and the Keynesian schools of thought. For most of the 20th century, however, mainstream economics mainly concentrated on quantitative economic policy and dealt with issues such as the optimal money supply or government spending. Qualitative or structural policies, such as political and economic reforms as well as the corresponding legislation, were neglected to a certain extent. Policy targets were commonly treated as given, i.e. derived from economic theory and economists' recommendations or other fields such as moral philosophy (Eggertsson, 1997, p. 1987–1988). In addition, neither politicians' incentives and behavior nor political processes were explicitly modeled (Eggertsson, 1997, p. 1191).

A stream of literature that focuses exactly on these issues neglected by the traditional policy analysis is the New Political Economy (NPE). The NPE could be characterized as an application of neoclassical microeconomic reasoning to processes that are either at the interface of politics and the economy or purely political. Strongly emphasizing methodological individualism, individual bureaucrats and politicians rather than organizations of the public administration or the government itself are treated as the relevant actors that maximize their individual utility (Ahrens, 2002, p. 40). Ahrens (2002) therefore describes the NPE "as an attempt to provide a rigorous and axiomatic general theory of the state, which interprets politics as a market for individual exchanges" (p. 40).

This general theory tries to incorporate various subfields of research that focused on different aspects of social and political exchange and—at least partly— lead to differing results (Besley, 2007, pp. 572–577). The most important of these subfields for the purposes of this study is public choice theory.[9] On the basis of the work of one of its most prominent scholars, James M. Buchanan, Besley identifies three key ideas of public choice analysis. The first idea is to model individuals as strictly seeking to "further their own narrow self-interest, narrowly defined, in terms of measured net wealth position, as predicted or expected" (Buchanan, 1989, p. 20). The second idea is that constitutions serve as constraints for the individual self-interest (Besley, 2007, pp. 574–575), which can be considered the essence of the following statement by Buchanan:

> To improve politics, it is necessary to improve or reform rules, the framework within which the game of politics is played. There is no suggestion that improvement lies in the selection of morally superior agents who will use their powers in some public interest. (Buchanan, 1989, p. 18)

The last key idea of public choice theory is its normative framework that sees outcomes purely in terms of their impact on the utility of individuals. In some accounts, this goes so far as to delegitimize a state intervention that increases total public welfare if it lowers the utility of one single individual (Besley, 2007, p. 575).

One of the main contributions of public choice theory to the understanding of economic development was to model the state by treating each public official and each politician as individual economic actors interested in maximizing their own utility and facing specific incentives. In this way, government failure became one of the key issues for economists, and is nowadays considered to have been the most important impediment for economic development in many developing countries (Rodrik, 1996, p. 12). This focus on state failure led to the notion that the essential conclusion from the public choice approach is to strive for a minimal state. This means that the scope of state action and regulation should

---

9   Whereas Besley (2007) refers to public choice theory as an antecedent of the NPE (p. 574-575), Ahrens (2002) asserts that public choice is one of various subfields of the NPE (p. 39-40). The present study follows the latter perspective.

be reduced as much as possible because government failures frequently produce results that are worse than market failures (Frey, 1988, p. 352).

Nevertheless, reasoning within the public choice framework has serious limitations. Not all decisions that politicians, legislators or public officials take may directly affect their individual utility or personal interest. In those cases, it could very well be that they act and vote according to what they perceive to be in the common interest of society (Ahrens, 2002, p. 46). While some contributions to the NPE do recognize that decision makers face certain constraints when they further their personal utility (Besley, 2007, 579–580), these constraints are usually not the main focus of mainstream NPE scholars. In particular, informal institutions such as cultural values and codes of behavior are commonly neglected for the sake of unambiguous theoretical models, even though early NPE scholars recognized their importance for a realistic analysis (Ahrens, 2002, pp. 45–46).

While these shortcomings are general in nature, they are of particular relevance for the issues analyzed in the present study. Theoretical microeconomic models based on utility maximization commonly require clearly defined, stable rules that are known to the relevant actors. It is questionable whether it is possible to identify such rules for complex economic and political processes in modern capitalist societies, but it is even more disputable whether such models have validity for processes that took place in pre-capitalist and non-Western societies such as late 19th century Japan, the East Asian Tigers prior to their fast economic growth or early post-communist Central Asia. It is reasonable to assume that informal cultural values and codes of behavior have a higher importance in such societies. Furthermore, formal constraints for the behavior of economic actors have changed profoundly in these societies at various stages of their development.

However, there is another branch of economic literature that deals precisely with the emergence of constraints for economic behavior and the analysis of both formal and informal constraints: New Institutional Economics (NIE). The term *institution* has been defined in varying ways in the literature. The definition that is most frequently used today was given by Douglass North (1990), who understood institutions as "the humanly devised constraints that shape human interaction" or less formally as the "rules of the game in a society" (p. 3). It is important to notice that this definition includes not only formal rules such as laws and regulations, but also informal rules such as cultural norms. Each enforced rule limits the set of feasible choices that economic and political actors face when taking a specific decision, because some options that are theoretically available may be illegal or socially unacceptable. In this way, institutions shape the incentive structure of an economy and influence its development toward growth, stagnation or decline (North, 1991, p. 97).

It should be mentioned that the NIE is actually not a single, coherent theory, but rather a whole field of research that intends to overcome some shortcomings of neoclassical economics in a variety of ways. From the perspective of the NIE, the most important shortcoming of the orthodox, neoclassical reasoning is that it is concerned only with the operation of markets under highly theoretical and abstract assumptions. It ignores the constraints that limit the functioning of the market mechanism in reality and the institutions that are indispensable for its functioning. Furthermore, neoclassical economics is primarily concerned with the operation of existing markets; it hardly provides insights into the emergence of a functioning market (North, 1994, p. 359).

Common, but rather unrealistic, assumptions of neoclassical economics that are typically revised and relaxed by the NIE include perfect information and the absence of transaction costs. At the same time, most works in the field of the NIE retain the actor-centered analytical approach based on individual rational behavior. Therefore, it can be considered an approach that does not try to replace neoclassical theorizing but rather to modify and extend it (Ahrens, 2002, p. 49). The two major branches of the NIE that originated in economics are associated with three Nobel laureates: Douglass C. North, Ronald Coase, and Oliver E. Williamson. Coase, Williamson, and subsequent scholars elaborating on their work have been primarily concerned with transaction costs and their impact on economic exchange. One of the main contributions of this literature was to explain why hierarchical organizations such as firms emerge (Coase, 1937; Williamson, O. E., 1971, 1975, 1985). The second branch of research initiated by Douglass North, which is more relevant for this study, focuses on two different but interrelated questions: (1) how do institutions influence the economic performance of a society and (2) which mechanisms lead to the emergence of institutions and their evolution over time (North, 1990, 1991, 1992). The former question can be analyzed as a first step from a static perspective where institutions are treated as exogenously given and economic actors face a "choice within rules" (Ahrens, 2002, p. 49). The second question explicitly requires a dynamic perspective where institutions are the endogenous variables. Economic actors face a "choice of rules" (Ahrens, 2002, p. 49) under these conditions. In the following sections, key characteristics of the NIE will be elaborated in detail in order to provide a clear and sound theoretical framework for subsequent sections of the present study.

2.2 The Fundamentals of the NIE

2.2.1 Objectives and Methodology

As elaborated in the preceding section, the New Institutional Economics deviate substantially from neoclassical economics in several aspects but retain key components of neoclassical assumptions and methodology. Following Ahrens (2002, pp. 53–57), the main assumptions, axioms and hypotheses of the New Institutional Economics will be specified here.

Probably the most important argument of proponents of the NIE is simply that institutions matter. This means that the rules and constraints that economic actors face in any given environment have an impact on their feasible choices and actions, thus the outcomes of economic exchange depend on institutions. However, each society is characterized by a multitude of rules and constraints. Certain rules may only be relevant for a part of the society while others apply to everybody; some rules are remarkably stable over time while others are subject to frequent changes. In general the institutional environment has to be distinguished from institutional arrangements. While the former is the relevant set of fundamental political, social and legal rules, the latter are arrangements of cooperation, competition or exchange between different economic actors or organizations (Davis & North, 1971, pp. 6–7). Together, the institutional environment and the institutional arrangements form the institutional matrix of a society (Ahrens, 2002, p. 51).

Table 2: Classification of institutions and enforcement mechanisms

Kind of rule	Kind of enforcement	Type of institution	
Convention	Self-enforcing	Type-1-internal	
Ethical rule	Via self-commitment of the actor	Type-2-internal	**Informal institutions**
Customs	Via informal societal control	Type-3-internal	
Formal private rules	Organized private enforcement	Type-4-internal	
Constitution, laws, regulations	Organized enforcement by the state	External	**Formal institutions**

Source: Voigt and Kiwit (1995).

In order to have a real impact on the behavior of economic actors, rules and constraints require specific *enforcement mechanisms* (Ahrens, 2002, p. 55). Which kind of mechanism is required depends on the characteristics of the corresponding institution. Some institutions are self-enforcing because a given economic actor would decrease his utility if he deviated from a rule even in the absence of enforcement mechanisms such as legal action by the police and courts. Others are enforced privately, for example certain rules in business associations, sports clubs or other private organizations. Finally, institutions such as laws or the constitution of a country are enforced through legal action (see Table 2).

In terms of methodology, most contributions to the NIE retain the *individual-actor approach,* which is central to neoclassical economics and the New Political Economy. This means that not specific interest groups, trade unions, business associations or the state are the relevant actors for the analysis, but that individual members of these organizations, each facing specific constraints and having individual interests, are the focus. The method of inquiry of the NIE has therefore been characterized as of an individualistic and deductive nature (Gronewegen, Kerstholt & Nagelkerke, 1995, p. 471). However, an economic actor also shares some of his interests with others. Hence, he is the member of a variety of organizations, defined by Douglass North (1990) as "groups of individuals bound by some common purpose to achieve objectives" (p. 5). Under specific circumstances and concerning particular issues, North therefore treats organizations as the relevant actors.[10] Organizations in the *Northian* definition include not only economic bodies such as companies, trade unions or cooperatives, but also political bodies (e.g. parties, parliaments or state agencies), social bodies (e.g. clubs, churches) and educational bodies (1990, p. 5).

It is commonly assumed that the economic actors that form the organizations are *individually rational* and may show *opportunistic behavior* in order to maximize their utility. However, these assumptions are not interpreted as strictly as in neoclassical microeconomics. While early contributions to the NIE commonly assume complete rationality, i.e. that preferences are both stable and consistent, recent research often tries to take a more realistic approach by viewing preferences as both incomplete and unstable over time (Ahrens, 2002, p. 54). Furthermore, Douglass North stresses (1990, p. 17–25) that uncertainty resulting from incomplete information and the limitations of an individual's intellectual "problem solving software" (p. 25) have a significant impact on human behavior and that the common neoclassical behavioral assumptions are in consequence unrealistic. While economic actors may behave rational in the neoclassical sense when facing choices that appear to be "regular, repetitive and clearly evident" (North, 1990, p 24), more complex decisions may lead to behavior that is ex-

---

10   Specifically, North argues that organizations are the key actors in the process of institutional change (North, 1990, p 73), which is discussed in detail in section 2.2.2 of the present study.

tremely difficult to predict without making the assumptions more realistic. In some of the more recent contributions to the NIE, the assumption of complete rationality is therefore substituted for bounded rationality (Ahrens, 2002, p. 54).

In the case of opportunistic behavior, it should be noted that contributions to the NIE usually do not interpret utility maximization in the narrow sense of wealth maximization, which is at least implicitly assumed by many works in other fields of economics. In reality, it is evident that individuals make decisions that do not serve their immediate economic interest. This includes diverse behavior from an anonymous free donation of blood to sincere dedication to ideological and religious causes—in some cases even the sacrifice of one's life for such causes (North, 1990, pp. 25–26). The question is whether this kind of behavior is so common that it makes the assumption of a rational and opportunistic *homo oeconomicus* useless for the analysis of human interaction. Contributions to the NIE have dealt with this problem by ruling out neither opportunistic behavior nor altruism while accepting that economic actors are not homogeneous. However, since it is extremely difficult for an individual to determine whether or not another economic actor will behave opportunistically ex ante, a key role of institutions is to suppress opportunistic behavior (Ahrens, 2002, p. 55).

As Ronald Coase stated, it is commonly said that the NIE started with his article "The nature of the firm" (Coase, 1937), with its explicit treatment of transaction costs (Coase, 1998, p. 72). Indeed, the realistic assumption that transaction costs exist, which means that economic exchange itself is costly, represents the most important distinction between the NIE and both classical and neoclassical economics (Ahrens, 2002, p. 52; North, 1990, p. 27) and is of major importance for the main contributions to the field. Transaction costs are for several reasons essential for economic decisions. North considers information cost defined as the "cost of measuring the valuable attributes of what is being exchanged and the costs of protecting rights and policing and enforcing agreements" (1990, p. 27) to be the most important kind of transaction costs. Since information in the real world is scarce (Eggertsson, 1997, p. 1189) an economic actor has to decide how much information about the desired good or service he wants to acquire. In most cases, it is rational from a utility maximizing perspective not to acquire all relevant information given the uncertainties and costs of information search (Ahrens, 2002, p. 54).

In addition to information costs, a multitude of further transaction costs such as the cost of "drafting, negotiating, and safeguarding an agreement" (Williamson, O. E., 1985, pp. 20–21) or the cost of enforcement (North, 1990, pp. 32–33) may be relevant for specific exchanges. In comparison with an ideal neoclassical world, the existence of transaction costs moves the possible frontier of production inwards because they have to be added to the cost of resource inputs and the cost of transformation in order to calculate the total cost of production (North, 1990, p. 28). In addition, transaction costs also affect political processes. While institutions are important for decreasing transaction costs for economic and political actors, it cannot be assumed that the optimal institutional framework for this purpose will emerge in any given society. As a consequence of institutional shortcomings, the neoclassical production frontier is moved inwards not just once, but twice (Eggertsson, 1997, p. 1193).

Under specific circumstances, it is also possible that institutions do not serve to *decrease* transaction costs, but to *increase* them. Ahrens notes that transaction costs also comprise the "costs of creating, monitoring, enforcing, and restructuring institutions" (p. 55). In a hierarchical institutional environment, rules may exist that determine the transaction cost for the restructuring of other rules. One example is a nation's constitution, which determines the rules that govern the process of legislation. For specific, far-reaching legislative changes, these rules are typically devised in a way that results in high transaction cost for the involved actors. An example would be a legislative change that affects basic constitutional rights. Through increasing the costs for restructuring existing rules, the stability of the institutional environment and the reliability of existing rules is increased, resulting in less uncertainty for economic actors.

The issues of transaction costs and uncertainty about the future lead to a further difference between the NIE and the traditional neoclassical framework. Since it is costly for an economic actor to obtain information about a potential contract partner and to monitor his actions after the contract is signed, complete contracts as assumed by economic theory are unrealistic (North, 1990, pp. 52–53). Instead, the NIE assumes that agreements in the real world are *relational contracts* that describe "shared objectives and general principles governing the relationship of contracting parties and show adequate procedures which guide future contractual arrangements" (Ahrens, 2002, pp 55–56).

While transaction costs and relational contracts are reasons why individuals may not achieve the same degree of utility as in a neoclassical world, it is also a matter of discussion in the NIE which utility functions individuals in the real world actually possess. As previously stated, personal wealth is not considered to be the only and not even necessarily the most important variable in the utility function. Which variables matter depends on the specific preferences of a given individual. In this respect, economic actors are not considered to be homogeneous because it is assumed that everybody makes decisions based on his personal *ideology* which is in turn based on his subjective perception of the reality (North, 1990, p. 23; 1992, p. 479). Since information is costly and hence incomplete, the model of the reality that a person constructs in his mind remains flawed and subject to changes. Furthermore, the way an individual interprets available information depends on factors such as past experience and cultural heritage. Therefore, the same piece of information may be interpreted differently by persons from different backgrounds (Ahrens, 2002, 56). Personal ideologies play a major role in explaining 'economically irrational' behavior as described above.

The last main assumption of the NIE to be introduced here is *path dependency*. Douglass North starts the preface of his 1990 book with the statement that "history matters" (North, 1990, p. vii). This notion is the essence of the concept of path dependency (Ahrens, 2002, p. 56). Path dependency states that historical events have a long lasting influence on present conditions, specifically on individuals' preferences and on the institutional environment in which they strive to achieve these preferences. Specific investments in human or physical capital that have been made in the past are one cause of path dependency. After the investment has been made, changes in the institutional environment could its value or even make it useless. As a result, actors would refrain from demanding these changes. Under such circumstances, the past investment has a sustained impact on the path of institutional development. Another cause of path dependency are network effects. Network effects refer to particular institutions that may have positive external effects for individuals if an increasing number of persons complies with them. Lastly, as explained above, the ideology of a person, which corresponds to his or her model of reality, is shaped by specific societal and cultural backgrounds. In this way, a "cognitive embodiment of institutions" (Ahrens, 2002, p. 56) exists. In other words, since culture and society are influenced by history and in turn influence the ideology of economic actors, modern day decisions of these actors are influenced by history.

2.2.2 Institutional change and its drivers

The proponents of NIE argue that institutions matter for economic and social exchange in a society and, therefore, for its path of development. Thus, it is of major importance to gain insights into the way institutions actually emerge and develop. However, research in the NIE differs in its approach to this issue.

Depending on the specific focus of scholarly publications, only specific institutions may be treated as endogenous and subject to change while others are simply assumed as a given. For research that is primarily concerned with the behavior of firms in a rather short term perspective, it is a reasonable approach to treat most of the institutional environment of a given society as exogenous and stable. Nevertheless, it is apparent that the rules and constraints of societies are not stable over time in reality there can be little doubt that the institutional environment of Asia today differs drastically from the one faced 500, 100 or even 50 years ago. If the path of economic development of a society is to be analyzed, as is the case in the present study, it is therefore indispensable to take a close look at the drivers, agents and mechanisms of institutional change. In a region such as Central Asia, where the transition process from a command to a market economy is still going on, the importance of institutional change is particularly apparent.

As elucidated in the preceding section, institutions differ concerning their degree of stability. Certain institutions survive even massive historical events such as revolutions and wars, while others change over the course of years or months even in times of relative political stability. Therefore, it makes sense to establish a hierarchy of institutions as a framework for their analysis. O. E. Williamson (2000, pp. 596–597) defines such a hierarchy based on the embeddedness of an institution in society. A rule that is deeply embedded in a society will change extremely slowly, while rules with a low degree of embeddedness are subject to frequent institutional change. This hierarchy corresponds to different levels of scientific analysis in the NIE (Figure 1). Contributions to the NIE that focus on a specific level of institutions have to treat this level as endogenous while institutions at higher levels are treated as a given (Williamson, O. E., 2000, p. 596, see also Eggertsson, 1990, p. xiii for a similar argument).

Informal institutions derived from traditions, religion and other customs are commonly considered to be at the top of the institutional hierarchy since they are deeply embedded in people's minds and in society. Most informal institutions tend to change very slowly (Roland, 2004, p. 116), according to O. E. Williamson (2000, p. 596, see also Figure 1), they only change over the course of centuries or even millennia. The lower levels of the institutional hierarchy are comprised by formal rules of the game such as laws (L2), governance structures such as private contracts (L3) and incentives resulting from prices and available quantities of desired goods (L4). For the purposes of this study, the first two levels are the most relevant ones.

It should be apparent that the different levels of the institutional hierarchy are not independent of each other, but interact in a variety of ways. This interaction plays an important role in understanding institutional change. Based on Dietl (1993), Ahrens (2002, pp. 62–64) argues that the institutions at the top of the hierarchy should be considered fundamental institutions, which provide economic actors with basic decision rights, but also duties. Rules at the level below are derived from fundamental institutions because these constrain the set of viable options when lower-ranking rules are chosen. If an institutional hierarchy of various levels is used as an analytical framework, there will be several stages of a choice of rules, which means that institutions at lower levels will always be derived from the institutions already chosen at the upper levels. Institutions at higher levels are generally more costly to change than those at lower levels (North, 1990, p. 83).

Figure 1: Hierarchy of institutions

Level		Frequency (years)	Purpose
L1	Embeddedness: informal insti-tutions, customs, traditions, norms, religion	10^2 to 10^3	Often spontaneous, non-calculative (caveat: see discussion in text)
L2	Institutional environment: Formal rules of the game—especially property (polity, judiciary, bureaucracy)	10 to 10^2	Get the institutional environment right. 1st order economizing
L3	Governance: Play of the game—especially contract (aligning governance structures with transactions)	1 to 10	Get the governance structures right. 2nd order economizing
L4	Resource allocation and em-ployment (prices and quantities; incentive alignment	continuous	Get the marginal conditions right. 3rd order economizing

L1: social theory
L2: economics of property rights / positive political theory
L3: transaction cost analysis
L4: neoclassical economics/agency theory
Source: O. E. Williamson (2000, p. 597).

While the interaction between institutions, and in particular between differ-ent levels of institutions, is important for understanding institutional change, it is not sufficient. Existing institutions represent constraints for choosing new rules, but they are not the agents of change. This role of inducing institutional change is fulfilled by organizations and the individual actors represented by them (North, 1990, p. 73). In this context, each individual actor is on the one hand an economic entrepreneur that tries to maximize personal wealth under the given circumstances. On the other hand, each actor also has a demand for specific in-stitutions that it tries to fulfill through cooperating with other individuals to promote institutional changes.

The interaction between organizations and the existing institutional envi-ronment in a society is the key to institutional change. In any given society, an organization such as a firm will already face an established set of rules and constraints that it has to adhere to. These institutions determine which activities organizations perceive as utility-maximizing. While the institutional framework in some societies sets incentives to invest in new, productivity increasing skills and knowledge, other societies may have institutions that make redistributive activities more attractive (North, 1990, p. 78).

The interaction is not a one-way street since organizations are also actors in the process of institutional change. A utility maximizing firm has basically two options: it can make choices within the given set of institutions or it can try to change the existing constraints. Whether the latter option is chosen depends on its perceptions on the costs and benefits of institutional change, since this desired change of rules will not come for free in most cases. If the perceived benefits of devoting resources to institutional change are negative, the firm would chose to invest in skills and knowledge that are deemed appropriate in the existing institutional setting (North, 1990, p. 79).

The level of resources that has to be devoted to the change in rules depends on the level and the kind of institution, which is not considered optimal. If two firms want to establish a business relationship, they will have the possibility to choose between different arrangements (Ahrens, 2002, p. 63), for example between a simple sales contract and a joint venture. While both alternatives have advantages and disadvantages, the choice itself is basically free of cost; the interaction of both parties determines the institutions that govern their future relationship. However, rules and constraints at higher levels of the institutional hierarchy are clearly more difficult to choose or change. In virtually all cases, institutional change at the level of laws and other state regulation will only take place as a result of interaction between political organizations such as parties, the parliament and bureaucratic agencies, or as a result of interaction between political and private organizations (e.g. through lobbying). A private organization will only devote resources to lobbying or similar activities if the cost of these resources is lower than the perceived benefits of the desired change in rules.

Institutional change can be advantageous for the development of an economy, but there are also evident examples where political negotiations or lobbying result in new rules that are not considered beneficial for the society as a whole. As previously mentioned, the existing framework of institutions sets the incentive for organizations and therefore also determines to a significant degree which path of institutional change these organizations will perceive as beneficial for them. This is the underlying reason why path-dependence is such an important concept for the NIE.

In addition, the direction of institutional development is influenced by the structure and characteristics of the relevant organizations. Different organizations compete with each other in a variety of ways. Companies compete with each other in the economic sphere and the outcome of this competition determines to a large degree to which industries productive resources, skills and knowledge will be allocated. Organized interest groups also compete for influence in the political sphere and the outcome of this power struggle has great influence on the direction of institutional change. The way in which interest groups organize and how they influence the economic development of a country has been the focus of the seminal works of Mancur Olson (1964, 1982). According to Olson's *Logic of Collective Action*, large interest groups face much bigger obstacles when forming effective organizations than small groups, because it is more difficult for them to overcome free-rider problems. He argues that in consequence, organizations representing narrow interests (for example a business association of a small number of companies in a specific industry) will have more influence on a society than it would be desirable from the standpoint of economic efficiency and welfare. Therefore, countries may often have institutions that do not benefit society as a whole but rather the redistributive interests of small groups (Olson, 1982, pp. 36–74).

Figure 2 represents a stylized diagram of institutional change based on the preceding elaborations and will serve as an important analytical basis for the following sections of the present study. The core of institutional change is the interaction between the existing set of institutions and organizations. Political, economic and other organizations have diverging interests concerning the institutional structure of the society. These are a result of the preferences of the individual members and the degree of collective action that these members are able to achieve. Organizations compete with each other in order to further these objectives. As a result of this competition, a societal desire to alter existing institutions arises, but the existing institutions restrain the alteration through setting higher or lower transaction costs for specific changes. The interaction between organizations determines the path of institutional change.

Figure 2: Stylized Northian model of institutional change

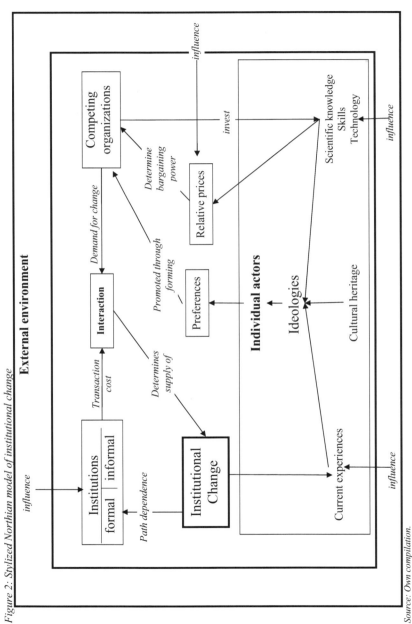

In addition to investing in institutional change, organizations also invest in skills and knowledge, which has great influence on various important factors in the process of institutional change. The scientific achievements and the development of new skills and technologies can have a profound impact on relative prices, which are in turn of decisive importance for the relative bargaining power of different organizations. Furthermore, these investments are in the long run an important source of change in the general scientific knowledge of the society. Together with the cultural heritage and current experiences of economic actors, the scientific knowledge determines an individual's mental model of the world, which finally shapes its ideology. In consequence, the investments in skills and knowledge may also alter the preferences of individual economic actors.

Changes in relative prices and changes in the preferences of individual actors are the two underlying reasons for institutional change according to North. He considers the former reason—which includes changes in the ratio of factor prices, changes in transaction costs and changes in technology—to be more important, whereas the latter represents a more difficult problem for a rigorous analysis (North, 1990, pp. 83–84). Preferences are based to a large degree on ideologies, which are subject to change for a variety of reasons. In the short term, ideologies change because individuals learn from current experiences; in the long term, ideologies change because the available scientific knowledge changes (see Figure 2). The path of this change is hardly predictable using the common (micro-) economic tools.

While ideologies of individuals have an important impact on the path of institutional change, this interaction is not one-sided. The process of institutional change itself has an influence on the current experiences of economic actors in a society and thus on their mental models and ideology. Moreover, the new institutional setting will in turn influence the power struggle between organizations and induce further institutional change in this way.

The described process is subject to exogenous influences from the external environment in a variety of ways. First of all, the external geopolitical environment can be a source of constraints that organizations and, in particular, political decision-makers have to respect. Furthermore, events in other countries can contribute to the current experiences of individuals and shape their ideologies and preferences. Finally, both the scientific knowledge and the relative price structure in a country are subject to external influences through an exchange of information and international trade.

It is theoretically possible that the various interrelationships between existing institutions, organizations, external environment and ideologies lead to an equilibrium where the institutional matrix of the society remains stable. Yet, such an equilibrium has never existed for a considerable period of time because all societies are subject to continuing changes in institutions. While Figure 2 illustrates the process of institutional change, it does not give an answer to the question what ultimately shapes the path of institutional development.

2.3 Institutions, the state, and the path of development

2.3.1 Enforcement and interplay of institutions

As became clear in Section 2.1, the way the state is perceived in economic research has changed over time and depends to a remarkable degree on the applied theoretical perspective. One extreme perspective is the idealization of the state as an impartial third party that strives to correct market failures for the benefit of the whole society. Such an idealization can only be the result of an approach which does not model actions of the state on the basis of an individual actor approach and explicit microeconomic assumptions.

This view is as a generalization hardly sustainable, as shown by both the real experience of many stagnating developing countries and virtually all contributions to economic theory. On the other side of the spectrum, economic models in public choice literature have come to the conclusion that the state is nothing more than a machine to redistribute wealth and income in a non-efficient way (North, 1990, p. 140). In contrast to the first perspective, this conclusion is based on an explicit modeling of individuals that work for the state and act in accordance with neoclassical microeconomic lines. In addition to the common assumption of rational behavior, such models inevitably also rely on specific assumptions concerning the relevant variables of the utility function of individuals. While the validity of these restrictive assumptions and the resulting conclusions for the reality has been subject to doubt, it is nevertheless not impossible to find examples of states that acted in ways that conform to the predictions of public choice models. In this way, the public choice literature contributes to an understanding of many of the economic failures in both developing and developed countries.

However, it should not be forgotten that not all economies show the same development and not all states seem to act in the same way, as economic history clearly shows. On the one hand, states in some economies have been characterized by maximizing the wealth of a small political elite at the expense of society as a whole, which seems to support predictions of models that assume the individual maximization of wealth by political decision makers. Zaire under President Mobuto is the most common example for such a *predatory state*. Common traits of predatory states are excessive taxation, overvalued exchange rates, and large but inefficient bureaucracies. As Ahrens (2002) notes, "governments of these states rely on rational strategies to enhance their exploitative power by pursuing economically irrational strategies of development" (p. 44). On the other hand, the type of state that is the focus of the present study, the *developmental state*, is supposed to have promoted the long-term economic development of countries such as South Korea and Japan. It is the aim of this section to analyze how the NIE can contribute to our understanding of these differences.

It is apparent that the state is, in reality, not a single entity that acts in a coherent way in order to reach clearly defined predetermined objectives. In all countries, the state consists of a wide variety of organizations which are in turn comprised of individuals. This includes legislative bodies such as parliaments, executive bodies such as a presidential administration, ministries or agencies, and judicative bodies, in particular courts. As neoclassical economics and its extensions in public choice literature and the New Political Economy, the NIE assumes that the individuals working in these organizations strive to maximize their own, individual utility. However, two questions arise: (1) What are the constraints that these individuals face when they maximize their utility? And (2): What variables actually contribute to the utility of individuals working in public organizations?

From the perspective of methodological individualism, it clearly makes no sense to characterize whole states or even organizations of the public administration with a single adjective such as "predatory" or "developmental" (Bates, 1999, p. 2). However, the state does not only consist of a multitude of different organizations and individuals, it is also a "nexus of institutions for social control, authoritative policy formation and implementation" (Ahrens, 2002, p. 105). As all organizations, public bodies interact with institutions. While they can induce institutional change, they also have to adhere to the institutional matrix that has developed through the path-dependent course of history. Institutions do not shape policy outcomes directly, but they do so indirectly by imposing incentives on decision-makers and structuring the decision-making process (Bates, 1999, pp. 1–2). In virtually all countries, formal rules exist to specify how members of political organizations, meaning bureaucrats and politicians, are chosen. The constitution and laws of a country formally determine how individuals for important political positions in the executive (e.g. president and regional governors) and the legislative (e.g. members of parliament) branches of government are selected. In democracies, the candidates for these positions are usually nominated by political parties, which have formalized rules on how to choose the individuals that will run for election. Furthermore, specific processes for hiring, firing, and promoting bureaucrats exist for most positions in the public administration in Western democracies. Once an individual has become a member of a political organization, it will still face specific constraints. Laws and the constitution determine the mandates of specific government agencies and officials, the instruments they are allowed to fulfill these mandates and procedures along which they must operate (Dethier, 1999, p. 6).

Within public organizations, rules exist that specify the duties and rights of each individual position. If these formal rules were always followed, the public administration of a country would resemble an ideal-type bureaucracy as specified by the sociologist Max Weber in "Wirtschaft und Gesellschaft" (1922/1985, pp. 124–130, [chap. 3 para. 3–5]). However, neither bureaucratic organizations nor political processes always function along the described lines in reality. While political processes and bureaucratic organizations in economically advanced Western democracies may usually be governed by the relevant formalized rules, their enforcement in several emerging and developing economies—such as the present-day Central Asian republics and the East Asian economies prior to their fast growth—is often subject to serious doubts. Therefore, theoretical models that compare the effects of different formal institutions on an economy while taking their enforcement for granted are of little substantial value when analyzing the path of economic development of real countries.

The interplay between different rules is one of the possible reasons for a lack of enforcement. Therefore, it is important to identify possible relationships between rules for the further analysis. Ahrens (2002, p. 52) provides one possible framework for the analysis of inter-institutional relationships from a theoretical perspective. For the purposes of this study, this framework has been slightly modified, the most important difference being the focus on rules instead of institutions. Two rules can be neutral to each other, i.e. the enforcement of one rule has no impact whatsoever on the enforcement of the other rule. They can also supplement or, in some cases, reinforce each other. In that case, the enforcement of one rule depends on the other (or the enforcement is even mutually dependent). However, there may also be rules that contradict each other, in which case the enforcement of both rules at the same time is impossible. Eggertsson (1997, p. 1192) therefore modifies North's definition of institutions as the "rules of the game", stating that only rules which are voluntarily obeyed or enforced through other mechanisms are institutions. When formal rules of the game established by the state are not respected or contradicted by privately enforced rules or informal constraints, they loose their relevance for economic outcomes. Following this definition, rules, but not institutions, can contradict each other. However, this contradiction may take different forms. It is conceivable that in one case, a specific (e.g. informal) institution completely substitutes a contradictory rule. I other cases, it may depend on the specific circumstances which of the two contradictory rules is enforced.

Concerning the enforcement of formal political and bureaucratic rules, special attention should be given to the interaction between these rules and informal institutions. According to North (1990, p. 37), informal constraints are the result of socially transmitted information and cultural heritage. In some instances, there may be mutual reinforcement between formal and informal rules, but it is apparent that this is not always the case (Ahrens, 2002, p. 52). By definition, the informal institutions of a society are not specified anywhere; neither the exact scope of their validity nor the relevant enforcement mechanism is apparent for an outsider. In all cases where formal rules are only insufficiently enforced and partly overruled by informal institutions, this represents a severe challenge to rigid economic analysis.

To summarize the insights of this section, it is important to notice that the quality of formal rules that govern economic and political exchange in a society is crucial for its economic development. However, this is not the only relevant factor from a new-institutionalist perspective. The degree of enforcement of rules is of major importance for the economic performance of a country. Furthermore, it has to be stressed that informal institutions are an important part of the institutional matrix of societies. Even when formal institutions change drastically in the course of historical events, informal constraints show a remarkable persistence (North, 1990, p. 37). The stability of informal institutions is an important rationale to explain the concept of path-dependence and incremental institutional change.

2.3.2 Informal institutions, ideology, and discontinuous institutional change

In virtually all modern societies, formal institutions have profound influence on the behavior of organizations and on the decisions of economic actors within these organizations. It is a reasonable supposition that the decision-making freedom of politicians and bureaucrats is in most cases more regulated than the freedom of private economic actors such as entrepreneurs. Institutionalized structures and procedures lead to determinacy of political life (Bates, 1999, p. 5). However, this determinacy cannot be exhaustive, since no formal institutional environment can be detailed enough to perfectly determine the decision of an individual actor in any theoretically possible situation. Therefore, there will always be choices of economic actors that do not exclusively depend on formal institutions, but also on other factors. It is apparent that in circumstances where formal rules such as laws are generally not detailed, weakly enforced or subject to essential and frequent changes, these other factors become significantly more important.

Situations that coincide with a considerable decrease in the influence of formal rules are major historical events. While North (1990, p. 89) argues that the single most important characteristic of institutional change is its overwhelmingly incremental progression, he acknowledges that events such as revolutions or a lost war with subsequent occupation by a foreign power substantially alter the formal institutional environment and are the source of discontinuous institutional change. One of the key arguments of Mancur Olson's book "The Rise and Decline of Nations" is that these historical events also lead to major changes in the structure of organizations, an emasculation of distributional coalitions and thus a decrease in the influence of vested interests (Olson, 1982, pp. 75–77). While there is serious doubt whether major historical events always have those consequences, Ahrens (2002, p. 337) points out that economic crises and regime changes can at least open a "window of opportunity" for economic reform, i.e. institutional change in the economic sphere. The German economist Walter Eucken referred to such favorable circumstances for reforms as "historischer Moment" (1952/1990, p. 251). It is of major theoretical and practical relevance to analyze which factors influence the path of institutional and economic development under such conditions. Since major historical events had a severe impact on the former Soviet Republics of Central Asia in the 1990s and on several economically successful East Asian developmental states in earlier decades, these issues are highly important for the present study.

From a theoretical perspective, the diagram of the Northian model of institutional change introduced in Figure 2 can serve as a starting point for determining which factors affect decisions when formal institutions are not decisive and the organizational structure is subject to major changes. The obvious complement to the formal institutional framework are informal institutions, and indeed, their importance in the course of formal institutional change should not be underestimated. As Douglass North notes, informal constraints persist even in course of major events such as the Russian Revolution, which could be considered the most complete formal transformation of a society (1990, p. 37). The sources of these informal constraints are culture and socially transmitted information (North, 1990, p. 37). However, it seems probable that rules based on culture, traditions, moral values and the like limit the feasible set of choices for decision makers only in specific cases and only to a certain extent. If this is true, the set of informal institutions would leave politicians, bureaucrats and others with a higher degree of decision-making freedom than specified, formal institutions would.

More decision-making freedom for political and economic actors increases the importance of their individual preferences for their choices. Following the assumption of the NPE and NIE that actors try to maximize their utility function under specific constraints, it has to be asked what the relevant variables of this utility function actually are. Theoretical contributions to the NPE generally rely on specific assumptions on what constitutes utility for state actors. It is often acknowledged that personal income and wealth are not the only decisive variables. Leading public choice scholar William Niskanen (1968) argued that "salary, perquisites of the office, public reputation, power, patronage, ease of managing the bureau, and ease of making changes" determine utility for bureaucrats, and that these individual variables are a function of the budget of the bureau they are managing (Niskanen, 1968, pp. 293–294). He concludes that budget maximization is an adequate proxy for bureaucrat's utility and elaborates a theoretically consistent model on this assumption. Other adherents to the NPE take similar approaches (Ahrens, 2002, p. 43). Concerning politicians, it has been a common supposition that staying in power is a crucial variable of their utility function (although staying in power can also be interpreted as a prerequisite for achieving other ends) (Ahrens, 2002, p. 43; Grindle & Thomas, 1989, pp. 220–221).

The New Institutional Economics does clearly not deny that all these factors are important variables of individuals' utility function. However, the NIE takes a broader, and therefore less definite, approach to the issue of economic actors' preferences. Referring to the model of institutional change in Figure 2, the preferences of individuals are fundamentally determined by their ideology. Their choices are essentially a result of preferences, incentives set by relative prices, and constraints as embodied in the existing institutional matrix. In order to understand how bureaucrats and politicians act when their decisions are not exclusively determined by binding rules, it has to be ascertained which ideology determines their preferences.

For the purposes of the present study, there is an additional reason why the ideology of politicians and public officials should be in the focus of the analysis. As described in the introduction, both Kazakhstan and Uzbekistan have been governed by authoritarian governments since their independence. The same holds true for important developmental states such as South Korea, Taiwan and Singapore in the initial phase of their fast economic development. There is no doubt that power struggles and competition between different individuals and organizations within the state apparatus also exist in authoritarian or even totalitarian political systems (Bates, 1999, p. 2). Nevertheless, it is reasonable to argue that in a non-democratic setting, the ideology of specific individuals, namely the president or other important political leaders, may have a seminal impact on the path of institutional change and, therefore, of economic development. Even if a "window of opportunity" has opened, the success of economic reforms is fundamentally affected by the determination and long-term vision of leading individuals, which could be called the critical actors for institutional change. If these leaders act because of their ideology or because of specific constraints in what they perceive as the national interest, they may serve as a substitute for the lack of institutions. In this way, *rules vested in persons* emerge (Ahrens, 2002, pp. 337–339). If the commitment to enforce these rules is perceived as credible by private economic actors, they will adjust their investment in skills and knowledge accordingly. Through the interrelationship between these investments, ideologies, choices, institutional change and path dependence described in Section 2.2.1, rules vested in persons may in the end lead to a new framework of formalized institutions.

What constitutes the ideology of economic actors in general and specific leaders in particular? According to North, ideologies are based on perceptions of reality. These perceptions in turn depend on scientific knowledge, current experiences and the cultural heritage of individuals (see also Section 2.2.1 and Figure 2). Note that cultural heritage from this perspective enters the process of institutional change in two different but interrelated ways. On the one hand, the cultural heritage is a seminal input to the development of informal institutions. These are enforced through various mechanisms and have to be obeyed by individuals when they take their decisions. Informal institutions are an essential part of the institutional matrix and therefore binding for any actor in a given society. On the other hand, the cultural heritage impacts individuals' preferences, even in the absence of constraints.

In the real world, there is no doubt that major differences between the ideologies of individuals exist because their cultural backgrounds and learning experiences differ (Denzau and North, 1994, pp. 3–4). This is particularly apparent when comparing different countries or different historical stages of development. It is questionable whether studies that base their conclusions on generalized assumptions on the variables of politicians' and bureaucrats' utility functions have a high explanatory value for major developments such as the *economic miracles* that took place in East Asia. The NIE cannot provide an answer as to which preferences critical actors of institutional change have, but it can provide a valuable framework for the analysis of specific historical and present cases. After summarizing the existing literature on the developmental state concept in the following section, the subsequent parts of the present study serve to analyze some of the most prominent examples of developmental states as well as the major economies of Central Asia by applying the NIE framework elaborated here.

3 East Asia and the developmental state in the literature: perspectives and disagreements

3.1 Methodology and research focus of the developmental state literature

Ever since it became apparent that several countries in East Asia had achieved what is commonly called an economic miracle, scholars of economics, political science and related fields have tried to determine the underlying reasons for this success. In particular, since the publication of Chalmers Johnsons "MITI and the Japanese Miracle" in 1982, a whole stream of literature appeared that analyzes the East Asian experience from different perspectives by either elaborating on his concept of the developmental state or criticizing it on the grounds of (mostly neoclassical) economic theory. This research is based on a variety of different perspectives that coincide with differences in the degree of abstraction and the treatment of specific policies and institutions as endogenous or exogenous variables. As is common in social sciences, the findings of scholars differ remarkably, and while some conclusions are mutually reinforcing or at least complementary, others are clearly contradictory.

A major reason for the diverging conclusions of research on East Asia is the varying degree of generalization that different publications strive for. As indicated by its title, "MITI and the Japanese Miracle" is exclusively focused on Japan and the activist role of the Japanese state in the economy. Other extensive contributions on the developmental state that Chalmers Johnson himself considers to be among the most important (Johnson 1999, p. 35) include Robert Wade's "Governing the Market" (1990), which is focused on Taiwan, and Alice Amsden's "Asia's Next Giant" (1989) on the role of the state in the South Korean economy. In contrast to these publications that attempt to draw conclusions based on the evidence of single, but economically very successful, economies in Northeast Asia, other contributions provide a comparative perspective on East Asia by incorporating evidence from other countries. This often includes the city states of Singapore and—in some instances—Hong Kong and also the comparatively less successful Southeast Asian economies of Malaysia, Indonesia and Thailand (for example Campos & Root, 1996; Root, 1996; World Bank, 1993). These studies represent attempts to draw generalizable lessons from all the high-performing Asian economies.

Scholarly publications on the economic development of East Asia differ not only in their country-specific focus, but also concerning the research question they attempt to answer. According to Vu (2007, pp. 27–28), the literature on the developmental state deals with three different fundamental questions:

(1) What roles do developmental states play in the successful industrialization of their countries?

(2) What do developmental states share and what is generalizable about them?

(3) Why did developmental states emerge where they did but not elsewhere?

To put it even simpler, research has been aimed at answering *what* the authorities in developmental states do, *how they are able* to do it and *why* they do it. While the first question is mainly concerned with the policies that governments in East Asia pursued, the second question relates to the specific institutions and the organizational structures that characterized these states. For answering the third questions, the analysis of exogenous constraints faced by decision makers are of major importance. It is apparent from the perspective of the NIE that the three questions are closely interrelated. On the one hand, institutions represent constraints for political decision makers and thus shape policies; on the other hand, the institutions themselves are partly the result of political decisions. Similarly, the geopolitical environment is a source of constraints that affect political decisions and the path of institutional development, but it is to a certain degree also the result of political decisions taken in the past. Therefore, publications on East Asia often deal with several of these questions at the same time, whether explicitly or implicitly.

The way in which these questions are addressed in terms of methodology is generally similar. The developmental state literature differs from most current research in economics, including the NIE, since it does not follow a deductive approach based on specific assumptions on the characteristics and behavior of economic agents. In contrast, the central publications derive their conclusions in an essentially inductive way from historical experiences of economic development. This was also the methodology of both Friedrich List and his successors of the German Historical School which was dominant in many continental European countries before the Second World War and influential until the 1960s even in the United States (Chang, 2003, pp. 5–7). Two general approaches in the literature on East Asia can be distinguished. The major early publications, in particular Johnson (1982), Amsden (1989), and Wade (1990/2004), focus exclusively on one country, and are broadly structured along chronological lines. Thus, they essentially represent historical narratives that introduce implications for economic policy and—to some degree—economic theory. Most of the major subsequent publications do not focus on one country, but are comparative studies. While not explicit about the theoretical foundations of their methodology, it can be argued that these latter studies essentially follow John Stuart Mill's methods of induction. Conclusions are usually inferred by comparing several East Asian countries that show a similarly successful economic development (and therefore based on the method of agreement). In some cases, this approach is complemented by contrasting the successful economies of East Asia with countries in other developing regions. These analyses are thus based on the method of difference. The World Bank study on the East Asian miracle (1993), as well as the contributions of Root (1996) and Campos and Root (1996), are examples of the former approach,[11] while Evans (1995) and Haggard (1990) contrast the East Asian experience with that of Latin American economies and (in the case of Evans) India.

The following section gives a short overview over the main topics and findings of research on the economic development of East Asia in accordance with the three questions specified above in order to set the basis for a more detailed analysis of institutional developments in the subsequent sections.

3.2 The key issues of the developmental state literature

3.2.1 Economic policies in East Asia: the controversial role of the state

If a country, or a group of countries, achieves remarkable rates of economic growth while other economies stagnate, it is apparent that the policies of the high-growth countries will be subject to analysis by both researchers and practitioners of economic policy. Indeed, the economic policies of the HPAEs have been the focus of a large part of economic literature on East Asia; however, they have also been the topic that raised most controversy among economists and scholars of related fields. The key issue in this debate is the role of the state in the East Asian economies and, in particular, the importance of government interventions for economic growth.

There are three different perspectives on this issue in the scholarly literature (see Evans, 1998, p. 67; Wade, 1990/2004, pp. 22–29; World Bank, 1993, pp. 82–85). One school of thought attributes the rise of the East Asian economies to a very restricted role of the state that enabled the invisible hand of market

---

11 Since Root (1996) explicitly deals with the fact that the Philippines and Indonesia were not as successful as other HPAEs, his approach also includes some elements of the method of difference. However, this is not his key focus.

mechanism to allocate resources in an economically efficient way. This perspective has been called the *free market explanation* (Wade, 1990/2004, p. 82) or the *neoclassical perspective* (World Bank, 1993, p. 82). On the other side of the spectrum, there have been several scholars, such as Johnson, Amsden or Wade, who claim that activist and selective interventions played a major role for East Asian economic development. This has been called the *governed market explanation* (Wade, 1990/2004, p. 24), the *revisionist view* (World Bank, 1993, p. 83), the *industrial policy model* (Evans, 1998, p. 67) or the *developmental state view* (Aoki, Kim, & Okuno-Fujiwara, 1997a, p. xv). Finally, several attempts have been made to find a middle ground between this *free market vs. government intervention* dichotomy. While there are important differences between these approaches, they agree that governments did play an important role in East Asian growth and that interventions took place. Commonly, it is argued that only some interventions (if any) had a positive effect on economic growth, and that the defining characteristic of these specific interventions was that they were market-conforming. However, it has to be noted that these attempts to find a middle ground do not represent a coherent third school of thought of their own, since they differ significantly in their conclusions and their proximity to the other two perspectives.

The free-market explanation

As summarized by Wade (1990, p. 22), proponents of a free market explanation for the East Asian miracle argue that Japan, and later the Tiger States, were economically successful because their governments hardly interfered with the market mechanism. There are two commonly cited advocates of this view: Hugh Patrick and Edward Chen. Hugh Patrick interpreted "Japanese economic performance as due primarily to the actions and efforts of private individuals and enterprises responding to the opportunities provided in quite free markets for commodities and labor" (Patrick, 1977, p. 239, cited in Johnson, 1982, p. 9; Wade, 1990/2004, p. 22; White & Wade, 1988, p. 4). Edward Chen argued that in Japan, South Korea, Taiwan, Hong Kong and Singapore "state intervention is largely absent. What the state provided is simply a stable environment for the entrepreneurs to perform their functions" (Chen, 1979, pp. 183–184, cited in Wade, 1990/2004, p. 22; White & Wade, 1988, p. 4; World Bank, 1993, p. 82). The key argument of this perspective on East Asian growth is that governments played only a minor role in the economy and instead allowed markets to be at the center stage of economic life (World Bank, 1993, p. 82). Market-friendly policies in East Asia allegedly included a stable fiscal and monetary policy that resulted in low inflation; flexible labor markets and the exploitation of comparative advantages through competitive exchange rates, openness to trade and foreign investment (Haggard, 2004, p. 54). According to Stephen Haggard (2004), the free market explanation for East Asian growth was dominant in the literature on East Asia until 1982. He claims that John Williamson's list of the policy prescriptions of the *Washington Consensus* (Williamson, J., 1990) could have been easily taken from the early literature on East Asia (Haggard, 2004, p. 54).

The governed market explanation

The free market interpretation of East Asian growth has been harshly criticized by scholars because of a perceived lack of factual validity, particularly concerning the economic policies of Japan, South Korea, and Taiwan (World Bank, 1993, p. 83). Therefore, other explanations for East Asian growth have emerged which concede that the state had a larger role in the economy than asserted by proponents of the free market view. The importance of industrial policies and government guidance of the private sector in the East Asian economies was already stressed by some scholars in the 1970s (Wade, 1990/2004, pp. 24–25). However, Haggard (2004, p. 54) asserts that the real beginning of the counter revolution to the neoclassical arguments started with the publication of Chalmers Johnson's "MITI and the Japanese miracle" in 1982. According to Johnson, the market-based explanation is clearly insufficient in explaining the Japanese miracle. In contrast, he claimed that industrial policies promoting the investment in certain strategic industries were an essential cause of Japan's fast economic growth (1982, pp. 9–11). From this perspective, the state's role is to serve as a guide for the path of economic development and to "lead the market in critical ways (World Bank, 1993, p. 83).

Other prominent scholars that adhere to this perspective on East Asian growth, which the World Bank has termed *revisionist*, are Alice Amsden (1989, 1991, 1995), Robert Wade (1988, 1990, 2008), Ha-Joon Chang (1993, 1999, 2003), and Peter Evans (1995, 1998). It should be noted that proponents of this perspective do not argue that the mere fact that the governments of some East Asian economies pursued industrial policies is sufficient to explain their superior growth. Rather, it is argued that the quality of industrial policies and the combination of these policies with other factors were of vital importance for their success. Amsden stresses that industrialization outside of Western Europe and North America has generally involved a high degree of state intervention. However, South Korea has been more successful than non-East Asian countries, because the government set stringent performance standards for the recipients of subsidies (Amsden, 1989, pp. v–vi). Wade (1990/2004) calls his own perspective the *governed market theory* and identifies three key factors for the superior performance of East Asian economies:

(1) very high levels of productive investment, making for fast transfer of newer techniques into actual production;

(2) more investment in certain key industries than would have occurred in the absence of government intervention; and

(3) exposure of many industries to international competition, in foreign markets if not at home. (Wade 1990/2004, p. 26)

Thus, he argues that sector-specific industrial policies are only a part of the explanation for East Asian growth.

Attempts to find a middle ground

The attempts to find a middle ground between the *governed market* and the *free market* explanations are manifold. A common approach is to admit the existence of interventions in some East Asian economies while justifying them from a perspective that remains, in principle, neoclassic. An approach, which is clearly very close to orthodox neoclassical reasoning, is what Wade terms the *simulated market explanation* (Wade 1990, p. 23–24). Proponents of this view, such as Jagdish Bhagwati and the former World Bank chief economist Anne Krueger, argue that governments in East Asia intervened actively in the economy, but only in order to offset existing artificial market distortions. This is particularly stressed concerning measures such as export subsidies. While Krueger concedes that some of the Asian Tigers intervened in the economy through setting incentives for exports through subsidies and similar measures, she argues that these measures essentially counterbalanced incentives for import-substituting production, resulting in domestic incentives that were reasonably uniform. Furthermore, she points out that no specific industry was supported through these incentives to export because they applied to all commodities (Krueger, 1990, pp. 108–109). Similarly, Bhagwati argues that the East Asian Tigers were economically successful because they followed a so called *export promotion strategy*, that is characterized by "the adoption of a structure of incentives which does not discriminate against exports in favor of the home market" (Bhagwati, 1988, pp. 30–31).

Similar to the perspective of Bhagwati and Krueger, the *profit-investment nexus model* of Akyüz and Gore (1996) admits the importance of interventions for East Asian growth while stressing the importance of interventions that were non-selective in the way that they did not explicitly promote a pre-determined industrial structure or specific companies. However, Akyüz and Gore do not claim that the interventions were market-conforming in the sense that they counterbalanced existing market distortions. While the proponents of both the *industrial policy explanation* and the more market-friendly perspectives usually focus their argument on the allocation of resources, Akyüz and Gore assert that accumulation rather than allocation was decisive for the impressive performance of East Asian economies (1996, pp. 462–463). Moreover, they state that the governments in East Asia played a crucial supporting role in capital accumulation through policies which promoted corporate profits and household savings (1996, pp. 466–468).

The World Bank published one of the most comprehensive studies on the East Asian miracle in 1993. In this study, the World Bank calls its own perspective on East Asian economic policies the *market-friendly view* (1993, pp. 84–86). While this view was already developed in an earlier World Development Report focusing on a general analysis of the experiences of developing countries (World Bank, 1991), it is argued that its key conclusions are also valid for East Asia. According to the market-friendly view, "the appropriate role of government (. . .) is to ensure adequate investments in people, provision of a competitive climate for enterprise, openness to international trade and stable macroeconomic management. But beyond these roles, governments are likely to do more harm than good." (World Bank, 1993, p. 84). While the World Bank study concedes that governments in some of the most successful East Asian economies carried out significant interventions, it is argued that "East Asian success sometimes occurred *in spite of* rather than *because of* market interventions" (World Bank, 1993, p. 86, italics original).

Despite these statements, the World Bank admits the considerable importance of interventions in some East Asian countries, particularly the most successful economies in Northeast Asia, in an extensive assessment of economic policies in the same study (World Bank, 1993, pp. 89–102). According to this assessment, the policies which were conducive to economic growth do not only include broad interventions aimed at promoting exports, but also selective interventions that served "very narrow promotion targets" (World Bank, 1993, p. 90) by supporting specific industries and firms. In addition, it is acknowledged that "some selective interventions went beyond helping markets perform better. Rather, they guided and in some cases even bypassed markets" (World Bank, 1993, p. 90). These findings clearly represent a sharp contrast to the basic principles of the World Bank's *market-friendly view* that were specified earlier, and are not consistent with a strict interpretation of these principles.

The *market enhancing view* advocated in the collective volume of Aoki, Kim, and Okuno-Fujiwara (1997b) represents an explicit attempt to overcome the dichotomy between explanations for the East Asian miracle that advocate either state-led development or the predominance of market-coordination (Aoki, Kim, & Okuno-Fujiwara, 1997a, pp. xv-xvii). As argued in the contribution of Aoki, Murdock, and Okuno-Fujiwara (1997, p. 1), the proponents of the market enhancing view differ with advocates of other perspectives concerning the way coordination failures were resolved in the high-performing Asian economies. It is asserted that most research in the field has conceived the market and interventions of the government as two alternative resource-allocation mechanisms. In contrast, the market enhancing view is summarized as follows:

> Instead of viewing government and the market as the only alternatives, and as mutually exclusive substitutes, we examine the role of government policy to facilitate or complement private-sector coordination. We start from the premise that private-sector institutions have important comparative advantages *vis-à-vis* the government (. . .). We also recognize that private-sector institutions do not solve all important market imperfections and that this is particularly true for economies in a low state of development. (. . . .) The market-enhancing view thus stresses the mechanisms whereby government policy is directed at improving the ability of the private sector to solve coordination problems and overcome other market imperfections. (Aoki, Murdock, & Okuno-Fujiwara, 1997, pp. 1-2)

As summarized in this section, the discussion between advocates of different explanations for the East Asian miracle presented here has mainly concerned the choice of economic policies. Different conclusions on the degree of interventionism in the East Asian economies and the relationship between state interventions and economic development have been the source of disagreement. As the advocates of other attempts to find a middle ground between the *free market* and the *governed market* explanations, the proponents of the *market-enhancing view* admit the existence state interventions in the HPAEs. Aoki, Murdock, and Okuno-Fujiwara (1997) do not explicitly address the dispute on the historical reality of interventionism in East Asia. However, they largely follow the perspective of the World Bank study (1993). This means that the existence of selective, targeted industrial policies is admitted, but they are not given the same importance as in the publications of Johnson, Wade, Amsden, or Chang. Instead, the proponents of the *market-enhancing view* argue that the main role of the governments in the HPAEs was to "complement and foster private sector coordination" (Aoki, Murdock, & Okuno-Fujiwara, 1997, p. 8). This shifts the focus from the economic policy approach pursued by the East Asian governments toward specific mechanisms and institutions at the intersection between state and business. These issues have also been dealt with by other scholars and will be discussed in detail in Section 3.2.2.

Perspective adopted in the present study

The debate on the role of the state in the East Asian miracle has not ended. However, it has to be noted that the free market explanation, which fully negates the importance of state interventions for East Asian growth, has not been advocated in recent publications. In this sense, scholars have reached a basic agreement that activist economic policies were pursued in several of the most successful East Asian economies. Yet, the nature and consequences of these policies is still controversial. The simulated market perspective, according to which interventions essentially counterbalanced each other, would implicate that the state used policies to correct for state failure—either its own failures caused by previous interventions or the failures of other states that implemented trade barriers hindering the optimal allocation of resources on an international scale.

In spite of the prominent proponents of this hypothesis, this is generally not the approach that scholarly publications in the field have maintained over the last years. Instead, it is commonly acknowledged that interventions went significantly beyond this in at least some of the high-performing Asian economies. If they had a beneficial influence on East Asian development, the achievement was to correct for market failure, and not for state failure. Whether this was indeed achieved or not is a further source of controversy. Scholars such as Johnson, Wade, Amsden, and Chang have always maintained their support for the industrial policy explanation for East Asian growth. As was noted here, the World Bank (1993, p. 86) claimed that growth sometimes happened in spite of, and not because of, interventions. Nevertheless, even the World Bank study acknowledged that selective interventions were important for the successful development of some HPAEs. Therefore, Chang (2003, p. 49) goes so far as to assert that there is nowadays a broad consensus that the successful economic performance of Japan and the Asian Tigers (except Hong Kong) was caused by activist industrial, trade and technology policies.

Despite Chang's claim that there is a consensus, it is highly probable that other scholars still disagree with him on this issue. However, a comprehensive and definite test of the varying perspectives of research on the East Asian economic policies is very hard to realize and certainly beyond the scope of this study. In this instance, a researcher sometimes has to decide which explanation is the most plausible, without being able to base his evaluation on hard data. In the subsequent sections, the present study will follow the argument of Wade (2008), who asserted convincingly:

The fact that they [the East Asian capitalist economies; M.S.] had intensive government 'intervention' does not mean that the intervention was important to their subsequent growth, of course. (. . .) But we now have detailed studies of how these industrial policies worked, and these detailed studies make it plausible that the policies had an important effect. (p.18)

It is thus postulated that at least Japan, Taiwan, Singapore and South Korea, during their fast catch-up growth, conformed to a high degree to Johnson's notion of a developmental state, whereas the newly industrializing economies in Southeast Asia may only show some characteristics of this concept.

To sum up the literature, four main conclusions on the economic policies of the high-performing Asian economies will be drawn here to set the foundations for the analysis in the subsequent sections of the study:

(1) The successful East Asian economies provided a comparatively stable macroeconomic environment that was generally supportive of private business.

(2) East Asian governments pursued policies that supported capital accumulation, raised the overall level of investment and promoted economic development.

(3) In addition to interventions promoting capital accumulation, selective interventions that supported specific industries occurred.

(4) In spite of some commonly acknowledged failures, selective interventions were overall not harmful, but rather supportive of economic development.

A developmental state from this perspective is a state that intervenes in the economy on the one hand to raise the overall level of capital accumulation and on the other hand to promote specific industries that are considered to be of particular value for the overall economic development of the society. It is furthermore characterized by carrying out these interventions effectively to sustain a high economic growth rate over a long period of time—in the case of the HPAEs over several decades. Since capital accumulation and manufacturing industries are promoted, economic growth is based on a constant upgrading of the economy toward more capital-intensive, and at a later stage, knowledge-intensive, industries. While this prerequisite is usually not made explicit, it can be inferred that virtually all contributions to the developmental state literature implicitly label a developmental state as such only if it is, or has been, successful in promoting sustainable economic growth.

3.2.2 Effective governance as a prerequisite for the developmental state

Even though there is no agreement on the type of policies that were commonly followed by the East Asian economies, their performance makes it apparent that their economic policy was comparatively successful. This does obviously not mean that economic policies were always optimal and no examples of failed policies exist. Of course, it is theoretically possible that the East Asian countries would have grown even faster if other policies had been chosen in specific situations. Nevertheless, it is reasonable to argue that economic policy in the HPAEs was generally more conducive to economic growth than in virtually all other developing and emerging economies.

It has to be stressed that the choice of good economic policies is only a part of a successful economic policy. As Root notes, a government may formulate appropriate policies, yet at the same time lack the capacity to implement them, or to "deliver what it promises" (1996, p. 147). Indeed, it has been argued that economic and industrial policies which were (at least superficially) similar to the strategies of the high-performing Asian economies lead to deleterious effects in other countries (Haggard, 2004, p. 56). It is thus not only of great interest to analyze according to which processes economic policies were chosen in the East Asian economies, but also to assess what factors facilitated the implementation of these policies. While the debate on economic policy that was outlined in the preceding section has not led to a consensus among economists, it is therefore complemented by a second debate on the institutional foundations of the East Asian miracle (Cheng, Haggard, & Kang, 1998, p. 88; Haggard, 2004, p. 56).

A term that is often used in research on this topic is *governance*, which can be defined as

> the traditions and institutions by which authority in a country is exercised. This includes the process by which governments are selected, monitored and replaced; the capacity of the government to effectively formulate and implement sound policies; and the respect of citizens and the state for the institutions that govern economic and social interactions among them. (Kaufman et al., 1999, p. 1)

Important contributions to the research on the specific characteristics of governance in East Asia have been made by Root (1996, 1998), Haggard (1990, 2004), Evans (1995, 1998), and Ahrens (2002). According to Evans, the challenge of economic research in this field is to link the apparent disparity in the economic performance of different countries to underlying differences in the structure of states and the relations of states with the society (Evans, 1995, p. 44).

The definition of governance stated above also includes the process of government selection and, thus, the regime type of a country as a key characteristic of its overall governance structure. However, Root argues convincingly that regime type, at least in the broad sense of a dichotomy between democracy and authoritarianism, does not explain variations in economic growth across Asia. Instead, he claims that other differences in the governance structure of the East Asian economies may provide explanations for their superior performance and their ability to formulate and implement appropriate policies (1996, pp. 170–181; 1998, p. 60). This relates to two key elements of the governance structure that are commonly highlighted in the literature on East Asia: (1) the bureaucracy and (2) the interface between the state (in particular the bureaucracy) and business elites, or, in a more general sense, between the state and society as a whole (see for example Root, 1996, p. 5; World Bank, 1993, pp. 167–188).

The importance of the bureaucracy

As the title of "MITI and the Japanese Miracle" indicates, the pivotal importance of the bureaucracy for economic development in East Asia was already a key argument of Johnson's pioneering work. In the last chapter of the book, Johnson (1982) summarizes his insights on Japan by specifying the following four constituting elements of the developmental state, three out of which deal explicitly with the bureaucracy:

> The first element of the model is the existence of a small, inexpensive, but elite bureaucracy staffed by the best managerial talent available in the system. (....)
>
> The second element of the model is a political system in which the bureaucracy is given sufficient scope to take initiative and operative effectively (....)
>
> The third element of the model is the perfection of market-conforming methods of state intervention in the economy. (....)
>
> The fourth and final element of the model is a pilot organization like MITI. (Johnson, 1982, pp. 315–320)

While Johnson explicitly sees a concern with industrial policy as the essence of the developmental state (see preceding section), the elements of his model are in principle also compatible with more market oriented perspectives on economic policy (Wade, 1990/2004, p. 26). As stressed by Cheng at al. (1998, p. 88), as well as Evans (1998, p. 68), even champions of a minimalist government can agree that the competence of the bureaucracy is essential for successful economic policy. However, Evans argues that bureaucratic capability is even more important for more interventionist explanations of East Asian growth (Evans, 1998, p. 68).

The overall influence of the bureaucracy on economic policy and its power vis-à-vis politicians, society, the private sector and interest groups have also been key issues in other contributions on East Asia. According to several accounts (World Bank, 1993, p. 167; Akyüz et al., 1998, p. 28), the foremost institutional characteristic of East Asian bureaucracies has been the insulation of economic technocrats, i.e. their ability "to formulate and implement policies in keeping with politically formulated national goals with a minimum of lobbying for special favors from politicians and interest groups" (World Bank, 1993, p. 167). Particularly in post-war Japan, the bureaucracy disposed of significantly more power and responsibilities than it is common in Western economies (Johnson, 1985, p. 61; World Bank, 1993, pp. 168–169). As summarized by Johnson, Japan's elite bureaucracy "makes most major decisions, drafts virtually all legislation, controls the national budget, and is the source of all major policy innovations in the system" (1982, pp. 20–21). The overall division of power between politicians and bureaucrats and the degree of bureaucratic autonomy has been different between the high-performing Asian economies and between different phases of development in Japan. Nevertheless, the primacy of the bureaucracy over the legislature in important areas has been considered a common characteristic of all HPAEs. As the World Bank (1993) summarized:

> One of the distinct features of the budgetary process in all the HPAEs is the primacy given to the bureaucracy over the legislature in drafting laws. Though the legislature must approve the laws, the bureaucracy studies, analyzes, and drafts the bills. It has considerable control over the agenda and can use this to minimize political pressure. (p. 170)

In order to ensure that the economic bureaucracy has the capability to perform its crucial and extensive responsibilities, the ability of the state to attract highly qualified individuals to public service, and particularly to the economic bureaucracy, is generally considered vital. The World Bank identifies three general principles of successful bureaucracies in East Asia: (1) Merit-based recruitment and promotion, (2) an incentive-based and competitive compensation; and (3) a well-defined, competitive career path with ample rewards for those at the top (World Bank, 1993, pp. 174–175).

Johnson (1985, pp. 59–60) identified the intrinsic meritocracy that governed hiring and promotion in the Japanese economic bureaucracy as an important foundation of its attractiveness for qualified graduates. A major part of this meritocracy is compulsory and extremely selective examinations for civil service applicants (Johnson, 1982, pp. 57–58). While similar exams have been used to select bureaucrats in South Korea (Root, 1996, p. 21; World Bank, 1993, p. 175), recruitment in other successful East Asian economies such as Taiwan and Singapore has taken place in a variety of different ways along essentially meritocratic lines (Evans, 1998, p. 71). Once candidates achieve a position as a public official, bureaucrats in Japan, South Korea and Singapore receive salaries that are comparable or even superior to those of employees in the private sector (World Bank, 1993, pp. 176–177). While the average salaries of public officials in Taiwan have been considerably lower than in the private sector for the period of its fast economic growth, technocrats in economic planning agencies receive much higher salaries than those in other agencies (Cheng et al., 1998, pp. 99–100). Less developed East Asian economies have generally provided compensation packages to bureaucrats that were less competitive compared to the private sector (World Bank, 1993, p. 177).

Evans (1995) summarizes that the public service of developmental states in East Asia approximates an ideal type Weberian bureaucracy in several aspects, in particular concerning highly selective meritocratic recruitment, long term career rewards and corporate coherence. While he agrees with other accounts that this creates certain autonomy of the East Asian bureaucracies from interest group pressures, he argues that it is misleading to describe public agencies and technocrats as insulated since the state and in particular the bureaucracy maintained a concrete set of ties to society. He labels this combination of independence and social ties *embedded autonomy* and considers it to be a decisive factor for East Asian growth (Evans 1995, pp. 12–13).

The state-society interface

According to Evans (1998), the connection between state and society was made on two levels. On a basic level, the East Asian governments succeeded in making their commitment to the economic development of their nations credible. In addition to this broad ideological connection, there is a set of concrete interpersonal ties, organizations and institutions that characterized the government-business relations in East Asia (Evans, 1998, p. 74). Although other publications do not use Evans' term of *embedded autonomy* to describe the close ties between the state and society in the successful East Asian economies, there is a notable consensus on their importance for the successful formulation and implementation of economic policies. There was an active participation of societal groups in the policy making process of the high-performing Asian economies, despite the authoritarian nature of some governments in the period of rapid economic development (Root, 1996, pp. 11–15; 1998, pp 68–72). In particular, the participation of major private businesses in this process has been an important participatory mechanism in East Asia (World Bank, 1993, pp. 181–188; Evans, 1998, pp. 74–78).

One of the main functions of the government-business interface is to share information between private companies and the relevant public agents. This enables the bureaucracy and political leaders to gather information on the condition of the economy, the situation of private businesses, and new trends in technology. Moreover, feedback on the effects of existing regulations and previously implemented economic policies could be gathered (Root, 1998, pp. 69–70; World Bank, 1993, p. 187). In this way, businesses have notable influence on the formulation of new policies. Furthermore, the flow of information also goes from the state to the private sector and is crucial in the effective implementation of policies (Evans, 1998, p. 77). This can also increase the credibility of the state's commitment to these policies (Root, 1998, pp. 69–70; Stiglitz, 1996 p. 163). In the East Asian developmental states, the continuous interaction between economic bureaucracy and private business was a precondition for the implementation of what Evans has called the *support performance bargain* (Evans, 1998, p. 76). This means that the state apparatus on the one hand supported specific companies and industries through subsidies and similar measures. On the other hand, the impact of these measures and the performance of supported companies is closely monitored, as Amsden (1995, p. 795) stressed.

The actual organization of government-business ties has varied among the high-performing Asian economies (Evans, 1998, p. 76). An essential mechanism in the state-business interface of several East Asian countries are credible intermediary organizations such as autonomous business associations which served to share information between companies and the state and mediated in case of conflicts (Root, 1998, p. 69). In addition, deliberation councils, which bring together bureaucrats of specific agencies and private industry, have been frequently emphasized in the research on East Asian institutions (Root, 1998, p. 69–70; Stiglitz, 1996, p. 164). These councils are of major importance in Japan and South Korea and also have also been emulated to a certain degree in Malaysia beginning in the mid-1980s (World Bank, 1993, pp. 181–184). Taiwan and Singapore have used different channels of communication. In Singapore, private citizens review government policies and commented on them by serving as directors of government statutory boards and as members of ad hoc advisory boards (World Bank, 1993, p. 184). In contrast to the previously mentioned countries, formal connections between government and business are much less prominent in Taiwan (World Bank, 1993, p. 184; Evans, 1998, p. 77). However, the high importance of state-owned companies in the Taiwanese economy results in a considerable influence of the state on the smaller companies of the private sector (World Bank, p. 1993, p. 185). Furthermore, periodic large-scale conferences that bring together economic policy makers, business leaders and academics have been held (Evans, p. 1998, p. 76). Proponents of the *market enhancing view* furthermore stress the importance of banks and credit markets as intermediaries between East Asian governments and the private sector. According to Aoki, Murdock, and Okuno-Fujiwara, state interventions in the financial sector that credibly signal the government's commitment to sustainable economic growth will foster the long-term orientation of banks. This would increase their willingness to invest in information-gathering, give long-term credits and to carefully monitor their debtors (Aoki, Murdock, & Okuno-Fujiwara, 1998, pp. 8-11).

The capability and organization of the bureaucracy, as well as the functioning of the state-business interface, have differed between the East Asian Tigers and their less successful counterparts in Southeast Asia. As summarized by Doner et al. (2005, pp. 334–336), the ideal-type of a meritocratic bureaucracy, which has close ties to the private sector and whose economic policies are coordinated by a pilot agency, is largely present in South Korea, Taiwan, and Singapore, but only to a limited degree in Malaysia and Thailand and even less in Indonesia or the economically struggling Philippines. The differences are found in the sphere of the state-business nexus. While the public-private collaboration is governed by transparent rules in South Korea, Taiwan, and Singapore, the transparency of rules is evaluated as significantly lower in the other Southeast Asian economies (Doner et al. 2005, p. 335).

In contrast to scholars who emphasize the strength of the developmental states vis-à-vis weak, subordinated and repressed societies (see Leftwich, 1995, p. 405), Root argues that states in the high-performing economies are best described as *strong but limited*, which distinguishes them from most other states in the developing world. The East Asian states were strong in the sense that they possessed institutional arrangements that enabled them to resist the pressures of narrow interests, and they were limited in the sense that the power of governments and the bureaucracy was constrained by binding rules and credible commitments (Root, 1996, pp. 141–143). A meritocratic, autonomous, public bureaucracy along with close and transparent ties between the state and private companies are important institutional foundations of such a state. From this perspective, the stability and transparency of the consultative mechanisms involved in the process of policy making in East Asia also served to tie the regime's hands to policies once they had been chosen (Root, 1998, p. 69).

3.2.3 Conditions for the emergence of a developmental state

As elaborated in the preceding sections, there is a fundamental consensus in the literature that governments in the high-performing Asian economies pursued policies that were in most cases conducive to economic growth and that they created institutions which not only helped them formulate and implement these policies, but also credibly signaled their commitment to the pursuit of economic development. However, the question remains as to why the governments of several East Asian countries created such institutional structures, while the governments of most other emerging and developing countries around the globe did not. As Vu (2007, p. 27) points out, this is essentially an historical issue and of vital importance for any conclusion on the lessons that can be learned from the East Asian experience. What were the underlying reasons for the apparent commitment of East Asian bureaucrats and even authoritarian rulers to the economic development of their nations and for their ability to achieve this objective?

Several scholars have attempted to answer this question. A common focus of this research has been the historical, cultural and geopolitical context of economic development in East Asia. In particular, the different set of exogenous conditions that were faced by East Asian political decision makers compared with leaders in Latin America or Africa are considered an important explanatory factor for the different development path of these regions. These conditions represented constraints that committed decision makers to pursue the economic development of their nations instead of extracting resources in a predatory manner. From this perspective, the historic, cultural and geopolitical context is interpreted primarily as a source of limitations. Conversely, it has been stressed that some conditions specific to the high-performing Asian economies were supportive to these countries' capacity for pursuing a strategy of economic growth and furthermore provided opportunities for development that were not present for countries in other regions.

The importance of culture

An explanation for East Asian growth that is often heard in public discussion and the media is the specific cultural heritage of countries in the region and the virtues of supposed Asian values for economic development. In particular, the importance of Confucianism is commonly stressed as the source of these values in Japan, Korea and the ethnically predominantly Chinese nations (the V.R. China, Taiwan, Hong Kong and Singapore), as several authors point out (Rowen, 1998, p. 20; Root, 1996, p. 2).

However, there is a consensus in economic research that this explanation is not sufficient and even misleading. A counter-argument is that most countries that have been shaped by Confucian values for centuries were actually poor until recently and some still are (Rowen, 1998, p. 5). Indeed, while Confucianism has been interpreted as the cultural foundation for East Asian economic development in recent decades, it had been considered the reason for economic backwardness and poverty of the region prior to the Asian miracle (Akyüz et al.,

1998, p. 27; Rowen, 1998, pp. 21–22). In addition, Root points out that the beginning of economic success of some East Asian countries actually corresponds with a shift away from Confucian principles by leaders such as Park Chung-hee of South Korea and Lee Kuan Yew in Singapore (Root, 1998, p. 61). However, this does not mean that some values typically associated with Confucianism, in particular the high importance which is traditionally given to education, did not contribute to the economic development of the region in a significantly positive way (Rowen, 1998, p. 22).

The importance of external threats

If one takes into account that the countries which became economically successful through the East Asian miracle were comparatively poor before, the focus invariably shifts to the specific conditions in the initial phases of their fast growth. In this respect, a factor that is commonly acknowledged in the literature as being fundamental for the commitment of some East Asian leaders to economic growth is the existence of vital external threats to the national survival of their countries (Woo-Cumings, 1998; see also Doner et al., 2005, p. 339; Haggard, 2004, p. 71; Kang, 1995; p. 584). However, it should be noted that the prevalence of such threats differed drastically between the HPAEs. The challenge that the People's Republic of China represented for the survival of Taiwan as a de facto sovereign entity after 1949, as well as the fierce and persistent conflict between North and South Korea after the end of the Korean War in 1953, are the most eminent and widely discussed of these threats. As extensively elaborated by Meredith Woo-Cumings (1998, p. 322), economic growth was seen as indispensable for achieving military security in these countries, and therefore created a national determination to the pursuit of economic development.

Similarly, it has been argued that the danger of becoming a colony of the Western powers was a key incentive for the pursuit of economic reforms in late-19th century Japan (Cumings, 1984, pp. 8–9; Grabowski, 1994, p. 414). In the case of Singapore, it has been argued that a sense of vulnerability was created by the separation from Malaysia in 1965 in combination with severe riots between ethnic Chinese and Malays and Britain's announcement that it would withdraw its military forces (Doner et al., 2005, p. 347). In contrast, there were no eminent external threats to Malaysia, Indonesia or Thailand (Perkins, 1994, pp. 660–661).

Natural resources

Another difference between the HPAEs is the varying endowment of natural resources. Japan and the four Asian Tigers are only scarcely endowed with natural resources. In addition, these five countries have a high population density, which makes them land-scarce and labor-abundant. As a result, these countries could hardly expor natural resources or agricultural goods. In contrast, Malaysia, Thailand, and Indonesia are much better endowed with natural resources and major exporters of goods such as oil, tin, rubber, and rice. As several scholars argue, the scarcity of natural resources in Japan and the Asian Tigers imposed harder budget constraints on the governments of these countries and caused them to focus on industrialization and growth in manufacturing (Akyüz et al., 1998, pp. 18–19; Doner et al., 2005, pp. 339–340; Kosai & Takeuchi, 1998, p. 314; Perkins 1994, p. 656).

Special relations with the United States

While the governments of some successful East Asian countries had to take their political decisions under stringent exogenous constraints, the same countries also faced some conditions that improved their decision-making freedom, specifically their ability to pursue growth-oriented policy. For South Korea, Taiwan and Japan, the privileged partnership of these countries with the United States was such a condition. According to Cumings (1984, p. 24), the direct economic and military aid that the United States gave to South Korea and Taiwan from 1955 till 1978 surpasses the support that virtually all other emerging or developing countries received during this period. Japan benefited significantly from US military procurements and started its post-war economic take off with the start of the Korean War in 1950, whereas South Korea and Taiwan later benefited from a surge in demand caused by the US engagement in the Vietnam War (Woo-Cumings, 1998, p. 329). In addition to direct financial support, the US also had a decisive influence on economic policy by sending economic advisors to Taipei and Seoul (Woo-Cumings, 1998, p. 330). In this way, the privileged partnership with the United States was an additional constraint for policy makers in these countries.

The importance of the colonial heritage

An additional geopolitical condition that may have contributed to the economic development of the HPAEs was the influence of Japan on its comparatively less developed neighbors. Amsden (1995, p. 796) argues that Japan, the first non-Western country to industrialize, was perceived as an economic role model and benchmark by its neighbors. While this may be true for all countries in the region, the influence of Japan on South Korea and Taiwan, which were both Japanese colonies before 1945, was much more direct and profound. While the colonial rule imposed severe hardships on the native population and has been characterized as brutal and ruthless, it may have also laid some foundations for the later success of the South Korean and Taiwanese economies. This includes not only the improvement of the physical infrastructure, but also a transformation of the institutional environment and the industrial structure present (Kohli, 1999; see also Cumings, 1984, pp. 10–12; Vu, 2007, p. 31; Woo-Cumings, 1998, pp. 324–326).

Furthermore, it is sometimes noted that the East Asian economies benefitted from an unusually equitable distribution of wealth and the absence of a dominant economic class at the beginning of their economic take-off. In South Korea and Taiwan, these initial conditions were at least partly the result of colonialism because land reforms had been carried out under the colonial administration and the Japanese largely controlled business. Furthermore, the Second World War and the following events led to a similar situation in Japan. In Thailand, which was never colonized, and in developmental states with a European colonial heritage, these conditions were not met to the same degree (Aoki, Murdock, & Okuno-Fujiwara, pp. 24–25).

A comprehensive theory on the emergence of developmental states: the contribution of Doner et al. (2005)

An important and comparatively recent contribution to the research on the emergence of developmental states has been made by Doner et al. (2005) in the journal *International Organization*. While virtually all other publications on this issue focus on the importance of one of the factors described above, Doner et al. (2005) attempt to draft a theory on the emergence of developmental states by taking into account all the relevant factors. This theory is not only intended to be systematic, but also to be exhaustive in the way that it establishes all conditions that are necessary and sufficient for a developmental state to emerge (Doner et al 2005, p. 330).

Doner et al.'s (2005, p. 328) hypothesis is that developmental states will emerge if three conditions are fulfilled. Two of these conditions have already been mentioned: the existence of vital external threats to national security and a lack of easy revenue sources caused by scarce natural resources. The third condition is a political regime that faces the credible threat of popular uprisings in the case of deteriorating living standards, which forces the regime to rely on broad coalitional commitments to different popular sectors to maintain its power (Doner et al., 2005, p. 331).

Figure 3: Line of argument in Doner et al. (2005)

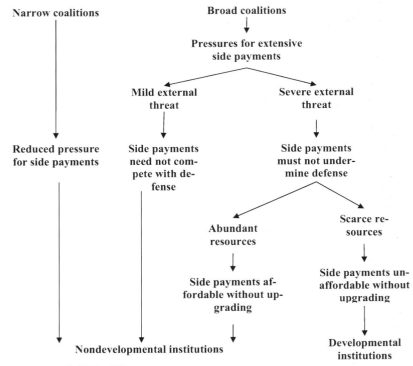

Source: Doner et al., 2005, p. 330.

The corresponding line of argument is summarized in Figure 3. Regimes that rely on broad coalitions face the pressure to deliver extensive side payments to their supporters. If the country faces external security threats in addition to these pressures, side payments have to compete with defense spending. Doner et al. (2005) argue that both side payments and defense spending are affordable for governments that can dispose of abundant resources, while governments that lack these easily available revenue sources are essentially constrained to follow a policy of development through industrial upgrading. As a consequence, a combination of the three described constraints, a condition termed *systemic vul-*

nerability, is considered to be a both necessary and sufficient condition for the emergence of developmental states (Doner et al, 2005, pp. 329–330). According to Doner et al. (2005), South Korea, Taiwan and Singapore all faced this condition, while the comparative abundance of natural resources in the Southeast Asian countries Malaysia, Thailand, Indonesia and the Philippines resulted in intermediate regimes. These intermediate regimes were characterized by less bureaucratic capacity and less encompassing public-private linkages (see Table 3).

Doner et al. (2005) validate their hypothesis using a purely qualitative approach based on facts taken from the existing literature on East Asia. As can be seen in Table 3, Doner et al. (2005) use the predominant religion, homogeneity of ethnicity, colonial heritage, openness to foreign capital as control variables in their qualitative analysis. This means that they do not consider these factors, which have been suggested by other scholars as relevant for the success of East Asian economic development, as having any relevant explanatory power for the emergence of developmental states (Doner et al., 2005, p. 336).[12] In the case of ethnic homogeneity, colonial heritage and openness toward foreign capital, they base this argument on the observation that the three states, which they define as being developmental—South Korea, Taiwan and Singapore—do not share the same characteristics. In the case of the shared Confucian heritage of these three states, they base this notion on the same arguments that were mentioned at the beginning of this section (Doner et al., 2005, p. 336).

---

12   Please note that the term control variable is commonly used with a different meaning in experiments and statistical analyses. The use of the term within the present study, specifically in Table 3, follows the definition in Doner et al. (2005, pp. 336-337) in order to give an accurate reflection of their work.

Table 3: Variables of Doner et al. (2005)

	Control variables				Independent variables			Dependent variables	
	Colonialism	Foreign Capital	Ethnicity	Religion	Coalitions	External threats	Natural resources	Bureaucratic capacity	Public/ Private Linkages
NICS									
Korea	Japanese	Closed	Homogeneous	Confucian	Broad	Severe	Scarce	Strong	Embedded/ encompassing
Taiwan	Japanese	Closed	Homogeneous	Confucian	Broad	Severe	Scarce	Strong	Embedded/ encompassing
Singapore	British	Open	Heterogeneous	Confucian	Broad	Severe	Scarce	Strong	Embedded/ encompassing
ASEAN-4									
Indonesia	Dutch	Open	Heterogeneous	Islam	Broad	Mild	Abundant (oil)	Weak	Clientilist
Malaysia	British	Open	Heterogeneous	Islam	Broad	Mild	Abundant (rubber, tin)	Moderate	Mixed
Philippines	U.S./ Spanish	Open	Heterogeneous	Christian	Narrow	Mild	Abundant (sugar)	Weak	Clientilist
Thailand	Independent	Open	Heterogeneous	Buddhist	Narrow	Mild	Abundant (rice)	Weak to moderate	Mixed

Source: Table from Doner et al. (2005, p. 337); sources for specific entries given there.

One important implication of the model of Doner et al. (2005) is that the political leaders of the three mentioned Asian Tigers took the lead in building developmental states because of the constraints they faced, and not because they were "more brilliant or benign, than their counterparts throughout the developing world" (p. 330). Interpreted in a strict manner, this means that it does not matter who has political power in a country. Neither a political leader's ideology, as determined according to North by his mental model of the world, nor his intellectual capacity would have influence on the emergence of a developmental state. Apparently, Doner et al. (2005) are aware that this conclusion may be exaggerated. They concede: "we treat leadership and agency as epiphenomenal out of our methodological concern for parsimony, rather than any ontological conviction that agency and leadership never matter" (Doner et al., 2005, p. 331). They maintain that this approach toward the importance of political leadership is valid as long as no evidence against the sufficiency and necessity of *systematic vulnerability* is presented—in other words, as long as their theory is not falsified (Doner et al. 2005, p. 330–331).

4 The developmental state and economic theory: implications, theoretical lineage, and the need for further research

4.1 Varying models and definitions

Research that takes into account the experience of several HPAEs has often stressed the differences in economic policies, institutional structures and external conditions for these countries. Nobel laureate Paul Krugman asserted succinctly in his paper "The Myth of the Asian Miracle" (1994) that "the extremely diverse institutions and policies of the various newly industrialized Asian countries, let alone Japan, cannot really be called a common system" (Krugman, 1994, p. 78). Similarly Stephan Haggard stated that research has "hit the point of diminishing marginal returns in the quest for a unifying 'model' of East Asia's growth" (Haggard, 2004, p. 74).

However, the fact that institutional arrangements have taken a variety of forms, and that economic policies have varied both between different countries and over time, does apparently not mean there is nothing to be learned from East Asian experience. One approach to this issue that was taken by a large number of contributions, including the previously cited World Bank Study (1993), the contributions of Root (Campos & Root, 1996; Root, 1996) and a paper published by Krugman's fellow laureate Joseph Stiglitz (1996), is to identify generalizable lessons on a high level of abstraction, while neither denying the existence of major differences between the economies in the region nor emphasizing specific institutional arrangements as indispensable.

Another approach to account for the apparent differences between the high-performing Asian economies is to distinguish between several models of development within the region. As elaborated in the preceding section, Doner et al. (2005) regard South Korea, Taiwan and Singapore as developmental states, while they consider Malaysia, Thailand, Indonesia and the Philippines to be intermediate states (Japan and Hong Kong are not tackled in their paper). Similarly, other authors distinguish between a Northeast Asian and a Southeast Asian model of development, usually including Singapore—which is Southeast Asian geographically—in the Northeast Asian group and excluding Hong Kong altogether on the grounds of pursued economic polices (Akyüz et al. 1998, p. 7; Kosai & Takeuchi, 1998, pp. 314–315). Including Hong Kong in the analysis and stressing its common characteristics with Singapore as city states, Perkins (1994, pp. 655–656) distinguishes three models: the state-interventionist export led model of Japan, South Korea and Taiwan, the free port service commerce dominated model of Singapore and Hong Kong and the natural-resource-based model of the Southeast Asian countries Thailand, Indonesia and Malaysia.

For the purposes of the present study, it should be stressed that the aim is not to identify a common East Asian model, but rather a model of the developmental state. Despite the basic consensus on some essential characteristics of a developmental state, in particular the importance of the bureaucracy and the state-business nexus (as has been outlined in section 3.2.2), there are nevertheless a variety of definitions. This is partly a result of the different research aims of publications and, to a lesser degree, the result of the country focus of contributions. Some definitions explicitly apply to only one specific country or region, while others only refer to characteristics of a state that could in principle be realized in any country. Closely related to the definition of a developmental state is therefore the question of which countries actually are developmental states.

Because of the seminal importance of Chalmers Johnson's "MITI and the Japanese Miracle", the definition devised there, based exclusively on the Japanese experience, is still the most renowned and frequently cited. Johnson defined the developmental state as a plan-rational state, contrasting it with the Socialist command economies of the Eastern Bloc, which he considered to be plan-ideological, and the Western regulatory states, which he described as market-rational (Johnson, 1982, p. 18). Furthermore, he argues that the essence of a developmental state is that it gives "greatest precedence to industrial policy, that is, to a concern with the structure of domestic industry and with promoting the structure that enhances the nation's international competitiveness" (Johnson, 1982, p. 19). Since Johnson's definition rests on the description of the behavior of developmental states (and Western market economies) as *rational,* it leads to the theory-related question of how rationality and rational behavior are defined in this context. Even though Johnson does not explicitly address this question, it can be inferred from his analysis that he considers a state to be rational if it strives primarily (or even exclusively) for the objective of general economic development. His distinction of plan-rational, market-rational and plan-ideological states hints toward a typology of states, a consideration that is explored in another section.

Other scholars use definitions quite different from Johnson's; however these usually do not contradict his proposition. One example for such a definition, provided by Castells (1992), and later approvingly cited by Johnson (1993, p. 64), is that

A state is developmental when it establishes as its principle of legitimacy its ability to promote and sustain development, understanding by development the combination of steady high rates of economic growth and structural change in the productive system, both domestically and in relationship to the international economy. (Castells, 1992, p. 56)

Further definitions are given by Meredith Woo-Cumings (1999), who defines the term developmental state as "a shorthand for the seamless web of political, bureaucratic, and moneyed influences that structures economic life in capitalist Northeast Asia" (p. 1). Doner et al. (2005) define developmental states as "organizational complexes in which expert and coherent bureaucratic agencies collaborate with organized private sectors to spur national economic transformation" (p. 328). While Woo-Cumings' definition explicitly refers to Northeast Asia, a region that does not include Singapore by common definitions, Doner et al. (2005) posit, that Singapore is a developmental state, but that Malaysia, Thailand, Indonesia and the Philippines are not. In contrast, other contributions, such as Jomo (2004) and Vu (2007), do refer to Southeast Asian economies as developmental states.

Leftwich (1995, pp. 400–401) takes an even broader approach by attempting to construct a model of the developmental state. He does this by taking into account not only evidence from the previously mentioned high-performing economies of Northeast and Southeast Asia, but also from the People's Republic of China and Botswana. He then defines developmental states

as states whose politics have concentrated sufficient power, autonomy and capacity at the centre to shape, pursue and encourage the achievement of explicit developmental objectives, whether by establishing and promoting the conditions and direction of economic growth, or by organizing it directly, or a varying combination of both. (Leftwich, 1995, p. 401)

These alternative definitions are clearly not devised to be mutually exclusive, but rather stress different aspects of state behavior. While Johnson stresses the basis on which decisions are taken (rational or ideological), as well as the purpose of state action (regulation or planning), the other definitions essentially refer to the relationship between the state and society. Castells (1992) emphasizes the source of legitimacy of the state, or its justification for exercising authority over the society. Meanwhile. Woo-Cumings (1999) and Doner et al. (2005) point to specific mechanisms of interaction between state and private actors. Leftwich's (1995) definition stresses both the importance of central power and capacity and the objectives it pursues when exercising this power.

4.2 Toward a typology of states

The question that results from these different definitions—and from the notion of the existence of developmental states in general—is whether they can be justified on theoretical grounds. Three characteristics of the state represent the essence of the above cited definitions (with the possible exception of the region-focused statement of Woo-Cumings (1999):

(1) Developmental states are committed to the economic development of their country's society;

(2) they pursue activist policies that involve the mid- to long-term planning of economic development;

(3) they have the capability of choosing and implementing economic policies that are overall adequate for achieving their objectives. This capability rests mainly on a competent (economic) bureaucracy and an effective interaction between state and business.

If the arguments of the proponents of the developmental state concept are correct, it should be possible to distinguish developmental states from other types of states through analyzing these three aspects.

As noted above, Johnson (1982) defined the developmental state by contrasting it with two other types of states, which he termed plan-ideological and market-rational. Since he uses the term *rational* essentially as a synonym for a genuine commitment to economic growth, it can be inferred that plan-ideological states differ from developmental states in the first aspect. However, both types of states are similar in using planning and active state-involvement for achieving their objectives. Looking at the states that Johnson considered to be plan-ideological, namely the Soviet-type planned economies (Johnson 1982, p. 18), it can furthermore be argued that they did have the ability to implement policies in accordance with government decisions, even though the kind of policies chosen where not conducive to sustainable economic development. This leads to the conclusion that plan-rational and plan-ideological states differ mainly in their overall objective, but show similarities in their methods and capabilities. Non-socialist totalitarian regimes, fascist states for example, may also fit into the plan-ideological category, since they always represent combinations of heavy state interference in the society with a specific ideological commitment. Because of this ideological commitment, economic growth cannot be more than a secondary objective for such states.

The third type of state that Johnson (1982) identified is embodied by the developed Western economies, which he considered to act in most instances market-rational. Similar to developmental states, they act rationally in the way that they pursue economic development and revise policies that are not conducive to this goal. However, they exhibit a lower degree of interference with the private sector and the market mechanism. In terms of bureaucratic capability, it is difficult to gain insights on market-rational states from Johnson's account, since he does not deal with the developed Western economies in great detail. On the one hand, it can be inferred that the economic success that characterizes these economies would not have taken place without a sufficient degree of state capability. On the other hand, the regulatory policies that are, according to Johnson, the focus of Western economies (Johnson, 1982, pp. 18–19) may be less demanding than the developmental, activist policies of plan-rational states. Nevertheless, it is reasonable to argue that a possible difference in bureaucratic capability is not the main distinguishing characteristic of these two types of states. Instead, the distinction relies mainly on the second aspect specified above, namely the degree of involvement in the economy and the degree of economic planning by the state. Figure 4 represents a very basic illustration of the typology of states according to Johnson (1982).

In addition to some theoretical issues that will be discussed in subsequent sections, Johnson's (1982) typology of states has one major and obvious shortcoming: it is apparent that not all countries fit into the three categories. To a certain degree, this is the consequence of the economic environment in 1982, when "MITI and the Japanese Miracle" was published. Johnson describes Japan— arguably the economically most successful country of 1960s and 1970s—as a third type of economy by comparing it with other prevailing types at the time, the Western market economies and the Soviet-type economies. The book ends by reflecting on the lessons that the United States may learn from Japan (Johnson, 1982, pp. 323–324). For several reasons, this is not the approach that has been followed by subsequent scholars and it is not the approach followed here. The economic environment has changed drastically over the last decades. Soviet-type economies essentially vanished, while most market-regulatory Western economies only showed incremental institutional change. Moreover, Japan proved to be economically much less competitive after 1990 than it had previously been. Johnson's analysis in "MITI and the Japanese Miracle" ends in 1975, a time when the wealth and productivity gap between Japan and the Western economies had either, in the case of most European countries, ceased to exist or, in the case of the USA, narrowed substantially. Even though Japan would show superior growth rates for the 15 years after the time-frame of Johnson's analysis, its economic development leads to the conclusion that the institutional characteristics of the Japanese developmental state were more suited to catch-up growth in times of economic backwardness than for competing at the world's economic and technological frontier. Further support for this argument can be found in the development of the East Asian Tigers, particularly South Korea, which suffered an economic breakdown in the Asian crisis of 1997 and has resorted to more market-oriented economic policies since.[13]

Figure 4: Typology of states according to Johnson (1982)

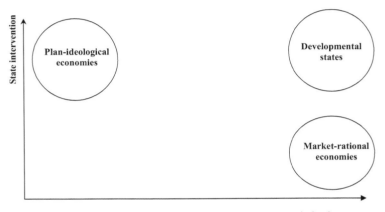

Source: Own compilation.

As a consequence of these profound developments, there has been a shift of the comparative toward contrasting the East Asian developmental states with emerging and developing economies, rather than with regulatory states or with (nowadays virtually non-existent) industrialized socialist economies. However, it is hard to see how most developing countries would fit into the threefold typology specified above. Nevertheless, there is a term that is not only frequently used to describe a certain type of developing economies, but is sometimes contrasted with the notion of a developmental state: the *predatory state* (see, for example, Evans, 1989). As noted in Section 2.3.1, members of governments and bureaucracies in predatory states are individually rational in the sense that they aim to extract resources from the economy in order to maximize their personal utility (Ahrens, 2002, p. 44). This is different from a rational state in the way

---

13   For a detailed analysis of the change in Korean economic policies, see Pirie (2008).

Johnson used the term. Even though the predominance of this individual economic rationality distinguishes predatory states from plan-ideological states,
both types of states have in common that they differ from developmental states
in lacking the dominant overall commitment to economic growth. However, the
differences between developmental states and predatory states are probably
much more profound. Whereas the state apparatus of plan-ideological states
such as the former Soviet Union essentially functioned according to a set of coherent rules, such rules seem to be largely absent in predatory states such as
Mobuto's Zaire. As a consequence, it can be argued that predatory states do not
only lack the commitment to growth, but in most cases also lack the bureaucratic
capability to successfully implement policies.

Figure 5: Typology of emerging and developing economies

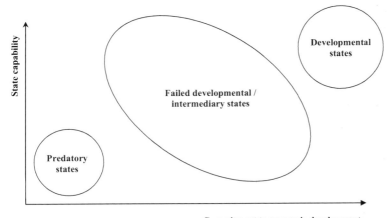

Source: Own compilation

Although the notion of the predatory state has been frequently used in the
literature on state failure in developing economies over the last decades, it
should be apparent that not all developing countries conform to this concept.
Rather, the state acts in a variety of ways in different countries, and while the
extremely successful East Asian economies represent one extreme, Zaire under
Mobuto and other predatory regimes in sub-Sahara Africa represent another. In
contrast, regimes in states such as pre-1990 India or in the large Latin American
economies are clearly not exclusively predatory, but they are also not developmental states by common definitions. These countries have been referred to as

failed developmental states (Herring, 1999) and intermediary states (Evans, 1989, 1995). As a result, a typology of states that is focused on developing and emerging economies rather than on industrialized countries arises, which is illustrated in Figure 5.

4.3 The theoretical lineage and implications of the developmental state argument

If activist policies and planning are indeed considered to be one of the foundations of the superior performance of developmental states, such as South Korea and Japan, this should also be justified on theoretical grounds. As previously mentioned, "MITI and the Japanese Miracle" marked the start of a counter-revolution against the neoclassical explanation for the superior performance of the Japanese economy. However, while Johnson explicitly rejected the purely market-based explanation (Johnson, 1982, pp. 9–10), his own contribution is not a theoretical explanatory account searching for causality, but a rather descriptive historical study (Kang, 1995, p. 567; Woo-Cumings, 1999, p. 2). Other proponents of the developmental state concept have been much more explicit in elaborating the implications of their research for economic theory and for the policy recommendations of international organizations such as the World Bank and the IMF (Amsden, 1989, pp. 139–155; Chang 1999, pp. 185–192; Wade, 1990/2004, pp. 350–353; 2008, pp. 15–23).

These scholars criticize the neoclassical/neoliberal paradigm on several grounds. A crucial target of their criticism is the notion that the functioning of the price mechanism guided by the invisible hand of the market is sufficient to ensure economic development. Chang (1999, p. 186) considers this notion misleading because it fails to account for market failures adequately. However, he considers the failure of most neoclassical accounts to distinguish between dynamic market efficiency and static market efficiency to be the more important issue in this controversy (Chang, 1999, pp. 186–187). Similarly, Amsden points out that market-optimist economists often use economic laws to analyze economic growth that were initially formulated to explain resource allocation and consequently static efficiency (Amsden, 1989, p. 139).

The distinction between short-term allocative efficiency and long-term dynamic efficiency is dispensable if theoretical models that assume economic agents with perfect foresight are an adequate representation of the reality, which is considered dubious on both empirical and theoretical grounds (Chang, 1999, pp. 184–186). Furthermore, it is argued that the common neoclassical assumption of rising marginal cost is misleading, since manufacturing processes are often characterized by substantial economies of scale and learning effects. The corresponding risk of not being able to achieve the minimum firm size and production numbers to reap these benefits may cause investors (in particular in emerging economies with a low stock of capital) to invest less in manufacturing industries than would be economically efficient (Wade, 1990/2004, pp. 351–352).

While the reasoning of proponents of the developmental state concept challenges prevailing recommendations of neoclassical economics, they are of course not without predecessors in the economic science and related fields. This refers both to the applied methodology and the conclusions of their research. The idea that state intervention can increase the prosperity of an economy can be traced back to the mercantilism of early modern days (Woo-Cumings, 1999, pp. 4–5). Furthermore, the infant industry argument is central to the work of Chang and Amsden. According to this argument, which was conceived by the German economist Friedrich List (1789–1846), new industries in economically backward countries cannot compete against their developed counterparts from advanced economies without state interventions to protect them in the early stages of their development (Chang, 2003, pp. 3–5). Other predecessors who provided theoretical inputs for the reasoning of developmental state scholars include Alexander Gerschenkron and his account on economic backwardness (Gerschenkron 1962; see for example Amsden, 1989, p. 13; 1991, p. 793; Chang, 2003; p. 7; Wade, 1990/2004, p. 351) and Joseph Schumpeter's work on the dynamic efficiency of markets (Schumpeter, 1938; see for example Amsden 1989, pp. 140–141).

As a result of his critique of recommendations arguing for the benefits of a minimal state, Chang (1999) advocates the model of a developmental state that assumes four additional functions:

(1) the coordination of economic processes, in particular through promoting complementary investments (pp. 192–193);

(2) consensus building through the provision of an entrepreneurial vision on the future of the economy (pp. 193–195);

(3) the construction of institutions conducive to achieving this entrepreneurial vision (pp. 195–196); and

(4) actively manage conflicts that arise out of the structural change resulting from industrial and economic growth (pp. 196–198).

4.4 Conclusions and the need for further research

It is a legitimate critique of the neoclassical paradigm that it fails to take into account the theoretical contributions of other schools of thought and research in other disciplines. However, it is also valid to argue that the critics of neoclassical economics sometimes go too far in their rejection of the prevailing economic reasoning and therefore dismiss valuable insights altogether (Vartiainen, 1999, p. 202). In particular, important contributions to the literature on the developmental state have shortcomings concerning the theory of its main subject-matter: the state itself. Johnson has been criticized for emphasizing that the Japanese economic bureaucracy acted in a rational way, without explaining "how and why the angel of rationality got things right in Japan" (Cumings, 1999, p. 64). Kang (1995) makes an even stronger argument when he points out that political processes and resulting problems of rent seeking and bureaucratic control are not explicitly addressed by Johnson (1982), Wade (1990/2004) or Amsden (1989). Criticizing Johnson and Wade, he argues:

> In Johnson's work, an enlightened and selfless political elite is fully cognizant of economic imperatives and lacks any political exigencies that might inhibit the pursuit of those imperatives. This elite is further able to design an institutional structure that will costlessly and efficiently meet those goals. Problems of bureaucratic control and discretion, rent seeking by economic actors, legitimacy, and political power do not come into play. The preceding citation is especially pertinent, as Wade relies heavily on Johnson's conception of the developmental state in building his own argument. (Kang 1995, p. 567)

Similarly, Kang (1995) comments on Amsden's "Asia's Next Giant": "For a book that emphasizes the role of the state, Amsden has left us with surprisingly little knowledge of either politics or the state itself" (p. 568).

As outlined in Section 2 of the present study, the dominant perspective on the state within economics has shifted several times. Prior to the advent of public choice and the NPE, the state was often treated as an impartial actor that was assigned the responsibility of raising the average welfare of society, either through managing business cycles by pursuing Keynesian economic policies or by implementing other interventions. To a large extent, the advocates of the developmental state assume a similar perspective.

In contrast to Johnson (1982), Amsden (1989), and Wade (1990/2004), Chang (1999) has dealt more explicitly with the question on the underlying reasons for the benevolent behavior of some states. He points out:

Rightly or wrongly, politicians and bureaucrats, regard themselves as guardians of public interests (. . .). This is partly because the process of "political" (as opposed to "economic") socialization inculcates self-oriented views into people but also because there are more institutional constraints on self-seeking in politics than in the marketplace. (Chang, 1999, p. 190)

Thus, Chang (1999) sees institutional constraints as one key to explaining the existence of developmental states. Kang (1995) argues that the shortcomings of the developmental state literature could be accounted for by analyzing the East Asian experience on the grounds of the New Institutional Economics (Kang, 1995, p. 587).

Since then, institutions have indeed explicitly been analyzed by scholars dealing with East Asia (see Haggard, 2004; Root, 1998; Yamamura, 1995, the collective volume of Aoki, Kim, & Okuno-Fujiwara, 1997b; and conference proceedings edited by Hayami & Aoki, 1998). However, most of these contributions are limited to a comparative institutional analysis that aims at identifying similarities between the East Asian states and does not involve much theorizing (see Root, 1996). In other words, this research has dealt to some degree with the question as to which institutions exist (or used to exist) in East Asia, but has hardly focused on the process of institutional change. In addition, the state is often conceived exclusively as the originator and designer of institutions without paying much attention to the complexity of the underlying processes and the relevant incentives and constraints. Other contributions have a narrower focus and address the functions which specific institutions, such as rules and incentives relevant for the transfer of technologies, perform (Itoh & Urata, 1998; Kim & Ma, 1997). These specific institutions are consequently explained in more detail and depth. Nevertheless, a comprehensive and exhaustive analysis of the emergence of developmental states from the perspective of the New Institutional Economics is still lacking. The following section of the present study aims to fill this gap.

PART II:

THE EAST ASIAN DEVELOPMENTAL STATES FROM THE PERSPECTIVE OF THE NIE

5 Institutions and policies of developmental states: a comparative analysis

5.1 Methodology and objectives of the case studies

Part II of this study consists of several case studies that serve two essential objectives. The first objective is to analyze which conditions were responsible for the emergence of developmental states in East Asia from the theoretical perspective that was outlined in Section 2 based on the Northian NIE. The emergence of a developmental state is the result of the process of institutional change, which is therefore the primary focus of the following sections. The second objective is to add new insights to research on the question of which institutional characteristics distinguished the East Asian developmental states from other, economically less successful states. In order to gain a comprehensive picture of the institutional arrangements in East Asia, all countries that the World Bank considers high-performing Asian economies will be taken into account, with the exception of Hong Kong that followed very liberal economic policies by international standards. The focus of the analysis will be on the countries that are considered to be the clearest examples of developmental states and that started their economic catch-up earliest: Japan, South Korea, and Taiwan. The developmental city-state of Singapore will also be analyzed in some detail, whereas only some aspects of the economic history of Malaysia, Thailand, and Indonesia will be taken into account. This is due to the fact that these countries showed only some of the characteristics of developmental states and were economically less successful than Japan and the Asian Tigers.

As George and Bennett (2005, p. 130) note, there is an important difference between *prediction* and *explanation* that researchers should acknowledge. While there are some non-explanatory predictions, there are also theories that offer an explanation for processes, but do not predict the outcome of such processes, such as the theory of evolution (George & Bennett, 2005, pp. 130–131). The Northian theory of institutional change is also an example of such a theory: it offers an explanatory theoretical framework which can be used as a starting point to analyze the process of institutional development, but it does not offer falsifiable predictions on its outcome. As elucidated in Section 3, the same is true for the vast majority of research on the emergence of developmental states. Most of the existing literature on the question of why developmental states evolved in East Asia aims at identifying one of the decisive conditions and to explain its importance for the emergence of a developmental state in specific countries. This research does clearly not attempt to provide exhaustive, falsifiable theories that take into account all relevant factors.

As a consequence of the nature of the existing research on the developmental state and the applied theoretical framework, the main purpose of the following case studies is not to test existing theories, but rather to develop a new perspective on the emergence of developmental states. Applying the method of process-tracing as outlined by George and Bennett (2005), the fundamental causal mechanisms leading to the emergence of developmental states will be identified. As George and Bennett note, process-tracing has major similarities to presenting a historical explanation for a specific outcome in several aspects. However, in contrast to common historical narratives, process-tracing is aimed at presenting an analytical explanation for the outcome that is not only theory based but also explicitly focused on specific variables (George & Bennett, 2005, pp. 92–97).

The model of institutional change that was illustrated in Figure 2 gives a basic structure to the analysis. As this figure shows, there are four issues that are particularly relevant in this respect and represent the fundamental variables of the analysis. First of all, the pre-existing environment in terms of both formal and informal institutions is the starting point for any institutional development. Furthermore, as elaborated in Section 2, according to Douglass North, organizations and their entrepreneurs are the agents of institutional change. Since organizations are defined as "groups of individuals bound by some common purpose to achieve objectives" (North, 1990, p. 5, see also Section 2.2.2), it must be analyzed which groups were influential in the process of institutional change and what determined their relative bargaining power. In addition, the ideologies, shaped by the cultural heritage, current experiences and knowledge of the individuals that comprise these societal groups are of major importance, since they are the driving force behind to individuals' preferences. It should be noted that neither ideology, nor the institutional environment or the structure of organizations represent independent variables—on the contrary it is the essence of the NIE that they mutually influence each other. The only independent variable in the analysis will be the external environment, which may have had a determining impact on the path of institutional change in developmental states at several moments in history through altering relative prices, shaping current experiences of actors or directly influencing institutions and the structure of organizations.

While it is not their main purpose, the case studies will also serve as a probability probe for the contribution of Doner et al. (2005), which represents a clear exception from the literature since it does aim at providing a falsifiable theory on the emergence of developmental states. In their contribution, Doner et al. (2005) argue that their theory would either be falsified if it is proven that developmental states emerge in countries where the three conditions which indicate *systematic vulnerability* are not present, or if developmental states do not emerge in countries where those conditions are met (Doner et al., 2005, pp. 330–331). According to their own standards, a falsification of the theory would thus require to test it against evidence from countries that are not within the scope of their contribution. This is not the approach followed here, since the countries that will be analyzed in the following case studies were—with the notable exception of Japan—already the subject of the analysis of Doner et al. (2005). However, the explanatory power and coherence of the theory developed by Doner et al. will again be evaluated in the light of the theory-based institutional analysis in the following case studies on East Asia. Since the NIE, as developed by North, clearly stresses the importance of ideology, the focus will be on the question whether political leadership—and consequently the ideologies of political leaders—is indeed a negligible factor for the emergence of developmental states, as Doner et al. (2005) postulated.

Since the concept of the developmental state was not developed deductively from theory, but rather inductively from empirical observations, the question as to the best definition for a developmental state is not only of a theoretical nature. It is also, as previously noted, a geographical question. However, there is another relevant dimension that has not yet been taken into account in the present study: time. Institutional change is continuous and there has apparently never been a standstill in this process. As a consequence, there never existed a completely stable institutional equilibrium corresponding to a developmental state. Rather, phases of several decades existed in the institutional development of specific East Asian economies where the states assumed roles that were on the one hand interventionist and on the other hand conducive to economic growth.

While institutional change continued incrementally during those phases, it should nevertheless be possible to find some common, institutional characteristics that contributed to this positive role. After analyzing the process of institutional change in the successful East Asian economies along historical lines, each case study is concluded with a section that summarizes insights on these characteristics. Some of these characteristics may have evolved during specific *historical moments* that coincided with profound changes in formal institutions (see Section 2.3.2) at the beginning of the emergence of developmental states. However, the different forms of inter-institutional relationships (see Section 2.3.1) also make it plausible that those institutions that already existed a long time before the fast growth of East Asian altered their influence on the economy as a result of their interaction with broader change in the institutional environment. In this respect, it is particularly interesting to analyze the interaction of informal institutions and formal rules on different levels of the institutional hierarchy (see

Section 2.2.2, specifically Figure 1) in order to evaluate on which hierarchical level the characteristic institutions of the East Asian developmental states were actually located.

At the end of Part II, final conclusions on the institutional characteristics of developmental states will be drawn, focusing on issues previously neglected by the literature and new insights that were gained through the applied theoretical perspective.

5.2 Japan as the archetype of the developmental state

5.2.1 Phases of institutional development

5.2.1.1 From the onset of the Meiji Restoration to World War II

As elaborated in Section 2 of this study, institutional change generally happens incrementally. However, there are certain moments in history where the validity of a significant portion of the rules of a society is cast into doubt, and a window of opportunity for profound reforms emerges. The Meiji Restoration of 1868, which the former minister of foreign affairs and finance, Kiichi Aichi described as "our entry into the modern World" (Aichi, 1969, p. 21), without any doubt represents such a moment. Since the Meiji Restoration marks the start of the developmental orientation of Japan (Johnson, 1983, p. 11), it serves as the starting point of the analysis in this study.

In the middle of the 19th century, Japan had been ruled by the Tokugawa Shogunate for 250 years. While this period was characterized by internal and external peace, Japan was, with some smaller exceptions, virtually isolated from foreign influences and, in particular, from trade (Grabowski, 2007, pp. 530–531). According to Maddison (2005), only extremely restricted Japanese trade with China, Korea and the Netherlands took place. The Japanese themselves were not allowed to travel abroad or even build seafaring vessels. Spanish and Portuguese traders, who had gained some influence on Japan, were expelled from the country in the 17th century (Maddison, 2005, p. 15). However, this was not the only obstacle to economic development as the economic historian Angus Maddison (2005) summarizes:

> The system of hereditary privilege and big status differentials, with virtually no meritocratic element, meant a large waste of potential talent. (. . . .) The Tokugawa system was inefficient in its reliance on a clumsy collection of fiscal revenue in kind and over-detailed surveillance of economic activity. It also imposed restrictions on

the diffusion of technology. The most important was the ban on wheeled vehicles on Japanese roads and the virtual absence of bridges. These restrictions were imposed for security reasons, but made journeys very costly and time consuming. There were restrictions on the size of boats, which inhibited coastal shipping and naval preparedness. There were restrictions on property rights (buying and selling of land), arbitrary levies by the shogun, and debt defaults by daimyo and samurai which could push bankers and merchants into bankruptcy. The policy of seclusion, rebuffing all direct or diplomatic contact with the west, was due to security considerations but was a serious constraint on economic growth. (p. 20)

In spite of these obstacles, Maddison estimates that Japan's GDP per capita in 1850 was slightly higher than China's and India's. Nevertheless, Japan was economically a backward country when compared to any of the major Western powers (see Figure 6). The question is why the inefficient institutional environment that characterized Japan during the Tokugawa Shogunate remained in place with only minor changes over such a long period. The key to this question seems to lie in the structure and bargaining power of societal groups.

Figure 6: Per Capita GDP of selected countries 1850

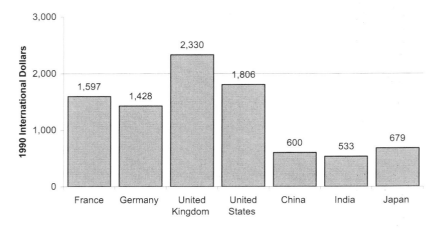

Source: Data from Maddison (2010).

The effective governance of Japan during this time was in the hands of the Shogun, who, from his seat in today's Tokyo, was the overlord for a small number of feudal lords of the upper-class samurai. In contrast, the emperor of Japan—the Tennō, seated in Kyoto—had more of a symbolic function and little political power. The dominance of the Shogun was not limited to the political and military sphere. Cultivated land that generated about 25% of Japan's total rice revenue was occupied by the Shogun and his leading retainers, compared to only 0.5% held by the emperor and the aristocracy in Kyoto (Maddison, 2005, p. 17). The monopoly of violence[14] was in the hands of Japan's military elite, the samurai, who comprised a notable 6% of the population, but consumed a remarkable quarter of the total GDP (Maddison, 2005, p. 20).

Most of the GDP in pre-industrial Japan was produced by a large group of farmers. According to Grabowski (2007, pp. 532–533), this group actually had more bargaining power than common characterizations of the Tokugawa Shogunate as a stagnating feudal society might imply. Since the structure of social relationships in villages was close-knit, farmers were able to effectively organize collective action, such as protests and uprisings, in order to limit taxation and overly predatory behavior of the authorities (Grabowski, 1994, pp. 8–9; 2007, p. 534). Nevertheless, the isolation from international trade meant that both farmers and merchant capital were lacking a viable exit option from the institutional environment (Grabowski, 2007, pp. 530–531). The dominance of the Shogun regime and the warrior class was strong enough to enforce economically ineffective institutions for a long period of time. This refers, in particular, to the institutionalized isolation of Japan and to the obstacles for economic development summarized in Maddison (2005). Since the isolation also represented a barrier for foreign knowledge, which was rarely overcome, it had significant lock-in effects for the institutional development of Japan as it limited the learning process of all individuals and any consequent changes in ideologies.

The situation of Japan in the middle of the 19th century could therefore be characterized as essentially stable. Under these conditions, institutional change would only happen incrementally through relative price changes, changes in preferences and new scientific knowledge generated within the country. However, this stable situation ended rather abruptly in 1853 due to major changes in the external environment. That year, an American fleet of war ships, the so-called *black ships*, appeared in Tokyo Bay with the request to negotiate a treaty of amity and commerce on behalf of the American President. While earlier attempts of Western powers to end Japan's isolation were shaken off by the Shogun's regime, the credible and repeated threat of the American representatives to use force led to a treaty in 1858. This treaty opened six Japanese ports to foreign trade, allowed only moderate import restrictions and admitted American consuls

---

14   A "sword hunt" that disarmed all citizens but the samurai occurred in 1588. Primitive firearms, which had been introduced to Japan by the Portuguese, were banned in 1615 (Maddison, 2005, p. 17).

to Japan. Similar treaties with the UK, France, Russia and the Netherlands had to be agreed to within the next weeks (Aichi, 1969, pp. 21–22; Maddison, 2005, p. 20).

This important development had a momentous impact on the Japanese institutional and organizational environment in a variety of ways. Since the different factors that drive institutional change are interrelated, it is difficult to identify causal relationships with well-defined exogenous and endogenous variables. Arguably, the most important immediate result of the altered external environment was a loss of bargaining power for the Shogun and the feudal elite of higher-ranking samurai vis-à-vis other societal groups. This loss of power was amplified by the fact that the Shogun died in 1858 and his successor was only 12 years old (Maddison, 2005, pp. 20–21). In 1867, the Shogunate was overthrown by an alliance of two feudal lords and the imperial court in Kyoto, with the aim of reinstating the political power of the emperor for the first time since the 12th century (Maddison, 2005, p. 21). In January 1868, the emperor Meiji officially became the head of state, hence the term Meiji Restoration. The following years were characterized by a profound modernization, or to be more specific, a Westernization of Japanese institutions. The legal equality of different social classes, private property rights on land (including the possibility to sell it) and the freedom to choose any occupation were established, while the ban on exports was lifted (Grabowski, 2007, p. 535).

This exogenous shock thus had remarkable impact on the Japanese institutional environment. The bargaining power of different societal groups was significantly altered. The previously marginalized elite of lower-raking samurai played a strong role in the restoration (Goldstone, 1991, p. 434). The opening of Japan not only changed the relative prices of goods, but also led to an influx of knowledge and new ideas. From a Northian perspective, the blend of current experiences, scientific knowledge, and cultural heritage comprise a decision maker's mental constructs, and, consequently, his ideology. Changes in ideology result in different preferences of the decision makers and, therefore, induce further institutional change. As Goldstone (1991) noted, "the ideology of the restoration was explicitly conservative," meaning that "obedience to traditional authority (that of the emperor), rather than a challenge to traditional authority, was the leading principle of mobilization behind the Meiji leaders" (p. 432).

In spite of this ideological principle, the Meiji Restoration did not result in a sustainable concentration of political decision-making power in the hands of the Japanese emperor. According to Silberman (1970), the Meiji leaders had the perception that the emperor's importance was sustained by his infallibility. Therefore, "to allow the emperor to make mistakes would result in vitiation of the basic symbol of legitimation for the new government" (Silberman, 1970, p.

358). Despite their loyalty to the emperor, the leaders of the Meiji Restoration were aware that the specific succession criteria of the Japanese monarchy did not always result in a person with the necessary capability for major political decisions (Silberman, 1970, p. 358). Silberman (1970) concludes that over the whole period from the Meiji Restoration until the 1920s, the allocation of decision-making powers at the highest level of Japanese government was characterized by "the absence of a formal, clearly defined, and differentiated structure of decision-making. Throughout this entire period the *structure*, and therefore the processes, remained informal, illusive, ambiguous, and highly particularized" (1970, p. 347). The formal institutions that govern political processes were apparently not the decisive rules for the distribution of decision-making power.

In the years immediately after the Restoration, Japan was effectively ruled by an oligarchy whose structure and membership is difficult to specify to this day. From this condition, a specific group of men known as the *genrō* (meaning *elder statesmen*) evolved. These men effectively and actively ruled Japan from around 1890 until approximately 1900. The *genrō* were an informal, consensus-based group that was originally comprised of seven men who had previously held high offices in the bureaucracy (Silberman, 1967, p. 82; Silberman, 1970, p. 347).

Researchers generally agree that the Meiji oligarchy did not maximize its utility as a function of the variables that public choice scholars such as Niskanen typically assume (compare Section 2.3.2). As Raphael and Rohlen (1998) note, the *genrō* "were nationalists to the end, putting the interests of the nation above all else, including personal gain" (p. 281). However, it is difficult to determine with certainty why this was the case. From a Northian perspective, the ideology of an actor is a result of his mental model of the world, which is shaped by both cultural heritage and current experiences. While the quote from Raphael and Rohlen (1998) seems to refer to an *inherent* commitment of the new elites that may have been the result of cultural values and the samurai background of the *genrō*, other scholars stress the importance of the experiences of the preceding years, such as the evident backwardness and vulnerability of Japan, for the commitment of Japanese leadership to modernization (Grabowski, 2007, p. 540). In order to make this commitment known and credible, the slogan of *rich country, strong military* was used to proclaim the new overarching goal of the state (Johnson, 1983, p. 11).

The new leaders decided to use Prussia as a model for the new constitution, adopted in 1889, and civil service reforms (Lehmbruch, 2001, pp. 59–61).[15] As noted by several authors (Kohli, 1999, p. 101; Woo-Cumings, 1993, p. 43), the Prussian model was consciously adopted because it offered a way to achieve Western rationality and modernity without accepting Anglo-American liberalism. Arguably, the commitment of political decision makers to modernization on the one hand, and traditional authority, as well as a strong state, on the other, is a key explanatory factor for the specific role in the economy that the Japanese state assumed over the next few decades.

The new leaders created an immediate reform with far reaching consequences: the end of feudalism, implemented through a land reform in 1873. In consequence, the samurai army was replaced by a conscript, peasant-based army (Fulcher, 1988, p. 234; Maddison, 2005, p. 21). In Northian terms, the demand for pre-modern warfare and its relative price had decreased drastically, which meant that the members of the traditional elite had to find new sources of revenue. This was particularly important for lower ranking, less wealthy, samurai. From the perspective of the developmental state concept, it is particularly interesting how these societal changes affected the bureaucracy and its role within the economy. Again, the blend of cultural heritage and current experiences is an important explanatory factor for these developments. Traditionally, merchants were at the bottom of the social status hierarchy (Fulcher, 1988, p. 233).[16] To engage in commercial activities would have led to a drastic loss of status for former samurai. While some accepted this, many sought to pursue a path that did provide economic rewards without a loss of status, and becoming a successful civil servant was an opportunity to do so (Silberman, 1966, p. 162).

Prior to 1868, the basic requirement to enter the civil service was to be born at least as a lower-ranking samurai (Silberman, 1966, pp. 159–60). Even though the percentage of commoners in upper civil service remained very low, important changes took place after the Meiji Restoration. During the Tokugawa Shogunate, the rank of a civil servant's family within the different layers of the elite had been the decisive factor for his advancement in the bureaucratic hierarchy. After 1886, a more meritocratic promotion process was implemented, and bu-

---

15   The continued similarity of Japanese and German institutions, in particular in the economic sphere, has been a topic of its own in the literature. See, for example, Streeck & Yamamura (2001); Yamamura & Streeck (2003) and the Varieties of Capitalism approach of Hall & Soskice (2001).

16   The society that existed during the Tokugawa Shogunate consisted of four orders: samurai, peasants, artisans, and merchants, in descending order of social status (Dore 1959: 57-60, cited according to Grabowski 1994: 14).

reaucrats originating from lower-ranking samurai families were able to attain even the highest positions (Silberman, 1966, pp. 160–161). One of the key factors for the promotion of bureaucrats from traditionally lower-ranking families was to have acquired Western education (Silberman, 1966, pp. 163–165). Silberman (1966) concludes that by 1873, the new bureaucracy confirmed largely to the Weberian concept, in spite of a lack of formalized achievement criteria (pp. 170–171). This lack was gradually filled over the course of the next few years and by 1900, entry into the civil service, as well as promotion and retirement procedures, were governed by a set of clearly defined rules (Silberman, 1995, p. 154).

The traditional disregard for commercial activities, in combination with the apparent need for economic modernization, sheds further light on the reasons for the important role of the Japanese state—and, in particular, the bureaucracy—in the emerging market economy. According to Allen (1968, pp. 134–135), the economic activities of the early Meiji governments went significantly beyond what was even at that time considered to be the appropriate role of the state in the economy. The government was particularly concerned with the establishment of modern manufacturing industries in Japan and tackled this issue in different ways: through setting up state-owned factories in target industries and through granting financial and technical assistance to private companies by disseminating imported machinery at low prices and inviting foreign specialists (Allen, 1968, p. 134). The constraints faced by political decision makers were an important reason for this strong support. In contrast to Western economies that could protect their industries through tariffs, Japan was committed to free trade through the unequal treaties forced upon it by Western powers.[17] Furthermore, it should be noted that Japan had been a virtually closed country prior to 1868, and there were consequently no merchant houses with pre-existing close commercial ties to the developed economies. Transaction costs and, in particular, information costs involved in the establishment of modern industries were exceptionally high for private businesses. Under these conditions, the government concluded that direct involvement in the economy was the adequate way to achieve development (Chang, 2003, p. 46–47; Johnson, 1982, p. 25).

However, the government involvement in the economy was at most partially successful. While the introduction of foreign knowledge and technology was important for the further development of the Japanese economy, sectors with

---

17   In 1875, the United States, which had played a key role in opening the Japanese market, had an average tariff rate of 40-50% according to Chang's estimates (2003, p. 17), whereas Japan was constrained to a tariff below 5%.

little government involvement contributed most to economic growth. Examples include agriculture and light industries such as textiles. Since the majority of state-owned enterprises were financially unsuccessful, the government largely withdrew from direct control and ownership of companies in the 1880s; the importance of private enterprise significantly increased over the following years (Allen, 1968, p. 135; Raphael & Rohlen, 1998, p. 281). However, Allen (1968, p. 136) maintains that this withdrawal was only a change in the means of state control over the economy and not a shift toward laissez-faire. Formerly state-owned enterprises, such as the shipbuilding industry, received large subsidies (Chang, 2003, pp. 46–47). The private companies that generally profited most from the privatization were a small number of business houses that became known as the *zaibatsu*. Even though these companies were private, they maintained close ties to the government. Serving as "agents through whom the Government operated in executing its economic policy" (Allen, 1968, p. 136), the *zaibatsu* invested in industries that were considered to be in the interest of national economic development (Allen, 1968, p. 136; Johnson, 1982, p. 23). Furthermore, the state maintained a decisive influence in the allocation of capital through controlling the banking system, which was closely linked to the *zaibatsu* (Fulcher, 1988, p. 245). At the same time, efforts of the Japanese government to improve the educational basis of the population, which had been undertaken since the early days of the Meiji-government, had been fruitful. While only about 15% of the population had been literate in 1968, Japan had a primary school enrolment rate of 96% in 1905 (Raphael & Rohlen, 1998, p. 285).

Figure 7: GDP per capita of selected countries 1900

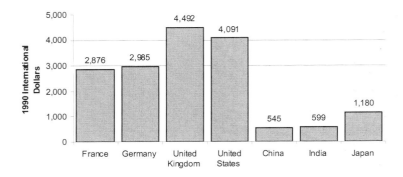

As Figure 7 shows, Japan's economic development in the second half of the 19th century was significantly more successful than that of China, the previously dominant economic and cultural power in East Asia. Whereas the Chinese GDP per capita amounted to 88% of the Japanese value in 1850, according to Maddison's estimations (2010), it was only 46% of the Japanese GDP per capita in 1900. The advantage that Japan had gained in the economy also transferred to the military sphere. After defeating China in the first Sino-Japanese war (1894–1895) and Russia in 1904, Japan became the major regional power (Kohli, 1999, p. 100). As a result of these wars, it was able to gain Korea and Taiwan as colonies.

In contrast to its evident success compared to other Asian countries, Japan's economic performance compared to Western economies is less clear. The Japanese GDP per capita amounted to 29% of the British GDP per capita in 1850 and to an even lower 26% in 1900.[18] However, the 18 years from 1950 till 1868 were apparently still part of the Tokugawa period, thus the lackluster economic performance of Japan in these years is not surprising. Focusing on the last three decades of the 19th century, the Japanese economy did show stable and positive economic growth rates, as can be seen in Table 4. While it did grow faster than the dominating economy of the time, the United Kingdom, in all three decades, the economic catch-up of Japan in terms of per capita GDP was rather limited when taking into account the enormous initial wealth differences. Japan compares even less favorably with the United States, whose economy grew faster than Japan's in two out of three decades.

Table 4: Economic performance of selected countries 1870–1900

		1870–1880	**1880–1890**	**1890–1900**
Cumulated Real GDP per capita growth in PPP [%]	**Japan**	17.1	17.2	16.6
	USA	30.2	6.5	20.6
	UK	9.0	15.3	12.0
Economic catch-up of Japan [percentage points]	**Toward the USA**	-3.0	2.7	-1.0
	Toward the UK	1.7	0.4	1.0

Source: Own calculations based on Maddison (2010).

---

18   Percentages calculated based on Maddison (2010).

The political power structure in Japan changed around the turn of the century. While the first university trained civil servants hired after 1868 gradually came to dominate the bureaucracy, the *genrō* essentially retired from day-to-day politics, but maintained some influence on major policy decisions and the selection of prime ministers. At the same time, political parties emerged and became gradually more important, leading to shared responsibility of parties and the bureaucracy for most political decisions (Silberman, 1970, pp. 347 and 359–360). The state further withdrew from direct inference in the economy of the homeland, while maintaining its dominating influence in Korea and Taiwan. Johnson (1983) characterizes the time from 1900 until the mid-1930s as "a period of more or less orthodox laissez faire," even though he acknowledges that the government maintained some direct influence in specific industries (Johnson, 1983, p. 11). Particularly important was its investment in iron and steel manufacturing in 1896 through the foundation of the Yawata steel works, which were controlled and operated by the Ministry of Agriculture and Commerce (MAC) (Johnson, 1982, pp. 86–87). In addition, Japan had recovered its tariff autonomy in 1911, and the free trade regime that had been forced upon it was replaced by politics that were comparatively protectionist (Chang, 2003, p. 48).

The First World War had a profound and positive impact on the Japanese economy. Trade grew dramatically, and a Japanese chemical industry was started during the war due to the absence of German competition (Johnson, 1982, pp. 89–90). However, this boom was followed by a recession that lasted throughout the 1920s and worsened during the world recession of the 1930s (Johnson, 1982, p. 96). In the political sphere, the *genrō* completely disappeared from decision making for reasons of age and retirement. In consequence, an unclear allocation of decision-making power for long-term decisions emerged that resulted in conflicts between various structures in Japanese politics until the Second World War (Silberman, 1970, p. 347). Among the organizations that participated in this power struggle were the political parties, the increasingly powerful and independent *zaibatsu* that maintained close links to specific parties, the anti-capitalist and expansionist military, and a variety of groups within the bureaucracy (Fulcher, 1988, p. 246).

Within the bureaucracy, the new Ministry of Commerce and Industry (MCI)[19] was not yet powerful compared to other ministries and a pilot agency, which has been considered important for a developmental state by several au-

---

19 The Ministry of Agriculture and Commerce (MAC) was dissolved in order to form the Ministry of Commerce and Industry (MCI) and a separate Ministry of Agriculture in 1925 (Johnson 1982, p. 83).

thors, had not yet emerged in Japan. However, the MCI was the source of an important institutional innovation in 1927: the creation of the first deliberation council that brought together bureaucrats and all leading businessmen. As a result of the meetings of this council, the Yawata steel works were finally amalgamated with private firms (Johnson, 1982, p. 102). Furthermore, Japanese bureaucrats continued to introduce foreign influences into Japan. While the adoption of a five-year plan for economic development is an example for Soviet influence on Japan, Germany continued to be the most important role model, especially after 1930 (Johnson, 1982, pp. 105–106). A result of this German influence was the *Important Industries Control Law*, passed in 1931, which legalized self control of the dominant companies through cartel-like agreements, including production limits, fixed prices and obstacles for the entry of new competitors (Johnson, 1982, p. 109; Lehmbruch, 2001, pp. 75–76;). These policies are evidence of both the reluctance of the *zaibatsu* to be controlled directly by the state and of the state's continued aversion toward liberal economic policies in the modern sense of guaranteeing and promoting competition and free market entry.

From today's perspective, the most striking characteristic of the ambiguous decision-making structure that had evolved in the 1920s was the inability of the civilian government to control the military, which acted virtually independent after 1930 (Fulcher, 1988, pp. 239–240). Particularly interesting is that this change in behavior was not the result of a change in formal institutions—the independence of the military from the civilian government had been guaranteed by the constitution since 1890. The control that the civilian government and the bureaucracy had previously exercised was a rule vested in persons, namely the *genrō*, but it had not developed into an equivalent, formalized institutional structure.

Table 5: Economic performance of selected countries 1900–1940

		1900–1910	1910–1920	1920–1930	1930–1940
Cumulated Real GDP per capita growth in PPP [%]	**Japan**	10.5	30.1	9.1	55.3
	USA	21.3	11.9	11.9	12.8
	UK	2.6	-1.4	19.6	26.0
Economic catch-up of Japan [percentage points]	**Toward the USA**	-2.6	4.3	-0.8	11.2
	Toward the UK	2.0	9.0	-3.3	7.9

Source: Own calculations based on Maddison (2010).

While the power of the military increased, the political parties lost their influence after 1930 and were merged into a single organization in 1940. Fulcher (1988) considers the military and economic expansion of Japan prior to 1930 to have been rational in the wake of foreign threats in the 19th century and the increasing need for self-sufficiency caused by the globally protectionist policies in the interwar period. However, he argues that the military expansion of Japan became increasingly irrational "in the sense that it became heedless of costs and consequences, and self-destructive" (Fulcher, 1988, pp. 244–246). This irrationality led to the outbreak of the Second Sino-Japanese War in 1937, which evolved into the Pacific theatre of the Second World War after the Japanese attack on Pearl Harbor in 1941.

However, the increasing influence of the military also coincided with more rapid economic growth than Japan had experienced before. In the decades from 1900 to 1940, Japan showed a less stable economic development than in the last decades of the 19th century. While growth had slowed after 1900, the First World War resulted, as previously mentioned, in fast economic growth in Japan, which caught up with the leading Western economies to a notable degree (see Table 5). It again lost some ground vis-à-vis the USA and UK in the 1920s; however, the economic expansion after the beginning of the war efforts in Asia was dramatic and the economic catch-up that Japan achieved unprecedented in earlier decades.

5.2.1.2 Institutional change during the war and occupation period

Both the war and the subsequent occupation of Japan by the United States were periods of increasing state control over the economy, albeit the reasons for state control and the organizations responsible for enacting and implementing the corresponding policies and institutions in both periods differed. During the war, the bureaucracy, the military and the *zaibatsu* continued to be the relevant centers of political and economic decisions. The structure of the Japanese industry had already changed away from light industries, such as textiles, toward heavy industries in the 1930s. After 1937, this transformation was heavily promoted through state interventions (Johnson, 1982, pp. 157–158) because it was fundamental for the war effort. Even though the *zaibatsu* were the apparent beneficiaries of these policies among private companies, they were also forced to accept more state involvement in their business than before the war (Johnson, 1982, pp. 160–165). The bureaucracy itself was reorganized in order to improve the organization of the industrial war production. In 1939, the Ministry of Commerce was reorganized into vertical bureaus, one for each strategic industry (Johnson, 1982, p. 83).

In 1943, the MCI was dissolved and a new Ministry of Munitions with further reaching powers was created (Johnson, 1982, p. 168).

Aoki (1997, pp. 238–239) identifies five major institutional changes that reflected the altered role of the state in the economy:

(1) Essential shareholder's rights were restrained since the government assumed control over the selection of top management of private companies and set dividend ceilings. Furthermore, large stockholders were heavily taxed.

(2) The government drastically reduced the number of commercial banks and assigned a single bank as financial intermediary for each munitions company.

(3) Industrial controlling associations, supervised by bureaucrats, were formed as intermediaries between the economic bureaucracy and private enterprises.

(4) Small and medium suppliers that were technologically backward were assigned to specific major companies for technological assistance.

(5) A worker's association for moral enhancement and mutual aid of the families of drafted blue- and white-collar workers (the Industrial Patriotic Society) was formed.

These institutional innovations aimed at facilitating the mobilization of resources during the war and thus drew the Japanese state much further away from the ideal of a regulatory state that is commonly recommended by today's economists.

After its disastrous defeat in the Second World War, Japan was occupied by a foreign power for the first time in its history. Between August 1945 and spring 1952, the country was effectively controlled by the USA, specifically by the Supreme Commander for the Allied Powers (SCAP), General Douglas MacArthur (Allen, 1968, p. 141). At the same time, the United States replaced Germany as the most important foreign influence on the Japanese intellectual discourse and had an important impact on institutional development over the following decades, despite notable and decisive continuity in some areas (Lehmbruch, 2001, p. 87).

The American occupation of Japan was indirect in the sense that the SCAP did not replace the Japanese government, but gave orders to it and worked through the existing institutional and organizational structures. Nevertheless, it had both a direct impact on institutions and an indirect impact on the path of institutional change because it profoundly changed the distribution of power between different societal groups. While the analysis of previous periods of Japanese institutional development has already shown that the external environment shaped the institutions of Japan in a variety of ways—for example, through changing relative prices and ideologies of decision-makers—the occupation years were certainly exceptional in the sense that foreign influence was both direct and coercive.

The most apparent direct influence of the occupational authorities on Japanese institutions was the new, liberal democratic constitution, which was drafted under American guidance and enacted in 1947 (Johnson, 1982, p. 43). Since Article 66 (2) of the new constitution explicitly requires that the ministers as well as the prime minister have to be civilians, the impact of the occupation on the distribution of power between different groups is also apparent. Not only was the military completely removed from political life, but the *zaibatsu* were deeply transformed, while the labor movement was promoted. Furthermore, the landlord class was essentially eliminated through a redistributive land reform in 1947 (Pempel, 1999, p. 162). In contrast, civilian public service was only partly subject to the imposed changes. While the formerly prestigious Home Ministry was dissolved, the economic bureaucracy did not face similar restructuring. Instead, the loss of power that other organizations faced enabled the economic bureaucrats to expand their influence. However, the crucial decision-making power was in the hands of the U.S. occupational authorities and represented a constraint to bureaucratic influence (Johnson, 1982, pp. 23–24 and 41–44).

The transformation of the *zaibatsu* mainly affected the holding companies, particularly the ownership structure. Despite their size, the *zaibatsu* conglomerates had been essentially family-owned companies up to this point. During the war, the separation of ownership and control of the *zaibatsu* (which had already been stronger than in other companies) was strongly promoted by the government through this reduction of shareholder's rights. After the war, both owners and top managers of the *zaibatsu* were heavily affected by the occupational authorities' purge of war criminals. The wealth of *zaibatsu* families was de facto confiscated and shares were redistributed to small individual investors. Preference in this process was given to employees of the companies (Jackson, 2001, pp. 142–144).

In contrast to the ownership structure of the private sector, several wartime institutional developments were only slightly altered. As Aoki (1997) notes, the close relationship between a single bank and the *zaibatsu* successor companies remained intact in most cases to ease the problem of bad debts accumulated during the war. Similarly, the exclusive supply relationships between several small and medium-sized companies and a single large, technically advanced company continued. The industrial controlling associations were succeeded by controlling associations that were closely connected to the economic bureaucracy, while the wartime worker's organization was dissolved. However, the organizational structure of the latter evolved into the company-based unions typical for post-war Japan (Aoki, 1997, pp. 239–240).

The day before the first occupation troops reached Japan's main island, the wartime Ministry of Munitions was renamed Ministry of Commerce and Industry overnight in order to downplay the bureaucrats' importance in the Japanese war effort. While the SCAP held a small number of individual bureaucrats responsible and purged them, the structure of the ministry was left unchanged and there was a notable continuity of personnel. In the following years, the economic bureaucracy did not only increase its role in the economy because other previously powerful groups had lost their influence, but also because they assumed new responsibilities for the emergency reconstruction of the war-torn economy at the request of the occupational authorities (Johnson, 1982, pp. 172–174).

However, administrative functions of the economy were initially not concentrated with the ministry. A priority production system under the supervision of a new agency, the Economic Stabilization Board (ESB), was set up to increase the production in key sectors. Priority was given to coal production in order to relieve the energy shortage; in addition, steel and fertilizer were designated industries. Already in 1945, the SCAP had ordered the creation of another government agency, the Board of Trade (BOT), to control imports and the export of the occupied country. The amount of trade in the first years of the occupation was very limited, which increased a rapid inflation that had been caused by expansionary monetary and fiscal policies such as the priority production system. In the geopolitical sphere, the beginning cold war had increased the geostrategic importance of Japan for the US government, which ordered the SCAP to make economic self-sufficiency its main objective for Japan (Johnson, 1982, p. 189). As a result, policies aimed at increasing Japanese trade, reducing inflation and balancing the national budget were drafted by the occupational authorities and implemented in the following year. There was also an important development within the Japanese bureaucracy when the BOT was combined with the Ministry of Commerce and Industry to form the new Ministry of International Trade and Industry, the MITI, in 1949 (Johnson, 1982, pp. 187–191). The powers of the ESB were transferred to MITI in 1952 (Johnson, 1982, p. 220).

Table 6: Japanese economic development 1940–1945

	1940	1941	1942	1943	1944	1945
GDP per capita (PPP) [1990 international dollars]	2,874	2,873	2,818	2,822	2,659	1,346
GDP per capita (PPP) relative to USA [%]	41	35.01	28.93	24.5	21.56	11.50

Source: Data on GDP per capita from Maddison (2010), data on GDP per capita relative to USA are own calculations based on Maddison (2010).

Obviously, the economic performance of Japan in the 1940s was profoundly shaped by the war. As Table 6 shows, the Japanese GDP per capita in purchasing power parity remained stable from 1940 until 1943, declined in 1944 and collapsed in 1945 when the war was fully affecting mainland Japan. Throughout this period, Japan's economy was losing ground relative to the USA, whose economy benefitted from the demand increase caused by the war. Due to US assistance, the GDP per capita rebounded in the immediate post-war years (see Table 7), but remained below the pre-war level.

Table 7: Japanese economic development 1946–1950

	1946	1947	1948	1949	1950
GDP per capita (PPP) [1990 international dollars]	1,444	1,541	1,725	1,800	1,921
GDP per capita (PPP) relative to USA [%]	15.70	17.34	19.03	20.12	20.09

Source: Data on GDP per capita from Maddison (2010), data on GDP per capita relative to USA are own calculations based on Maddison (2010).

5.2.1.3 Institutional change during the post-war miracle

In 1952, after authority over major decisions had been gradually transferred from the occupational authorities to the Japanese government, Japan regained its status as an independent country. This resulted in another notable change in the external environment that affected the process of institutional development, although less profound than earlier changes. Even though the United States renounced their formal authority over Japanese matters, they retained some influence as the country's most important ally and donor of economic aid.[20] The political decisions in Japan were furthermore constrained in 1952 when the country joined the International Monetary Fund and the World Bank, in 1955 when it joined the General Agreements of Tariffs and Trade (GATT) and in 1964 when it was admitted to the Organization for Economic Cooperation and Development (OECD). Through these organizations, Japan's trading partners were able to pressure the government for a liberalization of the Japanese economy (Johnson, 1982, pp. 220 and 263).

As Chalmers Johnson's exceptionally detailed description shows, the political and economic discourse of the 1950s and 1960s was characterized by an intense power struggle between interest groups that preferred economic planning and activist policies and groups that were in favor of economic liberalization (Johnson, 1982, pp. 198–242). As elaborated in the previous section, the influence of the Japanese bureaucracy on the economy in general and the role of the economic ministry (the MCI and later the MITI) had increased after the war due to the disappearance of other powerful groups from the decision-making processes. In order to understand the internal decision-making process of Japanese ministries and their relationship with the elected government, it is essential that only the position of the minister is occupied by a politician while all other positions, including the vice minister, are filled by career bureaucrats (Johnson, 1982, pp. 51–52). In contrast to the formally subordinate vice minister, ministers have often lacked both internal backing within the ministry and the necessary in-depth knowledge of internal proceedings and relevant preceding legislation (see for an example Johnson, 1982, p. 45).

Nevertheless, the democratization and economic recovery of Japan inevitably lead to the emergence of new and influential organizations. After the creation of the Liberal Democratic Party (LDP) in 1955, a party that would rule Japan continuously from its creation till 1993, politicians started to rival the influence of bureaucrats on major decisions (Muramatsu & Krauss, 1987, 516–518; Johnson, 1982, p. 427). It is important to note that neither the LDP nor the bureaucracy as a whole, and not even specific ministries, always act as an organization that adheres to the Northian definition of "groups of individuals bound by some common purpose to achieve objectives" (North, 1990, p. 5). Instead, there is a power struggle of individuals with different preferences within the formally recognized organizations that may result in the formation of different factions.

---

20   Economic aid was complemented by a drastically increased US-demand for Japanese products during the Korean War (1950-1953) (Johnson 1982: 200).

These will commonly share some objectives and act as a single organization in the Northian sense to promote them, but the factions will disagree on other issues and act as separate organizations in the corresponding processes.

Within the LDP, Johnson (1982, pp. 46–47) identifies two main factions: one made up by former public officials that usually supported an increasing influence of the bureaucracy and one made up by *pure* politicians. Within the economic bureaucracy, there was considerable debate on the right economic policies and the corresponding institutions both between different organizations and within these organizations. MITI rivaled for influence with ministries such as the Ministry of Finance (Johnson, 1982, p. 275) and other government agencies, such as the Fair Trade Commission (Johnson, 1982, p. 175).

In the discussion on economic policies in the 1950s, the position of MITI was to promote heavy and chemical industrialization through activist policies (Johnson, 1982, p. 228). Furthermore, the bureaucrats within the Ministry were generally against a thorough liberalization of the Japanese economy, especially against opening it for foreign capital, since they feared that such a process would decrease their role in the economy or even eliminate MITI's raison d'être (Johnson, 1982, pp. 228 and 249). This preference of actors within a bureaucratic organization to maintain the importance of their bureau is essentially consistent with the common assumptions of public choice theory. However, MITI had to face both national and international pressure for the liberalization and internationalization of the Japanese economy. The international pressure was on the one hand a result of Japan's special relationship with the United States, but it was certainly severely strengthened by the compulsory requirements of the international organizations to which Japan had been admitted. In Japan, there were supporters of internationalization within the private sector, the elected government, other parts of the bureaucracy and, to a lesser degree, within MITI itself. As Johnson (1982) notes, MITI in the 1960s and 70s was characterized by the competition between the industrialist faction, favoring tight state control, and the younger international faction, that was more willing to accept the necessity (and in some cases also the benefits) of liberalization. While the former was dominant in the 1950s, its influence within the ministry was gradually weakened over the following years (Johnson, 1982, pp. 79–80).

On the national scale, the supporters of trade liberalization prevailed finally in 1960 (Johnson, 1982, p. 251) and the Japanese economy was opened gradually over the following two decades. The environment for interventionist policies of the economic bureaucracy changed as a result. MITI lost most of the explicit control powers over the domestic private sector that had been acquired during the war and occupation period. However, it was able to maintain decisive influence through so called *administrative guidance*. This means that it issued directives, requests, warning, suggestions and encouragements that were formally not equivalent to laws, even though informal enforcement measures made administrative guidance in some forms indistinguishable from legal orders (Johnson, 1982, pp. 265–266).

Furthermore, the economic bureaucracy adapted to the new circumstances through a variety of institutional innovations aimed at increasing the competitiveness of Japanese companies while simultaneously decreasing or postponing the pressure of foreign competition. In order to achieve the former objective, the *Industrial Structure Investigation Council* was formed. This council brought together the leaders of Japan's industry and had the objective to compare Japanese industries and companies with their counterparts in North America and Western Europe in terms of their competitive ability, taking into account characteristics such as export ratios, economies of scale and concentration (Johnson, 1982, p. 253). The latter objective became an issue when liberalization was extended from openness to trade toward openness to foreign direct investment after 1964. As a reaction, MITI implemented a variety of very specific rules and measures that in their totality "had the effect of turning Japan's capital 'liberalization' into a strictly pro forma acquiescence in international conventions" (Johnson, 1982, p. 278).

Despite the notable power that the bureaucracy, especially MITI, retained over the economy in the post-war period, its influence was never unrivalled and declined gradually during the period of liberalization. On the one hand, the power of the bureaucracy was limited due to the existence of several influential organizations in the Northian sense, i.e. interest groups that collaborated to promote their objectives. On the other hand, Japan's liberal democratic constitution, which provided for a free press, independent courts and an active civil society, lead to various mechanisms of accountability, despite the single-party rule that Japan experienced for most of the post-war period.

Even though Johnson's analysis is famous for his widely cited statements that in Japan "the politicians reign and the bureaucrats rule" (Johnson, 1982, p. 154) and that "the bureaucracy makes policy and the Diet merely rubber-stamps it" (Johnson, 1983, p. 60), he gives several examples of cases when politicians acted against the will of the bureaucracy and prevailed. One of the most prominent cases is the *Special Measures Law for the Promotion of Designated Industries*, drafted by MITI in 1963, that would have given it significantly more control over the private sector economy (Johnson, 1982, pp. 257–258). In spite of MITI's vigorous support, it was never brought to a vote in the Diet by the government after being widely criticized by business associations, banks, the Ministry of Finance, and other bureaucratic agencies such as the Fair Trade Commission, which saw itself as the warrantor of free trade and anti-monopoly regulations (Johnson, 1982, pp. 258–260). Other scholars (Muramatsu & Krauss, 1987, p. 516; Kosai, 1987, p. 555) argue that Johnson generally overestimated the power of MITI and underestimated the power of politicians, parties, and the Diet.

At the end of the 1960s and during the 1970s, the criticism of MITI's economic policies, aimed at the promotion of industry and essentially neglecting non-economic issues, were becoming more widely criticized in the public since they were linked to increasing pollution and damaging the foreign relations with the United States (Johnson, 1982, pp. 284–285). Demands for effective environmental policies became more and more vociferous (Streeck & Yamamura, 2003, p. 8). MITI's reaction was to shift its support toward knowledge-intensive industries ranked high on the value chain that would cause less pollution (Johnson, 1982, p. 291). At the same time, new pressures for less bureaucratic control of the economy came from the increasingly powerful private companies (Encarnation & Mason, 1990, pp. 25–27; Johnson 1982, pp. 287–288) that had previously benefitted from protectionist policies and other supportive measures. These developments and the shift in public opinion against interventionist policies decreased the power of the MITI; however, it regained some of its previous authority when economic issues once again became a top priority in the wake of the oil shock in 1973 (Johnson, 1982, p. 297). Nevertheless, it never achieved the elevated position within the bureaucracy that it had enjoyed before as more checks on its power were implemented through court decisions resulting from inter-bureaucratic struggles (Johnson, 1982, pp. 298–301; Streeck & Yamamura, 2003, p. 8).

Table 8: Japanese economic development 1950–1990

	1950	1960	1970	1980	1990	2000	2008
GDP per capita (PPP) [1990 international dollars]	1,921	3,986	9,714	13,482	18,789	20,738	22,816
GDP per capita (PPP) relative to USA [%]	20.09	35.19	64.63	72.28	80.99	72.85	73.18

Source: GDP per capita from Maddison (2010), GDP per capita relative to USA own calculations based on Maddison (2010).

When Johnson published "MITI and the Japanese Miracle" in 1982, Japan had managed to catch up from around 20% of the US-American GDP per capita (PPP) in 1950 to more than 70% (see Table 8). Economic growth had been exceptionally strong for three decades, and it continued to be strong in the 1980s before declining drastically after 1990. The economic liberalization and the decline of state involvement in the economy that Johnson described for the 1960s and 1970s continued in the following decades. It is indeed an interesting question at what time Japan ceased to be a developmental state in Johnson's sense. According to Streeck and Yamamura (2003, p. 5), Japan continued to be fundamentally developmentalist after the 1970s; however, the characteristics that had previously been considered vital for Japanese economic success were afterwards considered to be responsible for the economic failures of the 1990s (Streeck & Yamamura, 2003, p. 9). The consequential pressure for institutional change in the direction of a more liberal variety of capitalism has certainly resulted in a major transformation of the Japanese economy, even though it might retain important differences to Western economies (see Yamamura & Streeck, 2003). This pattern of gradually declining state intervention seems to be characteristic for developmental states, as the case studies on South Korea and Taiwan show in the following sections.

5.2.2 Conclusions from the institutional development of Japan

Due to its long history as an industrialized country competing with the advanced Western nations, Japan offers eminently important lessons for the issues under study. Japan is the archetype of the developmental state, since this concept was first and foremost defined as a description for the role of the Japanese state in the economy and extended to other countries afterward. As a result of the notable changes in the institutional and organizational environment during its long quest for economic catch-up with the West, the question arises at what phase of its institutional development Japan actually became a true developmental state.

The originator of the term developmental state, Chalmers Johnson, does not give an unambiguous answer to this vital question. As previously mentioned, Johnson asserted that the emergence of the Japanese developmental state began after the Meiji Restoration (1982, p. 20). However, he also noted that "MITI and modern Japanese industrial policy are genuine children of the Shōwa era" (Johnson, 1982, p. 33), which began in 1926. He also stated in another instance that the learning and adaptation process that resulted in the economic achievements of Japan began after the financial crisis of 1927 and ended after the oil show in 1973 (Johnson, 1982, p. 306). Consequently, Johnson chose 1925 as the actual beginning of his analysis in "MITI and the Japanese Miracle," but also took into account some developments from 1868 to 1925.

Indeed, most relevant characteristics of the Japanese institutional environment underwent important changes. These were already noted by Johnson and analyzed in more detail by Raphael and Rohlen (1998), who argued that it makes sense to distinguish the pre-war Japanese model that followed the Meiji Restoration from the model adapted in the 1950s and 1960s. They also note that it might make sense to distinguish between even more models of Japanese economic development, depending on the chosen time frame, the level of analytical detail and the country experiences to which Japan is compared (Raphael & Rohlen, 1998, p. 266–269).

The question of at what point in time Japan became a developmental state is relevant for the delineation of a model of the developmental state. As much as the variations and similarities between different high-performing Asian economies may help to understand the decisive factors for their success, the temporal variations of the Japanese institutional environment contribute to the understanding of its key characteristics with respect to economic development.

There are some general principles and elements of Japan's institutional environment that remained largely stable throughout the period of catch-up with the West beginning in 1868. Within the span of a generation after the Meiji Restoration of 1868, a rule-based administrative structure started to govern the Japanese bureaucracy that essentially remained in place at least until the 1990s. According to Silberman (1995, p. 153), the key elements of this structure are:

(1) Candidates for the upper civil service role must have higher education in law, political science, economics or public finance if they do not apply for an administrative role that is specifically technical in nature.

(2) They must pass highly competitive written and oral tests for the upper civil service that focus on the subjects mentioned above. Graduates from Tokyo University have been by far the most successful in these tests over the course of the years.

(3) Successful candidates enter at the lowest level of the upper civil service and advance gradually at a highly predictable rate through the hierarchy. There is no link between lower and upper civil service that allows mobility between them.

(4) Promotion up to the middle levels is mainly based on seniority, and at higher levels based on a combination of performance and seniority.

(5) Career path centered primarily on a single ministry.

(6) Service-wide uniform career period of 20 years of service or 60 years of age that grants the right to a retirement income.

(7) Protection from arbitrary dismissal through clearly defined and known laws and regulations.

Japan's bureaucratic promotion system is an example of a closed multi-track system. This means that there are several tracks, such as lower, intermediate and higher service, and the entry of a bureaucrat into one of these tracks is determined by the examination he takes. The system is closed in that it does not permit civil servants to change from a lower track to the higher, and it furthermore does not allow the lateral entry of outsiders from the private sector or politics (Kim, 1995, pp. 529–530). The vital importance of a meritocratic and relatively autonomous bureaucracy is the most commonly noted element of successful developmental states. The Japanese experience has supported this argument strongly since the late 19th century.

While the institutions governing the recruitment and promotion of bureaucrats may have remained virtually unchanged, there were some changes to the overall influence of the bureaucracy on political and economic decision-making. While there seems to be a consensus that the Japanese bureaucracy has been exceptionally autonomous and influential both in the pre-war and post-war periods, its influence was rivaled by the military from the 1930s up to 1945, and by political parties before and after this period. Furthermore, the organizational structure of the bureaucracy itself changed at various points in time. In particular, the emergence of a clear pilot agency—which Johnson considered to be a vital element of the developmental state (1982, p. 319)—did not take place in the first decades after the Meiji Restoration. Johnson states that MITI's predecessor, the MCI, was not a powerful ministry in 1925 (Johnson, 1982, p. 99), but is unclear about the time when it became a pilot agency. As he notes, the ministry incrementally increased its power over the next few decades by merging with other, specialized agencies, but never became all-powerful (Johnson, 1982, pp. 319–320). The manifold evidence of struggles between different centers of bureaucratic power that was described in the preceding sections, and also described by Johnson, supports the latter claim.

The role that the state, and specifically the bureaucracy, assumed in the Japanese economy has shifted not only twice, as Raphael and Rohlen's distinction between a pre-war and post-war model might suggest, but several times between the Meiji Restoration and 1975, which marks the end of the time frame of Johnson's analysis in "MITI and the Japanese Miracle." As described in the preceding sections, the interventionist politics of the years immediately following the Restoration were quickly scaled down to the benefit of more private sector involvement that remained under government guidance. This guidance decreased in the decades after 1900 but intensified again after 1935. State guidance reached previously unknown levels in the 1940s when the economy was mobilized for war and remained high until the early 1960s, when it began to decline gradually. After the adoption of the Meiji Constitution in 1890, the most fundamental formal institutions changed only once again during this period, when the new, democratic constitution was enacted in 1947. Since both the 1940s and 1950s mark a peak in state interventionism, the changes in the role of the state in the economy were not directly connected to changes in the constitution. Instead, it is necessary to look for other institutional changes that caused these shifts, which could either be found on lower levels of the formal institutional hierarchy or among informal institutions. According to the model of institutional change that served as the basis for the analysis, the underlying processes causing these changes should be related to developments in the external environment, organizational power structure and the ideology of actors.

Several major developments in the external environment profoundly influenced the Japanese institutional environment. The most obvious case is of course the opening of Japan by American war ships after centuries of isolation. In the following years, the unequal treaties with Western powers imposed liberal trade policies on Japan. When its economic growth and the European countries' relative decline in power shifted the geopolitical conditions, Japan used its regained autonomy to protect itself not only from foreign political influence, but also from unwanted economic influence. As Cumings noted (1984, p. 12) it essentially withdrew from the world system in the 1930s to pursue economic self-reliance with its colonies. However, this does clearly not mean that Japan isolated itself from all foreign influences—rather the opposite is the case. Since the Meiji Restoration, the aim of catching-up with more advanced economies was pursued by using these economies as reference models. Even though institutions from several countries were adapted, the learning process was selective since its beginning, focusing on Germany and amplifying this focus in the 1930s and 1940s. After the war, the USA assumed a prominent position in the geopolitical environment of Japan, not only through imposing some institutional changes in the immediate post-war period, but also as its main foreign ally. Nevertheless, Japan remained selective in its learning process. The United States and West Germany were seen as reference models for its desirable industrial structure (Johnson, 1982, p. 256), but the measures that were implemented to achieve this structure were apparently quite different from the economic policies that the referenced economies pursued.

Whether Japan was already a developmental state during the period from 1868 to 1925, or whether it became one in 1925 (or even 1949), is a matter of perspective and a matter of definition. Taking Johnson's model of a developmental state as presented in the last chapter of "MITI and the Miracle" (Johnson, 1982, pp. 315–320) at face value would lead to the conclusion that a genuine developmental state came into being after the war, when MITI was formed. However, the comparison of Japan with other countries that have been referred to as developmental states by later authors—in particular with South Korea, Taiwan, and Singapore—might lead to a less restrictive definition of a developmental state, since the institutional environments of these countries apparently showed major differences. What should be concluded from the Japanese case study at this point is that a particular institutional environment should not be overemphasized as defining for a developmental state. The developmental state should be treated as a dynamic concept, in which both the level of state involvement in the economy and the manner of state involvement may vary significantly over time.

5.3 The industrialization of South Korea and Taiwan

5.3.1 Phases of institutional development

5.3.1.1 The institutional heritage of Japanese colonialism

While some major works on the developmental states of South Korea and Taiwan have not given much attention to the period of Japanese colonial rule that began around the beginning of the 20th century and lasted until 1945,[21] it seems that there is now a consensus that it did have a long-lasting impact on the institutional environment of these countries (see Cumings, 1984; Kohli, 1999; Maddison, 2005, p. 25, Vu, 2007). The underlying reason for this partial neglect of a possible positive legacy of Japan in its former colonies is mainly due to the extreme hardships and subjugation that was imposed on the local population, particularly in Korea (Hechter, Matesan & Hale, 2009, pp. 39–40, Kim, 2007, pp. 21–25).

---

21   Amsden deals with this issue briefly (1989, pp. 31–35); Wade dedicates even less space to the Japanese colonial period (1990/2004, pp. 73–75).

The main reason for this impact is the different role that colonies played within the Japanese empire compared to the role of the colonies in Western powers. As historian Bruce Cumings (1984) noted quite early:

> The place to begin in comprehending the region's economic dynamism is with the advent of Japanese imperialism. Japan's imperial experience differed from the West's in several fundamental respects. It involved the colonization of contiguous territory; it involved the location of industry and an infrastructure of communications and transportation in the colonies, bringing industry to the labor and raw materials rather than vice versa; and it was accomplished by a country that always saw itself as disadvantaged and threatened by more advanced countries. (p. 8)

In addition, Woo-Cumings (1995, p. 440) notes another general characteristic of Japanese colonialism that distinguishes it from the rule of Western powers: the massive presence of Japanese bureaucrats in its dependencies. Because of the generally accepted vital importance of the bureaucracy for the developmental state, this is certainly important for the issues analyzed here. Despite the generalizable characteristics of Japanese colonialism, there were also major differences between Japanese rule in Taiwan and Korea that had a long-lasting effect on institutional development. These differences were to a large degree due to the diverging exogenous constraints in terms of the existing institutional environment, power structure of established societal groups and the prevailing ideologies of the local population that Japan faced when taking control of the two territories.

Taiwan became a Japanese colony after the First Sino-Japanese War in 1895. Until this time, the island had been a peripheral part of China that had only been inhabited by an aboriginal population until the 18th century. Most land and wealth at the end of the 19th century was in the hands of a small class of absent Chinese landlords. Through a land reform carried out by the Japanese shortly after taking control, land rights were removed from this group and transferred to local landowners that became, to a certain degree, supporters of the colonial regime (Wade, 1990/2004, p. 73). After some initial uprisings that were brutally suppressed by the military and Japanese police forces, the local resistance gradually eroded and virtually disappeared until the 1930s (Hechter et al., 2009, p. 39).

In contrast to Taiwan, Korea already enjoyed centuries of independent national history with a common language, ethnicity and culture (Amsden, 1989, p. 28). Furthermore, Woo Cumings (1995) notes that "for centuries, Koreans considered themselves superior to the Japanese, especially by virtue of Korea being closer to the fount of East Asian civilization, China" (p. 437). Despite this perception, it was a backward country compared to Japan at the end of the 19th century. Before becoming a Japanese protectorate in 1905 and a colony in 1910[22], Korea had been ruled by the Yi dynasty for more than 700 years and was a centralized, but rather weak, monarchical state. It was weak in the sense that royal authority was limited and could not fully exercise its rights, such as taxation, vis-à-vis the Yangban, a powerful aristocratic group that controlled substantial wealth in land as well as the central bureaucracy (Kohli, 1999, pp. 97–98).

Similar to Japan during the Tokugawa period, this unusually long period of relative political stability coincided with relative economic stagnation. The balance of power between the central state and the Yangban seems to have inhibited the necessary institutional change, even when the need for reforms became apparent after threats of foreign invasion beginning in the 1860s (Amsden 1989, pp. 29–31). While Korea had "one of the oldest and most sophisticated bureaucratic traditions in the world" (Woo-Cumings, 1993, p. 437), its traditional bureaucracy was not dedicated to the developmental goals of the later, modern state (Woo-Cumings, 1995, p. 438). Furthermore, even lower-ranking public servants, such as tax-collectors, were not salaried employees of the state, but a hereditary group (Kohli, 1999, p. 99), and were therefore hardly accountable to the superior levels of the bureaucratic hierarchy and much less to the public.

Even though Cumings (1984) stated that "Japan's administrative and coercive colonialism took two quite different societies and political economies, and molded them into look-alikes" (p. 11), the different conditions in both colonies lead to quite different results in terms of institutions, governance and economic development. Resistance against the Japanese dominance was far stronger in Korea than in Taiwan, and increased over the colonial period while it diminished in Taiwan (Hechter et al., 2009, pp. 38–41). Ironically, the long-term influence of Japanese dominance was probably higher and more profound in Korea than in Taiwan, in spite of this resistance and maybe even because of it.[23] As

---

22   Ironically, Japan forced Korea to accept open trade in 1876 by sending a large naval force—similar to the way in which Japan had been opened by an American warship only a few years earlier (Woo-Cumings, 1995, p. 440). Japan increased its influence on the Korean peninsula gradually over the following decades, competing until the First Sino-Japanese War (1894-1895) with China and until the Russo-Japanese War (1904-1905) with Russia (Maddison, 2005, pp. 23-24).

23   The higher importance of the colonial legacy in Korea is also indicated by the existence of several important contributions that trace the emergence of the Korean developmental state to Japanese colonialism (Eckert, 1990; Kohli, 1994 (reprinted as Kohli, 1999); Woo-Cumings, 1995; Kohli, 2004; Vu, 2007) and the relative lack of similar publications on Taiwan.

a consequence of the differing local conditions, the Japanese colonial administration often implemented its policies by setting incentives in Taiwan, but applying coercion in Korea (Cumings, 1984, p. 11). While Taiwan was governed
in an indirect way, giving notable powers to natives on the local level, Japanese
rule on Korea was much more direct and militaristic, leaving little room for the
participation of locals (Hechter et al., 2009, pp. 51–53). National resistance
against Japanese dominance and direct Japanese influence on Korea were, to a
certain degree, mutually reinforcing. Additional factors that contributed to the
increased Japanese influence on Korea were its higher geographical proximity
and its strategic importance during the Second World War.

Further differences in Japanese policy toward its two colonies can be identified in the area of land reform. Although land reform in Taiwan transferred the
ownership of land from absent landlords to their local tenants, the social structure of Taiwan itself did not change profoundly—small-scale tenancy was substituted for small-scale ownership, large farms were rare (Hechter et al., 2009, p.
45). In sharp contrast to Taiwan, the established landlords of Korea were not
absent from the new colony, and no similar reform was carried out. While land
was officially owned by the Korean monarch prior to Japanese dominance, it
had been effectively controlled by the Yangban. In order to gain the support of
this group and discipline peasants, this control remained essentially in place until 1945 (Cumings, 1984, p. 11; Hechter et al., 2009, pp. 45–46). Nevertheless,
the institutional change concerning land was profound. While Korean landlords
had relied on force in the case of conflicts with peasants before the colonial
time, the Japanese established a new system with alienable property rights guaranteed by law (Amsden, 1989, pp. 53–54). Compared to Taiwan, more Japanese
settlement took place in Korea (Amsden, 1989, p. 53) and, as a result, the Japanese emerged as an additional group of landowners apart from the local landlords. At the end of colonialism, between a quarter and a third of the arable land
in Korea was owned by corporations and entrepreneurs from Japan (Kohli,
1999, p. 114).

Apart from altering the structure of property rights in land, Japan also had a
profound impact on the development of the bureaucracy in its colonies. In the
case of Korea, the most important person in the construction of the new colonial
civil service was the assigned governor at the beginning of Japanese dominance,
Ito Hirobumi, who had been one of the most influential *genrō* and decisive for
the emergence of a strong bureaucracy in Japan (Kohli, 1999, pp. 101–102;
Woo-Cumings, 1995, p. 439). In contrast to Japanese politics concerning land
ownership, which had guaranteed the property rights of the established aristocratic elite, the reform of the bureaucracy alienated the Yangban from the colonial government. While the Yangban had previously controlled the civil service,

virtually all higher offices in the bureaucracy and governmental apparatus were given to Japanese (Hechter et al., 2009, p. 46). The appointment of lower level bureaucrats was modeled after the Imperial civil service of Japan and based on elaborate rules and regulations, to which Kohli (1994) traces the emergence of a rational character of the colonial administration (p. 1273).

Japanese rule of its colonies changed in several aspects over time, in particular after the beginning of the Pacific War. Initially, Japan aimed at the common colonial division of labor: Taiwan and Korea exported agricultural goods and raw materials to Japan, while importing industrial goods. Major efforts to raise agricultural productivity proved to be successful, even though the productivity increase in Korea lagged remarkably behind the improvements in Taiwan. In the 1930s, Japan largely pursued a strategy of autarchy with its colonies (which included Manchuria after 1932) and withdrew from world trade that it had entered reluctantly before the Meiji Restoration (Cumings, 1984, pp. 11–13).

The initial division of labor between Japan and its colonies, in particular Korea, was altered when Japan attempted to bring additional territories in China and Southeast Asia under control. Taiwan and Korea shifted from being peripheral areas in the Japanese Empire to semi-peripheral status, serving as a link between Japan proper and other areas. While limited industrialization took place in Taiwan, the government of Japan intensified its attempts to integrate the Korean and Japanese economies completely. This led to the promotion of heavy industrialization in Korea, which was spearheaded by the Japanese *zaibatsu*, who enjoyed a "capitalist paradise" of minimal taxes and business regulations (Woo-Cumings, 1995, pp. 442–443). Facing the challenges of war, a much larger territory to control and a growing Korean independence movement, it was attempted to achieve the support of Korean businessmen for the Japanese rule by including them in the industrialization drive (Kang, 1995, p. 578, Kohli. 1994, p. 1282). As a consequence of industrialization, the number of Koreans employed in the manufacturing industry increased extraordinarily, with estimates reaching as high as an increase from 10,000 industrial workers in 1910 to 1.3 million in 1943 (Kohli, 1999, p. 1284). In addition, the sizable number of Japanese-trained Koreans that had occupied lower-ranking posts in the colonial civil service moved up the bureaucratic hierarchy during the war, as Japanese bureaucrats were increasingly needed in other parts of the empire (Kohli, 1994, p. 1274).

5.3.1.2 Institutional developments from the end of the Second World War up through the early 1960s

After surrendering to the Allied Powers in 1945, Japan naturally had to forfeit colonies. While both Taiwan and Korea shared a Japanese legacy with some common characteristics—a strong bureaucracy and a fundamental physical and industrial infrastructure—there were also major differences. The most important among these were probably the much higher resentment of Koreans against the former colonial power and its local collaborators as well as the higher industrialization of Korea, which was concentrated in the North of the peninsula. The immediate post-war development path of Taiwan and Korea led on the one hand to further divergence, since both areas initially faced extremely different geopolitical conditions and societal developments, but on the other hand also to increasing similarity in other aspects.

Taiwan under Chinese rule

In accordance with the Cairo Declaration of 1943, Taiwan was returned to the Republic of China after the war, which was by then ruled by Chiang Kai-shek's nationalist party, the Kuomintang (KMT). According to Cumings (1984, p. 22), the colonial bureaucracy in Taiwan remained nearly intact, with Japanese personnel staying in the former dependency into 1946 to train Taiwanese replacements, and native bureaucrats of the colonial administration remaining in office. However, the economy was badly mismanaged by the new Chinese provincial government, which had taken over control of the industrial sector left behind by Japan. Conflicts between native Taiwanese citizens and the provincial government erupted in uprisings that were defeated with military help from the mainland, inflicting high numbers of victims (Haggard, 1990, pp. 77–78).

A dramatic shift in the societal power structure of Taiwanese society occurred only a few years after the end of the colonial period, in 1949. Since the 1920s, the Kuomintang had been fighting the communist party in a civil war, a conflict that had only been overshadowed by the defending China against the Japanese invasion. However, the army of the Nationalists was overwhelmed in 1949, and Chiang Kai-shek had to retreat with a number of between one and two million soldiers and civilians to Taiwan. As a result, the population of the island increased by almost 25%. The arriving mainland Chinese did not have any previous ties to the island and in consequence no social base, but the native Taiwanese were not organized in any political movement that could have acted as an opposition against the KMT (Wade, 1990/2004, p. 75).

The division of Korea after the Second World War

In contrast to the initial reunification of Taiwan with China that resulted from the Second World War, the post-war order resulted in the national division of Korea. The Soviet Union and the United States had agreed that the peninsula should be divided along the 38th parallel into two separate occupation zones. While communist dominance under the leadership of Kim Il-Sung was quickly established in the North, politics in the South were initially fragmented, leading to social dissent and major rebellions in 1946 and 1948. Contrary to Taiwan, most Japanese bureaucrats had fled the former colony soon after the war, even though some stayed as advisors to the American military government after being officially removed from their posts (Cumings, 1984, p. 23; Vu, 2007, p. 33). Despite some bureaucratic continuity, the effectiveness of the civil service was limited as a result of public resentment against Koreans who had cooperated with the colonial authorities (Cumings, 1984, p. 23). The main groups in the polarizing political conflict of the following years were communist and different conservative factions. The latter included both nationalists that had fought against the Japanese and Koreans that had served under them. Furthermore, it included some remnant members of the traditional Yangban elite and businessmen that had benefitted from the colonial industrialization drive (Amsden, 1989, pp. 36–37; Vu, 2007, p. 34). Even though the US-military government initially supported compromise and centrist movements, the increasing tensions both within Korea and on a global scale between the USA and the Soviet Union caused it to force communists out of South Korea and to support the staunch nationalist and anti-communist Rhee Syng-man. Rhee became president after elections, which were only held in the South, in 1948 (Vu, 2007, p. 34).

Shortly afterward, Rhee Syng-man proclaimed the Republic of Korea in the South and Kim Il-Sung proclaimed the Democratic People's Republic of Korea in the North. The United States and the Soviet Union withdrew their occupation troops from the Korean peninsula, leaving behind two essentially sovereign entities that did not recognize the other. In the south, Rhee Syng-man undertook several measures that would impact the path of institutional development through altering the organizational power struggle. While the substantial land holdings of the Japanese in Korea had already been redistributed by the American occupation authorities, a land reform was implemented between 1948 and 1950. While the old landlord class that had not been expropriated by the Japanese was also among the supporters of Rhee's regime—and the reform was therefore not as thorough as similar efforts in Japan and Taiwan—a notable redistribution of land took place (Koo, 1987, p. 170). Furthermore, the regime repressed all anti-American leftist groups, including workers unions, through an increasingly coercive state apparatus. At the same time, Rhee—who had been politically active against Japan during the colonial period—protected Korean bureaucrats and policemen that had been part of the Japanese administration by intervening against a law that would have purged them from working for the government (Vu, 2007, pp. 36–37).

A dramatic shift in the Korean economic and political history took place in June 1950: the Korean War began when North Korea's army passed the 38th parallel to invade the South. Since the North had benefitted far more from the heavy industrialization during the colonial period, North Korea was far more industrialized than the South, which had essentially remained a producer of rice and other basic agrarian goods with some light industry. Furthermore, its army had been reorganized and with equipped with new arms through Soviet aid. Since the military of South Korea was not sufficiently prepared for the invasion and only very limited American troops left on the peninsula, North Korea was able to conquer most of the South quickly. While the United Nations had condemned the North Korean invasion soon after it started in June, and encouraged member states to support South Korea, by August 1950 the allied South Korean and UN-forces, which were under American command, only controlled an area around the city of Pusan that made up around 10% of Korea. However, with significant American reinforcements arriving from Japan and the United States, the allied forces were able to push back the North Korean military, even venturing far north of the 38th parallel. At this point, the People's Republic of China intervened on the side of the North Korean government. Seoul was conquered by communist forces for the second time in January 1951, but re-conquered by the Allies two months later. The war eventually came to a strategic stalemate until 1953, with front lines close to the original border at the 38th parallel. Therefore, when an armistice was agreed upon in 1953, the new border between North and South Korea was close to the pre-war border with only slight territorial changes (Minns, 2001, p. 1030).

While the South Korean territory had hardly changed as a result of the war, it certainly did have an impact on the state, the economy, society and international relations of the country. The security threat from the North became the key factor in political and economic decisions. Obviously, this threat had been present before, but American and South Korean decision makers had not recognized it to a sufficient degree. The influence of the army, which had grown to six times of its pre-war strength, was significantly increased. In contrast, the old landlord class, which had already been severely weakened by the land reform and other developments, was completely abolished as a relevant group in the power struggle, since communist land reform in the occupied parts of the South had straightened out a lack of implementation of Rhee's pre-war reform (Cumings, 1984, p. 23). Furthermore, several policy objectives that Rhee had aimed for prior to the war—the repression of communist and other leftist groups, the concentration of power executive and the close alliance with the US—were achieved to an even higher degree than before as a result of the war (Vu, 2007, p. 38). According to Haggard (1990, p. 56), Rhee was rescued by the war, since his position as the defender against communism reduced American pressure for economic and political reform.

Similarities and differences

As Cumings (1984, p. 23) noted, the period from 1945 until the end of the Korean War in 1953 made capitalist Korea and Taiwan more similar than they had been during Japanese colonialism or ever before. In contrast to North Korea—but similar to Taiwan—South Korea hardly had any heavy industries, but it did have some light industries and a strong agricultural sector. The escape of Kuomintang supporters from mainland China not only brought an influx of high-level civilians to Taiwan, but also resulted in an oversized military under the command of Chiang Kai-shek. As already described, this was initially not the case in South Korea, however the Korean War resulted in a vast increase in the number of military personnel, and the size of the South Korean and Nationalist Chinese (Taiwanese) forces had become similar in 1953. Even though the migration from North to South Korea during the war was much smaller than the migration of KMT supporters to Taiwan, it was nevertheless notable since most migrants belonged to the educated and professional classes. In addition, the Korean War had not only strengthened the American political, economic and military support for South Korea, but also renewed the American support to the regime of the Kuomintang in Taipei, which had not received assistance after 1949 as a result of its failure to sustain its hold on mainland China (Wade 1990/2004, p. 82). As summarized by Cumings (1984, p. 23), both Chiang Kai-shek and Rhee Syng-man had achieved an ironclad commitment for defense against communism from the USA.

The similarities of Taiwan and South Korea in terms of their geopolitical and societal constraints resulted in economic policies that were broadly similar in the 1950s. Both countries pursued similar strategies of import substitution, financed by massive inflows of US financial aid (Cumings, 1984, pp. 23–25). Nevertheless, there were also continued differences, both in the way political regimes sought legitimization and in the manner in which economic policy was implemented. These differences are large enough to lead many scholarly contributions to a quite different evaluation of the success of both countries in economic development over the decade: Taiwan is commonly considered to have been more successful. As Table 9 shows, the growth of the Taiwanese real GDP per capita was much more stable in the years following the Korean War. In the last years of the 1950s, it was slightly, but consistently, higher than the growth of the South Korean real GDP per capita.

Table 9: Real GDP (PPP) per capita growth of South Korea and Taiwan 1954–1961 [%]

	1954	1955	1956	1957	1958	1959	1960	1961
South Korea	4.9	4,0	-1.7	4.9	2.3	0.7	-1.3	1.7
Taiwan	5.6	3.8	1.6	3.8	2.9	3.1	1.8	3.3

Source: Own calculations based on Maddison (2010).

The beginning of the KMT rule on Taiwan

Since 1949, Taiwan was dealing with two quite different political, societal and cultural legacies that would shape the path of institutional development: on the one hand, the legacy of native Taiwanese that had been altered by several decades of Japanese dominance; on the other hand, the legacy of the nationalist Kuomintang party and its mainland supporters. In the 1920s, the KMT had been organized essentially along Leninist lines. Its ideology on economic policy was, according to Haggard (1990, p. 77), characterized by combining the private ownership of productive means with extensive central planning and state intervention in an eclectic mix. While there were some attempts at economic and bureaucratic reform during the KMT rule of mainland China, both the party and the bureaucracy are considered to have been pervasively corrupt in the last years before being relocated to Taiwan (Haggard, 1990, p. 78). Furthermore, its effective political power and territorial reach on the mainland had been limited by internal factionalism, regional warlords and, later, the war against the Communists and the Japanese (Haggard, 1990, p. 77; Wade, 1990/2004, p. 195).

After being limited to rule Taiwan, the KMT's position in the internal societal power struggle of organizations was apparently completely different. Now, a government and military apparatus that had served to govern and control all of China was transferred to a small island of less than 10 million inhabitants (Root, 1996, p. 32). There can be no doubt that the state was in a strong and autonomous position relative to other societal groups. Taiwan was clearly not even in the most formal sense a democracy: it was ruled under martial law. Initially, the party itself was the source of certain constraints to the power of Chiang Kai-shek; however, he managed to centralize decision-making power in a party reform in the 1950s (Haggard, 1990, p. 80). Social groups, such as students and workers, were incorporated into the party structure and brought under state control in this way (Haggard, 1990, p. 81).

Despite the highly authoritarian single-party regime of Chiang Kai-shek, it did not attempt to monopolize every aspect of social and economic life. In particular, several scholars argue that economic policy was largely left to technocrats in the bureaucracy, with only limited input from the party (Haggard, 1990, p. 86; Root, 1996, p. 33; Wade, 1990/2004, p. 193). After relocating to Taiwan, the KMT government had taken over the centralized bureaucratic structure of the colonial regime and reinforced it (Wade, 1990/2004, p. 193); priority in bureaucratic reform was given to agencies responsible for disbursing US economic aid (Root, 1996, p. 34). While Chiang's regime was highly autonomous within Taiwan, the importance of American support in the face of a hostile geopolitical environment had an impact on policy choices. While there were some issues where the US merely encouraged policies, they were also instances where American influence effectively constrained the feasible choices of the Taiwanese government. An example of the former is land reform, which essentially reinforced and augmented the positive effects of the reform that had been carried out by the Japanese colonial government. Tenancy was further decreased by transferring property rights on large-scale holdings and land owned by the Japanese. The result was a renewed increase in agricultural productivity and an investable surplus (Haggard, 1990, p. 85; Wade, 1990/2004, p. 76). An example of the latter was the balance between private and public sector in the economy, where US aid officials argued in favor of a strong role of private ownership. The government finally had to accept a broad role of the private sector (Root, 1996, p. 34), even though state owned enterprises played a significant role. In spite of some disputes, Haggard (1990, p. 76) characterizes the US-Taiwanese aid relationship as largely harmonious.

Changing regimes in South Korea

In contrast to their policy in Taiwan, the United States insisted on the continuing existence of formally democratic institutions in South Korea, and imposed such institutions on Rhee Syng-man since the beginning of his presidency (Haggard, 2004, pp. 71-72). Even though Rhee had become gradually more authoritarian over time and his regime could not be considered a democracy in any but the most formal sense, he did face elections and a need to gather political, and particularly financial, support (Cheng et al., 1998, p. 100). This was done through the allocation of rents that resulted from the vast amount of US-financed aid and the import substitution policies. Chosen supporters in the private sector were the key beneficiaries. Furthermore, the bureaucracy was used for the patronage of political supporters. Even though the bureaucratic continuity in personnel between the colonial period and the initial phase of Rhee's rule has been noted, it is commonly agreed that bureaucratic capacity deteriorated in several ways (Woo-Cumings, 1995, p. 445). Cheng et al. (1998) characterize it as "both ineffective and disorganized, characterized by widespread corruption and patronage" (p. 100), even though they note the existence of developmental enclaves in some agencies. Competitive exams for bureaucratic recruitment continued to exist, but were almost completely ignored—over 95% of the higher civil service positions were filled according to other criteria (Evans, 1998, p. 73). As a consequence, the regime that Rhee headed before and after the Korean War has been characterized as blatantly corrupt and predatory by many accounts.

The gathering of political support through the allocation of rents was not sufficient to guarantee the survival of Rhee's regime at the end of the 1950s. According to Amsden (1989, pp. 42–52), there were three important conflicting views on the desirable path of political and economic development. These views were associated with the US aid mission, the student movement and the Korean military, respectively. The interaction of these three groups should set the basis for the development of the fundamental institutional environment over the next few decades.

The representatives of the United States had a much less harmonious relationship with Rhee Syng-man than with Chiang Kai-shek. They were generally unsatisfied with the economic achievements and political developments since the Korean War. The unwillingness of Rhee to normalize relations with Japan, which had, by this time, become an ally of the USA, was an additional source of disagreement (Amsden, 1989, p. 42). In the words of Amsden (1989), "the rancor between the two countries exceeded what could reasonably be expected from a corrupt aid recipient, a frugal aid donor and the inherent indignity of the aid relationship" (pp. 43–44). US aid dropped from $382 million in 1957 to $192 million in 1961, leading the Korean economy into a recession (Pirie, 2008, p. 66). The US aid mission generally argued for more restrictive fiscal and monetary policies in combination with privatization of the banking sector (Amsden 1989, pp. 43–44), thus policies that were in line with the concept of a liberal market based economy.

While the reduction of American aid exposed the economic problems Korea was facing, it was mainly the student movement that caused the end of Rhee's regime. In the face of blatant electoral fraud and the killing of a protesting high school student by the police, protests of students against the increasingly authoritarian and repressive regime had erupted throughout the country. Among the protesters were also previously repressed leftist groups that did not only call for political reforms, but also objected the decisive influence of the USA in internal Korean affairs (Amsden, 1989, pp. 42–43). Since neither the military nor the United States were willing to defend the regime, Rhee had to resign and escape from the country in 1961.

The result of Rhee's resignation was the Second Republic. The oppositional Democratic Party won the first elections and revised the constitution, changing Korea from a presidential to a parliamentary system. Previously repressed groups, in particular the worker's movement, increased in power. However, the new government achieved neither political nor economic stability. After economic turmoil, the short lived Second Republic ended in May 1961. At this time, the military, which had rejected to defend the Rhee regime, took the power in a coup d'état while the US remained passive (Kim, 2007, pp. 94–98). The new president, General Park Chung-hee, would lead South Korea for the next 18 years. His presidency is commonly considered to have been the key for the emergence of a Korean developmental state (see for example Minns, 2001, p. 1026).

While there were no similar political events Taiwan at this time, there were nevertheless important developments that led to a reorientation of economic policy. According to Haggard (1990, pp. 90–91), three issues that arose by the mid-1950s made the import-substitution strategy that the KMT had pursued since 1949 unsustainable. The first was slowing growth rates caused by the saturation of the domestic market for the products of Taiwanese companies. The second was corruption. The third, and most important issue, was an unsustainable deficit caused partly by an overvalued exchange rate. The need for policy change was further amplified by a change in the external environment as the USA increasingly pressed for less government control of the economy and signaled to end its economic aid to Taiwan (Wade, 1990/2004, p. 199). Thus, both Taiwan and South Korea were entering a new phase of economic and institutional development at the beginning of the 1960s.

5.3.1.3 The reorientation of economic policy in the 1960s

Around the turn of the decade between the 1950s and 1960s, both South Korea and Taiwan turned from an import substitution strategy to a more outward oriented approach commonly referred to as export promotion (Haggard, 1990, p. 25). This reorientation in economic policy corresponded to changes in the institutions governing the incentives for private economic actors. According to Haggard (1990), the governments of both Taiwan and South Korea used interventions in order "to reduce the risk of shifting into export business by providing various premiums and reducing information and transaction cost" (p. 93). Various measures including direct export subsidies, tax incentives, tariff rebates, and annual export awards, were used by the governments to promote the shift toward exporting (Amsden, 1989, pp. 66-69; Wade, 1990/2004, pp. 139-148)

In Taiwan, the reorientation took place despite almost total political stability and considerable bureaucratic continuity. As a consequence, the shift in Taiwanese economic policy was more incremental than in South Korea (Haggard, 1990, p. 93). Some major institutional and organizational innovations that had taken place in the 1950s were used as a basis for further improvements. In contrast, the strategic shift of South Korean economic policy was preceded by crucial political changes. In both cases, the reduction of American financial aid—and thus, a change in the external constraints—played a vital role in shaping the path of institutional, political and, eventually, economic development.

Taiwan at the beginning of the 1960s

In terms of personnel and bureaucratic structures, the new outward orientation of Taiwanese economic policy seems to have been caused, on the one hand, by a centralization of powers and, on the other hand, by the increasing dominance of reform oriented decision makers after 1958, which previously had to compete for influence with more conservative factions of the KMT. According to several accounts (Haggard, pp. 87–89; Wade, 1990/2004, pp. 389–393), the power struggle between these two groups within the government was decisive for Taiwan's path of economic and institutional development. The more conservative faction, which was powerful in the financial agencies and supported by the military, was focused on stability, supporting conservative fiscal and monetary policies and arguing against trade deficits. But the faction was also strongly in favor of a continuing dominance of state-owned companies, wanted to achieve a zero trade deficit through the control of imports and did not give great importance to industrialization. In contrast, the reformers, who were powerful in the industrial agencies, saw industrialization as their first priority. They argued that it would require less control of foreign trade, more competition between domestic companies and, overall, a stronger private sector. The conservative monetary and fiscal policies supported by the financial agencies were considered to be contrary to this objective, the reformers were not in favor of laissez-faire. The conflict between the two factions on economic policy also related to broader societal issues, since the governmental apparatus and state-owned companies were controlled by mainland Chinese, while the private companies were overwhelmingly in the hands of native Taiwanese (Haggard, pp. 87–89; Wade, 1990/2004, pp. 389–393).

After competing for influence with each other for most of the 1950s, the reformers' faction became dominant in 1958, when one of its leading figures, Chen Cheng, was appointed premier by Chiang Kai-shek. Chen succeeded in installing his supporters in virtually all key positions of the economic and financial bureaucracy (Haggard, 1990, pp. 91–92; Wade, 1990/2004, pp. 391–392). While changes in personnel and the subsequent reforms represent a shift in the Taiwanese economic policy and led to notable institutional change, it should not be disregarded that these changes took place under—and were apparently supported by—the continued central dominating authority of Chiang Kai-shek.

The reorientation toward more outward oriented economic policy was accompanied by major changes in the organization of the Taiwanese bureaucracy. As argued by Cheng et al. (1998, pp. 93–94), the Taiwanese non-agricultural economic bureaucracy can be divided into three parts, responsible for general economic planning, the control of foreign exchange and trade, and the administration of US aid, respectively. The key agency since the early 1950s had been the Economic Stabilization Board (ESB), which had been

> responsible for preparing plans, formulating monetary, fiscal, and trade policy, coordinating military and civilian expenditures, formulating the expenditure budget for the counterpart funds, screening private investment applications, and approving all large loans from domestic banks and all foreign loans of whatever size. (Wade, 1990/2004, p. 388)

While the ESB had apparently far-reaching powers on virtually all aspects of economic policy when it came to planning, it was not responsible for the influential task of setting the exchange rate and administering foreign trade during the period of import substitution. This was initially the responsibility of the Industrial Financial Committee (IFC) and, after 1955, of the Foreign Exchange and Trade Control Commission (FETCC) (Cheng et al., 1998, p. 93). All the named agencies lost power as a result of the reforms beginning in 1958, and the ESB was even dissolved in the same year. The agency that benefitted from these changes has been considered the pilot agency of the Taiwanese developmental state: The Council on United States Aid (CUSA), which became "the new super ministry" (Cheng et al., 1998, p. 94). It was renamed and given new responsibilities in 1963, when it evolved into the Council for International Economic Cooperation and Development (CIECD). While the councils were responsible for drafting the five-year plans of economic development and coordinating the activities of the ministries of economy and finance, they were less involved in the implementation and did not control monetary or fiscal policy (Cheng et al., 1998, p. 92). Furthermore, they had to compete over influence on economic policy with the regular line ministries and other bureaucratic agencies (Cheng et al., 1998, pp. 92–95; Wade, 1990/2004, p. 199).

In addition to the changes in bureaucratic organization, the reforms of the late 1950s and early 1960s also resulted in a different recruitment process. Even though political loyalty to the KMT regime remained an overriding condition for bureaucratic recruitment, the role of competitive exams was increased after 1960 (Root, 1996, p. 35). However, precisely the recruits of the leading economic agencies were often able to bypass the civil service examinations, since these agencies were independent from the regular bureaucratic structures (Cheng et al., 1998, p. 98). Nevertheless, Cheng et al (1998, p. 99) argue that the recruitment process for these agencies was actually more selective than for the general bureaucracy, relying mostly on direct hiring from elite universities, especially National Taiwan University, which guaranteed that candidates had already passed through a meritocratic and rigorous screening.

The most important policy changes that followed the reforms starting in 1958 from the perspective of neoclassical analysts were the liberalization of imports (even though it was only limited in extent) and the substantial simplification of the previous multiple exchange rate system, which had essentially lead to an overvalued currency and arbitrage at the expense of productive activities (Haggard, 1990, pp. 92–95). Alongside various other export-promotion measures, Wade stresses the importance of *export-processing zones.* In exchange for getting access to duty- and tax-free imported inputs and a simplified regulatory environment, firms within these zones have to export their all of their production (Wade, 1990/2004, p. 139). Moreover, Wade notes the increased focus of the Taiwanese government on heavy and chemical industrialization that started with the third multi-year development plan (1961–64) and continued in the subsequent plans (Wade, 1990/2004, p. 87). These policy changes coincided with an increasing importance of private sector companies, which were granted a more prominent role by the state. While only few public companies were denationalized, the overall share of the public sector in manufacturing fell significantly from 44% to 21% over the 1960s (Wade, 1990/2004, p. 88). Throughout the decade, the Taiwanese economy was characterized by massive capital accumulation and high growth rates in manufacturing (Wade, 1990/2004, pp. 88–89).

South Korea in the first years of the Park regime

As previously noted, the political and institutional developments that accompanied the shift to export-led growth in Korea were much more profound than in Taiwan. The differences between the short-lived Second Korean Republic and the authoritarian regime of Park Chung-hee are clear. After seizing power in

South Korea, Park banned all political parties and organizations, and imposed new controls on the press. Park had to return to nominally democratic rule in 1963, but the executive remained exceptionally strong, while the legislature was rather weak (Haggard, 1990, p. 63). However, there is also a consensus that Park's regime differed profoundly from preceding authoritarian regime of Rhee Syng-man. In contrast to Rhee, Park was strongly committed to economic growth and less preoccupied with political concerns (Koo, 1987, p. 173).

In sharp contrast to Rhee, Park Chung-hee had not been an activist against Japanese colonial rule, but had been born during the occupation and served in the Japanese imperial army in Manchuria at the end of World War II. In his book "The Country, the Revolution and I", published in 1963, he compared his seizing of power to the Meiji Restoration and attempted to draft the most important lessons that Korea should learn from the Japanese experience (Amsden, 1989, pp. 51–52). While Rhee had resisted the normalization of relations with the former enemy, Park did not and signed a corresponding treaty with Japan in spite of pronounced protests in 1965,[24] providing Korea with a new source of capital in the form of loans (Pirie, 2008, p. 66). This treaty also gave the foundation for the division of labor between Japan and its former colonies that would emerge over the following decades.

Domestically, Park continued the repressive policy toward leftist groups that Rhee had pursued. However, he also implemented severe repressive measures on the private business sector. A considerable number of businessmen were arrested on charges of corruption and accumulating illicit wealth through rent-seeking during the Rhee regime shortly after Park's coup. Furthermore, the government confiscated outstanding private shares of commercial banks, thus gaining control over the financial sector, while bargains were struck with private companies in the construction and manufacturing sector (Amsden, 1989, pp. 72–73; Cheng et al., 1998, p. 103; Haggard & Cheng, 1987, p. 111). Nevertheless, a more cooperative state-business relationship quickly emerged. Businessmen had to adjust to the new political conditions and were seeking the state's support. In addition, the government realized that the experience of established entrepreneurs was indispensable for further economic development (Cheng et al., 1998, pp. 103–104).

As a result of his much higher commitment to economic growth compared to Rhee Syng-man, Park also decisively influenced the path of institutional change. He was, in the words of Hilton Root, "the architect of modern industrial

---

24   For a summary of the discussion on the treaty that took place in South Korea in 1964-1965, see Haggard (1990, pp. 72-73).

society" and "an institution builder" (Root, 1996, p. 18). Haggard (1990, pp. 64–65) notes two important organizational innovations in the state apparatus. On the one hand, he reorganized the presidential mansion into four secretariats, two of them dealing exclusively with political affairs and the other two dealing with economic affairs. On the other hand, he created the Economic Planning Board (EPB), which would assume the role of the key economic planning agency over the next few decades, similar to MITI in Japan. Among several other powers, control of the state's budget was transferred from the Ministry of Finance to this new agency, leaving it only responsible for revenue and giving the EPB the predominant role in economic policy (Johnson, 1987, p. 154; Root, 1996, p. 20).

Contrary to the above mentioned coordinating councils that played a leading role in economic planning in Taiwan, the EPB was a regular ministry—as MITI in Japan—with considerable control over other ministries and intra-bureaucratic independence (Cheng et al., 1998, pp. 101–102). However, the EPB did, in contrast to MITI, not only rely on the knowledge of nationals, but also brought in foreign experts as senior advisers, particularly from the USA and Japan (Cumings, 1984, p. 29). While it certainly became a powerful agency, Johnson (1987, p. 154) argues that the EPB and the Korean bureaucracy in general were never as autonomous as their counterparts in Japan.

In terms of bureaucratic personnel, Park began with a clear cut, imposing mandatory retirement on the entire top tier of the civil service (Root, 1996, p. 21) and dismissing in total more than 35,000 civil servants (Cheng et al., 1998, p. 104). Competitive examinations that had largely been bypassed under Rhee became much more important and the overall meritocracy of bureaucratic recruitment and promotion was increased notably (Cheng et al., 1998, p. 105). Nevertheless, the bureaucracy that emerged under Park was clearly not a perfect meritocracy. As argued by Kang (1995):

> Park Chung-hee created a bifurcated bureaucracy, where domestic service ministries (Constructive, Agriculture, Home Affairs) were staffed with clientelistic appointments, allowed to be relatively inefficient, and served to satisfy the domestic patronage requirements faced by Park. On the other hand, the fiscal ministries (Trade and Industry, Economic Planning Board, Finance) were actively reformed by Park with an eye toward economic effectiveness and international competitiveness. Such a bifurcation allowed Park to pursue both an internal agenda aimed at retaining power and buying off supporters and an external agenda aimed at realizing economic growth with an eye toward creating legitimacy at home and increasing Korea's economic and political independence from other nations. (p. 575)

Concerning economic policy, South Korean government inaugurated its first five-year development plan after the military coup in 1962 (Amsden, 1989, p.

84)[25], in contrast to Taiwan, where the practice of drafting multi-year plans had already been adapted in the 1950s. This plan explicitly envisioned a synthesis of free enterprise and government guidance of the economy in selected industries (Haggard, 1990, p. 68). However, the economy only gradually became more successful. While the first years of Park's rule had been characterized by economic difficulties, the growth rates became much higher and stable after 1963. Economic reforms which led to "a rationalization of import controls, more stringent monetary policy, increases in taxation, greater export efforts, and significant devaluation" (Haggard & Cheng, 1987, p. 111) were initiated by the EPB, which was working closely with international advisors and drawing on their ideas (Haggard, 1990, p. 69–70; Haggard & Cheng, 1987, p. 111). Amsden (1989) instead stresses the importance of the sharp rise in subsidies to exporters that began in 1963 for the economic upswing. After this increase in subsidies, the exports of manufactured goods in 1963–64 became higher than in all years since 1945 combined (Amsden, 1989, pp. 66–67). The focus of the Park regime on exports became even bigger after 1965, when exporting was only incentivized by subsidies but even forced by coercive measures (Amsden, 1989, p. 69).

5.3.1.4 The maturing of the developmental state in South Korea and Taiwan

The 1960s are commonly considered to have been the key decade for the emergence of developmental states in Taiwan and South Korea. However, the institutional environment that emerged at this time did not remain completely stable and neither did external constraints, bureaucratic structures or economic policies. Concerning the international environment, it should be noted that the direct involvement of the United States in the domestic affairs of Taiwan and South Korea declined markedly. On the one hand, the US commitment to defend its East Asian allies seemed to decrease after Nixon announced a new foreign policy doctrine in 1969 (Cheng et al., 1998, p. 106). On the other hand, both countries actively sought to escape dependency, even though the result was rather a replacement of direct with indirect dependency (Cumings, 1984, p. 34). It is again of major interest to highlight both the notable similarities that these countries took in their developmental approach and the notable differences that continued to exist. Key differences include: the much higher degree of political sta-

---

25   A three-year development plan had actually been drafted in the last years of the Rhee regime in 1959, but it was only approved a few days before the end of the regime in 1960 (Cheng et al., 1998, p. 101).

bility in Taiwan, the much higher degree of stability in the bureaucratic structures in South Korea and the generally more interventionist economic policies in
South Korea, particularly in the 1970s.

Evolution of the South Korean developmental state

Over the 1970s and 1980s, the South Korean political system continued to be
much less stable than that of Taiwan. Nevertheless, the corresponding changes
in the bureaucratic structures were much less profound than those taking place in
the 1960s (see Section 5.1.3.1). Even though Park Chung-hee ruled the country
after the military coup for 18 years, the formal political institutions in this period
underwent several important changes: outright military rule after the coup
(1961–1963) was followed by a period of nominally democratic rule (1964–
1972)[26] which was ended by the declaration of martial law in 1972. The authoritarian rule of Park Chung-hee ended when he was assassinated in 1979. However, the following brief period of political liberalization came to an end by another military coup headed by Chun Doo-Hwan in 1980, who ruled South Korea
in an authoritarian manner until the democratization in 1987 (Cheng et al., 1998,
p. 89–90; Haggard, 1990, pp. 130–131).

Political instability in South Korea coincided with a relative stability in the
organization of the bureaucracy. As mentioned, the EPB in South Korea had a
more powerful and dominating position within the economic bureaucracy than
either the CEPD or the IDB in Taiwan, its position may have even been more
powerful than that of MITI in Japan. Cheng et al. (1998, p. 102) maintain that
the EPB de facto controlled the Ministry of Finance, which in turn controlled the
central bank and the South Korean banking system. Nevertheless, it was also
facing limits to its powers from within state structures. While Park Chung-hee
has been noted for the considerable autonomy he gave to economic technocrats—which were mainly working in the EPB—the authoritarian nature of his
leadership also enabled him to redistribute decision-making rights within the
state structures when the views of the EPB were not conforming his own. This is
evident in the well-known *Heavy and Chemical Industrial Plan,* which was
adopted in the early 1970s as a reaction to changing exogenous constraints, particularly the perception that of the US commitment to defend South Korea
against the North was increasingly unreliable (Kang, 1995, pp. 584–585; Minns,
2001, p. 1027). The formulation of the plan bypassed the supposed pilot agency

---

26   While there is consensus that this period can at best be considered a "controlled democracy" (Cheng et al., 1998, p. 89), Park only narrowly defeated the opposition candidate,
Kim Dae-Jung, in the presidential election of 1971 (Haggard, 1990, /p. 130).

as well as the Ministry of Finance (Cheng et al., 1998, p. 106). It was instead formulated by a small group of persons within the presidential administration that cooperated with the more industry-oriented Ministry of Commerce and Industry, and then administered by a newly formed Heavy and Chemical Coordination Council (Cheng et al., 1998, p. 106; Haggard, 1990, p. 131). As Cheng et al. (1998) note, this powerful council was headed by the Second Presidential Secretary, who was a "strong advocate of an extremely activist industrial policy that would involve the government in detailed sectoral planning" (p. 107).

The success of the highly interventionist economic policies of this plan is subject to discussion. In the renowned World Bank study on "The East Asian Miracle" (1993, p. 86), the plan is considered to be evidence for the notion that economic success in the HPAEs happened not because of, but in spite of interventions. In contrast, Amsden (1989, p. 152) stresses the accomplishments of the plan, whereas Haggard (1990, pp. 132–133) argues that there were some major achievements of the plan, but that it also led to major problems associated with an overheating economy: increasing debt, inflation and decreasing international competitiveness because of rising wages. Similarly, Pirie (2008) states that

> the heavy and chemical industrialization drive had bankrupted the Korean state. Critically however, the heavy and chemical industrialization drive had had basically been a success and created billions of dollars of new export capacity. This newly created export capacity provided the basis upon which a strong economic recovery could be constructed. (p. 76)

When the plan had to be scaled down at the end of the 1970s because it was unsustainable, the Economic Planning Board regained much of its influence (Cheng et al., 1998, p. 107). According to Pirie (2008), the EBP by this time consisted mainly of "American trained neo-classical economists" (p. 78).

Another result of the *Heavy and Chemical Industrial Plan* was a profound shift in the distribution of power between the government and societal groups. The government lost part of its bargaining power vis-à-vis the large private business groups (Amsden, 1989, p. 131). The *chaebol* had been the key agents of the heavy industrialization drive, which meant that they had increased their share in the South Korean economy, but that they were overextended in financial terms (Haggard, 1990, pp. 135–136; Minns, 2001, p. 1034). As Minns (2001) summarizes, "no government since the 1980s has been able to discipline or restructure the *chaebol*. Their sheer size, diversity, increasing control of finance and importance to the economy has fundamentally altered the balance between them and the state" (p. 1034). In the late 1970s and early 1980s, additional challenges to the state's power over the economy came from the increasingly strong worker's movement and the international environment, particularly since the USA pressured South Korea government for liberalization of its imports and financial markets (Amsden, 1989, pp. 133–135; Minns, 2001, pp. 1031–1032).

As a result of the changed power structure within the bureaucracy and between the state and other groups, South Korean economic policy was redirected toward liberalization and the degree of interventionism diminished beginning in the early 1980s. In particular, the state's control over the financial sector, which had been a key instrument of industrial guidance, decreased, enabling the *chaebol* to increase their power further by acquiring bank shares (Haggard, 1990, pp. 135–136; Minns, 2001, pp. 134–135). While the liberalization and the opening of the economy between 1980 and 1992 took place only to a very limited degree, it increased in pace and scope beginning in 1993 (Pirie, 2008, p. 77). The EBP led this process, but the influence of other economic ministries slowed it down (Pirie, 2008, p. 79). As a result of the comparatively slow liberalization, important issues, such as the financial structures of banks and the dominating industrial conglomerates, had not been sufficiently dealt with by 1997, which is often considered to have been a reason for the Asian Crisis that emerged in this year (see for example Minns, 2001, pp. 1037–1038; Pirie, 2008, p. 103). While Pirie (2008) considers the economic crisis after the end of the heavy and chemical industrialization drive to have been "the beginning of the end of the Korean developmental state project" (p. 76), he argues that the Asian Crisis of 1997 resulted in the definite shift of the South Korean economy toward a neo-liberal economic regime (Pirie, 2008, pp. 103–104).

Evolution of the Taiwanese developmental state

The Kuomintang continued to rule Taiwan in a highly authoritarian manner until some liberalization took place in the later 1980s. Chiang Kai-shek remained in power until his death in 1975. After a brief interlude of three years, his son Chiang Ching-kuo (who had previously been deeply involved in economic policy) became president and remained in this position until his death in 1988. For most of this period, the societal division between native Taiwanese and immigrants from the mainland (including their descendants) remained in place: mainlanders overwhelmingly controlled the state apparatus and the KMT (Wade, 1990/2004, p. 237), while native Taiwanese dominated the business community.

Within the Taiwanese bureaucracy, the allocation of responsibilities and powers continued to change between different agencies. The CIECD, which had emerged as the main planning agency in the 1960s, was renamed Economic Planning Council (EPC) in 1973 and downgraded to vice-ministerial rank at the same time, giving more power to the regular ministries (Wade, 1990/2004, p. 200). Only five years later, in 1978, it was again upgraded to ministerial rank, granted more powers and renamed Council for Economic Planning and Development. As Wade (1990/2004, p. 200) argues, this was a direct reaction of the Taiwanese government to the successful industrial development of South Korea and the powerful position of the Korean pilot agency, the Economic Planning Board. Already in 1970, a new agency, the Industrial Development Board (IDB) had been formed within the Ministry of Economic Affairs, which was given the task of turning broad guidance plans developed by the CEPD into detailed sectoral plans and implementing them (Wade, 1990/2004, pp. 201–202). In contrast to the CEPD, this gave the IDB close administrative contact to private businesses and considerable discretionary power over them (Wade, 1990/2004, p. 203). However, this intended division of work between the CEPD and the IDB also led to conflicts over decision making powers and specific economic policies over the following decades. According to Cheng et al. (1998), the IDB "emerged as the leading advocate and practitioner of industrial policy" under the given organizational conditions, while they note that the CEPD did never achieve the status of super ministry that its predecessors had in the 1960s (Cheng et al, 1998, pp. 95–96). Within the economic bureaucracy, the CEPD took a more market-oriented liberal standpoint in conflicts between the two agencies, whereas the IDB was more supportive of protectionism (Wade, 1990/2004, p. 204).

The more stable political rule in Taiwan coincided with a more incremental and generally more conservative approach to economic policy: there was no big push into heavy or chemical industries (Haggard, 1990, pp. 138–140). The more gradual changes in Taiwanese economic policy are commonly related to the autonomy of the economic bureaucracy from executive interference. This autonomy is considered to have been higher in Taiwan than in South Korea, despite the strong party organization of the KMT (Haggard, 1990, p. 140), the continued changes in bureaucratic structures and the bureaucratic cleavages mentioned above. Haggard argues that similar to Chalmers Johnson's description of Japan "the KMT reigned while the economic bureaucracy ruled" in Taiwan (Haggard, 1990, p. 141). Wade also stresses this similarity, but sees an apparent difference between Japan (and South Korea) on the one hand, and Taiwan on the other: public/private cooperation was far more apparent in the former (Wade, 1990/2004, p. 256). In contrast to Japan and South Korea, Taiwan did not rely on large private enterprises with close ties to the state in the modernization of industries, but on the continued dominance of large state-owned enterprises in capital intensive industries, which took a leading role in industrial upgrading efforts. As a result, the role of state-owned enterprises increased over the 1970s, spearheading the emergence of new industries (Wade, 1990/2004, pp. 97 and

109–111). In spite of the overall less interventionist economic policy of Taiwan when compared to South Korea, the government was also facing increasing pressure to intervene less, both from economists within the country and from the United States. By the mid 1980s, sector-specific industrial policies were becoming less common (Wade 1990/2004, 111–112), the change was again incremental. Pressures for a more democratic regime also began to emerge from various social groups, and Taiwan gradually became a democracy beginning in the late 1980s. In contrast to South Korea, Taiwan was hardly affected by the Asian Crisis of the late 1990s (Wade, 2000, p. 92).

5.3.2 Conclusions from the institutional development of South Korea and Taiwan

5.3.2.1 Conclusions on the emergence of developmental states

One of the most interesting aspects of the evolution of the role of the state in the South Korean and Taiwanese economies is the unusual parallels in the historical development of both countries. While the differences in their development are without any doubt important, and may indeed serve to draw important conclusions on the emergence of developmental states, the similarities in terms of colonial heritage, geopolitical environment and economic performance from the early 1960s till the 1990s are extraordinary.

From a theoretical perspective, tracing the process of the emergence of developmental states in both countries has important implications for the question whether political leadership and personal ideologies matter for the role that a state assumes in the economy. This obviously refers to the theory developed by Doner et al. (2005), who argued that the constraints faced by political decision makers alone are a sufficient and exhaustive explanation for the formation of developmental states. If this theory is correct, the emergence of a developmental state must have coincided with a change in the constraints leading to the condition of *systematic vulnerability* that is characterized by broad political coalitions, scarce resources and external security threats. If this is not the case, but the formation of the developmental state was instead closely associated with a shift in the political leadership of a country, this casts doubt on the explanatory power of Doner et al.'s (2005) theory.

Even though both Taiwan and South Korea were used by Doner et al. (2005) to develop their theory, more detailed analysis of the historical development that was carried out in the preceding sections provides important additional insights. A key issue for the evaluation of the theory of Doner et al. (2005) is the point in time when a developmental state actually emerged in both countries. In the case of South Korea, there is a certain consensus on this question. The Japanese colonial period is commonly characterized as having been an example of "predatory developmentalism" (Woo-Cumings, 1995, p. 445), which is evidenced by the fact that Korean food production increased significantly, while food consumption actually decreased, partly due to forced exports to Japan (Kohli, 1994, p. 1279). Concerning South Korea after the war, the time from 1945 until the early 60s is regarded as an interlude before a largely benign developmental state emerged after the coup of Park Chung-hee in 1961 (Woo-Cumings, 1995, p. 445). On Taiwan, Japan left a broadly similar colonial heritage, despite the notable differences that were described in the previous section. Furthermore, the similarities between South Korea and Taiwan continue in the mid-1960s, since there it is virtually undisputed that both states had become developmental by this time. Table 10 shows that both countries achieved an extraordinary economic growth that was associated with rapid catch-up toward the GDP per capita of the United States.

Table 10: Economic performance of South Korea and Taiwan 1950–2008

		1950	1960	1970	1980	1990	2000	2008
Real GDP per capita [1990 international dollars]	**South Korea**	854	1,226	2,167	4,114	8,704	14,375	19,614
	Taiwan	916	1,353	2,537	5,260	9,938	16,872	20,926
GDP relative to the USA [%]	**South Korea**	8.9	10.8	14.4	22.2	37.5	50.5	62.9
	Taiwan	9.6	12.0	16.9	28.3	42.8	59.3	67,1

Source: GDP data from Maddison (2010), GDP relative to USA are own calculations based on Maddison (2010).

The Japanese predatory developmentalism in its colonies was imposed on Korea and Taiwan and can only be explained through an analysis of the conditions faced by Japan. The relevant period of time for the analysis of the importance of political leadership in Taiwan and South Korea therefore begins after the colonial period. In Taiwan, a single political leader, Chiang Kai-shek, remained in power from 1945 until his death in 1975, ruling only the island after 1949. While Chiang Kai-shek's regime on mainland China is commonly considered to have been corrupt and ineffective, the same political leader apparently also headed a developmental state in Taiwan that emerged at some point in time after the KMT relocated to the island in 1949. Since the constraints that Chiang Kai-shek faced in Taiwan in terms of external threats and the abundance of natural resources were radically different from those he had faced as ruler of all China, this seems to be consistent with the theory of Doner et al (2005).

However, the development of South Korea represents a bigger challenge to the explanatory power of this theory. As noted above, the emergence of the South Korean developmental state is clearly associated with a change in political leadership, namely with the military coup lead by Park Chung-hee. Thereafter, the South Korean developmental state remained intact in spite of several further changes in leadership after the assassination of Park. Nevertheless, the fact that the governments prior to Park's coup, in particular the government led by Rhee Syng-man, are commonly considered to have been corrupt and ineffective—thus clearly non-developmental—casts doubt on the notion that political leadership is irrelevant for the emergence of a developmental state.

A closer analysis of the processes, leading to the emergence of developmental states and the changes in relevant constraints, may provide further insights for the evaluation of the theory of Doner et al (2005). The development of both countries in the 1950s is particularly relevant, since developmental states are usually considered to have emerged at the beginning of the 1960s. Obviously, the endowment of both countries with natural resources did not change in this period. Furthermore, the external threats that mainland China and North Korea respectively represented for Taiwan and South Korea were essentially already present in the 1950s, even though their intensity might have varied over the decades. If the role of the Taiwanese and South Korean states in the respective economies changed between the 1950s and 1960s, this change must have been caused by other conditions

As has been described, both South Korea and Taiwan sought to industrialize through import substitution in the 1950s. Doner et al. (2005) describe the process that caused the shift toward the export-oriented economic policies that are commonly associated with the developmental state as gradual. They argue that the conditions of systemic vulnerability in terms of scarce resources and external threats were present in the 1950s, but moderated through inflows of US financial aid. While it is acknowledged that neither Taiwan nor South Korea conformed to the concept of a developmental state in the 1950s, Doner et al. (2005) stress the achievements of the governments in terms of wealth-sharing mechanisms such as land reform. Institutional innovations that led to the emergence of developmental states in both countries were then caused by the unsustainability of import substitution after cuts in US aid (Doner et al., 2005, p. 341–344). Based on this line of argument, it should be concluded that Doner et al.'s (2005) theory on the emergence of a developmental state either requires a quite long timeframe or the explicit inclusion of foreign aid as an imperfect substitute for natural resources in order to hold true.

It should furthermore be noted that the comparatively positive evaluation of the economic development of Taiwan and South Korea in the 1950s is not un-disputed. In sharp contrast to Doner et al. (2005), Amsden (1991) argued that both Rhee Syng-man and Chiang Kai-shek were "egregious rent-seekers in the 1950's" (p. 286). If this judgment is taken at face value, the change in US finan-cial aid that took place at the end of the 1950s and beginning of 1960s gains fur-ther importance. If Amsden's evaluation is true, the existence of vital external threats and scarce natural resources would have hardly any apparent explanatory power for the emergence of a developmental state.

Further insights on this issue can be gained when not only the similarities, but also the remarkable differences between Taiwan and South Korea during this period are taken into account. As noted in the case study, Taiwan's econ-omy performed almost consistently better than South Korea's in the 1950s and its relationship with US donors was more harmonious. This is most notable when comparing economic growth in the decade after the Korean War. While South Korea achieved a cumulated growth of GDP per capita (in PPP) of 22.8% from 1953 to 1963, Taiwan achieved 42.4% in these years.[27] Moreover, Hag-gard, (1990) refers to Taiwan's economic import substitution policies as "self conscious," while he considers the economic policies of the Rhee regime in South Korea at this time "chaotic" (p. 89). He furthermore cites evidence that decision makers in Taiwan were already aiming at developing a self-sustaining and economically advanced country early on, in contrast to South Korea, where such objectives of policy making where not articulated prior to Park Chung-hee's military coup (1990, pp. 89–90).

This contrast between Taiwan and South Korea despite similar constraints leads to the conclusion that both Amsden's (1991) and Doner et al.'s (2005) equal treatment of the respective regimes is at least partly misleading. While South Korea under Rhee Syng-man seems to have corresponded quite closely to the notion of a predatory state and evolved into a developmental state by *shock therapy* after the military coup in 1963, the development in Taiwan was gradual. This shifts the focus back toward the issues neglected by Doner et al. (2005): political leadership and ideologies.

For the South Korean case, the importance of political leadership is clear due to the differences between the regimes of Park and Rhee despite only slight shifts in the external constraints. This does not mean that Park Chung-hee would also have created developmental institutions under different conditions. How-ever, it seems similarly unlikely that a developmental state would have emerged

---

27   Own calculation of growth rates based on GDP per capita data from Maddison (2010).

under Rhee Syng-man when taking into account the policies he pursued in the 1950s. Effectively, the fact that Rhee lost his power in 1960 casts doubt on the utterly deterministic perspective of Doner et al (2005). Implicitly, Doner et al. (2005) not only assume that constraints are the only decisive factor for political decisions, but also that politicians have the ability and the information to pursue virtually optimal policies, in other words: to construct a developmental state when it is adequate.

However, the Northian NIE acknowledges that actors have only a limited "problem solving software" (North, 1990, p. 25) and that they are, furthermore, not homogeneous because they possess different ideologies, shaped by their individual mental models of the world. Taking into account that the different ideologies of Park Chung-hee and Rhee Syng-man and—possibly—their different capacity to solve political and economic problems makes the emergence of a developmental state a complex issue. As a consequence, the development of a predictive theory on this issue, as attempted by Doner et al. (2005), may indeed prove futile. Nevertheless, it should be acknowledged that specific constraints alone do not seem to be sufficient to explain the emergence of a developmental state.

A further question is how the Taiwanese experience supports the argument of a leader's ideology as a determining factor for the emergence of a developmental state. The fact that Chiang Kai-shek had run a corrupt regime on the mainland before heading a developmental state on Taiwan casts doubt on any possible characterization as an inherently benevolent political leader. However, one has to notice that an individual's ideology from the perspective of the Northian NIE is not stable. While it is crucially influenced by the cultural heritage, it is also shaped by current experiences and knowledge and therefore subject to change. In other words, it is acknowledged that an actor is able to learn. While the discrepancy between Chiang Kai-shek's rule on the mainland and his rule on Taiwan may largely be explained by altered constraints, it should not be ruled out that a change in his ideology was also c. The economically more successful development of Taiwan in the 1950s when compared to South Korea, despite similar constraints, also supports the argument that ideological differences between Chiang Kai-shek and Rhee Syng-man existed and had a relevant impact.

What remains to be explained is the shift from import substitution toward the much more successful export promotion policies that took place in Taiwan around 1960. This shift happened more than a decade after the fundamental change of constraints and experiences associated with the relocation of the KMT from the mainland. The crucial reduction in US financial aid that has been noted by Doner et al. (2005) and other scholars, as well as the increasing doubts on the US commitment to defend Taiwan against the mainland at the end of the 1950s, should indeed be considered important in this respect. An explanation may arise from acknowledging that actors only possess incomplete information, political decision makers may thus not always know what the optimal economic policies actually are. Based on the knowledge on economic policy available to Taiwanese decision makers in the 1950s, pursuing import substitution may indeed have been a reasonable policy choice aimed at economic development. When this policy had become unsustainable, the commitment of the Taiwanese government resulted in a policy change.

A question that arises from acknowledging the importance of ideology is why the developmental states in Taiwan and South Korea remained intact after the death of Chiang in 1975 and the assassination of Park in 1979. As Table 10 shows, both economies continued to develop along broadly similar lines from 1963 till the Asian Crisis in 1997. Partly, the answer to this was given by Amsden (1991), who noted that "the state transformed the process of economic development and, in turn, was transformed by it" (p. 286). This statement suggests that a developmental state may sustain itself through its success, since economic development transforms the conditions for state action. However, it does not give insights in the causal mechanisms through which this self-sustainability is achieved.

Again, the NIE can fill this gap. As argued in Section 2, based on Ahrens (2002), there may exist *rules vested in persons* that rely on the commitment of political leaders to their enforcement. Which rules a leader chooses to implement is in turn based on his ideology and the constraints that he faces. Over time, he may attempt to formalize these rules and set high transaction costs for their change, so that formal institutions arise out of an ideological commitment. Furthermore, credible rules vested in persons that are conducive to economic growth will change the organizational power structure. If private businesses are among the main beneficiaries of these rules—as was the case in South Korea under Park—they will increase their bargaining power relative to the state, limiting the ability of subsequent leaders to reshape the institutional environment in an economically inefficient way. While Park Chung-hee faced a *window of opportunity* for institutional change after his successful coup, the institutional environment for subsequent leaders was already set and the importance of their respective ideologies, therefore, more limited.

Moreover, the importance of reference economies should not be underestimated. As noted in the case study on Japan, the Japanese political decision makers consciously decided to use Germany and later the United States as reference models concerning the desirable industrial structure. For Taiwan and, in particular, for South Korea, Japan itself served as a reference model in several aspects. Woo-Cumings (1995, p. 447) cites a survey on policy innovation in the Korean bureaucracy, which found that *foreign examples* were the most common source of new policies. Furthermore, the results of this survey showed that Japan was by far the most commonly used reference economy, followed by the United States and Taiwan.

The fact that Taiwan was also cited as an important reference economy leads to a further insight: the economic development of South Korea and Taiwan may have been mutually reinforcing. From the perspective of the NIE, this is a very reasonable argument. The mental models of the world that political decision makers and the individuals of the general public develop are apparently not only shaped by the developments that take place in their own country. In most cases, they will also be affected if a country that is geographically and culturally close, or in other aspects comparable, achieves a successful economic development. In this way, the economic competition between Taiwan and South Korea may have been an additional incentive for the political decision makers to pursue policies conducive to economic growth. This is not only supported by the survey cited above, but also by Wade (1990/2004), who observed that Taiwanese decision makers and commentators were closely aware of the developments taking place in South Korea (p. 200).

5.3.2.2 Conclusions on the institutional environment of developmental states

Until now, the conclusions have focused on the comparison between Taiwan and South Korea. In order to gain more insights on the nature of the institutional environment of developmental states, Japan should be added to the analysis. The resemblance between the Japanese and the South Korean developmental states has been widely explored, as was partly already described in section 3. As Woo-Cumings notes (1995, p. 447), post-war Japan shows the most immediate parallels to South Korea in terms of policies and bureaucratic structures, whereas the South Korean political system during the decades of high growth shows much more resemblance to pre-war Japan. The authoritarian nature of the Korean governments until the end of the 1980s and the influential role of the military under Park Chung-hee and Chun Doo-hwan show obvious similarities to the Japanese political conditions before 1945. Although Taiwanese economic policy was quite different in some aspects, particularly the use of state-owned enterprises, its political system did share the authoritarian nature with South Korea and pre-war Japan.

Since the differences and similarities between South Korea, Taiwan, and Japan are a topic that has already received considerable attention in research, I will limit the analysis here to several specific aspects directly related to the internal structure of the bureaucracy in developmental states. In particular, I analyze whether the strong role of a pilot agency that Johnson (1982) considered a key element of the Japanese developmental state was present in the same way in South Korea and Taiwan. Therefore, the role of the pilot agencies in the economy, their overall autonomy, and their position within the power struggle of bureaucratic organizations is discussed.

In the case study on Japan, the exceptional autonomy of the bureaucracy in general that was stressed by Johnson and other scholars both for pre-war and for post-war Japan has been described. Furthermore, it has been noted that the role of MITI after its formation 1949 was that of a pilot agency which had far reaching powers and was in command of several instruments to shape the path of economic development. However, it was also noticed that the influence of MITI was never without restrictions. While it reached the zenith of its influence on the economy in the 1950s, its relative power declined in subsequent decades. This decline had various reasons. One was the growing relevance of political processes and the LDP, which translated into an increasing awareness of the public opinion. Another source of limits for MITI's authority originated from within the bureaucracy, where other agencies gained influence in the bureaucratic power struggle.

The situation in South Korea and Taiwan was obviously different, since neither of the countries had functioning democratic institutions until the end of the 1980s. As argued by Woo-Cumings (1995, p. 446), South Korea's civil and military bureaucracies were not subject to any substantial checks from either the parliament or the electorate itself from the 1960s till the 1990s. The same is certainly true for Taiwan, where the regime was authoritarian throughout this period. However, the autonomy of the bureaucracy from the authoritarian governments was apparently limited. As Wade (1990/2004, p. 196) notes, president and premier in Taiwan had much more control over the apparatus of the economic bureaucracy than their Japanese counterparts; similarly, Cheng et al. (1998, p. 102–103) find that Park was firmly in command of economic policy making in South Korea. While the limits to bureaucratic power in Japan came from below, they came from above in Taiwan and Korea.

A similarity between Japan and South Korea, and Japan and Taiwan, is the importance of bureaucratic competition for constraining the authority of specific agencies. This is most apparent in Taiwan, where scholars commonly identify not one, but two pilot agencies for the time after 1970: the CEPD (as well as its predecessors before 1978) and the IDB. As described in the case study, the division of power between these two agencies, and the interrelationship between their tasks, led to various disagreements. In these conflicts, the IDB was an advocate of protectionism, whereas the CEPD favored liberalization. This is similar to the bureaucratic power struggle in Japan, where the MITI generally assumed the role of a proponent of interventionist industrial policies while other agencies promoted a more liberal, market-oriented economic policy. In both countries, a gradual and slow liberalization of the economy was the result.

The South Korean case is slightly different. As noted in the case study, the pilot agency of the South Korean developmental state, the Economic Planning Board (EPB), played a truly exceptional role within the bureaucracy. In terms of authority over other bureaucratic agencies, its control over the budget gave it an even more powerful position than MITI had enjoyed in Japan during the postwar decades. However, it was also noted that the most ambitious economic policies of the South Korean developmental state, the heavy and chemical industrialization drive of the 1970s, did not stem from the EPB, but from a group within the presidential administration. While the EPB itself was certainly involved in interventionist policies and planning, the proponents favored an even more activist approach toward economic policy, which was abandoned when the EPB regained its influence at the end of the 1970s. The pattern of this struggle for influence within the state apparatus is thus similar to Taiwan and Japan: a conflict about the adequate degree of state interventionism and economic liberalization.

5.4 Singapore: a developmental city-state?

5.4.1 Reasons for the emergence of different economic development strategies in Singapore and Hong Kong

Together with Taiwan and South Korea, Singapore and Hong Kong form the East Asian Tigers. However, Singapore and Hong King share some similarities that differentiate them from the two larger Tigers. The most obvious similarity is that both are city-states. As a consequence, the distribution of agricultural land, the modernization of agriculture and the power of rural elites were never issues that the governments had to handle (Haggard, 1990, p. 100), whereas Japan, Taiwan, and South Korea all undertook major land reforms at early stages of their economic catch-up. Furthermore, and in sharp contrast to South Korea and Taiwan, both Singapore and Hong Kong were only occupied for a very brief period during the Second World War by Japan, the archetype of a developmental state. Instead, both were British colonies, and thus share a legacy shaped by the country that is commonly perceived as the patron of free trade and laissez-faire economic policy. They also share some cultural traits, since both are predominantly inhabited by Chinese: Hong Kong because it was a British enclave on the Chinese mainland and Singapore because of heavy Chinese immigration during colonial times. In spite of these similarities, both city-states came to pursue economic development strategies that were quite different in some respects. While Hong Kong followed almost complete laissez-faire, the economic policy of Singapore was much more interventionist (Haggard, 1990, pp. 100–101). As a consequence, Singapore is commonly considered the only unambiguous example of a developmental state among the emerging economies in Southeast Asia (Doner et al., 2005, p. 336), whereas Hong Kong is virtually excluded from the literature on this concept.

Singapore was founded in 1819 by the British as a "transshipment point for trade with East Asia" (Haggard, 1990, p. 101). As a part of British Malaya, it grew into a metropolis, but served largely as an exporting port for Malay tin and rubber, with only minor manufacturing activities that were mainly under Chinese control (Haggard, 1990, p. 102; Huff, 2001, p. 295). During colonial times, it became a multiethnic society. Chinese became the largest ethnic group by 1827 (Leitch LePoer, p. 21), which explains why Singapore is commonly characterized as primarily Confucian in terms of cultural heritage (see Doner et al., 2005, p. 336; Rowen, 1998, p. 5). Indians became the second largest ethnic group by 1860 (Leitch LePoer, 1991, p. 23), but are today again outnumbered by ethnic Malays (Leitch LePoer, 1991, p. 79). While Singapore was occupied by Japan during the Second World War, it was reconstituted as a British colony afterward. In the years after the Second World War, Singapore was characterized by an extraordinarily militant worker's movement that caused massive strikes (Doner et al., 2005, p. 347). An independence movement began to emerge and led to the first elections in 1955 and the British promise to grant independence by 1957 (Haggard, 1990, p. 103).

Similar to Taiwan and Korea, Singapore did benefit from the institutional heritage of the colonial government in that it inherited a centralized and coherent administration. However, the first governments were "preoccupied with decolonization to the neglect of economic problems" (Haggard & Cheng, 1987, p. 104). The People's Action Party (PAP), which still dominates Singaporean politics today, came to power in 1959. At this time, it was split between a moderate faction (headed by Lee Kuan Yew) and a left-wing faction that was sympathetic to communism (Haggard, 1990, p. 104). The left wing was quickly purged after the elections, and the new government launched a plan that aimed at promoting industrialization through state action (Haggard & Cheng, 1987, p. 104). The Economic Development Board (EDB), which is commonly considered to have been the pilot agency of the Singaporean developmental state (see Doner et al.,

2005, p. 335), was founded by the PAP government in 1961 as one of several statutory boards (Haggard, 1990, p. 107).

An important objective of the moderate PAP faction was the unification of Singapore with Malaya. One the one hand, the unification was considered a necessity if Singapore wanted to retain its position as the region's trading center. On the other hand, it would weaken the city's strong political left (Haggard, 1990, pp. 104–105). The unification took place in 1963. However, it was very short-lived and ended only two years later. In the face of racial riots that emerged between Malays and Chinese in 1964, the government of Malaysia decided to expel Singapore from the federation in 1965, against the will of Lee Kuan Yew, the most important political figure in Singapore (Leitch LePoer, 1991, pp. 55–57).

As a result, Singapore was in an extremely difficult geopolitical and economic situation. Through tariff wars, the newly independent city-state was cut off from Malaysian markets and supplies; the import substitution strategy that had been envisioned within the federation had become unviable (Haggard & Cheng, 1987, p. 105). In addition, the British government announced in 1967 that it would accelerate its military withdrawal from Singapore, increasing the sense of vulnerability among the local political decision makers (Doner et al., 2005, p. 347).

This situation committed the Singaporean leadership to economic growth. However, it was not clear which path of development to follow. As a consequence of its geopolitical environment, Singapore attempted to leapfrog the markets of unfriendly neighbors and focused on full integration with the world economy (Doner et al., 2005, pp. 347–348). Lee Kuan Yew is cited by Huff (1995) as saying "we borrowed in an eclectic fashion elements of what Hong Kong was doing, what Switzerland was doing, what Israel was doing, and we improvised. I also went down to Malta to see how they ran the dry docks" (p. 1434).

While Lee mentioned neither Japan nor Taiwan or South Korea in this particular quote, there were nevertheless important similarities concerning economic policy from the mid-1960s onwards. As in the newly industrializing countries in Northeast Asia, the government assumed an important role within the economy, creating a capitalist developmental state. In Singapore, an important reason for government activism was the pre-existing industrial structure, which was characterized by a weak private sector that was concentrated in services (Haggard, 1990, p. 101) and the absence of a viable domestic manufacturing base. Facing the lack of a local entrepreneurial class that would be able to develop internationally competitive manufacturing industries, the government stepped in.

Lee did mention Hong Kong as a reference model in the quotation above; however, the historic and societal conditions of the other major East Asian city-state resulted in a quite different path of economic development. Similar to Singapore, Hong Kong had served since the first half of the 19th century as an entrepôt for the British Empire, in this case for its economic activities in China (Haggard, 1990, p. 116). After being occupied by Japan during the Second World War and then returned to the United Kingdom, the defeat of the Kuomintang government by the Communists on mainland China significantly altered the set of exogenous constraints. Hong Kong's trade with the mainland declined, especially after the United Nations imposed an embargo on China in 1951 (Haggard, 1990, p. 117). This loss of an entrepôt position as the center of regional trade is similar to Singapore. However, in contrast to Singapore, Hong Kong also benefitted from events on the Chinese mainland because it was subject to massive immigration, particularly through the relocation of businessmen from Shanghai after the Chinese revolution (Haggard and Cheng, 1987, p. 107). The political situation and economic hardships that predominated in the People's Republic of China were probably the main reasons that no strong independence movement emerged in Hong Kong. It continued to be ruled in a colonial manner that was not necessarily repressive, but certainly authoritarian (Haggard and Cheng, 1987, p. 108).

Since Hong Kong had inherited a local manufacturing sector from the Shanghai immigrants, the perceived need for state intervention was lower than in Singapore (Haggard, 1990, p. 115). Furthermore, the distribution of power in the societal power struggle was different in one very important aspect: after some labor activism in the immediate post-war years, the labor movement was exceptionally weak beginning in the 1950s, without any repressive government policies (Haggard, 1990, pp. 119–120). This is a sharp contrast not only to Singapore, but also to Taiwan, South Korea and pre-war Japan, where the labor movement was harshly repressed by the state since it was considered part of the political left. In consequence, the administration of Hong Kong faced less pressure to intervene because of existing competitive private businesses and relatively harmonious industrial relations that posed no imminent threat to the competitiveness of these companies. This may explain why laissez-faire persisted in Hong Kong, while interventionist developmental states emerged in Northeast Asia and Singapore. In addition, the continued influence of the United Kingdom may have preserved Hong Kong from diverging from its development strategy and move toward another reference model.

5.4.2 The institutions of the developmental state in Singapore

Singapore was politically stable after its separation from Malaysia. The People's Action Party has been in control up until modern day. Lee Kuan Yew remained in the office as prime minister until 1990, when he stepped down as the world's longest serving prime minister; he then held the advisory post of Minister Mentor until May 2011. The similarities to the long rule of the Kuomintang in Taiwan under Chiang Kai-shek and his son are obvious, with the exception that the rule of the PAP in Singapore was even more stable and political liberalization came even more gradually to the city-state.

Similarities between Singapore one the one hand, and Taiwan and South Korea on the other, continue in the bureaucratic sphere. It is generally agreed that Singapore's civil service is highly meritocratic and capable. According to the World Bank (1993, p. 176), it is a common perception that Singapore has the most competent bureaucracy among the emerging economies of East Asia. However, meritocracy in the recruitment process is not achieved through competitive examinations as in Japan, South Korea and (to some degree) Taiwan, but through requiring high academic standards in combination with personal interviews (Campos & Root, 1996, p. 142). The autonomy of the bureaucracy, in general, and the independence of economic decisions from political considerations, in particular, were very pronounced (Haggard, 1990, p. 113; Root, 1996, pp. 42–43). Furthermore, the Singaporean bureaucracy is particularly renowned for the competitive remuneration of civil servants and its freedom from corruption. Singapore is the only emerging economy where the salaries of public sector employees are on average higher than those of private sector employees at comparable positions, which has arguably contributed to attracting competent personnel and fighting corruption (Root 1996, pp. 46–48; World Bank 1993, pp. 177).

The differences between the Northeast Asian developmental states on the one hand, and Singapore on the other, are bigger in the sphere of state-business relations. The most apparent differences concern the attitude of the Singaporean state toward foreign investment and domestic private companies. As was summarized in previous sections, the governments of South Korea and Japan maintained close and cooperative relationships with a limited number of private domestic businesses. The economic development of Taiwan has relied on a combination of state-owned companies and smaller private businesses. In all three countries, the governments tried to promote the international competitiveness of domestic companies through a variety of measures including subsidies and protectionist policies (see Sections 5.2 and 5.3). In contrast to Japan, South Korea and Taiwan, state interventions in Singapore were not aimed at promoting the international competitiveness of domestic companies. The exact opposite was the case: while the Northeast Asian developmental states favored local firms and Hong Kong's economic policy remained neutral, Singapore favored foreign over domestic companies (Haggard, 1990, pp. 110–111).

One explanation for this difference is in the initial conditions faced by the government when Singapore became independent. As previously mentioned, the Singaporean private domestic sector had been always been weak, and it continued to be the weakest among the successful East Asian economies during the period of fast economic development (Haggard, 2004, p. 62). Furthermore, the smaller domestic market of Singapore, when compared to the Northeast Asian developmental states, and its long history as a center of international trade (Shin, 2005, pp. 386-387) made protectionist measures less feasible than in Taiwan or South Korea. Ethnic heterogeneity and the resulting tensions between Chinese, Malays, and other groups may have been an additional obstacle for the implementation of an economic strategy based on supporting selected private companies. As a result of these constraints, Singapore has been the only state among the commonly acknowledged developmental states that relied to a large degree on foreign direct investment by multinational companies to increase its manufacturing capacity. According to Jomo (2004, p. 60), this strategy was also based on the idea that foreign powers would develop a stake in the political survival of independent Singapore as a result of their companies' investments. In strategic industries where FDI could not be attracted to a sufficient degree, or where the involvement of foreign companies was not desired, the government stepped in through state-ownership in government-linked companies (GLCs) (Huff, 1995, pp. 1428–1429; Shin, 2005, pp. 386–387). Since 1974, the investment of the Singaporean state in domestic companies has been managed through a government holding company, Temasek Holdings, which serves as an intermediary between the government and the GLCs (Low, 2004, pp. 169-170).

Similar to its Northeast Asian peers, and different from Hong Kong, the Singaporean state has intervened in a variety of ways in the economy. However, while these interventions had a similar ultimate goal—the development of a competitive industrial structure with a strong manufacturing base—Singapore nevertheless followed a different approach. More than other East Asian economies, Singapore's economic policy focused on an objective that virtually all economists stress: macroeconomic stability. Precisely this objective was achieved through several pronounced state interventions in the economy, in sharp contrast to recommendations that stress the *inherent* stability of the private sector. The achievement of macroeconomic stability through interventions is considered the key lesson of the Singaporean experience (Huff, 1999, p. 36).

One area where the state intervened to a significant degree in the economy was the level of savings. According to Huff (1995, pp. 1426–1428; 1999, p. 37–38), the high savings ratio was not a result of voluntary behavior of economic actors or a deliberate reaction to state-set incentives, instead, the high level of savings was forced by the state through a variety of measures and rules. Savings were mostly generated by the public sector (Huff, 1995, p. 1426). In addition, private actors were forced to save through a compulsory social security scheme, the *Central Provident Fund* (Huff, 1995, p. 1428). The Singaporean social security system required compulsory contributions that amounted up to 50 percent of salaries (Stiglitz and Uy, 1996, p. 251).

An even more prominent intervention of the Singaporean state in the economy was the government's control over the wage level and labor relations (Haggard, 1990, p. 146; Huff, 1995, p. 1424). Keeping labor relations peaceful and wages at rates that promoted the international competitiveness of Singapore was considered indispensable for luring the required FDI to diversify and upgrade the manufacturing sector of the economy. Beginning in 1972, the main instrument to achieve this objective was the *National Wages Council* (NWC), a tripartite body that brought together the government, labor representatives, and representatives of both domestic and foreign businesses (Huff, 1995, p. 1424; Root, 1996, p. 48). The NWC was governed by two essential rules: confidentiality and unanimity (Root, 1996, p. 49). This guaranteed that open discussions could take place and that no decision could be imposed coercively upon one of the three parties (Root, 1996, p 49). While Root stresses the importance of the council for consensus building and its tripartism (1996, p. 49), Huff argues that the government was clearly in a dominating role. Huff (1995) summarizes:

> The National Wages Council could successfully establish itself as a body which achieved 'consensus' in line with government objectives because by the 1970s two of its constituents were the government, because no significant nongovernment trade unions existed in Singapore, and because employers apparently did not feel strong enough to break the cartel and bid up wage rates, despite incentives to do so due to Singapore's labor scarcity and desirability as a production base (Lim, 1987, p. 51). (Huff, 1995, pp. 1424–1425, source as given there)

The government's influence declined somewhat after 1981 but remained strong (Huff, 1995, p. 1424). Both Root and Huff agree that the decisions of the NWC, while officially not mandatory, were the determining influence upon the development of wages in Singapore (Huff, 1995, p. 1425; Root, 1996, p. 49). While it is a body that is governed by clear and formalized rules, its influence is thus a clear example of an informal institution. After a period of repression (Doner et al., 2005, p. 347), the PAP in Singapore forged a close relationship with unions and gradually achieved to control and utilized them for developmental goals after 1965 (Haggard, 1990, pp. 111–112).

The stability-oriented wage policies described above were mainly driven by the objective of attracting multinational companies to Singapore by guaranteeing competitive conditions for FDI. In addition, international investors were heavily subsidized through tax incentives and similar measures (Huff, 1999, p. 39). These incentives were clearly selective because they were targeted at specific industries chosen by the EDB, first on the basis of employment and growth potential and, in the later stages of economic development, on the basis of technical content and value added (Huff 1999, p. 39). Furthermore, the EDB compiled a list of desirable industries that was permanently updated. Applications to receive this *pioneer industry* status were evaluated on the basis of value-added and the linkages to other industries (Haggard, 1990, p. 113).

Apparently, the Singaporean state aimed at shaping the structure of its economy through selective incentives, similar to the other developmental states. Its approach for these incentives was more general and less focused on picking winners than was the case in South Korea, Taiwan, or Japan (Huff, 1995, p. 1433). However, the government was also directly involved in the economy through the government-linked companies. The importance of these GLCs for Singapore's development strategy is difficult to estimate. Low (2004, p. 161) cites two estimates for the contribution of government-linked companies to the Singaporean GDP. These differ greatly, ranging from a contribution of 60% of GDP to around 13% of GDP. According to Low, an important reason for the divergence of these estimates is the differing definitions on what constitutes a GLC. While the lower estimate only includes GLCs with a formal government shareholding of more than 20%,[28] higher estimates take into account that the government also exercises a notable influence in companies where it has a lower share of ownership (Low, 2004, p. 161). As previously noted, the government's main instrument for controlling its investment in the Singaporean economy is the holding company Temasek. Temasek has the objectives to serve as a monitoring arm of the government in business and to influence strategic decisions without intervening in the day-to-day management of companies (Low, 2004, p. 170; Sam, 2008, pp. 66–70). On the other hand, its investments shape the structure of the Singaporean economy. As Low (2004) summarizes:

---

28   This estimate distinguished between the share of GLCs and the share of the non-GLC public sector including statutory boards. The former was estimated at 12.9%, whereas the latter was estimated at 8.9%, resulting in a total of 21.8%.

Temasek will divest businesses which are no longer relevant or have no international growth potential. But rolling privatisation means from time to time, it will invest in new businesses to nurture new industry clusters in Singapore and still enhance long-term shareholder return. These are likely to be in new growth sectors which entail high risk, large investments or long gestation periods, where private enterprise in Singapore is unable or unwilling to assume risks. Temasek will be highly selective in making such new investment. (p. 170)

Thus, the government's direct involvement in the economy through the owner-ship of companies serves objectives that are clearly developmental. The varying characteristics of the state-business nexus in different developmental states do not inhibit that these states pursue broadly similar economic development strate-gies.

5.4.3 Conclusions: Differences and similarities between Singapore and the Northeast Asian developmental states

Singapore is quite similar to the Northeast Asian economies in terms of the au-thoritarian political conditions throughout the catch-up process, its highly meri-tocratic bureaucracy, the existence of cooperative mechanisms between the state and businesses, and the heavy investment in education. These characteristics of the highly successful East Asian economies were widely noted in the scholarly literature, in particular by the World Bank (1993). Even more than its Northeast Asian counterparts, Singapore can serve as the basis for a further major lesson that the World Bank drew from the East Asian experience: macroeconomic sta-bility should be a main objective of economic policy. Singapore has given the stability of prices, wages and the exchange rate a much higher priority than other East Asian countries. The most notable divergence in this respect is between Singapore and South Korea. As Figure 8 shows, the inflation of Singapore was substantially and consistently lower than that of South Korea from 1960 till 2000, even though the difference had diminished in the 1980s and 1990s.

Among the economies discussed so far in this study, South Korea has fol-lowed the most interventionist and selective approach to economic policy, with the possible exception of wartime Japan. Singapore is at the other side of the spectrum, even though some selective policies were noted in the case study. These were tax incentives for investments in specific industries and the use of state-owned enterprises to fill strategic gaps. While industrial policies in South Korea and Japan were sometimes proactively leading the market through exercising tight state control over specific private companies, the selective incentives in Singapore were aimed mainly at foreign companies.

Figure 8: Inflation rates of Singapore and South Korea 1960–2010 [%]

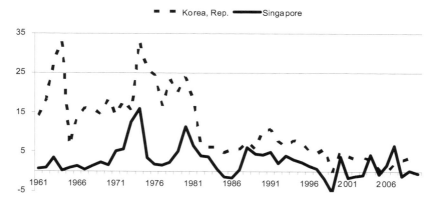

Source: World Bank (2011a).

An important lesson from Singapore is that its extraordinary macroeconomic stability was not accomplished *in spite of* state interventions, but at least partly *because of* state interventions. This, however, does not refer to all aspects of macroeconomic stability. Commonly recommended policies, particularly concerning conservative fiscal and monetary policies, certainly had a role in achieving stable conditions. However, the Singaporean state went significantly beyond such recommendations by controlling the development of wages. While virtually stable wages and the absence of labor disputes may certainly be considered essential constituents of a stable macroeconomic environment for investors and businesses in general, state interference with the market mechanism for setting wages clearly affects the allocation of resources in an economy.

The example of Singapore shows the diversity of developmental states in terms of their economic policies. The policies followed by Singapore resulted in an institutional environment for private business that was very different from the high-performing economies in Northeast Asia. Instead of nurturing domestic companies through protectionism as Japan, South Korea and Taiwan—an approach to economic development that has frequently been referred to as nationalistic—attracting foreign direct investment has been the main objective of Singapore since the 1960s. Giving priority to macroeconomic stability was instrumental for providing superior conditions for the manufacturing activities of multinational companies.

5.5 Emerging economies in Southeast-Asia from the perspective of the developmental state concept

5.5.1 The relevance of the emerging Southeast Asian economies

When the World Bank study on the East Asian miracle was published in 1993, it defined the group of the high-performing Asian economies as consisting of eight countries. These were Japan, the four East Asian Tigers and three emerging economies from Southeast Asia, Malaysia, Thailand, and Indonesia (World Bank, 1993, pp. 28–29). Other publications of the 1990s generally follow the same approach (see Akyüz et al., 1998; Amsden, 1991, 1995; Dowling, 1994; Campos & Root, 1996; Leftwich, 1995; Ng, Sudo, and Crone, 1992; Perkins, 1994; Root, 1996; Thompson, 1996), and conceive these three Southeast Asian countries essentially as a third tier of successful East Asian economies that followed the lead of Japan and the four Tigers in accordance with the famous *flying geese* metaphor.[29] A fourth Southeast Asian economy, the Philippines, formed the Association of Southeast Asian Nations (ASEAN) together with the three mentioned countries and Singapore in 1967. However, it is excluded from the group of the HPAEs due to its lackluster economic performance.[30]

The reasoning for the World Bank's perspective on the countries that were part of the Asian Miracle is apparent when the economic performance in the 20 years preceding the publication of the World Bank Study is evaluated. As Table 11 shows, Thailand, Malaysia and Indonesia where all among the world's fastest growing economies from 1973–1993, occupying respectively the third, eighth, and twelfth places in a ranking based on GDP per capita growth. While the three

---

29 This metaphor was already devised by Japanese economist Kaname Akamatsu in the 1930s and is commonly applied to East Asia in the way that industrial development is gradually transmitted from the lead goose, Japan, through various tiers of less developed economies. Whereas Japan would move up the ladder of industrial and technological development, some of its industries would move to the East Asian Tigers and then to Southeast Asia and China (Kojima, 2000, pp. 375-376).

30 Root (1996) also includes the Philippines in his analysis (pp. 111-138), but mainly to contrast it with the more successful East Asian economies.

countries had performed much worse than the Asian Tigers until the early 1970s, it seemed that they had begun a similarly successful catch-up process with the delay of at least one decade: their economic growth had been accelerating (World Bank, 1993, p. 28). Since the World Bank Study of 1993 considers the success of the interventionist development approaches of Japan, South Korea, and Taiwan to have been only possible due to "highly unusual historical and institutional circumstances" (p. 366), it has been concluded that the study actually recommends developing countries to follow the example of the Southeast Asian economies, whose policies were considered less demanding (see Akyüz et al., 1998, p. 7; Jomo, 2004, p. 57).

Table 11: Ranking of countries by real GDP per capita growth (PPP) 1973–1993

Rank	Country	Compound annual real growth rate 1973–1993 [%]	Cumulated real growth 1973–1993 [%]
1.	South Korea	6.65	262.28
2.	Taiwan	6.40	245.97
3.	Thailand	5.69	202.39
4.	Botswana	5.56	194.92
5.	Hong Kong	5.35	183.33
6.	Singapore	5.25	178.51
7.	China	5.20	175.74
8.	Malaysia	4.59	145.25
9.	Mauritius	4.14	125.18
10.	Cape Verde	4.11	123.83
11.	Oman	3.90	114.96
12.	Indonesia (including Timor)	3.55	100.91

Source: Own calculations based on Maddison (2010), data available for 172 countries and political entities.

More recent publications have drawn a quite different picture of the emerging economies in Southeast Asia, arguing that their economic performance has not lived up to expectations. Affected more profoundly in terms of GDP than the four Tigers by the East Asian Crisis of 1997, Malaysia, Thailand, and Indonesia have not been among the world's fastest growing economies since. According to Jomo (2004), the crisis "ended the Southeast Asian miracle" (p. 58). Furthermore, as has already been noted by some scholars quite early, these economies upgraded their industries much slower than the East Asian Tigers, due to giving less priority to the export of manufactures and a better endowment with exportable natural resources (Akyüz et al., 1998, pp. 18–19; Perkins, 1994, pp. 655–656). As a consequence, publications of the last decade have generally stressed the inferiority of the performance of Malaysia, Thailand, and Indonesia when compared to the successful economies of Northeast Asia and Singapore (see Jomo, 2003a; Doner et al., 2005; Jomo, 2004).

Table 12 compares the economic performance of Malaysia, Thailand, Indonesia and the Philippines since 1950. Thailand has had the most stable economic performance, whereas Malaysia has grown very quickly in the 1970s and 1990s but performed worse in other decades. Indonesia's performance has been more stable than Malaysia's, but at a lower level. Meanwhile, it is apparent that the Philippines have been consistently the worst performer since 1970. The Philippines are the only country among this group that did not achieve any catch-up with the USA in terms of per capita GDP since 1950 and even lost ground (see Table 13). As Table 13 shows, the growth performance of the other three Southeast Asian economies remains impressive even though they may not have met some optimistic predictions made in the 1990s.

As a result of their lack of catch-up with the East Asian Tigers and the perception that they have generally intervened less in the economy, scholars disagree whether Malaysia, Indonesia and Thailand should be considered developmental states or not. While Akyüz et al. (1998, pp. 18–22) notice important differences between the East Asian Tigers and their Southeast Asian followers, they also stress the similarities and argue that industrial policies have also been an important element in the growth experience of Malaysia, Thailand and Indonesia. Similarly, Vu (2007, pp. 44–47) argues that a developmental state emerged gradually beginning in the 1960s, while conceding that it has been less successful than in South Korea. In sharp contrast, Doner et al. (2005, p. 333)—as mentioned previously—consider Thailand, Malaysia and Indonesia, as well as the Philippines, to be intermediate states. In the light of the lackluster economic performance of the Philippines (see Table 12), there seems to be sufficient reason to criticize this approach of conceiving the four countries as one group.

Table 12: Economic performance of the ASEAN-4 in comparison

		1950–1960	1960–1970	1970–1980	1980–1990	1990–2000	2000–2008
Cumulated Real GDP per capita growth in PPP [%]	Malaysia	-1.9	35.9	75.9	40.3	59.1	26.1
	Thailand	32.0	57.1	50.8	81.4	38.1	36.8
	Indonesia	25.9	16.8	58.3	34.5	30.3	35.1
	Philippines	37.9	19.5	34.7	-7.5	8.2	23.1
Catch-up toward the US GDP/capita in PPP [percentage points]	Malaysia	-2.8	0.3	5.9	2.4	6.6	4.3
	Thailand	1.0	1.8	2.5	6.2	2.5	5.6
	Indonesia	0.5	-1.1	2.2	0.8	0.7	2.7
	Philippines	1.8	-1.3	1.0	-3.3	-1.1	1.0

Source: Own calculations based on Maddison (2010).

Table 13: GDP per capita (PPP) of Southeast Asian economies relative to the USA [%]

	1950	1960	1970	1980	1990	2000	2008
Malaysia	16.3	13.5	13.8	19.7	22.1	28.7	33.0
Thailand	8.5	9.5	11.3	13.7	20.2	22.5	28.1
Indonesia	8.4	8.9	7.9	10.1	10.8	11.5	14.2
Philippines	11.2	13.0	11.7	12.8	9.5	8.4	9.4

Source: Own calculations based on Maddison (2010).

Even though the performance of the emerging economies in Southeast Asia compares unfavorably with the developmental states in Northeast Asia and Singapore, an analysis of their development experience may be of particular value for the purposes of the present study. First of all, it should not be forgotten that the economic development in Malaysia, Thailand, and Indonesia may have been less successful than in Taiwan or South Korea, but it was much more successful than that of most other countries in the world. If the GDP per capita growth from 1950 to 2008 is taken into account, all three countries remain among the top 25 performers and rank higher than any of the large Latin American or African economies. In addition, they share important characteristics with the countries of Central Asia. Malaysia, Indonesia, and Thailand are not only better endowed with natural resources than the successful Northeast Asian developmental states, but they also share the characteristic of ethnically heterogeneous societies (Doner et al., 2005, pp. 336–340; see also Table 3 in Section 3.2.3). In Central Asia, all five republics are ethnically heterogeneous. Kazakhstan, Turkmenistan, and Uzbekistan are well endowed with natural resources (see Part III). Moreover, Malaysia and Indonesia share Islamic heritage with the five republics of Central Asia.

In the next sections, the development of Malaysia, Thailand, and Indonesia will be analyzed from the perspective of the NIE. As in the previous sections, Figure 2 (see Section 2.2.2) will serve as the analytical basis. Therefore, the analysis will focus on the external environment the countries faced, on the struggle between different interest groups, on the ideologies of key decision makers, and on the resulting path of institutional development.

5.5.2 Economic policies and institutions of the emerging Southeast Asian economies

5.5.2.1 Malaysia

It was already noted in Section 3.2.3 that the external environment for the Southeast Asian economies of Malaysia, Thailand, and Indonesia differed markedly from the one faced by other successful East Asian economies. Neither Malaysia nor Thailand nor Indonesia faced a particularly strong external threat. Furthermore, the political decision makers in these countries were not constrained by a vital partnership with the United States or any other developed economy. However, they faced domestic constraints that had a decisive influence on the path of institutional change, the economic policies that were pursued, and, eventually, on economic performance.

The territory of today's Malaysia became part of the British Empire beginning in the late 18th century with the acquisition of the island Penang. It remained a British colony until 1957. British domination was only interrupted by the Japanese occupation during the Second World War. The most important export goods produced in the colony were tin and rubber. According to Jomo and Gomez (1997, p. 344), Malaya (as it was called then) became the single most profitable colony of the British Empire. During this time, the British encouraged the massive immigration of Chinese laborers for the tin mines and rubber plantations on the Malayan Peninsula (Case, 2000, p. 135).

The ethnic heterogeneity that evolved became the most critical constraint for political decision makers. It had a profound impact on the organizational power struggle, shaping the path of institutional and economic development profoundly. During colonial times, the British acted as intermediaries between the Chinese and native Malays, which obstructed cross-ethnic encounters (Case, 2000, p. 135). The economic structure, which developed under the colonial administration, also shaped relationships between these ethnic groups (Jomo & Gomez, 1997, pp. 344–345; Pereira & Tong, 2005, p. 138). The native Malay, or *bumiputera*[31], comprised 52% of the population and dominated the post-colonial state apparatus. However, this group was economically marginalized because its economic activity was mainly limited to agriculture, specifically rice farming. This limitation had been supported by the British colonial administration. The Chinese minority, which made up around 35% of the total population, was more

---

31   The term bumiputera refers to all indigenous peoples in Malaysia, which includes ethnic Malays, indigenous peoples of Sabah, Sarawak and the Orang Asli in Peninsular Malaysia (Jomo & Wee, 2003, p. 444).

urbanized and dominated the economy together with foreign investors (Jomo & Gomez, 1997, pp. 344–345; Pereira & Tong, 2005, 138).

The political parties that eventually emerged were generally organized along ethnic lines. All prime ministers of Malaysia since independence have been members of the conservative United Malays National Organization (UMNO), which represents ethnic Malays. Already prior to independence, this party formed an alliance with the Malayan Chinese Association and the Malayan Indian Congress, respectively representing the minorities the Chinese and Indian ethnic minorities (Root, 1996, p. 69). While these parties have continued to cooperate in a political coalition since, the need for bargaining and reciprocity between the different ethnicities has been important for institutional developments. In this context, it should also be noted from a NIE-perspective that members of different ethnicities may have diverging ideologies, not only because of their differing cultural heritage, but also because of differences in professional and economic backgrounds.

The cooperation of parties, based on different ethnic groups in a common ruling alliance, meant that Malaysia was governed by a broad coalition in the sense of Doner et al. (2005, p. 354, see also Section 3.2.3). In order to maintain this coalition, the political decision makers faced the imperative to preserve social peace despite the relative dominance of ethnic Malays within politics and the state apparatus. As a consequence, a main focus of economic policy in Malaysia has been the reduction of tensions between the politically dominating Malays and the economically far more successful Chinese minority (Jomo & Wee, 2003, p. 441; Root, 1996, pp. 70–71). In the first decade of independence, the government was only moderately successful concerning this objective. As was noted in Section 5.4.1, Singapore had joined the Malaysia in 1963 but left the Federation two years later after Chinese-Malayan riots. Until 1969, the government pursued economic policies that were generally laissez-faire but involved limited import substitution industrialization; existing property rights from the colonial period were respected (Jomo & Gomez, 1997, pp. 346). The economic disparity between the two largest ethnic groups and the resulting tensions continued and even deepened in these years. After an election in May 1969, which showed increased support for opposition parties, severe riots between Chinese and Malays broke out in Kuala Lumpur (Case, 2005, p. 287; Pereira & Tong, 2005, p. 139).

After the incidents of 1969, the ruling coalition of the three parties named above was widened to include opposition parties with the aim of sharing economic wealth more equitable (World Bank, 1993, p. 158). As a result, the Malaysian state became much more interventionist through a strategy referred to as the New Economic Policy (NEP), which included a strong element of affirmative action (Jomo & Gomez, 1997, p. 346; Tan, 2009, p. 163). As Tan (2009) summarizes:

> The NEP was introduced in 1970 in response to pressure for greater government intervention from the emerging Malay middle class in general, and Malay businessmen specifically. The thrust of the NEP was largely shaped by these demands and involved the redistribution of wealth to this class through substantial increases in education, (public) employment and business opportunities, and the ownership of corporate equity with the aim of creating a Bumiputera (Malay) Commercial and Industrial Community (BCIC). (pp. 162–163)

According to Pereira and Tong (2005, p. 139), the NEP had two main objectives. The first objective was to eradicate irrespective or race, and the second objective was to "eliminate the identification of race with economic function" (Pereira & Tong, 2005, p. 319, see also Jomo & Wee, 2003, p. 444; World Bank, 1993, p. 158).

Despite these primarily redistributive goals, the NEP also resulted in some economic success. As Tables 12 and 13 show, Malaysia's economy was expanding rapidly in the 1970s, and the country achieved a notable catch-up toward the developed economies in terms of GDP per capita. The implementation of the New Economic Policy coincided with a reorientation toward exports and industrialization, including the establishment of free trade zones to encourage investments in manufacturing for export (Jomo & Gomez, 1997, pp. 354–355; Tan, 2009, p. 163). The export of manufactured goods was increased and Malaysia's dependence on primary exports was reduced. However, the degree of success in industrial upgrading that took place is difficult to determine. Tan (2009) argues that "Malaysia's manufactured exports were based on high-skill and technologically complex products" (p. 164), but Jomo and Gomez (1997) argue that "manufacturing in Malaysia is still limited to the relatively low-skill, labor-intensive aspects of production" (p. 355). The explanation for these superficially contradictory statements is that Malaysia was indeed involved in the production of technologically advanced products, in particular electronics, but only in low-skill and low value-added steps of the value chain. The NEP had relied heavily on foreign direct investment, funded by multinational companies that formed joint-ventures with domestic state-owned companies (Pereira & Tong, 2005, p. 139).

This reliance on foreign investors was partly due to considerations to bypass the dominant class of local Chinese businessmen, and resulted in an unfavorable international division of labor (Tan, 2009, p. 164). Local Malaysian firms were basically limited to the assembly of products as subcontractors of foreign companies (Tan, 2009, p. 164), in sharp contrast to Japan, Taiwan and South Korea where domestic companies were either dominating the value chain from the beginning or increased their control over time. Moreover, the relationship of the Malaysian government with domestic businesses has been characterized as contentious during the NEP, partly because of the strong affirmative action requirements (World Bank, 1993, p. 183). This is a further crucial difference between Malaysia and the countries analyzed in preceding sections of the present study.

According to Tan (2009, p. 165), bureaucratic failures have generally been considered an important underlying reason for the poor progress of technology transfer from multinational investors to local companies. Indeed, the World Bank (1993, p. 174) argued that Malaysia, Indonesia, and Thailand lag significantly behind the East Asian Tigers in terms of bureaucratic capacity, even though strong reform efforts were noted in the case of Malaysia. Furthermore, the World Bank study stated that the results of entry examinations for the Malaysian civil service were subject to affirmative action to the benefit of ethnic Malays (World Bank, 1993, p. 175). This is an interference with meritocratic recruitment and may have resulted in a lower bureaucratic capacity overall.

The NEP had further shortcomings in addition to the low degree of technological and industrial upgrading. While there was a remarkable success concerning the first objective stated above, the reduction of poverty (Pereira & Tong, 2005, p. 140), the achievements concerning the second objective were rather questionable. On the one hand, the ownership of ethnic Malays in corporate wealth did increase notably (Pereira & Tong, 2005, p. 140). On the other hand, a dynamic class of Malay entrepreneurs did not emerge (Tan, 2009, p. 166). According to Tan (2009, pp. 165-166), the preferential treatment of ethnic Malay capitalists did not coincide with performance targets, monitoring, and evaluation, resulting in inefficient structures that would not have been competitive without continued protection. Furthermore, the public sector became overexpanded which lead to vested interests within the state apparatus (Tan, 2009, p. 166). These policies led to increasing discontent among foreign investors and the ethnically Chinese business community in Malaysia, which eventually caused a reluctance to invest and capital flight (Jomo & Gomez, 1997, pp. 363-364).

When Mahathir Mohamad, who would dominate Malaysian politics for more than 20 years, became prime minister in 1981, Malaysia again reoriented its economic policy as a reaction to the growing discontent and the above-mentioned shortcomings of the NEP (Tan, 2009, p. 166–167). The redistributive efforts benefitting ethnic Malays were not abolished, but gradually diluted (Jomo & Wee, 2003, p. 444). The government increased its efforts to follow the reference models of the Tiger States and Japan substantially and became official in 1991, when Mahathir announced that Malaysia should *look east* for orientation (Haggard, 2004, p. 62; World Bank, 1993, p. 184). In the same year, he also announced the *Vision 2020* which emphasized Mahathir's intent to achieve developed country status by the year 2020 (Pereira & Tong, 2005, p. 140). In addition, public enterprises were privatized and measures to increase foreign and domestic private investment were implemented (Jomo & Gomez, 1997, pp. 365–366). The relationship between the state and business gradually improved beginning in 1986 and formalized consultative mechanisms were established in 1991 with the formation of the *Malaysian Business Council* (World Bank, 1993, p. 183–184). Moreover, the new prime minister undertook several measures to increase bureaucratic accountability (Root, 1996, p. 78). Similar to the pilot agencies in Northeast Asia, economic policy making was centralized in a single agency, the Economic Planning Unit (EPU), in the prime minister's department (Tan, 2009, p. 167). After lackluster results at the beginning, the efforts to improve the quality of the bureaucracy were amplified beginning in the early 1990s through the introduction of a new remuneration system based on incentive schemes and performance evaluations (Root, 1996, pp. 79–80).

In terms of economic policy, various export promotion measures were introduced (Rasiah, 2003, p. 49–50). As an example, free trade zones and export processing zone programs were expanded (Pereira & Tong, 2005, p. 140) Already in the early 1980s, a push into heavy industries began that was explicitly modeled after the Northeast Asian developmental states and in particular South Korea's heavy and chemical industry drive of the 1970s (Tan, 2009, p. 166–167; see also Section 5.3.1.4). Again, the government bypassed the Chinese-dominated domestic business sector, this time through creating a diversified state-owned corporation, the Heavy Industries Corporation of Malaysia (HICOM), which cooperated mainly with Japanese companies (Jomo & Gomez, 1997, p. 356–357). Beginning in the early 1990s, there were also increased state-led efforts to diversify the economy into high-technology sectors (Tan, 2009, p. 167). A state-owned holding company, Khazanah Nasional, was founded in 1993 to manage state assets and to make strategic investments, in particular in the high-tech sector. This holding company has been largely modeled after its counterpart in Singapore, Temasek (Demange, 2009, pp. 89–92). After these significant reforms, Malaysia seemed to be heading for sustained economic growth in the 1990s (Pereira & Tong, 2005, p. 140). However, some of the weaknesses of Malaysian industrialization in comparison to the Northeast Asian developmental states had remained. Tan (2009, p. 168) lists a very limited variety of produced goods, the domination of foreign firms, low levels of local content, low technological capabilities located in the country and the absence of independent marketing capabilities as characteristics of the Malaysian industry.

When the Asian Crisis emerged in 1997 after a collapse of the Thai currency, the baht, it seemed at first that Malaysia was less affected than South Korea, Indonesia, or Thailand itself (Case, 2005, p. 284; Jomo, 2006, p. 489). However, there had been a substantial buildup of portfolio investments in the years prior to the crisis, which made Malaysia vulnerable to capital flight (Jomo, 2006, p. 496). In contrast to the governments of South Korea and other East Asian countries, the Malaysian government did not respond to the crisis by turning to the IMF for assistance and embracing its neo-liberal prescriptions. Instead, Malaysia implemented capital controls and a fixed exchange rate for the ringgit (Jomo, 2006, p. 494-495). While Malaysia recovered faster from the crisis than either Thailand or Indonesia, its recovery in the years after the crisis lagged behind South Korea, which had followed the recommendations of the IMF quite closely (Jomo, 2006, p. 497). It is thus difficult to say whether the imposed controls eventually had positive or negative effects overall. However, economic growth seems to have slowed permanently in Malaysia. After the Asian Crisis and bailouts of domestic companies, the relationship between the government and the country's businessmen was considered an example for cronyism (Case, 2005, p. 193). Prime Minister Mahathir resigned in 2003 after more than two decades in power. Since then, there have been several swings between neo-liberal and interventionist economic polices (Case, 2005, p. 285-286).

To summarize, the economic and institutional development of Malaysia shows both major similarities and crucial differences to the developmental states discussed so far. When compared to the large majority of developing countries, Malaysia has experienced remarkable success in terms of industrialization and economic growth. This success was achieved in decades when substantial state interventions in the economy took place. Furthermore, the political decision makers in Malaysia explicitly used the East Asian development states as reference models, which resulted in several institutional reforms. However, Malaysia did eventually not achieve the same degree of industrial upgrading and sustainability in economic growth. To a large degree, this may be the consequence of different constraints that Malaysian decision makers faced when compared with their peers in Northeast Asia and Singapore. Instead of external threats to the survival of the country, Malaysian politicians were mainly constrained by internal political imperatives resulting from ethnic tensions. It has been considered a distinguishing characteristic of developmental states that their governments establish economic development as the basis of their legitimacy (see Section 4.1) The Malaysian government's legitimacy was not entirely based on this principle, instead, it had to balance this goal with the objective to redistribute wealth within the society in order to reduce tensions (Pereira & Tong, 2005, p. 141)

5.5.2.2 Thailand

Together with Japan, Thailand is the only high-performing Asian economy that was not colonized by economically more advanced countries prior to its own period of fast growth. As Feeny (1998, p. 413) notes, both countries signed important treaties with Western powers at approximately the same time. Furthermore, they both faced serious threats to their sovereignty from these powers. These notable historical similarities between Japan and Thailand led to several comparative studies on the economic history of both countries (see for example Ayal, 1963; Batson, 1980; Feeny, 1998; Yasuba & Dhiravegin, 1985).

For Thailand (or Siam, as it was called until the 1930s), the signing of the Bowring Treaty in 1855 is considered a turning point in its economic history, because it had to accept free trade on Western terms (Hewison, 2002, p. 231). This took place only a few years before Japan's opening to Western trade and influence. However, the Japanese Shogun regime had isolated the country almost completely from foreign influence over several centuries (see Section 5.2.1.1), while Siam had always maintained contacts with other countries (Abbott, 2004, p. 182). This relates to a difference between Japan and Siam that may have had a decisive influence on their development: Japan's location as an island nation. According to Feeny (1998, p. 415), Japan's location gave it a certain breathing space in the face of foreign threats, which permitted the pursuit of economic development. In contrast, the threat of colonization was immediate for Siam, which was surrounded by territories controlled by Western powers (Feeny, 1998, p. 415). Following a different line of thought, Doner et al. (2005) argue that Siam's "fortuitous positioning as a buffer between French and British possessions allowed Thai monarchs to preserve national sovereignty through negotiations rather than war" (p. 349). Furthermore, Siam, at this time, was land-abundant and labor scarce, in contrast to Japan which was labor-abundant and land-scarce (Feeny, 1998, p. 424). In consequence, Japan exported simple manufactured goods and faced the imperative to promote the accumulation of physical and human capital (Feeny, 1998; p. 415) in order to deal with budget constraints. In contrast, Siam's main export was rice, followed by other commodities such as tin, rubber, timber and sugar. The export of these goods rose sharply after the mid-19th century and they remained Thailand's main trade goods until the 1960s (Hewison, 2002, p. 231). The Thai leadership, therefore, faced less imperative budget constraints that that of Japan (Doner et al., 2005, pp. 349–350).

These differences in initial conditions are only some of the possible explanatory factors for the diverging development of Japan and Thailand (see Feeny, 1998, for a more comprehensive analysis). Nevertheless, they contribute notably to the understanding of this issue. According to Doner et al. (2005), the institutional development in Thailand between 1855 and 1945 was "impressive but limited" (p. 350). A centralized bureaucracy was established in 1892, which has had a continued powerful influence over policy making and public administration (World Bank, 1993, pp. 170–171). However, basic institutions such as property rights were neglected by the Thai leadership (Doner et al., 2005, p. 350).

In the 1950s, almost a century after the signing of the Bowring Treaty, Thailand's GDP per capita was not only much lower than that of Japan, but also considerably lower than the GDP per capita of colonial Malaya (see Table 13 in Section 5.5.1). The development of Malaysia and Thailand over the next 50 years was characterized by several similarities, but also crucial differences. While the political regime of Malaysia has essentially remained stable since independence, Campos and Root (1996, p. 41) argue that Thailand has been the most politically unstable among the HPAEs, despite its long history of independent statehood. After the shift from an absolute monarchy to a constitutional monarchy in 1932, Thailand's political environment has been characterized by a remarkably large number of coups and coup attempts. Most coups have been bloodless, with the king serving as a final arbiter tipping the balance in favor or against the coup (Campos & Root, 1996, pp. 41–44). According to Abbott (2004), the monarchy has served as a cementing force that "is thoroughly institutionalized in Thai public life and acts to hold the opposing forces together" (p. 187)

An important reason for this instability was a continuing threat from communist groups that was interdependent with external developments, such as the Vietnam War (Abbott, 2004, p. 185; Campos & Root, 1996, p. 42). The Thai state was apparently neither able to repress left-wing groups to the same degree as in Taiwan, South Korea or Singapore during the 1950s. In contrast, labor unrest was mitigated through the recognition of unions and collective wage bargaining in the early 1970s (Doner et al., 2005, pp. 350–351).

While these are all notable differences between Thailand and most of the developmental states discussed so far, the strong role of the bureaucracy within the state apparatus is a clear similarity. The Thai bureaucracy had always been powerful, but its role became even more important beginning with the regime of Field Marshal Sarit Thanarat, who took power in 1958 (Campos & Root, 1996, p. 155; World Bank, 1993, p. 171). According to Campos and Root (1996), macroeconomic management was almost entirely left to the bureaucracy under his rule. However, a clear pilot agency as in other successful East Asian economies has not emerged in Thailand. According to Abbott (2004, p. 193) there are a number agencies responsible for macroeconomic management, including the

National Economic and Social Developmental Board, the Office of Fiscal Policy in the Ministry of Finance, the Bureau of the Budget, the Board of Investment (BOI) and the Ministry of Industry. The BOI has generally been considered the most similar to pilot agencies in other developmental states in terms of their responsibilities; however, it is generally noted that its influence over other agencies has been significantly lower than that of MITI in Japan or of the EPB in South Korea (Abbott, 2004, p. 193; Doner et al., 2005, p. 335). Another agency, the Bureau of the Budget, has exercised tight control over the budget drafting process, cooperating partly with the Finance Ministry and the Central Bank but largely bypassing the cabinet) (World Bank, 1993, p. 171). This has contributed decisively to Thailand's success in monetary stability for most of the 20th century. Inflation was generally kept at levels lower than Malaysia and Indonesia, and even lower than South Korea or Hong Kong (World Bank, 1993, p. 171–172).

In contrast to the continuity in monetary policy, the overall approach to economic policy in Thailand has shifted several times. The relationship of the Thai state apparatus with society and businesses is one factor that accounts for these shifts. Similar to Malaysia, substantial Chinese immigration to Thailand had occurred since the late 19th century; there was an addition of one million Chinese to the population between 1880 and 1930 (Hewison, 2002, p. 231). As in Malaysia, the Chinese minority has achieved a strong position in the business sector and has been perceived, according to Campos and Root (1996), as "capitalist exploiters" (p. 92) by the Thai majority. As Campos and Root (1996) argue, the government-business nexus in period from 1932 to the late 1970s was characterized by the Thai-dominated public sector as "counteracting the economic power of the Chinese" (p. 92). At first, the government pursued an economic policy based on nationalism and haphazard state investment. After the coup of Sarit Thanarat, the approach toward economic policy became more coherent and shifted to import-substitution industrialization. This strategy was based on protectionist measures and support for the private sector, while state investment became more limited (Hewison, 2002, p. 232).

The Thai economic policy over the 1960s and 1970s has generally favored large companies and conglomerates over small and medium enterprises (Rock, 1995, p. 750). The relationship of these dominant companies with the state apparatus mainly rested on informal ties between businessmen and individual public officials (Campos & Root, 1996, p. 92–93). This created strong vested interests. According to Ng et al. (1992), the Thai "government lacked the capacity to pursue rational economic policies relatively free of pressures from particular interests up through the 1970s" (p. 223). As a result of pressures from domestic businesses that had benefitted from the import substitution policies, protection increased throughout the 1970s (Hewison, 2002, p. 234). As Tables 12 and 13 show, economic growth in Thailand was substantial in the 1970s, but much weaker than in neighboring Malaysia.

After an economic downturn and alarming balance of payment deficits following the second oil shock, a renewed reorientation of economic policy took place in the early 1980s (Campos & Root, 1996, pp. 93–94; Hewison, 2002, p. 234). The key agency of the economic bureaucracy, the Board of Investment (BOI), shifted from administrating the incentives associated with import substitution toward setting incentives that favored exports and labor intensity (World Bank, 1993, pp. 140–142). In the following years, there was a boom in exports. Foreign direct investment in labor-intensive manufacturing industries from the Northeast Asian HPAEs had an important role in this boom (World Bank, 1993, p. 142). At the same time, crucial reforms in the state-business nexus were implemented. In order to overcome the informal patronage system that had not alleviated a basic mistrust between the public sector and the private sector, formal communication channels were established (Campos & Root, 1996, p. 93). A peak forum for state-business interaction, the *National Joint Public and Private Sector Consultative Committee* (NJPPCC), was formed in 1981. This forum brought together high-level representatives from the relevant government agencies and from private sector associations, headed by the Prime Minister. Clientilism was sharply reduced and rents allocated through a more transparent system due to these reforms (Abbott, 2004, p. 190; Campos & Root, 1996, p. 93; Rock, 1995, p. 754; World Bank, 1993, p. 184).

According to Ng et al (1992, p. 223), the changes of the early 1980s increased the ability of state managers to pursue a coherent development strategy. They argue that Thailand became a developmental state at this time (Ng et al. 1992, pp. 219–220). However, there are other differences to the other developmental states that should be noted. It has been argued that Thailand's economic development has been based on its successful private sector, but that the Thai state is relatively weak vis-à-vis societal groups (Hewison, 2002, p. 229). Furthermore, Thailand has been considered the least interventionist among the three newly industrializing Southeast Asian economies, largely refraining from large-scale projects, but using selective tariff protection for chosen industries (Akyüz et al., 1998, p. 20). Abbott (2004) argues that policy implementation in Thailand has been much weaker than in other East Asian economies. In addition, he notes that factionalism in the state-business relations and the politicization of the bureaucracy increased again after an aborted coup in 1991 (Abbott, 2004, p. 191). When comparing Thailand with its southern neighbor, Malaysia, the stronger influence of domestic Thai business on the state has contributed to a different economic strategy and partly diverging results. As Jomo (2004) summarizes,

Malaysia has been more successful in technological upgrading, but the contribution of domestic companies to manufacturing industries has been marginal. In contrast, "Thailand has failed to attract higher technology FDI, but has preserved a modest role for Thai industrial enterprises" (Jomo, 2004, p. 65).

As has already been noted in the previous section, the Asian Crisis of the late 1990s had its origins in Thailand, which was one of the most affected economies. The response of Thai political decision makers was to embrace the help of the IMF more thoroughly than the Malaysian leadership. In the immediate post-crisis years, the government implemented reforms based on international advice and aimed at "liberalisation, deregulation, decentralisation, privatisation and a reduced role for the state" (Hewison, 2005, p. 310). The importance of local business and the Chinese business community in Thailand declined as assets were sold to foreign investors (Hewison, 2005, pp. 315–316). Thus, these policies fundamentally altered the partly cooperative relationship between the state and domestic business that had emerged since the 1980s. According to Hewison (2002), the anti-crisis measures "devastated Thailands pre-crisis capitalist class" (p. 240). After rising domestic resistance against neo-liberal economic policies, the businessman Thaksin Shinawatra, who promised to be more responsive to the needs of domestic companies, won the election for Prime Minister in 2001 (Hewison, 2005, p. 318). However, Thaksin lost his power after a military coup in 2006. The political instability that had characterized Thailand more than the other HPAEs also continued over the following years. Economic growth has rebounded after the Asian Crisis, but has not returned to pre-crisis levels.

5.5.2.3 Indonesia

The Indonesian economy has been the weakest performer among the three Southeast Asian countries. The lackluster economic performance coincides with severe institutional weaknesses: a lack of bureaucratic quality, a dysfunctional legal system, weakly protected property rights and a generally non-transparent business environment (Campos & Root, 1996, p. 120; Root, 1996, p. 90–91). In terms of the development of its political structures in the 1950s and 1960s, Indonesia shows some apparent similarities with South Korea. In South Korea, the nationalist regime of Rhee Syng-man, which was de jure democratic but had become gradually more authoritarian over time, was replaced through a military coup by Park Chung-hee in 1961. In Indonesia, the same happened to the increasingly authoritarian regime of Sukarno in 1965, when it was overturned through a coup d'état led by General Suharto (Vu, 2007, pp. 44–45), who then stayed in power until 1998. The military had already been quite powerful in politics during the last years of the Sukarno presidency. However, its political power had been mitigated by the president himself and the influential communist party (PKI), which had been promoted by Sukarno as a counterweight to the military (Campos & Root, 1996, p. 124).

It was after the coup led by Suharto that Indonesia began to show more similarities with the successful developmental states, particularly with South Korea and Taiwan. One similarity was the repression of the left. Suharto banned the powerful and large communist party, union leaders and students were arrested, and leftist bureaucrats purged, while the government was militarized (Vu, 2007, p. 45). The similarities continue in the realm of bureaucratic influence. According to Vu (2007, p. 43), a core of Western-educated technocrats had existed since the end of the Dutch colonialism in Indonesia; however, the influence of these technocrats was limited by the resistance of influential societal and political groups. After the military coup, the economic technocrats became much more influential because economic success was considered necessary to establish legitimacy for the new regime (Campos & Root, 1996, p. 125).

Based on the advice of the primarily US-educated technocrats, the Suharto regime pursued liberal, export-oriented economic policies aimed at attracting foreign investment and gathering the political support of Western countries in the 1960s and early 1970s (Vu, 2007, pp. 45–46). These involved good macroeconomic management, including stable prices and exchange rates (Campos & Root, 1996, p. 127). However, in the mid 1970s, economic policy shifted to a more nationalistic strategy, which relied on domestic capital and import substitution when the regime was threatened by anti-capitalist and anti-Western protests (Vu, 2007, pp. 46–47). Nevertheless, economic growth continued, even though Vu (2007, p. 46) argues that this growth was almost exclusively a result of windfall profits from the rising prices of Indonesia's oil exports. While some limited export promotion measures were adopted at the end of the 1970s, import substitution continued to be the priority of economic policy making until the mid-1980s (Rasiah, 2003, p. 45). The change at this time came as a result of falling oil prices. Reform-oriented policies aimed at deregulation, which had previously been advocated unsuccessfully by the technocrats, were now implemented as the government turned back to their advice in the face of economic crisis (Campos & Root, 1996, p. 127). A liberalization of import restrictions took place and export-oriented manufacturing increased in importance (Rasiah, 2003, p. 46–47).

As in Malaysia, the relationship between different ethnic groups has played an important role in shaping the institutional and economic development of Indonesia. While the Indonesian economy as a whole has been dominated by largely inefficient state-owned companies, the much more dynamic private sector has been overwhelmingly under the control of the Chinese minority since colonial times (Campos & Root, 1996, p. 129; Root, 1996, pp. 103–104), similar to Malaysia. However, the Chinese minority remained excluded from a direct influence on politics (Campos & Root, 1996, pp. 130). While the Malaysian development strategy, as embodied in the NPE, involved a strong element of affirmative action to increase the role of the ethnic majority in business, the liberal economic policies during the early years of the Suharto regime in Indonesia did not have a similar focus. The Chinese minority continued to dominate the private business sector and managed to forge alliances with politically influential military officers (Rasiah, 2003, p. 34). These alliances commonly involved granting the military officers shares in exchange for easier access to licenses and contracts, as well as protection from state harassment (Campos & Root, 1996, p. 131).

According to Root (1996, pp. 105–107), the Chinese minority generally lacks societal and commercial ties to the majority population. Instead, the minority is characterized by a high degree of social cohesion, which translates into informal mechanisms that ensure the enforcement of rules and contracts in business. As Root (1996) concludes, the existence of these informal institutions is the key explanation for the greater affluence of the Chinese minority in Indonesia when compared to the majority population (p. 107). While the formal institutional environment in Indonesia has always been characterized by the weaknesses noted at the beginning of this section, informal rules have served as an institutional equivalent for the Chinese minority.

Since the Chinese-owned companies had been the main beneficiaries of the interventionist policies prior to the mid-1980s, Chinese businessmen and their partners within the military initially resisted deregulation (Campos & Root, 1996, p. 135). Nevertheless, the deregulatory reforms took place in a climate of political tranquility. As Campos and Root (1996) suggest, this tranquility may be explained by the insight of the relevant groups that the high degree of government support for businesses had become unsustainable. Following the advice of the economic bureaucracy to liberalize the economy under these circumstances did not only involve credible perspective of a better economic performance, but also more inflows of funds from multilateral lending agencies (Campos & Root, 1996, p. 135).

Following the shift toward deregulation and export orientation, the inflows of FDI increased and the contribution of manufacturing to the Indonesian GDP rose sharply (Rasiah, 2003, p. 48). However, industrial upgrading and technology transfer remained limited; there has been little emphasis on conscious institutional development by the state (Rasiah, 2003, pp. 48–49).

5.5.3 Conclusions from the institutional development of Malaysia, Thailand, and Indonesia

A certain consensus on the achievements and failures of the three Southeast Asian economies analyzed in this section has emerged in the economic literature. It is apparent that the economic performance of Malaysia, Thailand, and Indonesia as a group is not comparable to the much more successful development of Japan, South Korea, Taiwan, or Singapore. A key difference between these two groups is the comparative lack of industrial upgrading of the three Southeast Asian economies (Akyüz et al., 1998, pp. 20–21; Doner et al., 2005, p. 328; Rasiah, 2003, p. 70). Furthermore, the Southern HPAEs—including Singapore—are distinguished from their Northeast Asian counterparts by their much higher hospitality to foreign direct investment (Jomo, 2004, p. 58; Kosai & Takeuchi, 1998, pp. 314–315)

Apparently, these differences are the result of other underlying factors that should be indentified in order to extract lessons from the Asian economic development. Concerning the limited degree of industrial upgrading and structural change, several scholars (Jomo, 2004, p. 65; Rasiah, 2003, p. 69) have stressed the lack of performance standards for state subsidies and other supportive measures in Malaysia, Thailand and Indonesia. In particular, incentives for private investment and export activities have generally not been tied to specific objectives, such as increased value-added or vertical linkages to other industries (Jomo, 2004, p. 65). Furthermore, efforts to promote technological change through the transfer of foreign technologies have been much weaker in Malaysia, Thailand, and Indonesia when compared to Singapore and the Northeast Asian developmental states (Felker, 2003). Ahrens (2002, p. 238) argues that severe skill shortages in Malaysia and Thailand have caused private companies to move their production facilities to other countries. Such shortages are on the one hand a result of a limited supply of labor in combination with fast economic growth. On the other hand, the Southeast Asian economies—in particular Thailand and Indonesia but to a lesser degree also Malaysia and Singapore—have not fostered education and skill formation of the general public to the same degree as South Korea or Taiwan (Booth, 2003, pp. 189–192).

While these differences in terms of economic and educational policies may explain the limited economic success of Malaysia, Indonesia, and Thailand when compared to the other HPAEs, it still has to be explained *why* these three different countries did not follow the example of their more successful peers in some important aspects. As noted in Section 4.2, two essential characteristics of developmental states distinguish them from other developing countries: the strong commitment of the government to economic growth and the capacity of the state apparatus to implement policies effectively and coherently. Judging from their development over the last five decades as described in the preceding section, the states of the third-tier HPAEs have not equaled Japan and the Asian Tigers in either of these two aspects. Following Doner et al. (2005, p. 328), the limited state capacity should not be seen independently, but as a result of the lack of commitment to economic growth.

The literature of the last years has attempted to give various answers to the question of why Malaysia, Thailand, and Indonesia have not achieved the same success as the Asian Tigers or Japan. However, another important question has been given much less attention: why have these three economies been much more successful than almost all other economies in the world? This critique particularly refers to Doner et al. (2005, p. 328), who postulate that Malaysia, Thailand, and Indonesia, together with the Philippines, belong to a group of *intermediary states*. As Tables 12 and 13 indicate, the Philippines have not achieved any notable and sustainable economic success since the 1950s. The same is true for other countries that have been referred to as intermediary states. Evans (1995) uses this term for Brazil and India, which only achieved remarkable economic growth rates in recent years and still have to prove the sustainability of this development. Since Malaysia and Thailand, and to a lesser degree Indonesia, did have a successful and sustainable economic development over several decades, grouping them together with these other intermediary states does not seem to be more reasonable than grouping them together with South Korea, Taiwan, and Singapore. A thorough analysis of the development of Malaysia, Thailand, and Indonesia should therefore answer why these economies have performed worse than the Tiger States and Japan *and* why they have performed better than most other emerging economies in the world. Using the Northian perspective on institutional change that was illustrated in Figure 2 (see Section 2.2.2) as the basis of this analysis, the pre-existing institutions, the external environment, and the ideology of relevant actors should be taken into account.

Several reasons for the lack of commitment to economic growth in Malaysia, Thailand, and Indonesia when compared to the more successful developmental states have already been explored in previous sections. The most prominent are the much better endowment of the three Southeast Asian economies with natural resources and the comparative lack of vital external threats. This relates to the external environment faced by the three Southeast Asian countries and to institutions and internal constraints resulting from the resource endowments. There is no reason to doubt the relevance of these factors for the severity of budget constraints and, consequently, for the incentive structure faced by governments. Economic development was less of an imperative for political decision makers in Malaysia, Thailand, or Indonesia than for Park Chung-hee, Chiang Kai-shek, Lee Kuan Yew or the post-war governments of Japan. While their endowment with natural resources and the lack of external threats may explain the lackluster economic performance of the three Southeast Asian economies when compared to Singapore and the Northeast Asian developmental states, these factors do not contribute much to an explanation for the good economic performance when compared to the large economies of Latin America and Africa. Apparently, the institutional environment of Malaysia, Thailand and Indonesia was more conducive to economic development than that of countries in other regions.

Of course, the better endowment with natural resources in comparison with the more successful developmental states does not mean that the leaders of the three Southeast Asian economies did not face crucial constraints. As has been noted, the governments of all Southeast Asian countries had to deal with the diverging interests of different ethnic groups. The influence of this heterogeneity on institutional and economic development is not easy to evaluate. As Doner et al. (2005) note, it has been argued in the literature that the ethnic homogeneity of Taiwan, South Korea, and Japan "has fostered the societal cohesion that ostensibly underlies developmental states" (p. 336). They refute this argument based on the example of Singapore, where a strong developmental state emerged in spite of ethnic heterogeneity. However, the last sections indicate that the presence of different ethnic groups has had a decisive influence on political decisions and, thus, also on the institutional development in Malaysia, Thailand, and Indonesia. Therefore, this issue deserves more scrutiny.

Malaysia, Thailand, and Indonesia have a Chinese minority in common, which has been economically more successful than the majority and dominated the business sector. In contrast, the governments and the bureaucracies of these countries were dominated by other ethnic groups. Different ethnic groups are at least partly governed by specific informal institutions and their members may have diverging ideologies. The case studies have shown that these conditions had a crucial impact on government business relations in Malaysia, Thailand, and Indonesia, which could not be characterized as cooperative for several decades. Formal consultative mechanisms similar to Japan, South Korea or Singapore did not evolve in Malaysia and Thailand until the 1980s, and they never evolved in Indonesia. To some degree, informal ties between specific public officials, politicians and Chinese businessmen may have been a substitute for formal channels of interaction. However, the examples of Thailand (prior to the 1980s) and Indonesia show that these informal ties were an insufficient substitute and led to problems such as patronage, intransparency and unpredictability.

Bureaucracies were generally less insulated from vested interests than in other developmental states. The question is why ethnic heterogeneity has not led to similar problems in Singapore. In contrast to Malaysia, Thailand, and Indonesia, people of Chinese ancestry are a clear majority in the city-state. The division between a Chinese-dominated business sector and a state apparatus dominated by other ethnicities has not been an issue in Singapore. Furthermore, it has to be noted that the conditions of a city-state are quite specific. Singapore's small geographical extension may have fostered the power of the state and thus compensated for the problems associated with ethnic heterogeneity in the larger Southeast Asian countries.

It still has to be explained why the Malaysia, Thailand, and Indonesia did experience a more successful economic development than most other developing and emerging economies despite mild resource constraints, a lack of apparent external threats and the problems associated with ethnic heterogeneity. The external environment offers one explanation for the economic success of Malaysia, Thailand, and Indonesia: the regional dynamic of East Asia as embodied in the *flying geese* metaphor. As a result of their economic success, Japan and later the Asian Tigers were induced to upgrade their industries toward more capital- and skill-intensive industries, which caused a relocation of resource-based and labor-intensive business activities (Akyüz et al., 1998, p. 22). The importance of this regional dynamic is evidenced by the increasing role of FDI from Japan and the Asian Tigers in the three Southeast Asian economies since the 1980s (Akyüz et al., 1998, p. 23).

However, any explanation that relates the success of Malaysia, Thailand, and Indonesia exclusively to the unusual success of economic policies pursued in other Asian countries is clearly unjustified. The most obvious evidence for this argument is the fact that other economies with a similar geographical proximity to the Tigers have not achieved a similar success. This refers not only to the previously mentioned Philippines, but also to Laos, Cambodia, Myanmar and the obvious case of North Korea. Vietnam became economically more successful in recent years, but was stagnating over several decades before.

Thus, the explanation for the development of Malaysia, Thailand, and Indonesia has to take both internal and external factors into account. One important internal factor is the ideology as embodied in actors' cultural heritage, knowledge, and current experiences. The geographical proximity to the economically most dynamic countries of the world offered a window of opportunity for growth to the Southeast Asian economies, but growth was not an inevitable result of the proximity. Instead, political leaders in some countries, most noticeable in Malaysia, consciously used the more advanced Asian economies as reference economies and adopted at least some of their successful policies and institutions.

The openness of Malaysia, Thailand, and Indonesia for foreign ideas and influence when contrasted with other countries in the region—most strikingly North Korea—certainly also shaped the ideologies of both political decision makers and the general public. Once a specific comparative perspective toward other countries has been firmly established in the ideologies of a society's members, it may shape the incentive structure for political decision makers. The sustained economic development of neighboring countries thus also poses a challenge to political leaders, who face an increased need to achieve similar economic success in order to foster their legitimacy. In this way, the regional dynamic of East Asia gained additional relevance for the Southeast Asian economies that were not too isolated from their geopolitical environment.

In addition, one has to notice the differences and interrelationships between Malaysia, Thailand, and Indonesia. In this context, one might shift the focus again to ethnic heterogeneity. While some difficulties resulting from heterogeneity have already been noted, it may have had a positive influence in other respects because it was the source of internal constraints for political decision makers. As was noted in the section on Malaysia, riots between ethnic Chinese and Malays threatened the power of the ruling multi-party coalition in 1969. In response, the ruling coalition was widened and a more interventionist economic policy aimed at promoting shared economic development, the NEP, was adopted. While the shortcomings of the NEP were described in Section 5.5.2.1, Ng et al. (1992, p. 220) state that the Malaysian developmental state emerged in the mid-1970s. They furthermore argue that Malaysia represented a stronger developmental state than Thailand or Indonesia because of its broad coalition and the imperative to maintain balance between the different ethnic groups (Ng et al., 1992, p. 223). Nevertheless, formal consultative mechanisms and a more cooperative relationship between private sector and state apparatus also emerged in politically unstable Thailand in the 1980s. One has to note that the Chinese minority represent a substantial percentage of the population in both Malaysia (23.7%) and Thailand (14%) (CIA, 2011). In addition, a considerable population of mixed Chinese-Thai ancestry exists in Thailand, where the Chinese minority has been much more integrated into the society than in other Southeast Asian countries (Thomson, 1993). Even though politics in both Malaysia and Thailand was dominated by other ethnicities, the large Chinese minorities could not be ignored completely and its presence was a crucial constraint for political decision makers. In Indonesia, where no formal consultative mechanisms in the state-business nexus emerged, the economically dominating Chinese minority only amount to less than 5% (Root, 1996, pp. 127–132).

6 A new perspective on the developmental state

6.1 The role of developmental states in the economy: balancing accumulation and allocation

There can be no doubt that accounts, such as Haggard (2004) or Krugman (1994), which stress the enormous diversity of institutions among the high-performing East Asian economies are correct in many ways. Even in the two spheres that are usually considered to be at the center of the developmental state, namely the meritocratic bureaucracy and the cooperative state-business interface, a wide variety of specific institutional arrangements can be found. Just taking into account the most commonly acknowledged examples of developmental states, there are notable differences in bureaucratic recruitment: in Japan and South Korea, meritocracy relied on entry examinations; in Taiwan and Singapore, examinations were complemented by other, less formalized rules based on previous academic performance. Nevertheless, there is no doubt that these four countries achieved an unusually high level of bureaucratic meritocracy. Different rules thus fulfilled the same function and worked similarly well. Further examples of such *institutional equivalence* can be found in the sphere of public-private cooperation. If ostensibly differing institutions fulfill the same function in different countries, this apparently inhibits the formulation of a definite and detailed model of the developmental state. However, this issue can be dealt with by shifting the level of analysis upwards toward the *functions* that the institutions perform for the economy.

This also relates to the institutions that govern the role of the state in the economy. The prevailing perspectives in the literature on the functions that developmental states assume in the economy have been outlined in Section 4. The most commonly cited view on this issue is Johnson's notion of a *plan-rational state*. As was elaborated in Section 4, most alternative definitions of the developmental state have made references to an active role of the state in the economy that involves planning, promoting structural change, and the coordination of economic processes. As argued most emphatically by Chang (1999, pp. 186–187; see also Section 4.3), the fundamental reason for the necessity of such a state lies in the failure of the market mechanism to achieve dynamic efficiency. For Chang (1999), an important role of the state in the economy is to coordinate "a simultaneous move from a low-equilibrium to a high-equilibrium" (pp. 193–194). The historical developments presented in the case studies can lead to new insights into the role that the East Asian developmental states played in this simultaneous move and into the reasons why they assumed such a role.

An important process that is involved in the transformation of an economy from a stable equilibrium at a low level of economic wealth to a new equilibrium at a higher level of economic wealth is clearly the accumulation of physical and human capital. Even accounts of the Asian economic development that are critical of the developmental state concept, such as the 1993 World Bank study, acknowledged the important role of some activist policies in promoting accumulation in the HPAEs (World Bank, 1993, Chapter 5).

It is not a groundbreaking argument that state intervention in the economy can accomplish a rapid accumulation of capital and other factors of production. In his article "The Myth of the Asian Miracle," Krugman (1994) stresses this point by comparing the East Asian economic growth to that of the Soviet Union. In the years after the Second World War, the Soviet Economy had shown an impressive performance and was growing at rates several times higher than that of the advanced Western economies (Krugman, 1994, pp. 62–63). The speed of the Soviet transformation from a peasant society to an industrialized nation was seen as a challenge to the Western belief in free markets. However, this growth was based completely on the mobilization of resources and accumulation, as Krugman argues "rapid Soviet economic growth was based entirely on one attribute: the willingness to save, to sacrifice current consumption for the sake of future production" (p. 63). He argued that the same was largely true for the economic growth of the East Asian Tigers, who had achieved extraordinary investment in physical capital, a rise in the employed share of the population, and massive improvements in the education of the work force (Krugman, 1994, pp. 70–72). In this sense, the governments in East Asia and the Soviet Union assumed similar functions in the economy.

However, this is clearly not the end of the story. While the role of the interventionist East Asian states and the Soviet state in their respective economies may share some basic similarities, there can be no doubt that they were extremely different overall. The Soviet Union did indeed achieve a catch-up from about 20% of the American GDP per capita (PPP) in 1949 to about 35% in 1960; it then remained more or less at this level until it collapsed—partly for economic reasons—in 1991.[32] At least in comparison to the Northeast Asian developmental states and Singapore, this is a very modest achievement.

---

32   Values for GDP per capita relative to the USA are own calculations based on data from Maddison (2010).

The extraordinary mobilization of productive factors and their accumulation may have been a similarity between the Soviet Union and the developmental states, but the allocation of these resources was not. Proponents of the developmental state criticize the recommendations of international organizations and mainstream economists for their focus on short-term allocative efficiency and macroeconomic stability over dynamic efficiency and economic growth (Amsden, 1989, p. 139; Chang, 1999; Wade, 1990/2004, pp. 350). This criticism may be legitimate. Nevertheless, it is evident that the allocation of resources is of tremendous importance for sustainable economic development. While it may be rather easy for an authoritarian government with coercive powers to achieve a rapid accumulation of capital, allocating resources in a way that makes the growth resulting from accumulation *sustainable* is a more challenging task.

Following Johnson's terminology of *plan-rational* and *plan-ideological* states, one may argue that the relevant decision makers within the Japanese state apparatus allocated resources based on reason, while Soviet decision makers followed a pre-determined recipe based on the dominant ideology. However, this is not a sufficient explanation for the superior economic outcomes of East Asian economic planning. For economists belonging to the Neoclassical, Austrian, and related schools of thought, *any* state intervention in the economy that goes beyond purely regulatory measures is considered harmful, no matter if it is based on ideology or reason. The key issue in this context is information. An economic order where free prices driven by the market mechanism allocate resources is considered superior to any alternative because it incorporates the knowledge of all relevant economic actors. As Friedrich August von Hayek (1969) argues:

> That we can never know what all the persons know whose knowledge is incorporated in the price mechanism, and therefore in the methods and the direction of production, is not just of theoretical importance. It also of great practical importance. The decisive reason why a market economy performs better than any other economic system is that its order incorporates more knowledge on facts than any human or even any organization can have. (p. 11, own translation)[33]

From this perspective, state interventions and planning, which clearly involve the manipulation of the price mechanism, imply the *presumption of knowledge*.

---

33   Original quote: Daß wir nie wissen können, was alle die Personen wissen, deren Kenntnisse in den Preisbestimmungsprozeß und damit in die Bestimmung der Methoden und Richtung der Produktion eingehen ist nicht nur theoretisch von großer Bedeutung. Es ist auch praktisch von großer Bedeutung. Daß in die Ordnung einer Marktwirtschaft viel mehr Wissen von Tatsachen eingeht, als irgendein einzelner Mensch oder selbst irgendeine Organisation wissen kann, ist der entscheidende Grund, weshalb die Marktwirtschaft mehr leistet als irgendeine andere Wirtschaftsform.

In an interventionist state apparatus, bureaucratic or governmental actors presume that they can choose an allocation of productive resources that is superior to the allocation that would have emerged through the free will of economic actors.

The question is how East Asian developmental states have been able to limit the problems arising from the presumption of knowledge. If Chang's (1999, pp. 186–192) argument that state intervention is necessary to overcome the trade-off between static and dynamic efficiency is true, a functioning price mechanism is not sufficient to attain the optimal rate of growth in an economy. As has been mentioned, Alice Amsden argued likewise by stating that the key to the superior South Korean economic performance was *getting the prices wrong* (Amsden, 1989, p. v) in order to achieve long-term dynamic efficiency instead of short-term allocative efficiency. One of the main prescriptions for developing countries that Wade (1990/2004) derives from the East Asian experience is to "channel (...) investment into industries whose growth is important for the economy's future growth" (p. 350). The question is of course *which* industries are important for future growth, and consequently *which* prices to get wrong and which wrong price level is adequate. Short-term economic growth may be generated by any policies that raise the level of investment, but growth can only be sustained over several decades if a competitive industrial structure emerges. Yet, if the state sets the wrong incentives, growth will not be sustainable.

There is no doubt that East Asian developmental states have been more successful than other activist states at achieving an overall beneficial allocation of resources. One important mechanism for achieving this is quite obvious: in all East Asian developmental states, private sector involvement and the importance of the price mechanism was much higher than in the Soviet Union or similar command economies. If the state raises the overall level of capital accumulation through promoting or even forcing savings, while leaving the decision on the use of resources to the private sector, the distortion of the market-driven allocation is only limited.

However, the developmental states in East Asia also implemented selective policies such as industry-specific tax incentives, subsidies and trade distortions that altered the allocation of resources profoundly. Pursuing such selective policies makes the presumption of knowledge an even more crucial issue: apparently bureaucratic or governmental actors who are responsible for setting selective incentives assume that they know which industries should be promoted in the interest of society. Nevertheless, the East Asian developmental states were the fastest growing economies of the world for several decades. Political and bureaucratic decision makers in these countries may have presumed knowledge, but historical evidence seems to show that their presumptions were overall correct. They seem to have found an adequate balance between fast accumulation and efficient allocation.

6.2 Transaction costs as the basis of the developmental state

The New Institutional Economics can help to understand how this successful presumption of knowledge was possible. As was elaborated in Section 2, proponents of the NIE are more hesitant to trust in the optimal allocation of resources through the market-driven price mechanism than other economists. The main reason for this is the existence of transaction costs. If transaction costs prevent an optimal allocation from emerging, state involvement may actually improve the way productive resources are used in the economy. According to North (1990, p. 27; see also Section 2.2.1), the most important type of transaction cost is information cost.

The key to von Hayek's quote above, and all conclusions derived from it, is that no individual and no organization can possess more knowledge than the economic actors of a society as a whole. As a general statement on overall knowledge, there cannot be any doubt that this postulate is true. However, it is also true that economic actors are not homogeneous and some have more knowledge than others. This knowledge is the result of information that actors acquired. For specific transactions, their knowledge enables well-informed actors to evaluate the utility of any alternative decision to an unusual degree. If these actors face constraints that force or incentivize them to act for the overall economic benefit of the society, it may be economically beneficial that they enforce a specific decision or at least set appropriate incentives for the society. To put it differently: if governmental and bureaucratic agents have for some reason an extraordinary advantage in terms of knowledge over the vast majority of private actors, it will be economically efficient if the state takes a leading role in the economy. However, it is highly probable that bureaucratic and governmental actors will only fulfill such a role to the overall benefit of society if they face appropriate constraints. The question is what leads to circumstances under which the state has significantly more knowledge that is relevant for the evolution of the economic and industrial structure.

According to scholars, such as Amsden, Chang, and Wade, the critical condition that made state intervention in the East Asian developmental states at least potentially beneficial was economic backwardness. As has been pointed out in Section 4.3, this argument is based on several prominent predecessors in economics, most notably on Alexander Gerschenkron (1962). For Alice Amsden, South Korea, Taiwan, and Japan are part of a generalizable paradigm of *late industrialization*, which is characterized by rapid economic catch-up through learning (Amsden, 1989, pp. 3–4; 2001, pp. 1–2). Since the focus of Amsden's analysis is the firm, the term *learning* in this context refers first and foremost to acquiring technological and managerial knowledge that is relevant for industrial production (Amsden, 2001, pp. 2–8). Learning, in this sense, implies the existence of advanced economies led by firms that are superior in terms of technology and management. For Amsden, the governments of economically backwards countries have the decisive role in initiating the process of learning through altering the incentives for firms (Amsden, 2001, p. 6). However, Amsden is not clear as to what actually prevents private companies in backward economies to acquire the relevant technological and managerial capabilities from other economies *themselves*.

Chang (1999) and Wade (1990/2004) are more precise about their perspective on the underlying theoretical reasons for the necessity of state intervention. Wade (1990/2004, p. 355) points out that entrepreneurs may lack the foresight or the capital to realize the long-term potential of specific industries. He argues that the lack of capital may be due to the weakness of capital and insurance markets (Wade, 1990/2004, p. 353). While the state's easier access to capital when compared to the private sector may be obvious in many backwards countries, it is much less apparent why the state, or actors working for the state, should have more foresight when assessing the long-term potential of an industry than private entrepreneurs and investors have.

Chang (1999, p. 186; 2003, p. 126) and Wade (1990/2004, p. 353–354) furthermore argue that market failures, particularly externalities, make state intervention a necessity for profound industrial transformation. As Chang (2003) points out, a shift toward a new industrial structure may not happen naturally even if it were socially desirable because "discrepancies between social and individual returns to investments in the high-value-added activities" exist (p. 126). In other words, a specific investment might have positive external effects— either for specific other investments or generally for the society—that are not mirrored in the individual cost-benefit calculations. In addition, Chang (1999, p. 192) argues that investment in new industries might not take place because private actors do not know whether complementary investments would come along. In a paper on Taiwan and South Korea, Rodrik (1995) takes a similar perspective, arguing that coordination failures impeded too much reliance on the market mechanism at the beginning of the economic take-off:

> For a number of reasons, the economic take-off could not take place under decentralized market conditions. Chief among these reasons are the imperfect tradability

of key inputs (and technologies) associated with modern sector production, and some increasing returns to scale in these activities. These conditions created a situation of coordination failure. In other words, while the rate of return to coordinated investments was extremely high, the rate of return to individual investments remained low. (p. 78)

While Chang (1999) concedes that investments in complementary projects may actually take place because private investors can also devise contracts between themselves, he maintains that "such a contract may be costly to draw up and monitor, especially when it involves a large number of agents" (p. 192). Transaction cost for monitoring (and possibly enforcing) private contracts is thus seen as a crucial reason for the existence of coordination failures and the necessity of state involvement.

However, the most important type of transaction cost in the Northian NIE, information cost, seems to be less present in the accounts of Wade (1990/2004), Chang (1999; 2003), and Amsden (1989; 2001). While Amsden stresses the importance of disparities between countries in terms of technological and managerial knowledge, differences in terms of information between different actors within a country are neglected.

Turning back to the historical evidence on the East Asian countries that was presented in the case studies, several circumstances relevant for the distribution of information are striking. As has been described, Japan was not only economically backward at the advent of the Meiji Restoration of 1868, it had also been a virtually closed country for several centuries. Contacts with foreign countries were limited to an extremely small number of individuals, imports and exports hardly took place. First of all, the long duration of isolation implies that a huge gap in information between virtually all economic actors in Japan and the economic actors of the dominating Western countries existed. This gap certainly involved the technological and managerial knowledge necessary for modern industries on which Amsden focused her analysis. However, the information gap was not limited to this type of knowledge. It also involved knowledge on the social and political conditions of other countries, on the evolution of these conditions over time, on the role that states in other countries assumed in the society and economy, on the specific path of development that other economies had followed and on many other relevant issues.

Remarkably, this lack of information applied to virtually *all* members of the Japanese society. This is an important difference between Japan and other countries that may have been similarly backwards in economic terms. In a country that is economically backward but not isolated, some individuals commonly maintain crucial ties to other, more advanced economies. These individuals may be diplomats or otherwise closely related to the government. However, there may also exist businessmen who export agrarian goods and basic commodities or import industrial goods. While the knowledge necessary to produce such goods may not be available to these individuals, they may possess relevant information on the types of goods produced in other countries and their respective quality, the relative prices of goods, the kind of skills necessary to produce certain goods, the potential demand of consumers in other countries for domestic products and many other issues. Therefore, the overall information gap faced by an economically backward country that has never been isolated is significantly smaller than the gap faced by an isolated country such as Japan in the 19th century. Furthermore, the distribution of information among members of the society should be much more uneven in a country that has not been isolated.

In pre-Meiji Japan, no individuals with important personal or business ties to other countries, especially to the advanced Western economies, existed. Japanese merchant houses were not only inexperienced with modern manufactures, they had also been limited to trade under the highly specific conditions of feudal Japan. The same is true for businessmen in Korea, which was similarly isolated during the Yi-Dynasty. The cost to obtain relevant information on other countries was certainly much higher in the late 19th century than today. Under these circumstances, it was highly implausible that private entrepreneurs would have been able and willing to carry the necessary information costs to establish a competitive industrial structure quickly. Furthermore, it could have been collectively inefficient if a multitude of private economic actors had incurred transaction costs to obtain the same information.

Facing these conditions, the Japanese authorities assumed a leading role in obtaining and disseminating information to society after the Meiji Restoration. As has been noted in Section 5.2.1.1, the state first established public enterprises in new industries after the restoration and then changed its strategy toward a more limited, indirect involvement. Despite these change in means, it continued to further the adaptation of foreign technology and investment in modern industries heavily.

Over the decades up to the Second World War, Japanese society continued to be heavily influenced by foreign countries in various aspects. However, the economy again became increasingly isolated from international trade after the government decided to aim for the autarchy of Japan and its East Asian colonies. When Japan reintegrated into the world economy after its disastrous defeat, its entrepreneurs faced a renewed lack of information. While Japanese businesses, especially the *zaibatsu*, had been capable of manufacturing industrial products that were advanced enough to enable Japan to wage a war for several years against a multitude of countries, they had not maintained business ties to foreign countries. Thus, Japanese businessmen were uninformed about the demand and overall conditions of international markets.

The conditions for businesses in Taiwan and South Korea after the end of the War were quite similar. As a result of Japanese domination and its aim for a self-sufficient *Greater East Asia Co-Prosperity Sphere*, the Taiwanese and Korean economies had been exclusively oriented toward Japan. The only ties to other countries that the small number of native businessmen had maintained until 1945 were cut when the war and colonialism ended. Any information about markets outside their home country was extremely limited.

Under the conditions of today's advanced economies, the presumption of knowledge is a severe problem in the formulation and implementation of selective industrial policies because there is usually no reason to believe that the state is better informed than the economic actors within the private sector. Basic information in such countries is available to anyone, but the past experience of entrepreneurs and businessmen working in a specific industry will in most cases actually give them an advantage in information over bureaucrats and governmental agents.

The conditions in East Asia were markedly different at the time when the developmental states in Japan, Taiwan, and South Korea emerged. The societies of these countries had an enormous need for information; however, the transaction costs involved with obtaining information were unusually high. As has been noted in the case study on Japan, the Meiji state reacted to this need by making foreign education a key requirement in bureaucratic recruitment. Obtaining knowledge and then using it to the benefit of the private sector may indeed have lowered the overall transaction costs to be carried by society. After the Second World War, the governments and bureaucracies of Japan, South Korea, and Taiwan maintained close relationships with the United States, economic aid missions were actively involved in policy making. All this implies that bureaucratic and governmental actors had a significant advantage over the private sector in terms of information on foreign countries and relevant knowledge for the establishment of modern industries.

The situation in Singapore was slightly different. As a transshipment port and British colony, there can be hardly doubt that Singaporeans were much better informed about the world than Koreans or Japanese prior to the beginning of rapid economic development. However, it has been noted in the case study that the private sector in Singapore was—in contrast to Hong Kong—weak and concentrated almost exclusively in services (Haggard, 1990, p. 101). Furthermore, Singapore's function as an entrepôt for raw materials from the Malayan peninsula ended with its independence in 1965. Consequently prior business ties of the private sector to Malaysia became obsolete. While the lack of relevant knowledge in the Singaporean private sector may have been smaller than in South Korea, Japan, or Taiwan, it was nevertheless significant when the government decided to pursue an economic strategy focused on growth in export-oriented manufacturing industries.

The conditions in Malaysia, Thailand, and Indonesia differed much more. In contrast to Japan and Korea, none of these countries had a history of seclusion. In contrast to Singapore, they also did not face a dramatic severing of existing economic ties and the resulting need for reorientation. In all three countries, a strong, Chinese dominated business sector existed, which maintained business ties to China and other countries. Exports of raw materials and agricultural products, such as rubber, rice and oil, for the global market had already been the basis of important international ties for several decades when the limited growth of manufacturing industries began in the 1970s. In this way, the three Southeast Asian economies shared more similarities with developing countries in Latin America or Africa than with their Northeast Asian peers. There does not seem to be a compelling reason to believe that governments and bureaucracies in these countries had more relevant knowledge for the establishment of modern industries than actors in the private sector.

6.3 The importance of reference economies

It has been argued in the last section that the gap between the information available to economic actors in the East Asian developmental states and actors in the advanced economies of the world was unusually high in the initial stages of East Asian economic growth. This section sheds more light on the type of information and knowledge that the developmental states acquired from economically more advanced countries.

As has been noted, economic backwardness has been considered the underlying reason for the necessity of an increased involvement of the state in the industrialization of developing countries. Amsden has been the most prominent proponent of the argument that industrialization in backward economies takes place through learning, meaning that firms from these economies adopt modern technologies developed elsewhere and learn from the managerial experience of advanced competitors. From Amsden's perspective, the role of the state in backward economy is mainly to alter market prices and incentives in a way that enables firms to adopt foreign technology and managerial knowledge. Important means to further this kind of learning are subsidies for nascent industries and protection from foreign competition on the domestic market.

This view will not be challenged here, but the relationship between the governments of backwards economies and the economically advanced states deserves some further attention. Again, the starting point of the analysis is the notion of the presumption of knowledge as the underlying reason for the failure of policies that alter market prices. It is without any doubt true that East Asian companies had a huge potential for learning when the HPAEs began their fast economic growth. The gap that Japan, South Korea, and Taiwan faced compared the leading Western economies in terms of GDP per capita and productivity was wide. But technological and managerial capabilities were not the only things that the East Asian countries could learn from the West, and learning was certainly not limited to economic actors in industrial companies.

In the case study on Japan, it became clear that especially the political leaders in the early Meiji period were highly interested in learning lessons from more advanced countries. While they promoted the adoption of foreign technology by Japanese companies, they also obtained information on the constitutions, laws, and regulations of other countries and consciously attempted to shape the formal institutional environment of Japan on the basis of this knowledge. This process was clearly not a pure imitation of the structures of a chosen country, but a highly selective take-over of specific rules. The information that was obtained from other countries, in particular from Germany, also included knowledge on the formulation, implementation, and results of economic polices. After the Second World War, the foreign influence became much more direct and even compulsory when existing institutions were complemented and partly substituted during the American occupation.

In South Korea and Taiwan, the importance of the USA as a foreign influence on the path of institutional was similarly important. For both countries, the USA was the primary strategic partner and US aid missions influenced the institutional environment and economic policy notably. However, the political leaders and bureaucrats of South Korea and Taiwan also looked for reference models elsewhere. As mentioned in the case study, a survey showed that South Korean bureaucrats saw Japan as the primary source of laws and policies that could be adopted. Since the diplomatic relations between South Korea and Japan have not been close and were rather difficult since the end of Japanese colonialism, this orientation toward Japan must have been due to other reasons. While geographical proximity certainly played an important role, it also seems highly probable that Korean bureaucrats simply saw Japan as an example of an extremely successful economy that had achieved this success under conditions that were broadly similar to those faced by South Korea. As the leaders of Meiji Japan, the South Korean bureaucrats and political leaders after the coup of Park thus consciously looked for suitable reference models in order to learn lessons on the path to economic success. As has been described in the case study, South Korea and Taiwan also mutually influenced each other in terms of policy formulation and institutional development. Singaporean leaders also heavily drew on the experience of several other countries in their quest for economic development of the city-state. Among the three larger Southeast Asian countries, Malaysia has been most explicit in learning from other East Asian economies (World Bank, 1993, p. 80). In particular, the heavy industrialization polices of South Korea served as an explicit reference model under the government of Mahathir in the 1980s (Tan, 2009, p. 166–167; see Section 5.5.2.1).

A specific issue in the context of using foreign countries as reference models for economic policy is the choice of strategic industries to be targeted by selective interventions. This issue is of crucial importance for the question whether the alteration of market prices through state action always corresponds to a presumption of knowledge by governmental and bureaucratic actors. In general, industrial policies that are not aimed at protecting existing industries for social reasons have the objective to establish new industries. These industries are chosen because scientists, politicians, or other experts expect them to be of vital importance for the economy in the future. In advanced economies, the chosen industries will often involve a high amount of new technology. Industries and products that are promoted through subsidies or similar measures in several countries today include solar energy, wind energy, and electrical cars. Such industries are not yet competitive in any country of the world without substantial state support. This means that supporting them involves a high degree of predicting the future, in other words: a notable presumption of knowledge.

The circumstances for state support in an economically backward country are radically different. When the Meiji state entered the world economy, it was not aiming to establish industries that would produce innovative goods not yet produced elsewhere. Its aim was to build industrial structures that had evolved over decades, or even centuries, in other countries as quickly as possible. Even after the Second World War, when Japan had been an industrialized country itself for several decades, it continued to look at other countries in order to emulate their industrial structures (Johnson, 1982, p. 256; see Section 5.2.2). The same is true for South Korea, Taiwan, and—to a lesser degree—the Southeast Asian economies. The industrial policies in these countries were aimed at establishing industrial structures on their own territory that already existed in more advanced economies.

The argument here is not that selective policies aiming at industries that exist elsewhere do not face the problem of the presumption of knowledge. The argument is that this problem is much smaller than in the case of selective industrial policies pursued by advanced economies. This is particularly true for economies that did not rely on substantial exports of natural resources and agricultural goods prior to the beginning fast growth. This enabled countries such as Japan, South Korea, and Taiwan to implement overarching development strategies that were modeled after the industrial structures of advanced economies without endangering the competitiveness of existing export sectors. Such an overarching strategy may have also benefitted from complementarities between different industries, which make specific industrial structures more efficient than others.

In the literature on the developmental state, the importance of the external, geopolitical environment for the commitment of political leaders and bureaucrats to economic development is frequently stressed. Indeed, there is no reason to doubt that the military threats posed to South Korea and Taiwan by North Korea and the People's Republic of China were elemental for the commitment of their authoritarian regimes to economic development and industrial upgrading. Similarly, defending the national sovereignty in the face of Western imperialism at in the 19th century certainly shaped the decision making process of political leaders in Meiji Japan. The Singaporean government confronted the necessity to vindicate the existence of the city as an independent country after 1965. As has been noted by Doner et al. (2005) and others, the external threats to Malaysia, Thailand, and Indonesia were much less serious. It was argued at the end of Section 5.5.3 that the presence of a large Chinese minority in Malaysia and Thailand was a crucial internal constraint that shaped political decisions and the path of institutional change toward the emergence of developmental states. However, it seems that this internal constraint was only an insufficient substitute for the external threats faced by other East Asian economies. The institutions characteristic for the developmental states in Northeast Asia and Singapore did not fully evolve in Malaysia or Thailand.

Other incentives that the external environment set for the governments of developmental states have received much less attention in the literature. The positive influence of the United States on the post-war development of Japan, Taiwan, and South Korea has been observed. The main focus in this respect has been on the benefits that the East Asian economies could reap from their good relations with the USA through financial aid, an increased demand for their goods (particularly during the Korean War and the Vietnam War) and their access to the large American market. However, the American influence was much more profound. As has been noted in the case studies, there were several instances where the US-aid missions decisively influenced the path of institutional development. While not insisting on laissez-faire or the complete abandoning of economic planning, the American influence—strengthened by the importance of

US financial and military aid—certainly contributed to the balance between market-orientation and state interventionism.

The relevant external environment of each East Asian developmental state furthermore included the other high-performing Asian economies. It is reasonable to argue that this crucially influenced the constraints and incentives that the decision makers faced in those countries. The economic success of countries that were geographically and culturally close and faced similar exogenous conditions may have served as evidence that industrialization and rapid economic growth were in fact possible. Through contributing the current experiences of both political decision makers and the society in general, this development shaped the ideologies of all relevant economic actors. As has been noted in the conclusions on the case studies, first and foremost in the section on Taiwan and South Korea, the success of the developmental states may have been mutually reinforcing.

Reference economies were certainly important for the emergence and progress of the developmental states. Learning from other countries, in terms of technology and also in terms of policies and institutions, enabled the late industrializers in East Asia to develop much faster than their predecessors in Western Europe and North America. While some institutions from other countries were imposed upon them through foreign occupation and colonialism, the learning process was in most of the cases deliberate, conscious, and selective. This relates to an insight that Gerschenkron already expressed in 1962:

> What makes it so difficult for an advanced country to appraise properly the industrialization policies of its less fortunate brethren is the fact that, in every instance of industrialization, imitation of the evolution in advanced countries appears in combination with different, indigenously determined elements. It is not always easy for advanced countries to accept the former, it is even more difficult for them to acquiesce in the latter. This is particularly true of the institutional instruments used in carrying out industrial developments and even so of ideologies which accompany it. What can be derived from a historical review is a strong sense for the significance of the native elements in the industrialization of backward countries. (Gerschenkron, 1962, p. 26)

This means that the institutional environment of a country will always be a blend of foreign influences with domestic conditions. In contrast to other developing countries, this blend resulted in extraordinary economic development in several East Asian countries.

6.4 The evolution of developmental states and the importance of conflict

The essence of the three preceding sections is that the developmental states in East Asia faced initial conditions that made interventionist measures a viable, and even an indispensable, tool of economic policy. The aim of this section is to draw conclusions on the way the role of the state in the economy changed during the decades of economic catch-up that characterized the successful East Asian economies.

The continuous economic catch-up toward the world's most advanced economies that several of the East Asian countries achieved coincides with continuous and overwhelmingly incremental institutional change. This institutional development was in turn interdependent with shifts in the organizational power structure, the ideologies of economic actors, changes in economic policy, and the transaction costs corresponding to political processes and economic exchange. In the preceding sections, it was pointed out that some of the most successful East Asian economies, most notably Japan, Taiwan, and South Korea, faced an exceptionally large gap in information toward the advanced Western economies at the time when developmental states emerged. Furthermore, it was suggested that the respective governments of these countries most probably had an advantage over the private sector in obtaining relevant information for the establishment of modern industries. Evidently, these conditions did not remain stable as the East Asian economies caught up with the West.

Generally, countries that are economically backward, or isolated from the international exchange of knowledge, have an extraordinary potential for development by learning from others. It was argued that under such conditions that state interventions may help exploit this potential by lowering the overall transaction costs for economic actors and causing a more rapid accumulation of production factors. However, the conditions for state involvement change as the backwardness of the economy diminishes and finally disappears. The accumulation of factors may eventually lead to diminishing returns. As a result, the importance of accumulation as an objective of economic policy gradually decreases. At the same time, industries shift slowly from the imitation and emulation of foreign methods and products toward innovation. Identifying an economically efficient allocation for resources that are partially or completely controlled by the state will become increasingly difficult. Thus, it is justified to argue that the coordination of economic processes through state interventions should diminish during the catch-up process in an ideal developmental state, while the coordination through market incentives should increase. In other words, the success of a developmental state may lead to its redundancy. In reality, this ideal progress of the role of the state in the economy never occurs as steadily or smoothly as described. Nevertheless, there is evidence for such an evolution in the most successful examples of developmental states in East Asia. As was described in the case studies, the role of the Japanese state declined over the post-war period. However, this process was not always continuous, and the economic problems that Japan faced since the 1990s raise the question of whether the shift in economic policy was fully successful. Taiwan's move toward less interventionism seems to have been almost fully gradual. In contrast, the role of the South Korean state was decisively altered by the Asian Crisis, which led to a sharp intensification of liberalization efforts that had been very limited before. Singapore's developmental state, which has always been comparatively less interventionist and more liberal than its Northeast Asian counterparts, seems to have changed less overall (Low, 2004).

Naturally, the knowledge gap between the East Asian developmental states and the more advanced economies diminished as a result of economic catch-up, as did the information advantage of the state over the private sector. By producing and exporting industrial goods under state auspices, companies in the East Asian economies gained experience and increased their stock of knowledge. The companies themselves thus steadily improved their capability to exploit the potential for industrial development that resulted from the international economic environment. At the same time, the presumption of knowledge became a more important issue for the formulation and implementation of selective economic policies by the state. At the initial stages of economic catch-up, the suitable path of economic development, in terms of products and industries to be supported, may have been comparatively apparent; however, this gradually changed as the East Asian economies moved closer toward the technological edge of the world economy. The presumption of knowledge thus became a bigger issue for interventionist economic policy making.

An important arrangement that helped the developmental states in East Asia to deal with this issue was the continuous exchange of information through a cooperative state-business nexus. In particular Ahrens (2002, pp. 229–231) and Root (1996, pp. 10–15) have stressed the *participation* of different societal groups, most importantly private business, in the process of economic policy formulation. Evans (1995) argued that the East Asian states were characterized by *embedded autonomy*, meaning close formal and informal ties between bureaucrats and other economic actors. However, Haggard (2004, pp. 61–63) notes that the prevalence of participatory mechanisms has varied substantially between the successful East Asian economies and also substantially over time. It is possible to argue that the differences between the East Asian countries represent deviations from the ideal developmental state that only emerged as a result of an optimization process in the most successful Northeast Asian economies. This would mean that a definite model of the developmental state could be found at the later stages of economic catch-up in Japan, South Korea, Taiwan, and possibly Singapore. However, this is not the perspective advocated here. Rather, it is argued that the essence of the developmental state concept is the *dynamic nature* of the institutional structures governing the role of the state in the economy.

Again, the model of institutional change, as illustrated in Figure 2 of this study, can contribute to understanding this issue. As has been noted, economic development and institutional change are closely interrelated. Already in Section 5.2.3.1, it was concluded that the economic growth of Taiwan and South Korea had an impact on the ideologies of both critical decision makers and the general public. As argued by Amsden (1991, p. 286), the economic success initiated through state interventions may have further strengthened the state's commitment to economic development. Here, the focus will be on the way economic growth shifted the balance of power in the organizational power struggle, which is decisive for the evolution of the institutional environment.

Many accounts on the developmental state characterize it as *autonomous* or *strong*, meaning that a developmental state is supposedly able to act largely independent of special interest groups and override the power of such groups to act in the national interest (Leftwich, 1995, p. 408). As noted in Section 3, Root (1996, 1998) complemented this notion by arguing that states in the HPAEs were not only strong, but also limited. According to Root (1996, pp. 141–142), a strong but limited government prevents *itself* from responding to special interests. While he sees institutions as the key mechanism to achieve limits to the power of the state, Root (1996) does not provide theory-based insights on the emergence of such institutions, except for stressing the importance of political leadership throughout his work (p. 143). As was mentioned multiple times throughout this study, other scholars, such as Woo-Cumings (1998) and Doner et al. (2005), have stressed the importance of exogenous constraints that limited the set of feasible choices, and eventually the power, of political and bureaucratic actors in East Asia. It has been argued here that *both* factors seem to have been relevant for the emergence of developmental states. However, analyzing the way in which the role of the developmental states in the economy changed during economic development requires shifting the focus toward other issues.

The shift toward less state intervention in the economy that can be noted in countries such as Japan, Taiwan, and South Korea after decades of state-led development can hardly be understood as an entirely voluntary withdrawal. As was described in the case studies, most notably in the section on Japan, the organizations that were chiefly responsible for interventionist economic policy-making faced increasing pressures to reduce their influence from a variety of sources. One important source of such pressures is the international environment. As the United States felt gradually more challenged by the raise in East Asian exports, American political leaders increasingly attempted to influence their Asian counterparts to liberalize their economies. Furthermore, the membership of the successful East Asian economies in international organizations and agreements, such as the OECD, the WTO and the GATT, put limits to the use of specific tools of industrial policy. In addition, the private companies, which had been the key beneficiaries of interventionist policies in some HPAEs, increased their influence in the organizational power struggle and became increasingly critical of state interference with their decisions. This was particularly important in Japan and South Korea, where large, diversified private conglomerates played the leading role in economic development. As a result of their focus on exports, these companies had developed close business ties with foreign countries. As was described in the case study on Japan, there were also instances where domestic companies wanted more cooperation with foreign investors than the economic bureaucracy was willing to permit.

There is one important reason to explain why states in East Asia responded to these pressures in a way that was successful that has not received much attention in the recent literature: the competition between various centers of power in the state apparatus. In his seminal account on the Japanese developmental state, Johnson (1982, pp. 320–322) notes the importance of conflict both within the bureaucracy and between the bureaucracy and political authorities. Even though his model of a developmental state stresses the importance of a pilot agency with a far-reaching jurisdiction (Johnson, 1982, p. 319–320), he argues that the competition between different bureaucratic agencies fulfills important functions for the developmental state. Most importantly, the competition between agencies serves as an important check on their respective influence (Johnson, 1982, p. 321). Therefore, later accounts that exclusively stress the *coherence* of the economic bureaucracy and public action (Evans, 1998, p. 69–72) seem to miss an important point.

While Johnson noted the importance of conflict between different bureaucratic agencies, or, more generally, between different centers of power within the state apparatus, the case studies in the preceding sections provide a more profound insight into the way it shaped the path of institutional development. It seems that a key function of bureaucratic conflict was to balance coordination by the state and coordination by market incentives. This is most apparent in the case of Taiwan, where two pilot agencies competed for influence after 1970: the interventionist Industry Development Board (IDB) and the more liberal Council for Economic Planning and Development (CEPD). In Japan, MITI assumed the role of the key proponent of industrial policies, whereas other agencies such as the Ministry of Finance and the Free Trade Commission (FTC) advocated more reliance on competition and the market mechanism. In South Korea, the highly interventionist policies of the Heavy and Chemical Industrialization Plan were drafted by a group within the presidential administration in cooperation with the Ministry of Commerce and Industry. When these policies were discontinued, the Economic Planning Board, which advocated less interventionism, regained much of its previously lost influence.

These bureaucratic agencies never acted entirely independently of other interest groups. Private companies striving for less state control over the economy found allies within the bureaucracy, as did politicians willing to respond to foreign pressures for more liberalization. As a consequence of bureaucratic competition for influence, each agency faced a constant need to justify its actions and policies. It seems probable that this need for justification was an important reason why state action was overall *rational*—as argued by Johnson (1982, p. 18)—and adaptive, as stressed by Root (1996, p. 15–16). The presence of agencies in favor of a more liberal approach to economic policy represented a potential threat to the power of economic planners and, therefore, increased their incentive to prove the viability of state interventions.

6.5 Conclusions: the key elements of the developmental state

It was argued at the beginning of Section 6 that the elaboration of a model of the developmental state based on the identification of characteristic institutions is made substantially more difficult because of *institutional equivalence*. Different developmental states in East Asia had varying institutions and achieved similar success in terms of economic development. Thus, it is not the aim of this section to delineate a list of institutions that constitute the model of a developmental state.

Instead, I attempted in the preceding sections to elaborate how the interaction between existing institutions, organizations, ideologies and the external environment shaped the emergence and evolution of developmental states. As a summary, Figure 9 illustrates these interrelationships. Since the New Institutional Economics serve as an analytical basis for the case studies in Part II of this study, Figure 9 shows some notable similarities to the model of institutional change illustrated in Figure 2 (Section 2.2.2).

Figure 9: Stylized model of a developmental state

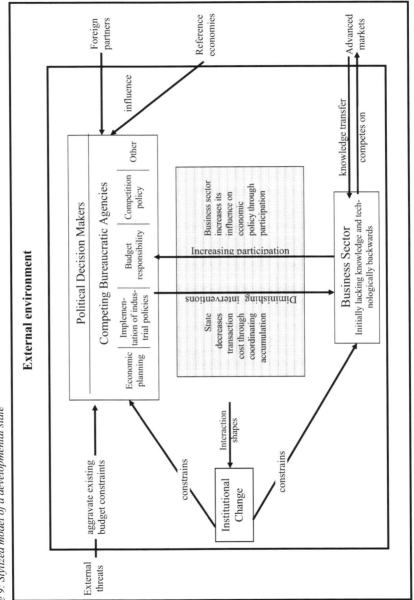

Source: Own compilation

An important characteristic of developmental states has been that they managed to achieve both a rapid accumulation of productive factors and a reasonably efficient allocation of these factors. The rules which governed accumulation and allocation of factors were developed through the interaction of the state apparatus and the private sector. At the initial stages of economic take-off, the state had a stronger role and promoted accumulation as the main objective. At later stages, the influence of the private sector became stronger, which resulted in a stronger focus on profitability and the efficient allocation of factors. Moreover, it is important to take into account that the state apparatus is not a monolithic organization. At least in some cases, different agencies within the bureaucracy were dominated by public officials with diverging ideologies. This is particularly notable in the case of Taiwan, where the interventionist IDB competed for influence with the more liberal CEPD. In inter-bureaucratic conflicts, specific agencies in the East Asian developmental states sometimes sided with private companies. Thus, the competition between different agencies also served as a constraint on the overall power of the state apparatus vis-à-vis the private sector.

Furthermore, both the private sector and the state apparatus in developmental states were influenced in a variety of ways by their external environment. In some publications on the developmental state concept, the relevance of foreign countries is mainly stressed in the context of external threats, which impose hard budget constraints on governments and make economic development an imperative. However, foreign countries had a much broader influence on developmental states. Japan, South Korea, and Taiwan maintained a close partnership to the USA after the Second World War. This partnership resulted in a notable influence of the United States on the governments and, eventually, on the institutional development of these countries, even though the US model of economic development was never fully embraced. Moreover, the bureaucracies and governments of all developmental states attempted to learn from the experience of other countries. In the case of Japan, Germany and the United States were important reference economies, while Japan itself, and later South Korea and Taiwan, served as a reference model for other East Asian countries. Furthermore, foreign countries also had a strong influence on the business sector. Technological capabilities and managerial knowledge were transferred from more advanced economies to East Asia. In addition, their continuing international experience and eventual partnerships with companies from advanced markets changed the ideologies of East Asian businessmen and altered the incentives they faced.

Lastly, the relevance of path dependency for the evolution of developmental states should be noted. A change in institutions represents a constraint for the future evolution of institutions. As a result, political decision makers may make their commitment to economic growth and, in particular, to private sector development credible through establishing institutions which bind the hands of the state apparatus and inhibit a future shift toward predatory policies.

PART III:

CENTRAL ASIA FROM THE PERSPECTIVE OF THE DEVELOPMENTAL STATE CONCEPT

7 Economic transition in Central Asia: A short overview

7.1 The Russian and Soviet legacy in Central Asia

7.1.1 The advent of Russian colonialism

As was noted in the case studies on the East Asian developmental states, the differing colonial heritage of each country has been considered to be among the key explanatory factors for diverging paths of institutional development. Especially in South Korea and Taiwan, the legacy of Japan is commonly argued to have contributed crucially to the emergence of developmental states. In contrast to East Asia, Central Asia was ruled for more than a century by a single, foreign power: the Russian Empire and the Russian-dominated Soviet Union that succeeded it. In this section, some basic characteristics of the Russian colonialism will be outlined.

On historic and cultural grounds, the area that is today occupied by Kazakhstan, Kyrgyzstan, Tajikistan, Turkmenistan, and Uzbekistan can be divided into two broad regions: the Kazakh steppe to the North and Turkestan, also referred to as Central Asia proper, to the South (Clem, 1992; see also Pomfret, 1995, p. 19). While both regions together form Central Asia according to the definition that is most commonly used today (and also used within this study), their colonial history and legacy differ in some aspects.

The Russian annexation of the Kazakh steppe began during the reign of Peter the Great in 1715, but was not completed until the mid 19th century (Hiro, 2009, p. 20–21). At this time, the region was inhabited by cattle-breeding nomads who lived in yurts and were divided into three different clans or hordes that were subdued by the Russian expansion one after another (Clem, 1992, pp. 28–29; Hiro, 2009, p. 21). With the Kazakh steppe already under its control, Russia expanded further south into Central Asia in the mid-19th century, competing with the British Empire (Pomfret, 1995, pp. 21–25). Step by step, the Khanate of Kokand, the Emirate of Bukhara, and the Khanate of Khiva were incorporated into the Russian Empire, before its expansion in the region came to an end when Trans-Caspia, a territory inhabited by Turkmen tribes, was subdued in 1881 (Clem, 1992, p. 30–31; Hiro, 2009, p. 25). While the Turkmen tribes were predominantly nomadic, the other peoples inhabiting this southern region, specifically the Turkic Uzbeks and the Persian-speaking Tajiks, had a long history of sedentary life (Hiro, 2009, p. 26). Cities, such as Tashkent, Bukhara, and

Samarkand, which were inhabited by these peoples, had once been among the principal cultural, economic, and scientific centers of the Islamic world. The different conditions that the Russian Empire encountered in the Kazakh steppe and in Turkestan resulted in diverging paths of development. In the northern steppe, inhabited by nomads, the Russian authorities found a considerable arable land surplus (Clem, 1992, p. 30). At the end of the 19th century, a massive inflow of Russian settlers to this region began, which would ultimately result in the Kazakhs becoming a minority in the territory they had traditionally inhabited (Clem, 1992, 30; Hiro, 2009, pp. 26–27). In Turkestan, no comparable settlement of Russians took place, the presence of a large sedentary population with established landownership meant that no surplus land was available (Clem, 1992, p. 32). Instead, the Russian presence was limited to mercantile interests in the cities and the military domination of the region (Clem, 1992, p. 31; Pomfret, 1995, p. 25). Thus, the history and the varying institutions of indigenous people—firmly established property rights to land in the South and nomadic lifestyle in the North—directly shaped further development in the different regions of Central Asia. Changes in the exogenous environment led to another development that would shape the economic future of Central Asia. As a result of the American Civil War, the Russian textile industry was facing a shortage of cotton supplies beginning in the 1860s (Clem, 1992, p. 31). Therefore, the cotton cultivation in Central Asia was increased sharply at Russian insistence (Hiro, 2009, p. 27). The fertile Fergana Valley, which today belongs largely to Uzbekistan, became the most important cotton-producing region in the Russian Empire (Hiro, 2009, p. 27).

According to Clem (1992), the differing characteristics of Russian colonialism in the Kazakh steppe and Turkestan are comparable to the varying forms that European colonialism took in other parts of the world. He argues that the Russian dominance of the steppe regions in the North was similar to European conquest of countries such as the United States, Australia, or Argentina. In these countries, extensive European settlement took place, and the often nomadic indigenous people were eventually displaced from their territories by the preponderance of immigrants that gradually expanded the frontier of their agricultural lands. In Turkestan, Clem considers the Russian expansion to have followed the pattern of the European imperialism of the 19th century. In the European colonies of this time, a large native population was subjugated, but not eradicated, by a relatively small number of intruders, concentrated in cities and towns, through superior technology and military power. These colonies essentially served as economic complements to the motherland through providing natural resources and agricultural commodities (Clem, 1992, pp. 21–25 and 32–33). In his analysis of the Russian expansion in Central Asia, Clem does not make any references or comparisons to the Japanese colonialism in East Asia. However, some similarities do exist, as has already been noted in the introduction to this study. As already noted in Section 3.2.1.1, Cumings (1984) states that:

> Japan's imperial experience differed from the West's in several fundamental respects. It involved the colonization of contiguous territory; it involved the location of industry and an infrastructure of communications and transportation in the colonies, bringing industry to the labor and raw materials rather than vice versa; and it was accomplished by a country that always saw itself as disadvantaged and threatened by more advanced countries. (p. 8)

Remarkably, all these characteristics also apply to the Russian and Soviet domination of Central Asia. While some resemblance, most notably the colonization of contiguous territory was present since the 19th century, the similarity became more pronounced after the Russian Revolution in 1917 and the emergence of the Soviet Union in 1922.

7.1.2 Central Asia as part of the Soviet Union

According to Pomfret (1995, p. 25), no fundamental economic transformation of Central Asia took place under the rule of the Russian Empire. This changed significantly when Central Asia became part of the Soviet Union. The essential role of the five Central Asian republics within the Soviet economic system was that of "producers of primary products, mainly, cotton, energy products and minerals" (Pomfret, 2003, p. 12). This is similar to the role that Korea and Taiwan played within the Japanese colonial empire prior to the Second World War. However, as was also described for Korea and Taiwan in Section 5.3.1.1, this is not the whole story. As Abazov (1999) summarizes in a paper on Kyrgyzstan:

> Throughout the Soviet era, the Soviet leaders interpreted the concept of economic modernisation as persistent and accelerated development of the industrial sector, collectivisation of the agricultural sector of the economy, centralised rational economic planning and economic equalisation. This policy sometimes ignored both cost-effectiveness and social factors. Only a belief in the unlimited potential of social engineering could explain the ways and methods of the economic development of Central Asia in general and Kyrgyzstan in particular since the late 1920s. (pp. 238–239)

While Abazov uses the term "rational economic planning" to describe the Soviet policies in Central Asia in this quote, it is obvious from the last part of his statement that they were not rational in the sense of Johnson's (1982) concept of a *plan-rational state*. Instead, Abazov's evaluation of the economic policies implemented in Central Asia during Soviet times seems quite close to Johnson's description of the Soviet Union as plan-ideological: policies were chosen based on ideological beliefs and not revised even when they turned out to be economically and socially ineffective. Although the general approach of planned, rapid industrialization was a similarity between Japan and the Soviet Union, the collectivization of agriculture and the Soviet focus on economic equalization were clear differences.

While the presence of the Japanese in colonial Taiwan and in Korea was higher than that of Westerners in their respective colonies, the presence of Russians in Central Asia was even more remarkable. The heavy Russian immigration into the northern parts of Central Asia that had been taking place since the 19th century continued throughout Soviet times (Abazov, 1999, p. 240). During the Second World War, a boost of heavy industrialization occurred in Central Asia when Soviet factories where transferred from frontline regions to more remote areas (Hiro, 2009, p. 59), similar to the industrialization that was carried out on the Korean Peninsula at the same time. As Abazov (1999, p. 240) notes, the Soviet industrialization in Kyrgyzstan even included the relocation of complete plants, together with their entire workforce. However, the main regional focus of industrialization was Tashkent, which was the only city that already had an industrial base from the pre-war period (Pomfret, 1995, p. 26). At the same time, Central Asia was subject to substantial immigration when Stalin decided to relocate entire ethnic groups that he considered potential security threats. The most important groups were Germans from the west and Koreans from the east (Pomfret, 1995, p. 26).

After the war, the relocation of industry from the western parts of the Soviet Union to Central Asia ceased. Central Asia's integration into the Soviet division of labor increased, and the production and processing of raw materials as the main economic focus of the region (Pomfret, 1995, p. 26). For analyzing the economic performance of the Central Asian republics after their independence, it is extremely important to notice that the Soviet Union was planned as a single economic unit (Pomfret, 2003, p. 12). While trade within the Union took place without attention to the borders of the Soviet republics, the Central Asian SSRs were closed to external trade (Pomfret, 2003, p. 12). As a result, economic linkages existed mostly to Russia in the North and between the Soviet republics of Central Asia, but not to the neighboring countries in the East and South.

7.2 The development of the five Central Asian republics after independence

7.2.1 The initial conditions of the Central Asian republics and their economic performance after independence

The five Central Asian republics differ from one another in a variety of aspects. However, they also share several characteristics that separate them as a group from virtually all other former Soviet Republics. Apart from a common historical and cultural background, the Central Asian republics also share the trait of having been the poorest and least industrialized parts of the Soviet Union, together with Azerbaijan (Pomfret, 2003, p. 12). Spechler additionally stresses that all are remote from important markets, and landlocked (2004, p. 63). Furthermore, they share some political conditions. As Olcott (1992, p. 108) noted in the early 1990s, all five republics were essentially forced to become independent when the Soviet Union dissolved. Since the borders of the republics within the Soviet Union had not been defined based on historical entities, none of the five countries had a prior experience as independent nation-states (Spechler, 2004, p. 62). With the exception of Kyrgyzstan, the presidents in the newly independent Central Asian countries all came from the Communist administrative hierarchy (Blackmon, 2005, p. 391; Pomfret, 2006, pp. 73). However, the Central Asian countries implemented quite different transition strategies. As a consequence of these similar conditions and diverging strategies, Pomfret (2010a; see also 2003, p. 17; 2007, p. 324; 2010b, p. 8) and others (Spechler, 2004, p. 61–62) have argued that the Central Asian economies development can be considered a natural experiment for the success of different approaches to economic transition.

The similarities between the Central Asian countries are also obvious from the perspective of the NIE as embodied in Figure 2 (Section 2.2.2). The set of formal institutions that actors in Central Asia faced in the initial stages of transition was virtually the same in all five republics (Perlman & Gleason, 2007, pp. 1330–1331). In addition, the fact that four out of five political leaders had a similar personal and political background might imply that they had comparable mental models of the world and, in consequence, similar ideologies. Furthermore, one might argue that the similar cultural and historic background of the Central Asian peoples resulted in comparable ideologies in the general public and a similar set of informal institutions. However, this is only true to a limited degree. Moreover, while the Central Asian leaders faced similar exogenous constraints in terms of governing a newly independent, landlocked country in the same geographical region, the conditions varied sufficiently to explain different transition strategies and economic outcomes.

The Central Asian presidents had considerable freedom of action concerning economic polices and reforms at the beginning of the 1990s (Pomfret, 2010a, p. 450). In particular, the formal institutional environment was questioned as a result of independence and the demise of communism. For this reason, it is possible that a *window of opportunity* for profound institutional change existed in Central Asia at this time. However, the differences in constraints faced by the political leaders were decisive for the further path of institutional change. Among the most important differences were the varying degrees of resource endowments of the five Central Asian countries. As Spechler summarizes, the smallest countries in terms of territory, Tajikistan and Kyrgyzstan, are generally considered to be resource-poor. In sharp contrast, Turkmenistan and Kazakhstan have abundant resources of oil and natural gas. Uzbekistan's economy has been dominated by cotton production since the Russian empire, but also has some resources in natural gas and gold (Spechler, 2008a, p. 39).

Figure 10: Population of the Central Asian countries at independence and today [in millions]

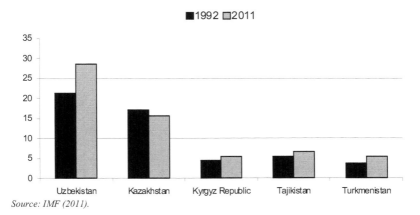

Source: IMF (2011).

Population also varies drastically between the five Central Asian states. As can be seen in Figure 10, Uzbekistan is the most populous country in the region, followed by Kazakhstan, which has a much larger territory. Kyrgyzstan, Tajikistan, and Turkmenistan are much less populous than the other two republics. Comparing these numbers to the HPAEs, Uzbekistan has today about the same population as Malaysia, and a slightly higher population than Taiwan. The three smaller republics have a similar population to the East Asian city-states, Hong Kong and Singapore, whereas Kazakhstan ranks between the city-states and Taiwan. All other HPAEs discussed here have a much higher population (IMF, 2011).

In sharp contrast to the Northeast Asian economies of Japan, South Korea, and Taiwan, but similar to the Southeast Asian HPAEs, all five Central Asian countries have an ethnically heterogeneous population. However, a key difference between the conditions in East Asia and the newly independent republics is the extraordinary importance of cross-border migration that has been taking place in Central Asia since the end of the Soviet Union. The importance of migration and the varying ethnic structure between the Central Asian republics has led to important differences in terms of the constraints that political leaders face.

As has been noted in the preceding sections, there was much more Russian migration to the northern parts of Central Asia, specifically the Kazakh steppe and cities in Kyrgyzstan, than to the south. As a consequence, the ethnic structure of Kazakhstan and Kyrgyzstan are somewhat similar (Hiro, 2009, p. 281). In 1989, there were almost as many Russians as Kazakhs living the Kazakh SSR, both groups comprising somewhat less than 40% of the population; Germans were the third largest ethnic group with slightly less than a million persons, making up about 5.8% of the population (Zardykhan, 2004, p. 68). In several regions, Russians outnumbered Kazakhs. In some cases by a ratio higher than three to one (Zardykhan 2004, p. 67–69). As can be seen in Figure 10, Kazakhstan is the only country that lost population since its independence. The main reason for this was the high emigration of ethnic Russians and Germans, who were disproportionately well educated and skilled (Pomfret, 2006, p. 43).

In 1989, the Russian population in Kyrgyzstan only amounted to 21.5% and native Kyrgyz made up slightly more than half of the population (Abazov, 1999, p. 240). The third largest ethnic group was formed by Uzbeks, with around 11%, while Germans only amounted to 2.3% of the total population (Abazov, 1999, p. 241). While emigration of Russians and Germans also took place in Kyrgyzstan (Abazov 1999, p. 249), their lower numbers and the higher birthrate in Kyrgyzstan compensated this loss of population.

Usually, these two northern republics, Kazakhstan and even more so Kyrgyzstan, are considered to have been the region's faster reformers in the early 1990s (Pomfret, 2006, pp. 6–7). This is also evidenced by the EBRD transition indicators. In particular, concerning privatization and the liberalization of prices and trade, Kyrgyzstan and Kazakhstan were considered to be significantly closer to a market economy than their Central Asian neighbors at the end of the decade (see Table 14). It seems that this is to a notable degree due to the constraints faced by its their political leaders; however, as in the case of the East Asian developmental states, there is also sufficient evidence to maintain that personal ideologies had some importance.

Table 14: EBRD transition indicators of the Central Asian countries, 1991 and 2000

	Kazakhstan		Kyrgyzstan		Tajikistan		Turkme-nistan		Uzbekistan	
	1991	2000	1991	2000	1991	2000	1991	2000	1991	2000
Large scale privatization	1.0	3.0	1.0	3.0	1.0	2.3	1.0	1.7	1.0	2.7
Small scale privatization	1.0	4.0	1.0	4.0	1.0	3.3	1.0	2.0	1.0	3.0
Enterprise restructuring	1.0	2.0	1.0	2.0	1.0	1.7	1.0	1.0	1.0	1.7
Price liberalization	1.0	4.0	1.0	4.3	1.0	3.7	1.0	2.7	1.0	2.7
Trade & Forex system	1.0	3.3	1.0	4.3	1.0	3.3	1.0	1.0	1.0	1.0
Competition Policy	1.0	2.0	1.0	2.0	1.0	2.0	1.0	1.0	1.0	2.0
Banking reform & interest rate liberalization	1.0	2.3	1.0	2.0	1.0	1.0	1.0	1.0	1.0	1.7
Securities markets & non-bank financial institutions	1.0	2.3	1.0	2.0	1.0	1.0	1.0	1.0	1.0	2.0
Overall infrastructure reform	1.0	2.0	1.0	1.3	1.0	1.0	1.0	1.0	1.0	1.3

Note: Indicators are measured on a scale from 1 (no reform) to 4+. Pluses and minuses are represented by the decimal place, e.g., 3+ and 3- are represented by 3.33 and 2.67.
Source: EBRD (2011).

As has been noted, Kyrgyzstan, the fastest reformer of the region in the 1990s, was also the only country with a president that did not come through the communist hierarchy. As Pomfret (2006) summarizes:

> Whether due to limited options or to the chance even that the incumbent leader had come from the Academy of Science rather than through the Communist administrative hierarchy as in the other Central Asian countries, the Kyrgyz Republic had by 1993 become the most liberal country in the region and the one most closely aligned with the "Washington Consensus" view of transition advocated by the IMF and the World Bank. In May 1993 the Kyrgyz Republic became the first Central Asian country to leave the ruble zone and issue its own national currency, and thereafter it was the first to bring hyperinflation under control. Its price and trade reforms were the most sweeping in Central Asia, and in 1998, it became the first of the Soviet successor states, including the Baltic countries, to accede to the WTO. (pp. 73–74)

Thus, it seems that the Kyrgyz political decision makers were consciously using the Western market economies—or at least the ideal market economy as embodied in the recommendations of Western-dominated international organizations—as the key reference models for their country. As a consequence, Kyrgyzstan received much more aid from international donors than any other country (Pomfret, 2006, p. 74). In the quote above, Pomfret explicitly makes a suggestion on the question as to whether the reform commitment was mainly due to exogenous constraints or to personal ideologies of political decision makers, specifically of the president in the early 1990s, Askar Akayev. In the present study, this important theoretical question was already explored in the context of Taiwanese and South Korean development. It was argued in Section 5.3.2.1 that both ideology and constraints mattered in these countries. In the case of Kyrgyzstan, there is no reason to come to a different conclusion.

Between 1991 and 1996, the Kyrgyz government also introduced a new legislative framework to govern the liberalized economy (Abazov, 1999, p. 243). However, this progress did not lead to the desired results. This may be due to the interaction of new, formal institutions with the informal institutional heritage. According to Pomfret (2006), market-unfriendly informal institutions related to the importance of personal contacts and corruption continued to dominate in Kyrgyzstan. Market-supporting formal rules were thus not sufficiently enforced (Pomfret, 2006, p. 74).

For Kazakhstan, the heavy presence of Russians has been one of the most influential factors in political affairs, as Zardykhan asserts (2004, p. 69). Maintaining the existing economic ties with Russia became a priority for the leadership under President Nursultan Nazarbayev, who attempted to construct a "viable successor organization to the USSR" (Pomfret, 2006, p. 40). However, Nazarbayev was also strongly dedicated to Kazakh nation-building. Due to higher living standards and human-capital endowments, Kazakhstan's political leaders were facing more favorable initial conditions for constructing a market economy than Kyrgyzstan's (Pomfret, 2006, p. 6). In the early 1990s, Kazakhstan started the transition toward a market economy fairly quickly, following the radical reforms that were implemented under Yeltsin in Russia at this time (Pomfret, 2005, p. 859). The unusually close ties in terms of both population and economic linkages were presumably a key reason for choosing the northern neighbor as a reference model. Similar to Russia, prices were liberalized quickly and rapid privatization was pursued. However, Kazakhstan remained in the ruble zone longer than Kyrgyzstan and did not focus on macroeconomic stability to the same degree (Pomfret, 2006, pp. 6 and 40). Concerning privatization, Kazakhstan was even faster than its two neighbors, becoming the first SSR to initiate a privatization program that covered almost half of medium and small enterprises in 1991 (Simon, 2009, p. 69). However, the success of this process had become doubtful in the mid-1990s, when privatization became increasingly associated with corruption and resembled the Russian reference model in creating powerful vested interests (Pomfret, 2006, p. 6; 2010a, p. 453).

A particularly important question in the context of nation building was the status of the northern regions, which were predominantly inhabited by Russians.

Nationalism of the previously repressed ethnic Kazakhs and the status of ethnic Russians inhabiting the northern regions adjacent to Russia were important issues for a newly independent republic (Hiro, 2009, 251–257) that had been thrown into relative geopolitical insecurity. There were fears that ethnic Russians would seek unification of the northern regions with adjacent Russia (Economist, 1997; Hiro, 2009, p. 254). An important measure to counter such movements and establish the sovereignty of Kazakhstan in the northern regions was the decision to move the capital from Almaty, close to the Kyrgyz and Chinese borders, to the small city of Aqmola in the northern steppe (Cumings, 2002, p. 15; Economist, 1997; Wolfel, 2002, p. 485–486). While this decision was already taken in 1991, the official inauguration of Aqmola, which was renamed Astana, as the new capital took place in 1997 (Economist, 1997).

In contrast to Kazakhstan and Kyrgyzstan, none of the three southern Central Asian republics has been considered a rapid reformer in the 1990s. Tajikistan is a special case in this context, because it is the only republic that did not emerge peacefully from the dissolution of the Soviet Union. Instead, it was characterized from 1992 to 1997 by a bloody civil war between the government, which was dominated by former communists, and predominantly Islamic opposition groups (Hiro, 2009, pp. 325–344; Pomfret, 2010b, pp. 2–3).

Turkmenistan is another country with extremely specific conditions. As a country that is only sparsely populated but in possession of large reserves in natural gas and oil and, in addition, an important exporter of cotton, Turkmenistan could expect unusually large gains in the terms of trade from the dissolution of the Soviet Union (Spechler, 2008a, p. 34). However, these gains made the emergence of a highly authoritarian political regime or, in the words of Pomfret (2006), "pathological political conditions" (p. 89) possible. As Spechler (2004) summarizes:

> President for Life Suparmurat Niyazov, a former Communist functionary, has encouraged a cult of personality that exceeds even that of Joseph Stalin in the late 1940s. Local newspapers have credited "Turkmenbashi" (father of all the Turkmen) with supernatural powers and divine ancestry. His book, Rukhnama (Spiritual Revival), must be studied in every school and government office. (p. 67)

The policies implemented under Niyazov made Turkmenistan the least reformed Central Asian country (Spechler, 2008a, p. 35). It should be noted that economic liberalization was never an objective for the regime, which focused instead on attaining economic independence (Pomfret, 2006, p. 89). While some limited privatization took place, overall resource allocation, except for small-scale trading in bazaars, has not been determined by free prices (Pomfret, 2006, p. 93). In addition, inflation amounted to more than 1000% for several years in the early 1990s, before it was brought down to double-digits in 1998 (Pomfret, 2006, p.

5). To some degree, profits from the exports of cotton, gas, and oil were used to finance import substitution projects such as oil refineries and textile plants. However their efficiency has been considered highly doubtful (Pomfret, 2006, pp. 94–95; Spechler, 2008a, p. 35).

The actions of the political leadership in Turkmenistan, specifically of President Niyazov, can be explained by an exceptional freedom of action to maximize his personal utility. This freedom was due to several factors, the most prominent among them the stupendous resource endowment of Turkmenistan. The threat to the regime from either secular or Islamic opposition groups was negligible (Hiro, 2009, p. 205). Furthermore, its specific geopolitical conditions kept Turkmenistan, as the most southern Central Asian republic, relatively free from any undesired foreign influence. Due to the profits from the export of the abundant natural resources, the leadership felt, in contrast to all other Central Asian republics, no need to work with international organizations such as the World Bank and the IMF (Hiro, 2009, pp. 205–206). As a consequence of this lack of exogenous constraints for the president, Turkmenistan under Niyazov seems to be the clearest example of a predatory state in Central Asia.

Uzbekistan, the most populous country in the region, is another country whose transition strategy has been sharply criticized by Western observers and international organizations. According to Spechler (2000b), this strategy was characterized by one key objective, namely "stability at any cost" (p. 295). While Uzbekistan's approach to transition was certainly more progressive than Turkmenistan, it is usually characterized as one of the slowest reformers in the former Soviet Union (Pomfret, 2006, pp. 25–26). Some authors (Reppegather & Troschke, 2006) have referred to the Uzbek strategy as a variety of *gradualism*, which is commonly associated with the transition of the People's Republic of China. While also referring the "Uzbek road" as "a sort of gradualism" (Spechler, 2000b, p. 299), one of the leading experts on Central Asia, Martin Spechler (2000b), stresses the differences to China:

> The "Uzbek Road" is *sui generis*—neither the liberal "shock therapy" recommended by the Washington consensus nor the gradualism practiced by China and, to a degree, by Hungary. Rather than proclaiming growth as its main goal, Uzbekistan has emphasized "stability at any cost." The authoritarian regime will assure stability by subsidizing employment, controlling prices on essential goods and services, privatizing the largest state-owned enterprises only gradually and partially, and pursuing self-sufficiency in energy and food supplies. Rather than devolving authority through early privatization by relying on whichever investors can be found, the state figures as "chief reformer." All outside ideologies—Communism, political Islam, or neoliberalism—are rejected. Insofar as any outside country is to be emulated, the model would be South Korea, Malaysia, Japan, or Turkey—not the USA (Abazov, 1998). (p. 295, source as given there)

Thus, he makes explicit reference to the East Asian developmental states that were analyzed in Part II of the present study, a point of view that Spechler also advocated in another publication (2000a).

In terms of initial conditions, Uzbekistan had both advantages and disadvantages compared to the other Central Asian economies. While all Central Asian countries are landlocked, Uzbekistan is, together with Liechtenstein, the only double landlocked country (Spechler, 2000b, p. 296), meaning a landlocked country that only borders other landlocked countries. As has been noted, its resource endowments are less abundant than those of Turkmenistan and Kazakhstan, but more than those of Tajikistan and Kyrgyzstan. While different estimations for the GDP per capita in purchasing power parity make comparisons between the Central Asian countries in the early 1990s difficult,[34] it is clear that Uzbekistan was poorer than Kazakhstan and Turkmenistan. However, Uzbekistan inhabited the most capable and effective public administration in Central Asia, since Tashkent had been the regional capital during Soviet times (Pomfret, 2003, p. 22).

The Uzbek transition strategy was gradual in the sense that small-scale privatization was undertaken quickly, while large-scale privatization and agrarian reform were only limited when compared to Kazakhstan and Russia (Pomfret, 2006, p. 27). Furthermore, the government has retained control over natural resource rents and, for the most part, over the financial sector (Pomfret, 2006, p. 27). Industrial policies aimed at import substitution were pursued through public investment in favored enterprises, specifically in chemical and petrochemical enterprises, as well as in cotton mills. Yet, as in Turkmenistan, Pomfret (2006, p. 29) considers these projects to have been largely inefficient. As a result of such policies, he characterizes the Uzbek development strategy as inward looking, even though its economy had a high export to GDP ratio (Pomfret, 2006, p. 29).

---

34   According to the estimates of the World Bank (2010), Uzbekistan was, at independence, poorer in terms of GDP/capita in PPP than Tajikistan and Kyrgyzstan. In contrast, it was richer than these countries according to Maddison's (2010) estimates. The estimates of the IMF (2011) occupy a middle ground, since they rank Uzbekistan above Tajikistan but below Kyrgyzstan.

Table 15: Real GDP growth of the Central Asian republics, 1991–2000 [%]

	1991	1992	1993	1994	1995	1996	1997	1998	1999	2000	Total 1991–2000
Kazakhstan	-11.0	-5.3	-9.2	-12.6	-8.2	0.5	1.7	-1.9	2.7	9.8	**-30.6**
Kyrgyzstan	-7.9	-13.9	-15.5	-20.1	-5.4	7.1	9.9	2.1	3.7	5.4	**-33.4**
Tajikistan	-7.1	-29.0	-16.4	-21.3	-12.4	-16.7	1.7	5.3	3.7	8.3	**-61.9**
Turkmenistan	-4.7	-5.3	-10.0	-17.3	-7.2	-6.7	-11.3	6.7	16.5	18.6	**-24.0**
Uzbekistan	-0.5	-11.2	-2.3	-5.2	-0.9	1.7	5.2	4.3	4.3	3.8	**-2.0**

Source: World Bank (2011a); cumulated growth own calculation based on World Bank (2011a).

The economic performance of the five Central Asian republics in the 1990s shows that each republic experienced economic troubles as a result of the transition from communism (see Table 15). This is not surprising, given similar recessions in Russia and in other countries that underwent the transformation from a planned economy at this time. Moreover, it is not surprising that Tajikistan, which suffered from civil war for most of the decade, experienced the sharpest decline in GDP. The development that has caused the most attention in economic research on the region was that Uzbekistan was by far the best performer. While the GDP of Turkmenistan declined about a fourth, that of Kazakhstan and of Kyrgyzstan, which has been considered an "early poster child for neoliberal reforms" (Spechler, 2004, p. 71), declined by around 30% in the 1990s. In contrast, Uzbekistan achieved a moderate decline of 2% (see Table 15). The difference in economic performance between the two most important economies, Uzbekistan and Kazakhstan, becomes smaller when performance is measured by GDP per capita (PPP) instead of total GDP (see Table 16). This is due to Kazakhstan's decline in population, caused mainly by the emigration of Russians and Germans. However, even by this measure, Uzbekistan was Central Asia's most successful economy in the 1990s.

The exact causes for the relatively good economic performance of Uzbekistan are not easy to determine. Since the country did not follow the advice of international organizations and Western mainstream economists, it was considered to be a paradox (Pomfret, 2006, p. 25). Pomfret (2010a, p. 452) offers three different, but not necessarily contradictory explanations: favorable conditions for Uzbek cotton and gold exports (see also Pomfret, 2006, p. 39), better economic administration than in the other republics, and the gradual transition strategy implemented by Islam Karimov's government.

Table 16: Real GDP per capita (PPP) growth of the Central Asian republics, 1991–2000 [%]

	1991	1992	1993	1994	1995	1996	1997	1998	1999	2000	Total 1991–2000
Kazakhstan	-11.6	-5.2	-8.6	-11.3	-6.6	2.0	3.3	-0.2	3.7	10.1	**-23.7**
Kyrgyzstan	-9.3	-14.9	-15.4	-20.0	-6.5	5.5	8.3	0.6	2.2	4.4	**-40.1**
Tajikistan	-9.1	-30.3	-17.7	-22.5	-13.7	-17.9	0.3	3.9	2.4	7.0	**-67.3**
Turkmenistan	-7.3	-8.0	-12.5	-19.4	-9.2	-8.4	-12.6	5.3	15.0	17.0	**-38.1**
Uzbekistan	-2.6	-13.3	-4.5	-7.0	-2.7	-0.2	3.2	2.6	2.8	2.7	**-18.5**

Source: World Bank (2011a); cumulated growth own calculation based on World Bank (2011a).

In contrast to the main export goods of Kazakhstan and Turkmenistan, oil and natural gas, cotton and gold exports did not rely on existing pipelines through Russia and could be redirected toward Western markets quite easily. In addition, the prices for cotton were on the rise in the early 1990s. However, they declined in 1996, which caused the government to impose import controls and a complicated, multiple exchange rate system (Pomfret, 2006, pp. 30–31; Spechler, 2000b, p. 301). This essentially leaves Uzbekistan's relatively capable administration, public investment and good economic management embodied in a successful transition strategy as the most likely reasons for its economic success. Empirical studies indeed seem to show that these are relevant explanatory factors for the so-called "Uzbek puzzle" (Pomfret, 2006, p. 28). These explanations might hint toward the resemblance of Uzbekistan with a developmental state.

7.2.2 The economic performance of the Central Asian republics since 2000

Taking a look at the development of the EBRD transition indicators for the Central Asian countries in the last ten years, it is striking how small the progress was compared to the 1990s (see Table 17 and Pomfret, 2010a, p. 454). Of course, Kazakhstan and Kyrgyzstan had already achieved high evaluations concerning small-scale privatization and price liberalization in the year 2000 (one might add the trade and foreign exchange rate system in the case of Kyrgyzstan). However, there was virtually no progress in other areas, specifically enterprise restructuring, competition policy, banking reform, the securities market, and infrastructure. With the partial exception of Tajikistan that emerged from civil war in

1997, the other Central Asian countries show a similar picture, albeit remaining at an overall lower level.

Table 17: EBRD transition indicators of the Central Asian countries, 1991 and 2000

	Kazakhstan		Kyrgyzstan		Tajikistan		Turkmenistan		Uzbekistan	
	2000	2010	2000	2010	2000	2010	2000	2010	2000	2010
Large scale privatization	3.0	3.0	3.0	3.7	2.3	2.3	1.7	1.0	2.7	2.7
Small scale privatization	4.0	4.0	4.0	4.0	3.3	4.0	2.0	2.3	3.0	3.3
Enterprise restructuring	2.0	2.0	2.0	2.0	1.7	2.0	1.0	1.0	1.7	1.7
Price liberalization	4.0	4.0	4.3	4.3	3.7	4.0	2.7	2.7	2.7	2.7
Trade & Forex system	3.3	3.7	4.3	4.3	3.3	3.3	1.0	2.0	1.0	2.0
Competition Policy	2.0	2.0	2.0	2.0	2.0	1.7	1.0	1.0	2.0	1.7
Banking reform & interest rate liberalization	2.3	2.7	2.0	2.3	1.0	2.3	1.0	1.0	1.7	1.7
Securities markets & non-bank financial institutions	2.3	2.7	2.0	2.0	1.0	1.0	1.0	1.0	2.0	2.0
Overall infrastructure reform	2.0	2.7	1.3	1.7	1.0	1.7	1.0	1.0	1.3	1.7

Note: Indicators are measured on a scale from 1 (no reform) to 4, with pluses and minuses, e.g., 3+ and 3- are represented by 3.33 and 2.67.
Source: EBRD (2011).

Table 18: Real GDP growth of the Central Asian republics, 2001–2010 [%]

	2001	2002	2003	2004	2005	2006	2007	2008	2009	2010	Total 2001–2010
Kazakhstan	13.5	9.8	9.3	9.6	9.7	10.7	8.9	3.3	1.2	7.0	**120.8**
Kyrgyzstan	5.3	0.0	7.0	7.0	-0.2	3.1	8.5	8.4	2.9	-1.4	**48.2**
Tajikistan	10.2	9.1	10.2	10.6	10.5	6.7	7.0	7.8	7.9	3.8	**123.2**
Turkmenistan	20.4	15.8	17.1	17.2	13.0	11.4	11.8	10.5	6.1	8.1	**241.4**
Uzbekistan	4.2	4.0	4.2	7.7	7.0	7.3	9.5	9.0	8.1	8.5	**95.5**

Source: World Bank (2011a); cumulated growth own calculation based on World Bank (2011a).

While the progress of the Central Asian countries concerning further economic reforms has been lackluster since the end of the 1990s, their economic performance improved drastically. As Tables 18 and 19 show, the economic development of Central Asia after the turn of the millennium differed drastically from the 1990s. All five republics recovered from recession and showed, with minor exceptions, positive growth rates in both total GDP and GDP per capita throughout the decade.

By both measures, sparsely-populated Turkmenistan, which is among the countries with the largest reserves of natural gas in the world (Pomfret, 2010a, p. 455), was clearly the best performer (see Tables 18 and 19). This was mainly due to rapidly soaring oil and gas prices, which had been stagnating for most of the 1990s (Pomfret, 2010a, p. 454–455). There seems to be no evidence at all that improved economic policies, a more effective administration or similar factors have had a decisive influence on this development. Compared to the previous decade, the EBRD transition indicators for Turkmenistan even worsened in the field of large-scale privatization (see Table 17). As Pomfret (2010a, p. 454) states, the value of Turkmen GDP increased because of higher export prices, but the production of gas grew only very slowly while non-gas output stagnated. Furthermore, one has to keep in mind that the reliability of economic data for the five Central Asian republics is questionable, due to the political conditions in the region and the crucial importance of black markets. This is a general problem; nevertheless, there are important differences between the countries in the region. Turkmenistan is considered to have the least reliable data among all former Soviet republics (Pomfret, 2010b, p. 7). While the death of president Niyazov in 2006 sparked hopes of political and economic reforms, Pomfret (2010a) argues that the actual steps toward liberalization undertaken by the new president Berdymukhammedov "were largely cosmetic and serious economic reforms minimal" (p. 455).

Table 19: Real GDP per capita (PPP) growth of the Central Asian republics, 2001–2010 [%]

	2001	2002	2003	2004	2005	2006	2007	2008	2009	2010	Total 2001–2010
Kazakhstan	13.7	9.8	8.9	8.8	8.7	9.5	7.7	2.0	-0.4	4.4	**101.5**
Kyrgyzstan	4.5	-0.8	6.0	5.9	-1.2	2.1	7.7	7.5	2.0	-2.2	**35.8**
Tajikistan	9.0	7.9	9.0	9.3	9.1	5.2	5.4	6.1	6.1	2.0	**94.7**
Turkmenistan	18.7	14.1	15.4	15.5	11.4	9.9	10.3	9.0	4.7	6.7	**196.9**
Uzbekistan	2.9	2.7	3.0	6.5	5.8	6.0	7.9	7.2	6.3	7.0	**71.1**

Source: World Bank (2011a); cumulated growth own calculation based on World Bank (2011a).

Tajikistan is another country that has been comparatively successful by economic measures in the decade since 2000. In addition, it is among the Central

Asian countries that improved at least concerning some transition indicators over the last decade (see Table 17). Nevertheless, its achievements are limited. In the year 2000, Afghanistan was the only Asian country with a significantly lower GDP per capita in purchasing power parity (Pomfret, 2010b, p. 7). Furthermore, Tajikistan is the poorest of all transition countries (Spechler, 2008a, p. 37). After the civil war, Tajikistan's approach toward transition has been comparatively liberal. However, Pomfret (2010b, p. 11) argues that the implementation of policies has been poor overall. According to Spechler (2008, p. 37–39), Tajikistan's large-scale industry remains unreformed and uncompetitive: the well-being of its citizens relies to a large degree on remittances from Tajiks working abroad (mainly in Russia) and attempts to attract foreign investment have been largely unsuccessful.

Even though there had been predictions that economic liberalization would finally pay off for the rapid reformers (Pomfret, 2010a, p. 454; 2010b, p. 11), Kyrgyzstan showed the worst economic performance of all Central Asian countries in the last decade. An important reason for this development was political turmoil. While president Akayev had always been the most liberal among the Central Asian political leaders, he increasingly resorted to ruling and permitted the enrichment of relatives and friends (Pomfret, 2010b, p. 17). Perceptions that he had a regional bias in terms of favoring the north of the country over the south lead to his resignation in the so-called Tulip Revolution in 2005 (Pomfret, 2010b, p. 17). His successor, Kurmanbek Bakiyev, had to resign in April 2011 in the face of severe riots between the ethnic groups of Kyrgyz and Uzbeks in the south of Kyrgyzstan (Economist, 2011a; 2011b).

Keeping in mind the three most important characteristics of a developmental state—a strong commitment to economic development, an economic policy approach that involves crucial state intervention, and a capable, effective state apparatus—it is apparent that none of the three smaller Central Asian countries resembled such a state in the past two decades. According to Pomfret (2010a, pp. 457-458), Tajikistan shows characteristics of a failed state. This evaluation is largely based on the 1990s, when the country decayed into chaos. However, even after 1997, the central government had to share the control over Tajik territory with local warlords and the implementation of policies has been poor (Pomfret, 2010b, p. 11). This is a sharp contrast to any characterization of a developmental state.

Kyrgyzstan represents a slightly different case, because the apparent commitment to economic reforms that the government showed in the 1990s might lead to inferences that the political leadership had a genuine commitment to economic growth. However, embracing the recommendations of economically liberal international organizations represents an obvious divergence from the path of development pursued by countries such as Japan or South Korea. It is impossible to know how the Kyrgyz economy would have developed with a different strategy. Indeed, the country's high dependence on foreign aid and its weak bargaining position toward donors make it debatable whether the political decision makers actually had the possibility to consider a markedly different transition strategy. The development of Kyrgyzstan in the last years, with two regime changes in the face of popular uprisings and inter-ethnic tensions, is no reason for optimism that the country will be able to effectively implement a coherent and successful economic strategy in the near future.

Turkmenistan is different from both Tajikistan and Kyrgyzstan in that it achieved unusually high rates of economic growth and political stability over the last few years. However, the characteristics of its political regime seem to prohibit any comparison with the East Asian developmental states. While several countries in East Asia also had authoritarian regimes during periods of fast economic growth, the isolation of Turkmenistan and the opacity of economic and political conditions in the country make it exceptional by international standards.

This shifts the focus to the two most populous countries and by far most important economies in the region: Kazakhstan and Uzbekistan. As was described in the preceding section, Uzbekistan was, for most observers, the surprise of the 1990s, because it experienced an unusually small recession after the dissolution of the Soviet Union and became the best performer among the Central Asian economies despite Western criticism of its gradual transition strategy. However, Uzbekistan did not manage to achieve a similarly successful development in the last decade. As Tables 18 and 19 show, it was the worst performer of the region in terms of GDP per capita growth, with the exception of politically unstable Kyrgyzstan. Instead, it seems that Kazakhstan has become the region's most important political and economic power.

Figure 11 compares the total GDP of Kazakhstan and Uzbekistan over the last two decades. As can be seen, the Uzbek GDP has been smaller than the Kazakh in all years since both countries became independent, in spite of the smaller population of Kazakhstan (see also Figure 10). This was obviously due to a higher GDP per capita and interrelated with human capital. However, the gap seemed to disappear in the early 1990s: while Kazakh GDP declined sharply due to the transition recession and the heavy emigration of skilled German and Russian minorities, Uzbekistan's GDP remained almost at the same level. As Figure 11, as well as Tables 18 and 19, shows, this convergence seems to have ended in the late 1990s. Since then, Kazakhstan consistently achieved higher economic growth rates than its southern neighbor. This represented a challenge to Uzbekistan, whose government had pretentions toward regional leadership before

(Cummings, 2002, p. 17; Pomfret, 2010a, p. 455)—a position that Kazakhstan now attempts to assume (Schmitz, 2009, p. 15).

Figure 11: GDP of Kazakhstan and Uzbekistan, 1990–2010 [constant 2000 US$]

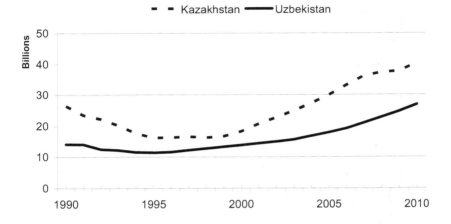

Source: World Bank (2011a).

Obviously there are several exogenous factors that explain the successful economic development of Kazakhstan after the turn of the millennium. Not only did oil prices increase drastically, there was also a surge in production from Kazakh oil fields due to new discoveries. Moreover, new pipelines independent from Russia were opened, which improved Kazakhstan's bargaining position. Thus, Kazakhstan benefitted in a variety of ways from the oil boom (Pomfret, 2010a, p. 454–456). Uzbekistan is roughly self-sufficient on oil and natural gas, which means that the direct effects of the oil boom on the economy were essentially neutral (Pomfret, 2010a, p. 455).

While these exogenous factors are of extraordinary importance, one also has to notice the continuing differences in economic policy and transition strategy between Kazakhstan and Uzbekistan. Uzbekistan, which has been more closed toward foreign trade and influence than Kazakhstan since the beginning of transition, has become even more isolationist and inward looking in some aspects. Foreign exchange controls were implemented in 1996 in the face of declining cotton prices. While these were officially removed in 2003, Pomfret (2010b, p. 14) argues that practical limitations on access to foreign currencies remain and lead to the misallocation of resources and the protection of domestic producers. The United States and international organizations, such as the EBRD, revoked their limited financial assistance to the country in 2004 due to human rights violations and a lack of economic reforms (Economist, 2004). In 2005, the United States was in turn asked to vacate their military air base in Uzbekistan, which had been the heart of US operations in Afghanistan (Economist, 2005; Gleason 2006).

Kazakhstan has also shifted its transition strategy to some degree. Due to the rapid reforms that the Kazakh government undertook in the early 1990s, the country is still much more liberal and market-oriented than its southern neighbor. Spechler (2008) summarizes:

> Privatization has proceeded farther in Kazakhstan than nearly any other Central Asian country, with two-thirds of all firms already in the private sector by 2006 according to the EBRD. Prices are almost completely market based. Banking and other financial institutions are much better established than elsewhere in the region. (p. 33)

However, he notes that Kazakhstan is still an example of *state-led capitalism,* because state-owned companies continue to be dominant in strategic industries and account for a significant share in gross investment (Spechler, 2008a, pp. 33). Pomfret (2010a, p. 457) argues that the management of Kazakhstan's economy and the institutions governing it have improved in the 2000s. When the world financial crisis broke out in 2007–2008, the Kazakh government reacted by increasing its involvement in the economy. A national wealth fund was founded in 2008 with the objective of directing investment into infrastructure and industrial diversification (Scharff, 2010, p. 2).

This combination of state involvement, good economic performance, and comparatively good economic management might suggest that, in contrast to the 1990s, it is now Kazakhstan, and not Uzbekistan, which shows more resemblance to the East Asian developmental states. In any case, both the development path and the importance of these two economies seem to suggest the need for the analysis of their institutions in more detail in the following section.

7.3 Diverging transition strategies of Kazakhstan and Uzbekistan: the importance of constraints and ideologies

7.3.1 Kazakhstan's path from rapid reformer to state-led capitalism

7.3.1.1 Political conditions

Since the last years of Soviet rule, one person has dominated Kazakhstan's politics: President Nursultan Abishuly Nazarbayev. Assuming the top-office in the Kazakh SSR in 1989, Nazarbayev reluctantly lead the country into independence two years later (Heinrich, 2010, p. 27, Olcott, 1992, p. 111). While the political conditions in Kazakhstan were comparatively pluralistic and elections competitive in the first years after independence, the regime has become more authoritarian over time (Cummings, 2002, p. 7; Pomfret, 2006, p. 40).

The increasing authoritarianism in Kazakhstan has been frequently criticized by international organizations (OSCE, 2011) and Western observers (Cummings, 2002; Davé, 2009). However, the lack of a true democracy does not necessarily represent an obstacle for economic development, as several successful East Asian economies show. Indeed, scholars also note some aspects of Nazarbayev's regime that could be beneficial from an economist's standpoint. Davé (2009) notes that, while on the one hand disbursing resources to his kinship and friends, Nazarbayev "also allowed much economic freedom to the country's budding entrepreneurs and offered rapid career mobility to the growing class of skilled professionals, technocrats, and top bureaucrats" (p. 248). Cummings (2002, p. 21) argues that pragmatism has been more important than ideology in Kazakh politics. While Perlman and Gleason (2005) assert that the Kazakh elites may use "administrative reforms as a way to channel resources to themselves," they maintain that these elites have realized "that the best way to maximize the resources subject to corruption is to be in control of a growing economy and to create surplus through government efficiency" (p. 101). To a notable degree, these three statements could also be used to describe the characteristics of several East Asian developmental states.

From the perspective introduced in the present study's sections on East Asia, the key issue in the context of political is the participation of different societal actors in decision-making. Specifically, participatory mechanisms in economic policy making are of utmost importance from the perspective of the developmental state concept. As has been mentioned, Kazakhstan did indeed show some participatory mechanisms that were in line with the Western model of democracy in early 1990s. According to Cummings (2002, p. 7), Kazakhstan had a comparatively outspoken media in the initial years of independence. The first constitution adopted in 1993 established a semi-presidential republic in Kazakhstan (Heinrich, 2010, p. 27). However, this relatively liberal period ended shortly afterward. While president Nazarbayev exercised informal power over the parliament and constitutional court almost from the beginning (Cummings, 2002, p. 7), revisions of the constitution in 1995 and 1998 strengthened the power of the President at the expense of the parliament (Heinrich, 2010, p. 27–29). In 2007, an amendment was passed that allows Nursultan Nazarbayev to run for president an unlimited number of times, but limits future presidents to two terms (Heinrich, 2010, p. 28). Furthermore, the media was brought under tightening state control beginning in 1997 (Cummings, 2002, p. 8). Cummings (2002) asserts that "by 2002 executive dominance had supplanted the attempts at pluralism in the early years of independence" (p. 9). According to Davé (2009), Kazakhstan's political system is best characterized as "a hybrid of Soviet-era institutions and practices overlaid with some formal and cosmetic elements of Western democratic systems and models of governance" (p. 252).

It is apparent from these accounts that participatory mechanisms that are commonly associated with Western democracy are hardly present. Over the last two decades, Nursultan Nazarbayev has achieved the adoption of formal institutions that concentrate political power in his hands to an unusual degree. Nevertheless, this does clearly not mean that he is able to maximize his personal utility without facing constraints. One important constraint that shaped political choices and institutional development to a significant degree has already been mentioned in the preceding sections: the ethnic heterogeneity of Kazakhstan, in particular the presence of a Russian majority in the northern regions. In this context, one might also add the inner structure of the Kazakh society, which is formed by kin-based clans, or hordes, that continue to be of great importance (Schatz, 2004). According to Cummings (2002, p. 14), the issue of Kazakh-Russian multi-ethnicity dominated politics until around 1995 when the Russian emigration and the higher Kazakh birthrates made the dominance of the Kazakh ethnicity apparent. Since then, this issue has been overshadowed by concerns of intra-Kazakh balance between the three different traditional hordes (Cummings, 2002, p. 14).

An interrelated constraint to the decision-making freedom of the President arises from the international context. Because of the difficulties to establish the legitimacy of the new Kazakh government over the Russian population in the north, foreign policy has been used as a legitimating tool by President Nazarbayev (Cummings, 2002, p. 17). While cooperating closely with Russia, he tries to balance Russian influence by maintaining comparatively close relations with Western countries and the People's Republic of China. Kazakhstan is a member of several international organizations such as the Organization for Security and Co-operation in Europe (OSCE) and the Shanghai Cooperation Organization (SCO), which brings together the Central Asian countries, Russia, and China. There is evidence that Nazarbayev considers these memberships to be a crucial component of his foreign policy. Through the membership in the OSCE—which was presided by Kazakhstan in 2010 (Interfax, 2010)—Western countries do seem to have a certain influence on the regime. When Nazarbayev recently decided to cancel the presidential elections in 2012 and 2017 in order to stay in power until 2020, it was Western criticism that caused him to revise his decision and to call for early elections in 2011 (Neef, 2011).

While the position of the president himself seems to be virtually uncontested in present-day Kazakhstan, important intra-elite cleavages and limited political competition exist at lower levels. Even though the parliament and politics in general are dominated by the Nur Otan party, headed by Nursultan Nazarbayev, several opposition parties exist and are a viable political force within certain constraints (Bowyer, 2008, p. 5; Heinrich, 2010, pp. 32–34). Perlman and Gleason (2005, p. 108) argue that the debate and contestation over policy alternatives in Kazakhstan is more open than in all other Central Asian countries. According to Bowyer (2008), a genuine debate and discussion even takes place in the lower house of parliament, despite the affiliation of all its members with the Nur Otan party. However, the cleavages within the parliament are mostly along regional, and not ideological, lines (Bowyer, 2008, p. 5).

7.3.1.2 Government-business relations

In his speech on the *Strategy 2030,* Nursultan Nazarbayev stated that one of the basic principles of Kazakhstan's economic policy should be "limited interference of the state with the economy combined with an active role thereof" (Nazarbayev, 1997). Nazarbayev (1997) adds on this by stating:

In the economy the state must play a substantial though limited part in creating legitimate limits of the market in which the private sector is offered a leading part. We mean finalizing formation of the legal basis that would provide for registering ownership rights, on shaping up competitive markets and reliable means of antimonopoly regulation, on maintaining fiscal and monetary policy, on developing a network of social protection, on providing for the development of requisite infrastructure, education, health care, and on pursuing effective environmental policy. If, for the time being, the markets are weak and underdeveloped, if the market space is encumbered with fragments of the administrative system, the state must interfere having in view development of the market and clearing of the space. (Nazarbayev, 1997, Section. 3, para. 3)

Thus, in spite of stressing state-activism, the role that Nazarbayev supposedly envisioned for the Kazakh state in the economy is largely in line with the recommendations of international organizations and most Western economists. While referring to several of the most successful East Asian economies as reference models, the key lesson Nazarbayev draws from their experience seems to be macroeconomic stability. As it says in the *Strategy 2030*:

> To become the first ever Asian Snow Leopard, we must deem, as a priority, utilization of the best international experience in the field of macroeconomic indices-low inflation, low budget deficit, steady national currency, high rate of savings. Such formula proved effective for Japan, Korea, Indonesia, Taiwan and Chile. Hopefully, it would prove as effective for Kazakhstan. So far we have never faced the alternative: inflation or economic growth. We must never forget that our finite goal is economic growth, and macrostabilization is but a means of gaining this objective. (Nazarbayev, 1997, Section 3, para. 11)

This is close to the conclusions that the World Bank (1993) study drew from the East Asian miracle, which had been published only four years before Nazarbayev's speech. In general, Nazarbayev seems to embrace the model of a liberal market economy, open to foreign investment and trade, in the *Strategy 2030*. He quotes economists, such as Adam Smith and Ludwig Erhard, to support his arguments. Obviously, this does not necessarily mean that he had a genuine commitment to liberal economic policy. Nevertheless, it is true that Kazakhstan belonged to the formerly communist countries that quickly implemented consequent liberal reforms and abolished most forms of public control over the economy from a formal point of view (Libman, 2010, p. 53–54). In addition, the unusually high levels of foreign direct investment in Kazakhstan seemed to be evidence of such a commitment. Nevertheless, the Kazakh state never retreated to a purely regulatory role. Furthermore, the *Strategy 2030* was announced in 1997, and the conditions have changed notably since then. The main changes concerning the role of the Kazakh state in the economy have taken place in the area of the state-business nexus, which is of utmost importance for the implementation of any economic strategy. These changes concern not only the mechanisms that the state uses to interact with foreign and domestic private companies, but also, and most strikingly, the level of influence that the state exercises. As in other areas, the development of Kazakhstan shows some parallels with Russia in this respect.

In the first decade after independence, the Kazakh state established a regime with two different forms of government-business relations (Libman, 2010, p. 54). This refers, on the one hand, to the state's relationship with domestic business groups, which had close informal ties to the president and his family, and, on the other hand, to foreign investors, primarily in the mining and energy sector, who enjoyed important privileges (Libman, 2010, p. 54). It is not easy to determine the relative bargaining power of the state vis-à-vis these groups. Apparently, the Kazakh state decreased its formal role in the economy to a remarkable degree during the 1990s. While this is an essential component of the transition process from a command economy toward a market economy, the loss of control of the central government of Kazakhstan seems to have gone further in some aspects than in other formerly communist countries. According to Schmitz (2009, pp. 12–13), regional elites gained significant influence on the economy and administration at the expense of the central government in the 1990s. The competition between regional and central authorities apparently led to uncertain and in-transparent conditions for foreign investment because of bureaucratic arbitrariness (Schmitz, 2009, p. 13). At the same time, foreign investors were able to attain control over the Kazakhstan's most attractive assets in the mining and energy sector and achieved a stronger position than in other formerly communist countries such as Russia (Libman, 2010, p. 54). Pomfret (2010a, p. 457) argues that these investors were only under weak state control in the 1990s. The state's relationship with domestic companies was quite different from that with foreign companies, because the state remained in a more powerful position. Similar to Russia, the quick privatization of the state's assets led to the emergence of large private business groups. However, Kazakh private business continued to depend more on governmental support and their personal ties to the President than their Russian counterparts (Libman, 2010, p. 54).

As has already been noted in the preceding section, the political conditions in Kazakhstan changed since 2000 in that power was concentrated more in the center, and specifically in the hands of President Nazarbayev. At the same time, the government has initiated a re-nationalization process in the economy (Libman, 2010, p. 54–55). Most importantly, the Kazakh government has been attempting to regain the control over strategic industries related to the extraction of raw materials, a policy that has been referred to as economic nationalism (Schmitz, 2009, p. 8–9). According to Libman (2010), these changes mean that "the very core of one of the government-business relations models was redefined" (p. 55). While the Kazakh government has also increased its control over domestic businesses, this shift was less pronounced since it had always been in a comparatively strong position toward them (Libman, 2010, p. 55). Nevertheless, it is apparent that the central government has become stronger in the bargaining process with other economic interest groups.

Some of the most important mechanisms and organizations at the intersection of state and business in Kazakhstan are the *Foreign Investor's Council*

(FIC), the association *Atameken*, and the national wealth fund *Samruk-Kazyna*. The *FIC* was formed in 1998 as an advisory body to promote the dialogue between the government and foreign investors. It is chaired by President Nazarbayev (FIC, 2011) and has two major objectives: submitting economic policy recommendations of the foreign investors to the government and analyzing policy issues at the instruction of the President (FIC, 2011). While the FIC serves as a communication channel between the government and foreign companies, *Atameken* has the same function between the government and the domestic private sector. Atameken is an association of more than 1000 enterprises from different sectors that serves as an important communication channel between the government and private companies and may facilitate some participation of business in economic decision-making. Recent press releases seem to be evidence of the importance of this organization. Timur Kulibayev, who has been chairman of Atameken since 2010, was also appointed head of Samruk-Kazyna in April 2011 (Interfax, 2011a). He is President Nazarbayev's son-in-law and considered to be on the short list of potential successors (Interfax, 2011a). Thus, the president's family is profoundly involved in the management of this influential fund. Furthermore, there have been several reports arguing that a political party might evolve from the organization of Atameken (Interfax, 2011b; Maratov, 2011; Ostapenko, 2011). While this party would be loyal to the President, it would also compete with Nur Otan for influence and may give a voice to private companies, specifically to small and medium businesses, in the political arena (Maratov, 2011).

Both the FIC and Atameken are mechanisms that have the aim of facilitating the communication between government and business. While this may also lead to the exertion of influence by the government—or, in some cases, by the businesses—these organizations are not means of direct government involvement in the economy. The national wealth fund Samruk-Kazyna represents a different case. It was formed in 2008 through merging the state holding Samruk with the development fund Kazyna (Scharff, 2010, p. 2) and has been one of the most important instruments that the state has used to exercise its influence in the economy in recent years. The holding Samruk had already been founded two years earlier as a tool to manage and coordinate major state-controlled companies in the areas of natural resources and infrastructure (Libman, 2010, p. 55; Schmitz, 2009, p. 14). At the recommendations of McKinsey, it was modeled after the funds of Singapore (Temasek Holdings) and Malaysia (Khazanah Nasional) (Schmitz, 2009, p. 14; see also Sections 5.4 and 5.5.2.1). While Samruk originally had the official objective to further the privatization of the state-controlled businesses, the state has actually increased its control throughout the economy in the wake of the financial crisis of 2007–2008 (Scharff, 2010, p. 13).

The increased involvement of the state in economic affairs is also mirrored in the president's statements. While he embraced an overall liberal approach to economic policy in his *Strategy 2030*, his rhetoric seems to have changed in important aspects since. At the beginning of his annual address to the people of Kazakhstan in the year 2008, he stated: "We should continue our strategic focus on Kazakhstan's industrialization, on our joining the community of the world's 50 most competitive nations and on forming a select group of 30 corporate leaders to advise on these goals" (Nazarbayev, 2008). Furthermore, he argued in favor of a new tax code to promote the diversification and modernization of the Kazakh economy (Nazarbayev, 2008). Both statements seem to hint toward a more activist role of the government, and particularly the focus on diversification and modernization through government-induced incentives is similar to the economic policies pursued in the East Asian developmental states. However, important questions remain. First of all, it is unclear whether the commitment of the Kazakh government, specifically of President Nazarbayev to economic development, industrialization, and diversification is genuine. Even if this is the case, it remains to be seen whether the Kazakh state apparatus actually has the capabilities to implement effective measures to promote this development.

7.3.1.3 The public administration

In contrast to Japan or Korea, Kazakhstan did not look back to a long history of well-organized and effective public service. Statehood essentially came with the Russian colonization to the previously nomadic people of the Kazakh steppe. The informal institutions that govern the attitudes of Kazakh bureaucrats have been shaped both by the Soviet legacy and by cultural values predating Russian influence in the region. According to Libman (2008), these cultural values may have contributed to evaluations that saw the Soviet administration in Asia as more corrupt than its counterpart in the European part of the Soviet Union. The Soviet legacy itself had probably both positive and negative aspects. There is no doubt that the Soviet public service was both inefficient and subject to remarkable corruption. Nevertheless, the Soviet state apparatus was more effective than the administration of many developing countries in the sense that it was firmly in control of the country's territory, able to exercise power, to implement decisions taken at the center and to regulate social life. Furthermore, "the Soviet administration featured typical bureaucratic elements such as formal rules, hierarchy of offices and recruitment of personnel according to meritocratic principles" (Schiek & Hensell, forthcoming 2012, para. 7).

Despite some positive aspects of the Soviet legacy, Kazakhstan did not face particularly good circumstances in terms of bureaucratic quality when it became independent. Kazakhstan inherited a civil service regime that the World Bank (1997) categorized as an *open system* from the Soviet Union. This means that:

> Civil servants are employed by individual units under contractual arrangements similar to those applicable in the rest of the economy. Rules may be provided to regulate the activities, but not the specific employment situation, of civil servants, which is governed by regular labor legislation. This was the civil service system of the USSR; it is still in place in a number of former socialist countries, including Kazakstan [*sic!*]. (World Bank, 1997, p. 29.)

Even though meritocratic elements in the recruitment and promotion process of bureaucrats existed, Emrich-Bakenova (2009) argues that "technical qualifications were less important for career advancement than political and ideological considerations" (Emrich-Bakenova, 2009, p. 718). Thus, the Soviet civil service was far from the meritocratic bureaucracy that is generally considered a characteristic of the East Asian developmental states. The World Bank (1997) considered switching from an *open system* to a *statutory system* a key priority of civil service reform in Kazakhstan. In a statutory system, specific rules for *all* civil servants are defined by the state. These rules would ensure the "equal access of citizens to the civil service based on their talents, and promotion based on merit" (World Bank, 1997, pp. 25–26).

Kazakhstan became the clear front-runner for civil service reform in Central Asia after a Presidential Decree in 1995. As Emrich-Bakenova (2009) stated, this decree was a great step forward because it promoted formal institutions based on merit and professionalism against the political-ideological norms of the old Soviet bureaucracy (p. 718). The reform process continued in 1997, when improvements of the bureaucratic recruitment and promotion were named a key priority of the *Strategy 2030*. New legislation to ensure a meritocracy was adopted and an agency to oversee the implementation of rules and regulations was established in 1998 (Emrich-Bakenova, 2009, pp. 724–725). The new Civil Service Law of 1999 for the first time distinguished between political and administrative civil service positions and specified qualification requirements for the latter (Emrich-Bakenova, 2009, pp. 725).

The government has undertaken steps toward a reform of the bureaucracy. The significant improvements in the Kazakh civil service are also acknowledged by a more recent analysis of the World Bank (2005). It is argued (World Bank, 2005) that:

> The Kazakh civil service system remains one o f the most advanced among Central and East European and CIS states, and is built on a strong institutional foundation, The focus on stabilization and institutional development, which has dominated the process over the last four years was the correct one, and the result is a strong basis for further development of the civil service. (p. 51)

However, the advancements of the civil service reforms in Kazakhstan have also been cast into doubt. The most recent country study of the Bertelsmann Foundation on Kazakhstan argues that the attempts to completely overhaul the organization of the bureaucracy were partly characterized by unclear implementation that resulted in job duplication. Furthermore, the study asserts that bureaucratic recruitment is still dominated by political loyalty (Bertelsmann Foundation, 2009a, p. 18). Similarly, Emrich-Bakenova (2009) cites a variety of studies which showed that formal rules are often bypassed. In particular, this refers to the rules for recruitment, performance evaluation, and promotion (Emrich-Bakenova, 2009, pp. 727–728). Furthermore, the issue of politization continues to be an important problem, particularly at higher positions within the hierarchy (Emrich-Bakenova, 2009, pp. 734–736 and 738–739).

According to Emrich-Bakenova (2009, pp. 731–732), the general competitive recruitment process is also bypassed for graduates of the *Bolashak Program*, a scholarship program that the government set up in 1993. Through the Bolashak Program, students from Kazakhstan get the possibility to study at prestigious Western and East Asian universities under the condition that they come back to work in Kazakhstan for at least five years (Abazov, 2006, p. 6). Official sources state that the selection process for this program is highly competitive (Center for International Programs, 2011); however, there have also been charges of corruption against the selection committee (Emrich-Bakenova, 2009, 731–732).

Despite the described shortcomings, it is apparent that the Kazakh government has implemented market reforms effectively (Bertelsmann Foundation, 2009a, p. 17), that there was progress in the field of corruption (Bertelsmann Foundation, 2009a, p. 18), and that there are "pockets of elites that continue to be extremely well trained" in the public administration (Bertelsmann Foundation, 2009a, p. 8). However, research on the Kazakh bureaucracy has been very limited overall, and it is difficult to gain a thorough insight on its internal structures. Thus, it is not easy to weigh the positive and negative aspects of the civil service in Kazakhstan. Measuring bureaucratic quality is always a difficult task and no evaluation can claim to be reflective of all relevant aspects and be entirely objective. A set of indicators that captures some of the most important factors that are important in this context are the Worldwide Governance Indicators. These are meta-indicators calculated on the basis of other evaluations by the World Bank. For the purposes of the present study, the indicator for *government effectiveness* is most important. This indicator represents an attempt to measure "perceptions of the quality of public services, the quality of the civil service and the degree of its independence from political pressures, the quality of policy formulation and implementation, and the credibility of the government's commitment to such policies" (World Bank, 2011).

As Figure 12 shows, Kazakhstan's government effectiveness, as measured by the Worldwide Governance Indicators, was a very low level in 1996 when they were first compiled. Only slightly less than 10% of the countries taken into account ranked lower according to the World Bank's evaluation. Judging from the development of this indicator, the civil service reforms undertaken by the Kazakh government have had a notable positive effect. With the exception of a setback in 2002, Kazakhstan has consistently improved its government effectiveness since 1996, even though it still ranks below 50% of the analyzed countries.

Figure 12:   Government effectiveness in Kazakhstan as measured by World Governance Indicators

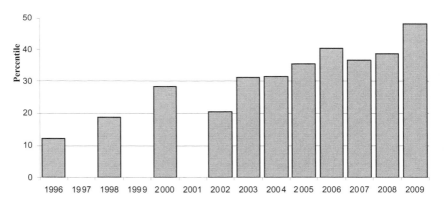

Source: World Bank (2011b).
Notes: "Percentile" refers to the percentage of countries that rank lower than Kazakhstan in a given year. The Worldwide Governance indicators were not compiled for years before 1996 and only on a two-year basis between 1996 and 2002

There are many questions that remain to be answered if the analysis of the Bertelsmann Foundation is correct and there are some agencies with a high bureaucratic quality and effectiveness within an overall weak public service; it has to be analyzed where these "pockets of elites" are. As Section 5.3.1.3 notes, the Korean bureaucracy in the early years of the developmental state under Park has been characterized as bifurcated (Cheng et al. 1998, p. 104; Kang, 1995, p. 575). This means that economic agencies were overall effective and governed by meritocratic processes whereas domestic service ministries were characterized by clientelistic appointments and inefficiency. Hence, the continued presence of non-meritocratic informal rules in the Kazakh public service may not necessarily impede the emergence of a developmental state.

Furthermore, it was noted in the sections on East Asia that not all East Asian developmental states achieved a meritocracy through transparent and competitive examination processes. An example is Taiwan, where precisely the recruits of the most important agencies of the economic bureaucracy were able to bypass the general civil service examinations (see Section 5.3.1.3). Thus, the fact that the regular recruitment process is sometimes bypassed in Kazakhstan is not sufficient to conclude that a meritocracy is absent. Specifically, the exemption of *Bolashak* graduates from the general recruitment process may also have positive effects. It has already been noted that the Kazakh leadership has been quite open to foreign influence since independence. The fact that the government actively promotes a civil service career for persons who have studied in advanced Western and East Asian economies may be interpreted as evidence for a credible commitment to reform.

7.3.2 Uzbekistan: gradualism or stagnation?

7.3.2.1 Political conditions

Similar to Kazakhstan, but in contrast to all other Central Asian countries, Uzbekistan has been ruled by a single person since its independence: President Islam Abdug'aniyevich Karimov. As Nursultan Nazarbayev in Kazakhstan, Karimov was secretary of the Communist Party of the Uzbek SSR before he became president of an independent country. In sharp contrast to Nazarbayev, who lobbied the other Central Asian leaders to sign a new Union treaty in 1991, Karimov was the first politician in the region to lead his country toward more economic and political independence from Russia and the other former Soviet republics (Olcott, 1992, p. 111).

While the political conditions in Kazakhstan were initially liberal in some aspects and became more authoritarian over the next two decades, there is no similar development in Uzbekistan: virtually since its beginnings, the regime of Karimov has been highly authoritarian. While some secular and Islamic opposition groups emerged after 1989, they were quickly suppressed by the Uzbek security services in the first years of independence (Pannier, 2011, p. 606). According to the Freedom House indicators, both countries have consistently belonged to the category of countries that are "not free" from 1992 to today. However, the evaluation of both political rights and civil liberties was even worse for Uzbekistan than for Kazakhstan in every single year (Freedom House, 2011). While Kazakhstan closely followed the transition approach of its northern neighbor in the 1990s, Karimov took a much more independent stance. Already in 1992, he criticized the economic policies pursued by the other former Soviet republics in a publication titled *Uzbekistan: Its Own Road to Independence* (Hiro, 2009, p. 148–149). The economic policy approach that Uzbekistan pursued in the following years was indeed different from that of Russia or Kazakhstan. In his first years as the leading political figure of Uzbekistan, Karimov apparently first embraced a Turkish model of development before switching toward a Chinese model of development without specifying whether "Chinese" referred to the People's Republic or to Taiwan (Olcott, 1992, p. 127). According to Spechler (2004), Karimov then opted for "a development model independent of outsiders and loosely modeled after Korea and other Asian states" (p. 73). Later, the Uzbek leadership stressed the singularity of Uzbekistan by consistently referring to the "Uzbek model" (see Gulyamov,[35] 2011, p. 374; furthermore Pomfret, 2000, p. 734).

It is an interesting question whether the even more authoritarian stance of Karimov when compared to Nazarbayev and the more independent approach toward economic transition has been the result of differing constraints or of differing ideologies. According to the model illustrated in Figure 2 (see Section 2.2.2), the path of institutional change is determined by the pre-existing formal and informal institutional environment, the bargaining process between different organizations trying to promote their interest, exogenous factors (in particular the geopolitical environment), and the ideologies of economic actors as shaped by their mental models of the world. In the cases of Kazakhstan and Uzbekistan, it seems apparent that the ideologies of critical actors—Nazarbayev, Karimov, and a small number of other individuals—may have had an extraordinary influence on institutional development. Another important question would be whether the more authoritarian stance of Karimov, when compared to Kazakhstan or Kyrgyzstan, and the Uzbek transition strategy that was briefly described in Section 7.2 were dependent on each other.

According to Olcott (1992, p. 111), the decision to take a more independent stance toward Russia in the early 1990s was based on both personal ambition of President Karimov and the fact that Russia was not willing to pay higher, market-based prices for Uzbek cotton. It might also be the case that Karimov simply

---

35   Ravshan Gulyamov was Minister of Economy of Uzbekistan from October 2010 to August 2011 and is now Minister of Foreign Economic Relations, Investments and Trade.

felt less constrained in his decisions than Nazarbayev. In several ways, Uzbekistan faced more favorable conditions for independent statehood in the early 1990s. Uzbekistan had been subject to much less *Russification* than its northern neighbor in terms of both immigration and cultural influence (Clem, 1992, p. 28–33). It does not have a common border with Russia. While some minorities, especially Tajiks and Russians, are present in Uzbekistan, the titular nationality has a clear majority on the national territory: according to the 1996 census, Russians and Tajiks each amount to around 5% of the population while Uzbeks make up around 70% (CIA, 2011).[36] While significant emigration of Russians took place after independence,[37] this issue was far less important for Uzbekistan than for Kazakhstan, due to the much smaller share of the Russian population. Furthermore, the sedentary history of Uzbeks with longer traditions of statehood could be seen as an advantage for the emergence of a new, independent country.

In this way, Karimov may have seen less necessity to follow either the transition strategy of Russia or the policies recommended by international organizations. However, he faced two other important and interrelated constraints that have decisively shaped his policies since independence: on the one hand, the common border of Uzbekistan with Afghanistan and Tajikistan and, on the other hand, the threat of political Islam. In contrast to Kazakhstan, Islamist groups have been by far the most important opposition groups in both Uzbekistan and Tajikistan (Malashenko, 2005, p. 6). In Tajikistan, political Islam was an important factor in the civil war of the 1990s (Hiro, 2009, p. 335–344) and Afghanistan, after several years of civil war, came under the control of the Taliban shortly after the independence of Uzbekistan.

During the formation of an independent Uzbek state, several opposition groups emerged. An important issue was the emergence of Uzbek nationalism, which led to severe inter-ethnic tensions and bloodshed between the titular nationality and several minorities in 1989 (Hiro, 2009, pp. 135–136). Stopping these conflicts was one of Karimov's first objectives after being appointed party secretary by Gorbachev, and one of the immediate measures was a ban on public meetings and slowing the democratic process (Hiro, 2009, p. 137). At the same time, Islamic opposition groups emerged, which at least partly maintained close relationships with the Taliban in Afghanistan (Fredholm, 2003, pp. 2–4). Karimov incorporated nationalist and religious feelings in a moderate way in his policies, while beginning to suppress both secular and Islamist opposition

---

36   While official census figures put the Tajik population at around 5%, Tajiks themselves claim that is much higher and amounts to 25–30% (Foltz, 1996, p. 213).

37   According to Hiro (2009, p. 36), Russians formed 11% of the population of the Uzbek SSR in 1989.

groups (Hiro, 2009, pp. 138–153; Stevens, 2007, p. 53). As mentioned in Section 7.2.1, Spechler (2000b) has characterized Uzbekistan's transition strategy by the phrase "stability at all cost" (p. 295). While he was referring first and foremost to the economic policy approach pursued by Karimov, this statement is true for the political sphere as well. This also refers to the international context. Martin and Dina Spechler argue in a joint paper (2010):

> The chief objective of Uzbekistan's foreign policy since the country's independence in 1991 has been to preserve internal stability for its super-presidential, authoritarian regime. Preventing unwelcome interventions or pressures from outside actors has been instrumental to this goal, as has been recognized for some time. (p. 159)

As Nazarbayev, Karimov has attempted to balance the relationships of Uzbekistan with foreign powers in a way that does not make it too dependent on one partner. However, the international relations of Uzbekistan with other countries have been, in all cases, much more distant than those of Kazakhstan. The Bertelsmann Foundation characterized the foreign policy of Karimov as unpredictable for the international community (Bertelsmann Foundation, 2009b, p. 21). While Uzbekistan is member of several international organizations, such as the OSCE, IMF, or the SCO, this has not necessarily affected domestic and economic policies. The IMF withdrew its permanent representative without replacement in 2001 as a result of Uzbekistan's violation of its obligations as a member of the Fund (Spechler, 2003, p. 54). In particular in the first years of independence, Karimov embraced close relations to Western countries, especially to the United States, to show his intention to break ties with Russia (Pannier, 2009). His stance as an adversary of the rise political Islam may have helped him to maintain comparatively good relations with Western democracies (Pomfret, 2000, p. 740), despite the authoritarian nature of his regime. This was particularly true after the terror attacks in 2001, when the Taliban regime became the center of international attention (Gleason, 2006, p. 50). However, Karimov turned to Russia and China after Western criticism of his repressive measures toward uprisings in Andijan in 2005. Most offices of Western media and NGOs were closed, and the US forces stationed in Uzbekistan were asked to leave within six months. The relationship with the West warmed again to some degree after 2008 (Pannier, 2009; see also Gleason, 2006).

The political conditions in both the domestic and the international sphere have certainly shaped the Uzbek economic policies of the last two decades in a variety of ways. Karimov's aim to stay in tight control of political affairs would have been hardly compatible with a thorough economic liberalization based on free private enterprise. In contrast to Nazarbayev, he saw no reason to follow the Russian transition strategy too closely because Uzbekistan did not face the threat of a large Russian minority striving for the independence of territories adjacent to Russia. The fact that the Uzbek government referred to a several foreign countries as possible reference models could be interpreted as evidence for a relatively large decision-making freedom in economic policy making. Yet, all the mentioned approaches have a strong role of the state relative to the private sector in common, which would be in principle consistent with the political conditions in Uzbekistan.

While the exogenous conditions and the power struggle between different groups in the first years of independence seem to have had a crucial influence on the political and economic transition of Uzbekistan—and consequently on its institutional environment—one might also argue that ideologies, in particular the ideology of Islam Karimov, was important. As a Soviet-trained economist, he was much less inclined than Nazarbayev to embrace foreign advice and a complete makeover of the economy in a shock therapy from the beginning (Blackmon, 2005, p. 397). As Pomfret (2000) notes, the government kept tight control over the most important Uzbek exports, namely cotton and gold, instead of privatizing rents as in Russia and Kazakhstan. The resulting revenues were used to maintain the education and health care system to a higher degree than in other former Soviet republics (Pomfret, 2000, p. 739–740).

The good economic performance of Uzbekistan in the 1990s has led to a challenging situation for Western observers and economists, who criticized the political conditions, but simultaneously had to explain the economic success of a country that rejected commonly accepted policy recommendations. The less successful economic development in the second decade of independence, particularly when compared to Kazakhstan, alleviated this ostensible conflict. Perlman and Gleason (2005) note several positive aspects of Nazarbayev's regime in Kazakhstan (see Section 7.3.1.1). In contrast, their evaluation of Uzbekistan is much more negative. They argue that the Uzbek transition strategy has been "'piratical' wherein macro economic and administrative reforms are purely subterfuge and reform aims to direct both internal and external resources to the ruling elite no matter what the effect on the economy or government efficiency" (Perlman and Gleason, 2005, p. 101).

If this analysis reflects reality, Uzbekistan should be characterized as a predatory state. However, some doubts remain. Uzbekistan continues to spend a relatively high share of public revenues on education and the health care system (Spechler, 2008a, p. 41). Furthermore, the fact that Uzbekistan had the best economic performance of all formerly Soviet republics during the 1990s should not be forgotten. At the end of that decade, Pomfret (2000) noted that the Uzbek government did not invest in grandiose, representative projects such as the new Kazakh capital, Astana, or the new presidential palace of Turkmenistan. A nouveau riche class did not emerge to the same degree as in other former Soviet republics (Pomfret, 2000, p. 745). In 2003, Pomfret even argued that "government intervention, apart from the controls on cotton and wheat, tends to follow a version of the Asian developmental state model" (p. 22), even though he does not provide more details on the similarities between East Asia and Uzbekistan. Perlman and Gleason's statement above is from 2005—in the light of the notable continuity of political conditions, it would be surprising if Uzbekistan had become an outright predatory state so quickly. A more detailed analysis of the way the Uzbek state interacts with the economy is needed in order to get a better picture of its characteristics and will be provided in the following section.

7.3.2.2 Government-business relations

As has been noted in the previous sections, both the Uzbek leadership and outside observers have made references to other economies, in particular the successful East Asian economies, when describing the Uzbek approach to economic transition. However, it is subject to serious doubt whether significant similarities really exist. Even though Pomfret (2003) also made favorable comparisons between Uzbekistan and East Asia, he had argued earlier (2000):

> In the early 1990s the new government frequently invoked the Chinese model or the South Korean model as its blueprint for gradual reform leading to rapid economic growth. In fact, policies bore little relation to China's strategy of agrarian reform plus opening of the economy followed by a hands-off approach to new enterprises, and even less resemblance to Korea's market economy. (p. 734)

It is certainly true that Uzbekistan's economic policy has been far from a hands-off approach. The lack of resemblance to South Korea is less evident. As became clear in Section 5.3, South Korea underwent profound institutional changes from the beginning of its economic catch-up in the 1960s up to today. There is hardly any doubt that South Korea was a market economy by most standards in 2000, when the statement above was published. However, the significant amount of control over the private sector that the South Korean government had exercised in the early decades of fast economic growth make such a characterization more ambiguous.

After the first years of independence, the Uzbek government under Karimov stopped comparing its economic strategy to East Asian, Turkish, or other approaches. Instead, the singularity of the *Uzbek model* of economic development was continuously stressed. This model was first outlined in President Karimov's book "Uzbekistan: It's Own Way of Renovation and Progress" (1992) and rests on five core principles. Karimov (2010) summarizes these principles in a recent speech as follows:

(1) De-ideologization of the state system and priority of economy over politics.

(2) In the transition period from a planned and distributive system to the market system the state must take on the role of a principal reformer.

(3) To ensure the rule of law, i.e. the law is equal for everyone.

(4) Step-by-step and gradual implementation of reforms. We say: "Don't destroy the old house, until you build a new one."

(5) Implementation of a strong social policy during the transition period from one system to another.

In several aspects, these principles do appear to have been inspired by the experience of other countries. The first principle of de-ideologization of the state system is reminding of Chalmers Johnson's characterization of the Soviet system as *plan-ideological* and of the developmental state as *plan-rational* (Johnson, 1982, p. 18; see also Section 4.1). However, it may also be interpreted as a rejection of Western recommendations based on a positive, functional interaction between democracy and economic growth. "Priority of the economy over politics" refers to the priority of economic performance over democratic reforms. This prioritization reminds of one common definition of a developmental state, namely that it "establishes as its principle of legitimacy its ability to promote and sustain (...) steady high rates of economic growth and structural change in the productive system" (Castells 1992, p. 56; see Section 4.1. for the full quote). The same is true for principle two, which stresses the pivotal role of the state in the economy. While principle three is generally uncontroversial in the discourse on economic development, principle four is reminding of the gradual transition strategy of the People's Republic of China. Principle five is essentially a pledge that the state's policies will protect its citizens from the social hardships taking place in other transition countries.

The key issue is of course to which degree and in which way these principles have been followed in practice. The existing publications on the Uzbek economy can give some insights on this issue. Nevertheless, the limited scope of research—which is at least partly due to the difficult political conditions and the general intransparency in the country—inherently leaves some questions open.

The most striking characteristic of the role of the state in the Uzbek economy is its continued and profound involvement in it. The hierarchical structure of the Soviet economy was basically maintained in Uzbekistan. Libman (2010, p. 56) summarizes:

> Although the beginning of the 1990s witnesses a rapid small-scale privatization (. . .) the government still maintained control over the largest enterprises and the most attractive assets (. . . .) Moreover, in 1996 Uzbekistan introduced severe exchange controls restricting private economic activity across the borders, thus even going

back in terms of economic liberalization (cf. Pomfret 2006). Government holds direct or indirect stakes in almost all medium and large enterprises, which operate within the framework of numerous public holding companies, which often have de jure or at least de facto veto power in the corporate decisions. (. . . .) Uzbekistan has also extremely low acceptance of privatization among population even among other post-Soviet countries with their (. . .) legitimacy problems for property rights, especially those of large business (Капелюшников 2008). (Libman, 2010, p. 56; source as given there)

Similarly, Reppegather and Troschke (2006) argue that the de facto state-controlled sector is so prominent in Uzbekistan that truly private companies only have a subordinate or complementing role. Continuously since independence, the Uzbek government has not considered private business to be the engine of economic growth (Reppegather & Troschke, pp. 41–41).

While the independence of the domestic private sector has also decreased in Kazakhstan over the last decade, there is another crucial difference that should be noted: the much lower importance of foreign direct investment for Uzbekistan (Spechler, 2000b, pp. 298–299). Of course, foreign investment in Kazakhstan was mostly limited to the natural resource and energy industry, strategic sectors that remained mostly under direct state control in Uzbekistan. Indeed, Reppegather and Troschke (2006, p. 42) argue that the Uzbek government has considered virtually all sectors in the economy as strategic, because it is deeply involved in agriculture (particularly cotton), manufacturing industries, trade, the financial sector, and other areas. Even though there had been some industrialization in Uzbekistan, it was less industrialized than Kazakhstan when the Soviet Union dissolved and agriculture has continued to contribute very substantially to the Uzbek GDP (Reppegather & Troschke, 2006, pp. 30–31). Foreign investors play an important role in some non-critical sectors; examples include tourism and retailing of important consumer goods such as soft drinks and cigarettes (Libman, 2010, p. 56; Spechler, 2000b, p. 299). However, there are some exceptions from this rule: the South Korean companies Samsung and Daewoo carried out major investments in the production of electrical equipment and vehicle assembly, respectively (Spechler, 2000b, p. 299). As it seems, these investments were markedly influenced by the Uzbek government, which preferred the South Korean investors over their competitors from Western countries (Spechler, 2000b, p. 295). Furthermore, the government implemented an activist industrial policy. The current minister of the economy, Gulnara Saidova, stipulated at a conference in June 2010 that nine "high tech industries" have been established in Uzbekistan as a consequence these policies (Saidova, 2010, p. 10). [38]

As a consequence of the dominant role of the Uzbek state in the economy, the institutions and organizations governing the state-business nexus take a different form than in economies with a stronger private sector. Even in de jure private companies with a state-ownership significantly below 50%, state-appointed representatives seem to interfere with operations to a notable degree (Reppegather & Troschke, 2006, pp. 43–44). However, it is unclear which institutions and incentives these representatives face and what objectives are pursued through this profound involvement. As Libman (2010, p. 56) claims, the most influential businessmen in Uzbekistan do actually not have formal claims on assets (since these continue to be state-owned), but control specific sectors of the economy through close ties with the President. Reppegather and Troschke (2006) argue that government authorities do not control the companies too tightly in their day-to-day business, which is largely left to the respective managers. However, the state has the ability to impose decisions on the companies if it is deemed appropriate (Reppegather & Troschke, 2006, p. 44).

Due to the lack of a substantial private sector in Uzbekistan, formal associations that could serve as viable communication channels between the government and private business have hardly been analyzed in scientific publications on the region. Among the most important associations at the junction between business and government is the *Chamber of Commerce and Industry of Uzbekistan*. By its own account, the mission of this organization includes the representation of the interests of the rights of Uzbek entrepreneurs, as well as the attraction of foreign investment in modern manufacturing industries (Chamber of Commerce and Industry of Uzbekistan, 2011). It is hard to determine to which degree these objectives are actually pursued. According to Reppegather and Troschke (2006, p. 42), industrial associations in Uzbekistan are dominated by the state and only serve as an instrument for the implementation of industrial policies. However, there is hardly any research on this issue, and there is neither any strong evidence for this claim nor for other opinions.

---

38 The specified industries are: the car industry, the petrochemical industry, electrical engineering, oil and gas machinery, railway machinery, the textile industry, the construction materials industry, pharmaceuticals, and furniture production (Saidova, 2010).

7.3.2.3 The public administration

The quality of the Uzbek public administration has been a controversial issue in the literature. Several accounts have noted crucial positive aspects of Soviet heritage for the Uzbek bureaucracy. According to Reppegather and Troschke (2006), Uzbekistan was one of the first transition countries that quickly developed an effective way of collecting taxes on businesses. This enabled the Uzbek state apparatus to achieve a comparatively sound basis of revenue in order to maintain public spending and investment at a high level in the initial years of transition (Reppegather & Troschke, pp. 36–37). However, the most prominent advocate of the view that the quality of Uzbekistan's public administration represented an advantage over the other Central Asian countries has been Pomfret (2003, p. 22; 2007, pp. 330–331; 2010a, pp. 451–452; 2010b, p.13). As he summarized in a recent paper (Pomfret, 2010b):

> Uzbekistan inherited the most effective administrators in the region. The physical infrastructure, including both the domestic transport network and the irrigation canals crucial to the cotton economy, was relatively well kept up. Corruption was, and still is, widespread in all of Central Asia, but available evidence suggested lower levels in Uzbekistan than in the other four countries, implying more effective central control and (admittedly by the low standards of the region) a relatively high sense of public service. (p. 13, footnotes omitted)

The statement that Uzbekistan inherited the administrators hints toward the Soviet legacy of the country and in particular to the position of Tashkent as the regional administrative capital of Soviet Central Asia (Pomfret, 2010a, p. 451). Nevertheless, Pomfret does not rule out that "good technocratic leadership" (2003, p. 22) also had a positive influence on the bureaucratic capacity of Uzbekistan.

However, it has also been noted that the Uzbek government has only undertaken minor reform efforts concerning the civil service when compared to Kazakhstan (Emrich-Bakenova, 2009, p. 718; Perlman & Gleason, 2007, pp. 1338–1339). This evaluation is also reflected in the World Governance indicator for *government effectiveness*. The development of this indicator for Uzbekistan is illustrated in Figure 13. As Kazakhstan, Uzbekistan improved its evaluation in this indicator notably since it had been first compiled in 1996. However, the development was clearly less impressive than in Kazakhstan. While both countries were at a similarly low level in 1996, Kazakhstan ranked only slightly below the average of countries in 2010. In sharp contrast, Uzbekistan only managed to improve from being evaluated better than roughly 10% of the evaluated countries to ranking above 25% of the countries. Moreover, the development in Uzbekistan has been less consistent than in Kazakhstan, which showed an almost continuous improvement concerning the government effectiveness indicators since 1996.

Figure 13: *Government effectiveness in Uzbekistan as measured by World Governance Indicators*

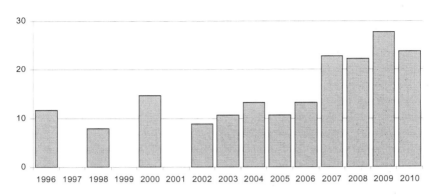

Source: World Bank (2011b).
Notes: "Percentile" refers to the percentage of countries that rank lower than Uzbekistan in a given year. The Worldwide Governance indicators were not compiled for years before 1996 and only on a two-year basis between 1996 and 2002.

The interesting question in this context is to find out whether the evaluation of the World Bank's indicator for government effectiveness actually represents a contradiction to the arguments of Pomfret (2003; 2007; 2010a; 2010b) and other scholars. First of all, it should be noted that the accounts that stress the positive aspects of the Uzbek public administration mostly focus on achievements in the early years of transition. In these years, the legacy of the Soviet Union had certainly a predominant influence on the quality of the bureaucracy in all newly independent Central Asian republics. It seems plausible that this legacy was more positive in Uzbekistan than in the neighboring countries, at least in terms of the capacity to implement decisions taken at the higher levels of the hierarchy. However, the Worldwide Governance indicators were compiled for the first time in 1996, several years after the Soviet Union dissolved. At this time, Kazakhstan and Uzbekistan were evaluated roughly equally. Kazakhstan then gained a remarkable advantage beginning in 1998 (see Figures 12 and 13). It may be the case that any advantage that Uzbekistan might have had in the early 1990s had basically disappeared until 1996, which would explain this evaluation. Furthermore, it is hardly subject to doubt that Kazakhstan has been more reformist since then, first and foremost in the years from 1996 to 2003. Spechler

(2008b, pp. 42–51) refers to this period as Uzbekistan's "lean years" and describes them as a retreat from the limited reforms that had been implemented earlier.

However, one should also keep in mind that no evaluation of bureaucratic capacity or government effectiveness is entirely objective. The Worldwide Governance indicators are meta-indicators based on a range of other evaluations, each representing a specific approach. These approaches are in several aspects reflective of certain underlying perspectives and assumptions of the organizations providing the evaluations. One example is the World Bank's inclusion of the public administration's independence from political pressures as one relevant attribute for the government effectiveness indicator. There are certainly good reasons for this. In some East Asian countries, such as Singapore, depoliticization has been considered a key characteristic of its effective public service. However, it was noted in this study's sections on East Asia and, in particular, for the case of Taiwan that a complete freedom of political influence was not given in all developmental states.

Similar issues also arise in other analyses of the Uzbek public administration. In a paper on recommendations for public administration reform in Uzbekistan, Ergashev et al. (2006) base their conclusions on the following arguments:

> First, *administrative management methods are incompatible with the efficient functioning of a market economy.* (. . . .) Second, *active government intervention in the economy and the use of administrative methods hamper market reforms and the development of private enterprise.* (pp. 32–33, italics original)

This line of argument shows that their assessment of the reform need for the Uzbek public administrations relies on economic schools of thought that generally perceive state intervention as harmful to development. Their analysis is thus not only focused on the public administration's effectiveness and efficiency, but also emphasizes its adequate role in the economy in a normative way. Other evaluations may implicitly be based on similar thinking. This is not an issue if liberal economic policies are indeed considered to be the best choice for developing and transition countries. However, it might be an issue if the most appropriate policies are not the ones recommended by the Washington-based international organizations, but the ones pursued by developmental states in the past.

Of course, this does not mean that criticism of the Uzbek bureaucracy from international organizations and liberal economists is generally not valid. Ergashev et al. (2006) argue that a variety of conditions exist that led to the need for reform, independently of the theoretical perspective the observer takes. In particular, they assert that narrow departmental and group interests play an increasing role within the bureaucracy. Furthermore, the public administration is subject to frequent reorganization while an integrated regulatory framework for operation of executive agencies is missing (Ergashev et al., 2006, p. 36).

Overall, it is hard to give a clear evaluation of the bureaucratic capacity in Uzbekistan. For Spechler (2008b), the quality of the bureaucracy seems to be the key impediment for a successful implementation of economic policies inspired by the East Asian developmental states. As he argues:

> Examples of the newly industrializing countries of southeast (*sic*) Asia are often cited in defense of state-guided development and export promotion, but those countries' success seemed to depend upon the existence of an honest and efficient bureaucracy ready to guide business into the proper channels with suitable rewards. (. . . .) Below the top echelons, by contrast to those in Singapore and Taiwan Uzbekistan's new civil service has been overworked and poorly paid, increasing both turnover and temptations to exploit one's position. Corruption and state capture prevent the kind of cooperation between business and government which allowed the "tigers" of southeast (*sic*) Asia to manage their export-led growth efficiently. (. . . .) Anecdotal and survey evidence of bribe-taking by government inspectors generally confirms the unsatisfactory reputation of Uzbekistan's bureaucracy. (Spechler, 2008b, p. 34, footnotes omitted)

These statements obviously suggest that the Uzbek public administration would not have the capacity to follow the example of the developmental states, even if the government headed by Karimov had a firm commitment to economic development as its key priority. In contrast, the most recent country study of the Bertelsmann Foundation (2009b) suggests that the government would have the capacity to concentrate the necessary resources for strategic reforms. The administration is highly centralized (Perlman & Gleason, 2007, pp. 1338–1339) and the Uzbek state enjoys a very strong position vis-à-vis all societal groups, which makes it unlikely that reform efforts would encounter significant opposition. From this perspective, it is the lack of commitment of the leadership and its focus on personal enrichment that has forestalled the implementation of reforms (Bertelsmann Foundation, 2009b, p. 19).

7.4 Conclusions: the Central Asian countries in comparative perspective

The preceding sections represented a brief summary of the economic literature on Central Asia with a focus on issues that are relevant for the present study. The key conclusion of these sections is that the available knowledge on the five Central Asian countries concerning these issues is quite limited. This is, on the one hand, due to the relatively intransparent conditions in all five republics, even though the level of transparency does differ to a significant degree. On the other hand, Central Asia is simply under-studied compared to other regions. This is particularly true in comparison to East Asia, whose economic rise has resulted in innumerable scholarly studies in economics and related fields. But it is also true compared to other regions such as Sub-Sahara Africa or Latin America, which have been within the focus of Western economists and observers for a longer time, probably as a result of colonial history and geographical proximity to Europe and Northern America.

The most important issue that has to be analyzed in more detail for the Central Asian countries in the context of the present study is the alignment of formal rules, official announcements, and de jure procedures with informal institutions, actual policies, and de facto practices. The existing literature deals with this issue to some degree, but it has clear limitations. In order to answer the research questions of the present study in a satisfactory manner, more knowledge about the reality of transition and reform processes in Central Asia is needed. As became clear in Section 7.2, the differences between the East Asian developmental states and the three smaller Central Asian countries are apparent. Therefore, Kyrgyzstan, Tajikistan, and Turkmenistan are not the main focus of the present study. In contrast, Kazakhstan and Uzbekistan seem to share at least some characteristics with the successful East Asian economies. Moreover, the presidents of both countries have made reference to East Asian countries in their speeches and announcements on the economic strategy of their governments. This is not surprising given the almost unprecedented achievements of the most successful developmental states in East Asia and the fact that all governments are commonly ready to express their commitment to economic development. However, it is clear that their factual commitment to this goal differs. It is inherently difficult to assess the commitment of a government or a political leader to economic growth by any possible means. Obviously, the economic performance of a country is influenced by manifold factors. Among these factors is the choice of the appropriate economic policies. Of course, even a government that is highly committed to economic development might choose policies that are inadequate.

In Kazakhstan, as well as in Uzbekistan, there have been some changes in economic policy over the last 20 years. However, these changes were arguably more profound in Kazakhstan, which shifted from a comparatively liberal approach to economic transition toward more state control. As a result, the similarities between Kazakhstan and the East Asian developmental states seem to have become more notable over the last decade. In the state-business nexus, several formal structures that remind of the East Asian state-led development approach are in place. Yet, it is hard to determine through the existing literature which functions these structures actually perform. Specifically, it is questionable whether the leading role that Samruk-Kazyna assumed in the Kazakh economy over the last years is developmental or whether it serves other, possibly predatory objectives. The same is true for intermediate organizations such as Atameken. Since there is hardly any research on this organization, it is hard to evaluate whether it is a functioning tool of participation in the state-business nexus or not.

In the case of Uzbekistan, the difficult and non-transparent conditions in the country have led to even less economic research on relevant aspects. The difference between formal rules and de facto practices seems to be even bigger than in Kazakhstan, which results in a limited validity of any research that does not have an empirical basis. In the 1990s, it seemed that the Uzbek government and its public administration had found a comparatively successful way of managing the economy through following a gradual approach to transition and maintaining investment in public goods at comparatively high levels. The increasing isolation of the country and the abandonment of some previously implemented reforms have cast severe doubt on this perspective. Nevertheless, it does not seem to be reasonable to characterize the Uzbek state as purely predatory. To get a better picture of the realities of economic development in Uzbekistan, one would have to analyze the informal institutions that shape the interaction of different administrative levels and economic actors.

The following section of the present study represents an attempt to shed some more light on these matters, through analyzing the information collected in more than 300 in-depth interviews with experts in both Kazakhstan and Uzbekistan.

8 Empirical study: insights on political and economic reform experiences in Central Asia

8.1 Objectives and design of the empirical study

As indicated at the end of the preceding section, the comparative lack of knowledge on Central Asia is an important obstacle for any conclusions on long-term economic processes in the region. It was already mentioned in the introduction that the issues and processes under study are inherently complex in nature. This is partly due to the large time frame that the analysis of the emergence of developmental states—or any other type of state—has to take into account. However, other reasons are much more important. States themselves are complex entities and their ties to society in general and the business sector in particular are manifold. Macroeconomic data does hardly tell anything about these relationships and is therefore only relevant as supplemental information for the analysis. Secondary data and indicators on issues such as government effectiveness, the rule of law, or corruption give a more detailed picture of the conditions for economic activity. Nevertheless, these indicators do not give much insight into the complexity of state-society interaction in Central Asia. In order to get a better understanding of the processes underlying the economic development of Kazakhstan and Uzbekistan over the last two decades, it is necessary to extend the publicly available knowledge. One way to do this is to learn from experts in the region through conducting interviews. While interview-based research is not widely used in economic research, it is common methodology in related fields such as sociology, political science and other social sciences.[39]

This section presents an interview-based empirical study carried out in Kazakhstan and Uzbekistan from September 2009 to March 2011. As a part of the research project *Emerging Market Economies in Central Asia,* a four-person team conducted more than 320 in-depth interviews. This project was funded by the VolkswagenStiftung and will result in several forthcoming publications aimed at exploring the institutional developments in Kazakhstan and Uzbekistan after the dissolution of the Soviet Union. Therefore, it has a broader research focus, which goes significantly beyond the developmental state concept analyzed here. Thus, the interviews were not exclusively carried out in order to

---

39   See Flick (2009, pp. 150-172), Gläser and Laudel (2009, pp. 11-22), and Hussy, Schreier, and Echterhof (2010, pp. 215-219) for an introduction to interview-based research.

serve as a basis for the present study. This has apparent results for the questions asked to interviewees and the information gathered.

As a first step of the research process, potential interviewees were divided into five focus groups on the basis of their professional background. These focus groups are:

(a) International organizations, academics and other experts with a general knowledge about the respective economy

(b) Public officials[40]

(c) State-owned companies

(d) Private domestic companies

(e) Foreign companies

The diverging professional backgrounds of the interviewees obviously resulted in different areas of expertise and different levels of knowledge on the relevant issues. For that reason, a different interview guide was developed for each group. The methodological literature on qualitative research generally distinguishes between different types of interviews according to their degree of standardization (see Gläser & Laudel, 2009, pp. 40–43; Hussy et al., 2010, p. 215). Overall, the interviews carried out for the purposes of the present study had a semi-standardized character. Questions in the interview guide had a predetermined wording and order, which was usually followed. However, the interviewer had the freedom to ask spontaneous follow-up questions or to change the order and wording of questions if deemed appropriate. In addition, interviewees were encouraged to share their knowledge about issues that were not anticipated in the predetermined interview guide but acknowledged as relevant for the research objectives of the study during the interview. When the interviewee indicated that he was not knowledgeable about certain issues or that he did not want to answer specific questions because of political sensitivity, the interviewers had the freedom to skip parts of the interview guide.

The methodological literature on interview-based research also distinguishes between different types of interviewees. A common distinction is between informants and respondents. According to Zelditch (1979), respondents are interviewed to get an understanding about issues and processes in which they are

---

40   The term public official was defined broadly within the project and includes all interviewees that are working within the state apparatus (excluding state-owned companies) or for the dominant political parties.

personally involved. Their personal experience, perspective and interpretation of specific issues and processes are the focus of the researcher's questions. In this way, respondents essentially provide information about themselves. In contrast, informants are interviewed because they are specialists in a relevant field and posses knowledge that is relevant to the researcher but not available through other sources. Informants are able and willing to provide presumably correct information about others. They are interviewed to obtain expert knowledge about events and processes that are not directly observable, not to compare diverging personal attitudes or perceptions (Zelditch, 1979, pp. 122–123; see also Gläser & Laudel, 2009, p. 12; Hopf, 1979, p. 35).

Within the scope of the project *Emerging Market Economies in Central Asia*, the interviews with the first focus group, namely international organizations, academics and other experts, clearly had the characteristics of informant interviews. As a result of their background, which was mainly in international cooperation and academia, the persons within this group had profound knowledge about the economic and political developments in the respective countries. They were able to provide sound information on the conditions for economic activity, the institutional environment and specific issues, such as the mechanisms and objectives of state intervention. In contrast, interviewees within the other four focus groups fall somewhere in between respondents and informants. On the one hand, they were asked questions about their personal experience concerning certain issues. As an example, interviewees from foreign companies were asked about their experience with agencies of the public administration in Kazakhstan and Uzbekistan. On the other hand, the same interviewees were also asked about their general perspective on issues such as the rule of law in the respective countries. Similarly, public officials were both asked about the recruitment process they underwent to obtain their current positions and about topics not directly related to their personal experience, such as the role of the respective governments in the economy.

The selection of interviewees within the specified target groups and relevant organizations was another important issue. Generally speaking, it is beneficial for the researcher to talk to decision makers at the top of the hierarchy in both the public administration and other organizations, because these persons are critical actors for the path of development and commonly have a broader knowledge about relevant matters. However, there are exceptions from this rule. George and Bennett (2005) find that researchers at times talk only to interviewees who are too high in a hierarchy and were often not closely involved in the relevant events or decisions. In addition, they might not recall the events under study as detailed as lower-level officials who worked on the specific issue every day (George & Bennett, 2005, p. 103). In Central Asia, the additional problem arises that the political conditions in the region make it more difficult to get access to high-ranking interviewees within the bureaucracy and state-owned enterprises. This makes fieldwork in the region a difficult undertaking. Within the research project, researchers attempted to get a general understanding of the institutional developments in Central Asia by talking to individuals at different levels of the hierarchy and by conducting a comparatively large number of interviews.

While the interviewees touched upon manifold topics as a consequence of the broad research objectives of the project, three issues are of particular relevance for the purposes of the present study, namely to analyze Kazakhstan and Uzbekistan from the perspective of the developmental state concept. In broad terms, these issues are the general role of the state in the economy, the state-business nexus and the institutions governing the public administration. Within these broader areas, subjects such as sector-specific industrial policies, ways to exchange information between the government and the business sector and the recruitment procedures in the bureaucracy were addressed. The general aim was to consolidate a large number of subjective perceptions into a comprehensive picture of the Kazakh and Uzbek economies.

As a consequence of the narrower research focus, not all interviews conducted within the scope of the research project provided relevant information for the present study. The focus of the analysis in Section 8.3 is therefore on the interviews with focus groups (a) and (b), namely international organizations and other experts, as well as public officials. This amounts to 30 interviews with focus group (a) and 8 interviews with focus group (b) in Kazakhstan (Section 8.3.1). The analysis of Uzbekistan is mainly based on 27 interviews with focus group (a) and 14 interviews with focus group (b).[41] The interviews with the other focus groups were used explicitly in the analysis whenever relevant and generally used as background information.

---

41   See Appendix B for background information on interviewees from focus groups (a) and (b).

8.2 Methodology for the analysis of interviews

During the field research, all interviews were audio-recorded if the interviewee did not object.[42] Each interview was then transcribed from the recordings. In the cases where the interviewee did not agree to an audio-recording, a second interviewer took detailed notes, which were compiled to a transcript of the interview as promptly as possible. Since the interviews took on average of one hour, the result of the transcription process was a vast amount of text that had to be analyzed in a systematic and structured way for the purposes of the research project and the present study. The social sciences have developed several methodologies for the analysis of verbal data. As noted by Hussy et al. (2010, p. 238), all of these methods have in common that they have the objective of understanding the meaning of information within the data. However, they are important differences in their analytical approach.

Some methods are highly flexible and give the researcher much freedom of interpretation. One example for such a method is hermeneutics, which are widely applied in law, philosophy and related fields. While the methodological literature on hermeneutics provides certain instructions and a basic direction on how to get an understanding of verbal data, this method essentially relates to a relatively free interpretation of the text by the researcher (Hussy et al. 2010, pp. 239–240).

Methods that are applied in fields that are more closely related to economics are usually characterized by a more rule-based approach. Two common methods in these fields are *coding* and *qualitative content analysis.* One can conceive hermeneutics and qualitative content analysis as representing opposing sides of the methodological spectrum in terms of freedom of interpretation, with coding lying in between.

As Schreier (forthcoming 2012) notes, there are major similarities, but also some crucial differences, between coding and qualitative content analysis. The most important similarity is that the text is structured by dividing it into parts and assigning these to different categories, also referred to as codes.[43] This sys-

---

42 6.92% of interviewees in Kazakhstan and 11.6% of interviewees in Uzbekistan objected to having the interview recorded.
43 In the methodological literature, the terms category and code are often used interchangeably (see for example Kuckartz, 2010, p, 57). This can lead to confusion because both not only the method of coding but also method of qualitative content analysis requires the development of categories/codes. In the present study, the term category (and subcategory) is generally preferred. However, code is used when citing other sources that use this term.

tem of categories, the coding frame, is usually structured in a hierarchical way through developing several top-level categories with subcategories. However both the procedure to develop the coding frame and the type of categories that is developed differs (Schreier, forthcoming 2012, chapter 4).

Table 20: Differences between coding and qualitative content analysis (QCA)

Coding	QCA
Analytic: How do categories relate?	**Descriptive:** How do data relate?
Codes are mostly inductive, data-driven	Codes are part inductive, part deductive
Iterative procedure	Linear procedure if possible
Focus on trustworthiness and credibility - creating and applying codes are one step - focus of code definitions is on the conceptual level - codes are not mutually exclusive - no segmentation necessary	**Focus on consistency** - creating and applying codes are different steps - focus of code definitions is on how to recognise instances of the concept in the data - subcategories for the same top-level category are mutually exclusive - before coding, material must be divided into units of coding

Source: Schreier (forthcoming 2012, chapter 4).

The differences between coding and qualitative content analysis are summarized in Table 20. *Coding* has its origins in grounded theory and is therefore based on an overall inductive approach aimed at generating new theory. As a consequence, the system of categories is not developed on the basis of an existing theory but devised while reading the interview transcripts. The categories are therefore not concept-driven but data-driven. Furthermore, the coding frame is continuously revised as the researcher achieves a better understanding of the information in the text, resulting in an iterative procedure. As stated in Table 20, the coding frame for qualitative content analysis is developed in part inductively and in part deductively. It is possible to use only inductively developed categories in qualitative content analysis. However, it is also valid to begin the development of the coding frame deductively by defining broad top-level categories on the basis of concepts derived from a theoretical framework. Depending on the applied theory and the objectives of the researcher, the deductively developed structure will then be complemented by categories that are inductively devised from the text and capture relevant aspects which had not been foreseen through the applied framework. This means that the development the coding frame may be iterative to a certain degree, nevertheless it is commonly attempted to arrive at the final coding frame early in the research process (Schreier, forthcoming 2012, chapters 4).

According to Kuckartz (2010), several types of categories should be distinguished. Among the most important are *factual categories*, *thematic categories* and *evaluative categories*. Assigning text to factual categories means that the interviewee has stated a specific, objectively true reality at this point in the interview. In contrast, thematic categories only have the function of a signpost that shows the researcher where specific issues are discussed. Evaluative categories are used when the researcher wants to gain a structured overview of the personal opinions that interviewees have concerning certain issues. Using evaluative categories requires the researcher to have more profound background knowledge, because it is often possible to interpret a particular statement in different ways (Kuckartz, 2010, pp. 61–62). Furthermore, statements expressing someone's personal opinion may be too complex in nature to simply classify along clearly defined evaluative categories.

The different types of categories that are used are also a further important difference between coding and qualitative content analysis. In both methodologies, thematic categories are devised that structure the text along the discussed topics and issues. However, qualitative content analysis involves, in contrast to coding, the development of evaluative subcategories. These subcategories do not only indicate what the interviewee talks about but also specifies and summarizes the meaning of his statement (Hussy et al., 2010, p. 246; Schreier, forthcoming 2012, chapter 5). One might also conceive the categories at higher levels of the hierarchical coding frame as variables and the subcategories at the lowest level as values a specific variable might have. Consequently, subcategories in qualitative content analysis have to be mutually exclusive (see also Table 20). This is not the case in coding, since an interviewee can easily touch upon different issues in the same statement, which would have to be assigned to different thematic categories.

These different methodologies for the analysis of verbal data were described here in some detail because the methodology applied within the present study actually incorporates elements of both coding and qualitative content analysis. As common for qualitative content analysis, a combination of deductive and inductive methods was used to develop a coding scheme (see Appendix A for the coding scheme). By far the larger share of the categories was conceived deductively on the basis of the Northian New Institutional Economics. Due to the broad scope of the NIE, these categories refer to a wide variety of relevant aspects, for example the actors and organizations involved in the process of institutional change or the enforcement of institutions such as property rights. Several categories were specifically devised to capture relevant aspects of the developmental state concept. This refers in particular to the categories on the state-business nexus, institutions governing the public administration and industrial policies (see Appendix A). During the process of reading the transcripts, a small number of inductively derived categories and subcategories were added to account for shortcomings of the drafted coding frame.

While the hierarchical structure of categories was constructed in a way that is typical for qualitative content analysis, the process of interview analysis and the type of categories had more in common with coding. The primary objectives of the interviews conducted in Kazakhstan and Uzbekistan was to gain new insights on the institutional environment of these economies and on the mechanisms and processes that shape the path of institutional change. Therefore, informants were asked mostly broad, open questions. Consequently, the answers are rather complex, providing detailed descriptions of events, experiences and personal opinions. If it is attempted to capture the essence of such statements through evaluative coding, there is a high probability that crucial information is lost by omitting the larger context of the answer. Moreover, even explicitly evaluative statements are not easily classifiable into mutually exclusive subcategories. As a result of the nature of the conducted interviews, most information in the transcripts was only coded with thematic categories. Evaluative categories were only used whenever the type of question was adequate and the given answers were sufficiently concise and unambiguous.

Due to the large number of conducted interviews and the resulting amount of verbal data, the use of the software MAXQDA proved beneficial for the interview analysis. This was particularly important for the purpose of the present study, because it facilitated the extraction of relevant statements for the developmental state concept from the extensive array of verbal data that was gathered in the research project. On the following pages, the results of this process are described in detail.

In order to make the presentations of the results in the following section transparent, individual interviews are referred to explicitly within the text. However, the political conditions in Central Asia make confidentiality a crucial requirement for interview-based research. Therefore, a label was assigned to each interview based on the country the interview was conducted in, the focus group, and an individual number. For example, interview K(b)1 was an interview conducted with a public official (focus group (b)) in Kazakhstan. Following the information given, the interviews from which this information was obtained are referenced. In this way, it is easy to recognize in how many interviews a particular statement was made. Furthermore, reader can trace the perceptions of specific interviewees through following the individual labels.

8.3 Results of the analysis

8.3.1 Kazakhstan

8.3.1.1 The role of the state in the economy: economic policies and objectives

In order to get a basic understanding of the functioning of the Kazakh economy, informants from the focus groups (a) and (b) were asked to describe the role of the state in the Kazakh economy in broad terms at the beginning of each interview. There was a general consensus that the Kazakh state does play a large role the economy. A term that was used by several interviewees in this context was "significant" (K(a)5; K(a)6; K(a)19; K(a)22). Many answers were solely focused on stressing the importance of the state's involvement in comparison to the Western market economies (K(a)9; K(a)10; K(a)11; K(a)14; K(a)16; K(a)17; K(a)18; K(a)20; K(a)22). However, there were also several interviewees who provided a more detailed picture. One important issue in this context was the worldwide economic crisis beginning in the late 2000s, which affected Kazakhstan notably. Apart from the overall negative effects of the crisis on the relatively open economy, the importance of the Kazakh banking sector, which had been growing rapidly in the preceding years, aggravated the economic problems (K(a)3). As in many other countries, the role of the Kazakh state increased through anti-crisis measures (K(a)3; K(a)5; K(a)6; K(a)24). This was mainly evidenced by the drastic increase in state-ownership through the holding Samruk-Kazyna (K(a)3; K(a)6; K(a)28); furthermore, the previously liberalized financial sector was put back under state control (K(a)5; K(a)6).

While the impact of the crisis on the role of the state is apparent, it was argued by a Kazakh expert (K(a)5) that the government may only be using the crisis as an excuse to increase its control over the economy. It was already noted in section 7.3.1 that the central government has redefined its relationship with private business in the second decade of independence. From this perspective, the crisis may have accelerated and amplified a process of renewed state-control that had begun several years before. As interviewee K(a)5 asserted, it seems probable that the state will not retreat from its new role in the economy after the economic crisis has passed:

> Considering the current crisis the government intervention into the market institution is very strong. In the past, for example, the state was in the regulating position but today it interferes in all institutions. I think it owns the controlling shares in all the banks and other financial institutions. (. . . .) I think the role will remain. The gov-

ernment is using the crisis as an excuse to take up these sectors of economy. Because when it disregarded, these sectors were almost falling apart.

Nevertheless, there was widespread agreement that the private sector in Kazakhstan is still more important than in other Central Asian countries. This is most obvious in comparison with Turkmenistan (K(a)2) and Uzbekistan (K(a)4). It was also argued by an interviewee (K(a)1) that the government's role in Kazakhstan as measured by state ownership has remained markedly more limited than in Russia.

This is in some ways surprising because Kazakhstan's economic development has followed that of its northern neighbor quite closely over the last two decades. Some parallels were already noted in section 7.3.1, and the interviews confirmed the importance of the political and economic developments in Russia for Kazakhstan. The relationship with Russia was further strengthened through a customs union comprising Kazakhstan, Russia, and Belarus (K(a)24; K(a)29), which was founded in 2010. When the interviewees were asked whether a particular country has served as a reference model for the Kazakh approach to economic policy, Russia was mentioned several times as the main influence (K(a)7; K(a)21) or as one of many influences (K(a)5; K(a)25). However, it was not the most frequently named reference country. Many more interviewees noted that countries of the European Union served as a model in some fields (K(a)6; K(a)10; K(a)14; K(a)15; K(a)19; K(a)26; K(a)28). In most of these interviews, European countries were referred to as one of several influences. Some interviewees also stressed the importance of a European reference model for a specific area. This includes France as a reference model for the legal system and formal political institutions (K(a) 10). Nevertheless, the most frequently named foreign influences in the interviews were clearly the East Asian developmental states (K(a)1; K(a)5; K(a)8; K(a)9; K(a)15; K(a)16; K(a)19; K(a)24; K(a)28; K(b)5). The most frequently named East Asian countries were Singapore (mentioned by ten interviewees), South Korea (mentioned by six interviewees), and Malaysia (mentioned by five interviewees).[44]

In this context, it is particularly interesting how the changes in the Kazakh transition strategy after the first decade of independence (see section 7.3.1) relate to potential foreign reference models. A public official (K(b)5) commented on this issue as follows:

From the historical perspective, the first consultants came from the West because the first financial support came from the western financial institutions: the World Bank,

---

44   Note that many interviewees named several foreign countries as influences on Kazakhstan.

EBRD, IMF. They brought their western ideologies and western approach. (. . . .) However, in the following years when the Asian states started to recover from the crisis of 1998, they experienced rapid growth and everybody started looking at Taiwan, Singapore, South Korea, China, so the role of the Asian consultants became more important. At the moment the experiences of Taiwan and Singapore are studied very thoroughly. In general, ADB and the Islamic Bank intensified their presence here. This is the reason why we have such a mixture of everything today. We are located between the East and the West and therefore, it's rather hard to understand what kind of model there is.

This statement seems to indicate that the shift toward more state control corresponds to a reorientation toward the East Asian inspired model of economic development. K(b)5 also noted a tangible impact of international advisors on the formal institutional environment of Kazakhstan:

> The main groundwork was formed at the end of 90s and the beginning of 2000s which was based on Western models. At that time the important institutions were established and as public officials, the people were pro-western oriented in technocratic sense. After we had refused their consultancy help and had realized that we are independent of these consultants, it was more difficult for them to give their recommendations, while it became easier for us to reject them. [The East Asians] showed us a different perspective. I am not saying it is wrong; it's just different but equally successful. This is why it could justify itself in their conditions.

While the shift toward using the East Asian economies as reference models seems to have affected the mental models of persons working for the Kazakh state apparatus, it is less clear whether Kazakhstan's leadership has a commitment to economic development and industrial upgrading that is comparable to the developmental states. A fundamental disparity between Kazakhstan and the most successful developmental states in Northeast Asia is the differing endowment with natural resources. With its relatively small population of around 16 million, Kazakhstan ranks 11th in the world terms of proven oil reserves and 15th in terms of proven gas (CIA, 2011). Furthermore, Kazakhstan differs from Japan, South Korea, and Taiwan because of its ethnic diversity and relatively secure geopolitical environment. Hence, the political leadership of Kazakhstan has been facing constraints that differed notably from Northeast Asia. As was noted in Part II of the present study, it is commonly argued that a combination of external military threats and a lack of easily extractable revenue from natural resources committed the governments of developmental states to pursue economic growth. Under these conditions, an essential objective of policies targeted at industrial upgrading and diversification was to increase the state's military capabilities. Kazakhstan's leadership neither faces the evident need to increase military spending drastically, nor does it face resource constraints comparable to the

Northeast Asian developmental states at the initial stages of their economic catch-up.

There are more similarities between Kazakhstan and the developmental states in Southeast Asia. Similar to Singapore after its independence from Malaysia, Kazakhstan had to prove its viability as an independent state after the dissolution of the Soviet Union. As was noted in section 7.3.1, Kazakhstan's ethnic diversity was a major issue in this context. This is a further resemblance to Singapore, but also to Malaysia, Thailand, and Indonesia. In all four Southeast Asian countries, the balance between different ethnic groups, in terms of economic well being and political power, decisively shaped the approach to economic policy over long periods of time (see section 5.4 and 5.5). In addition, the three larger southern HPAEs are relatively well endowed with natural resources.[45]

As a consequence of diverging constraints, the Kazakh government has been facing a different set of feasible choices than the leadership of the resource-poor developmental states. The post-war governments in Japan, Taiwan, and South Korea did not dispose of revenues originating from the extraction of natural resources, but they benefitted from substantial US aid. From this perspective, the Kazakh government has more decision-making freedom, because its budget is largely independent of its diplomatic relationship with a specific foreign power.[46] Instead, government revenue and the whole Kazakh economy are highly dependent on the oil and gas sector. A key question concerning Kazakhstan's path of economic development is whether this dependence will continue indefinitely or whether a substantial diversification will take place. As Table 21 shows, the contribution of agriculture to the Kazakh GDP has decreased substantially over the last 15 years, while that of services has remained more or less stable. The contribution of industry has risen by more than ten percent since 1995. However, it has to be noted that Table 21 is based on the World Bank's definition of *industry*, which includes activities such as mining and gas that are or primary importance for the Kazakh economy. The contribution of *manufacturing industries* alone to the Kazakh GDP has not changed much and was a slightly lower in 2010 than in 1995.

---

45   Malaysia, Thailand, and Indonesia rank 27th, 52nd, and 28th in terms of proven oil reserves and 16th, 38th, and 14th in terms of proven gas reserves, which is much higher than the other HPAEs. However, all three countries have a much larger population than Kazakhstan; therefore, their reserves per capita are decisively lower.

46   Theoretically, Kazakhstan might face declining revenues if its foreign relations deteriorate to a degree that causes major trading partners to enact significant sanctions against it. However, this case seems highly unlikely from today's perspective.

Table 21: Distribution of value added in the Kazakh economy, 1995–2010 [as % of GDP]

	1995	2000	2005	2010
Agriculture	12.9	8.7	6.8	4.8
Services	55.7	50.8	53.1	52.8
Industry	31.4	40.5	40.1	42.4
Manufacturing industry	*15.3*	*17.7*	*12.8*	*13.1*
Non-manufacturing industry	*16.1*	*22.8*	*27.3*	*29.3*

Source: World Bank, 2011a for Agriculture, Services, overall Industry and manufacturing industry. Value for non-manufacturing industry calculated as difference between the values for industry and manufacturing industry.

The importance of diversification was also reflected in the interviews. However, there were differing perceptions on the government's role in diversification. In the East Asian developmental states, industrial policies played a vital role in achieving diversification and in particular industrial upgrading. Clearly, the Kazakh state has not been laissez-faire over the last years and also intervenes in the market. However, it is not entirely evident whether interventions in Kazakhstan really contributed to a diversification of the economy. When asked about industries supported through specific government policies, many interviews referred first and foremost to the agricultural sector (K(a)5; K(a)8; K(a)10; K(a)11; K(a)12; K(a)17; K(a)19; K(a)21; K(a)23; K(a)28; K(b)2; K(b)3), which is also commonly supported through subsidies and protectionist measures in Western market economies. Several informants also noted policies aimed at the promotion of industrial diversification and upgrading (K(a)1; K(a)2; K(a)3; K(a)4; K(a)6). The government also attempted to promote the commitment of investors to long-term projects (K(a)1; K(a)2; K(a)3; K(a)4; K(a)7; K(a)11; K(a)23). However, there was substantial doubt over the credibility and effectiveness of these efforts. According to a Kazakh political analyst (K(a)16), the government does announce its support for specific projects, but these policies are not thoroughly implemented because "there can be a one time subsidy and everybody forgets about it after that." As a German expert (K(a)4) asserted, diversification has been taking place for a long time only on paper. Even a public official (K(b)6) noted that the targeted interventions of the Kazakh state have not been substantial and suffered from the lack of an overall systematic approach.

It seems that the recent economic crisis has had a profound impact on the direction and credibility of the Kazakh economic policy. Several interviewees asserted that government support for long-term investment projects and industrial diversification were very limited until recently (K(a)3; K(a)4; K(a)13; K(b)5). According to K(a)4, the Kazakh decision makers had not been fully convinced of the necessity of diversification until the recent economic crisis and decline in oil prices. Similarly, K(a)3 noted that the government's efforts to promote long-term commitment of investors to specific projects were increased as a result of the crisis. In slight contrast, a Kazakh expert (K(a)1) argued that the focus on diversification had already begun some years before the crisis and was actually overshadowed by the anti-crisis measures. Nevertheless, he stated that the Kazakh leadership's commitment to diversification as embodied in its more recent policies is credible:

> On the peak of the last years in 2006/2007 there were attempts to promote the diversification of economy through some break-through sectors such as IT and solar energy. The Government set up several industrial parks (. . . .) They [the sectors, M.S.] also were granted numerous tax incentives from the state. (. . . .) The years of vast money are over. Now the government has to economize, so don't expect any direct subsidies to hold. But maybe with the help of tax incentives (. . . .) There is a new so-called program of industrial development for 2011 to 2015. And that program sounds actually (. . .) very sensible (. . .). It doesn't contain anything on those fantastic breakthrough sectors but it's mostly about adding value. Going up at the value-added chain, so going from oil to oil refineries and chemistry, going from export of raw metals to advanced metal. Going from export of grain to a diversified vertical integrated agricultural complex. But credible.

Tax-incentives have been the main tool that the Kazakh government employed to support private investment in specific industries and projects (K(a)1; K(a)3; K(a)13). However, one has to note that the government's or the elite family's direct involvement in the economy through the ownership of companies may be an even more important instrument for the implementation of its economic development strategy. The mechanisms of the government-business interaction will be analyzed in detail in the next section.

8.3.1.2 Functioning of the state-business nexus

A cooperative relationship between the state apparatus and businesses has been considered a constituent characteristic of developmental states by virtually all publications in the field. Nevertheless, the concrete form of the state-nexus has varied substantially in East Asia, even among the most commonly accepted examples of a developmental state. While the state relied on large private business groups for the implementation of its industrial policy in South Korea and Japan, the Taiwanese state-business nexus has been characterized by the cooperation of large, state-owned enterprises with small and medium sized private companies. In Singapore, foreign investors played a leading role and were wooed by a public administration that was responsive to their needs. Foreign investment was complemented through the activities of state-owned companies and holdings. In the other Southeast Asian developmental states, foreign investors played a similarly important role. However, the state-business nexus in Malaysia, Thailand, and, in particular, Indonesia was generally less institutionalized and less stable than in Singapore and the Northeast Asian developmental states. The attitude of the state toward the domestic private business sector, which was commonly dominated by the local Chinese minorities, and the use of state-owned companies for the implementation of an economic strategy have varied over time in these countries (see section 5.5).

As has already been noted, the relationship of the Kazakh state with private business has also changed notably over the two decades of independence. After a period of relatively quick privatization and openness to foreign exchange, the state increased its control over the economy significantly. Nevertheless, the private sector remains more important than in other Central Asian republics. This was also reflected when the interviewees from focus groups (a) and (b) were asked about the most important players in the Kazakh economy. Several experts and public officials gave general answers referring to the president or other specific persons and agencies within the government as the key players in the economy (K(a)2; K(a)17; K(a)26; K(a)27). Furthermore, interviewees commonly stressed the importance of all foreign and domestic companies involved in the extraction of natural resources (K(a)7; K(a)15; K(b)5; K(b)7). When referring to specific companies, both state-owned and private companies were named. The most frequently named enterprise was the Eurasian Natural Resource Company (ENRC)(K(a)1; K(a)3; K(a)5; K(a)15; K(a)25), which is a diversified private company nominally headquartered in London but mainly active in Kazakhstan. The state-owned oil and gas company KazMunayGaz was also commonly mentioned (K(a)1; K(a)4; K(a)5; K(a)13; K(a)19), followed by the private mining company Kazakhmys (K(a)1; K(a)3; K(a)26), which is also headquartered in London.

It appears that both private and state-owned companies play important roles in the Kazakh economy. However, this conclusion deserves more scrutiny. While both Kazakhmys and ENRC are *de jure* headquartered in the United Kingdom, neither of these companies should be considered a foreign company, because both their assets and their major shareholders are located in Kazakhstan. It is furthermore questionable whether they should be considered private businesses. The two largest shareholders of Kazakhmys are the businessman Vladimir Kim, with a share of 28%, and the government of Kazakhstan, with a share of 26% (Kazakhmys, 2011). The company Kazakhmys is in turn the largest shareholder of ENRC with 26% of the shares, followed by the three businessmen Alexander Mashkevitch, Alijan Ibragimov, and Patokh Chodiev, who each hold 14.59%. The Kazakh Ministry of Finance owns 11.65% of ENRC's shares (ENRC, 2011). Thus, the government maintains a decisive influence over these joint-stock companies and seems to cooperate closely with several Kazakh businessmen.

The crucial influence of the government becomes even more evident when it is taken into account that one organization was named far more often as a key player in the Kazakh economy than any company: the state-owned wealth fund Samruk-Kazyna (K(a)2; K(a)3; K(a)4; K(a)5; K(a)6; K(a)11; K(a)21; K(a)25; K(b)5). As asserted by a Kazakh expert (K(a)5), "Samruk-Kazyna is almost our second government." It was also argued in the interviews (K(a)3) that this fund plays the key role in directing revenues from the export of natural resources into other companies and industries, and is thus essential in implementing industrial policies. As K(a)3 summarized:

> Samruk-Kazyna influences up to 50% of the economy today, because they created this welfare fund and also created the so-called oil-fund, which keeps about half of all foreign currency reserves of the country and as a crisis response more than 10 billion Dollar. Out of this, forty-something has been used for the support of the economy. So the government is now co-owner of 23% of two major banks, Kaskommertsbank and Halyk. This is how the money gets in. Bank Turanalem is now 75% government-owned and the new plan of the government through Samruk-Kazyna is to invest also into industrial projects in industries like the chemical industry or consolidation of metals mining and here this brings the big question of role of government and role of private sector going forward in Kazakhstan.

Samruk-Kazyna also owns 100% of the shares of the previously mentioned state-owned oil and gas company KazMunayGaz (Samruk-Kazyna, 2011). Thus, the wealth fund has become the most important linkage between the government and the economy as a whole.

Therefore, it may be argued that the Kazakh state-business nexus consists of three different mechanisms. The most important mechanism over the last years has been state-ownership in companies through Samruk-Kazyna. Public enterprises play a crucial role in the economy. However, state ownership is not limited to majority shares. The fact that the government also maintains shared ownership with private businessmen in several large companies may be interpreted as evidence of close and cooperative ties to a number of individuals that play leading roles in the Kazakh economy. The border between private and government-directed companies is therefore blurry in Kazakhstan. This is reflected in Forbes Magazine's well-known list of the world's billionaires. Five Kazakhs are on this list for the year 2011, including Timur Kulibaev, the CEO of Samruk-Kazyna and son-in-law of president Nazarbayev, as well as his spouse, the president's second daughter Dinara Kulibaeva. In terms of wealth, they are only surpassed by Vladimir Kim, a member of the Korean minority in Kazakhstan and main shareholder of Kazakhmys, and Alijan Ibragimov, one of the main shareholders of ENRC (Forbes, 2011).

Apart from pure state-ownership through Samruk-Kazyna and close ties to a number of selected businessmen, the state-business nexus in Kazakhstan is also characterized by institutionalized mechanisms linking the general private business sector with state actors. It was noted in numerous interviews that regular meetings take place between representatives of the state and the business sector (K(a)1; K(a)2; K(a)3; K(a)4; K(a)8; K(a)11; K(a)12; K(a)13; K(a)14; K(a)15; K(a)16; K(a)17; K(a)21; K(a)24; K(a)27; K(b)2; K(b)4; K(b)8; K(d)5). This interaction was generally seen as positive and, in some cases, also involves high levels of the state hierarchy and key decision makers such as the president, the prime-minister and the most important ministers (K(a)1; K(a)2). As summarized by K(a)2:

> There are forums that the government conducts on a regular basis (. . .). The government is actually trying to keep contact with the businesses. (. . .) the Ministry of Industry and Trade can come or Deputy Minister can come to such meetings and they can even put him on a spot and ask questions directly to him, give examples, and they answer it. (. . . .) They are quite open.

A large variety of employer associations exist in Kazakhstan that assume a major role in the state-business interaction. For foreign investors, the FIC, which has been briefly described in section 7.3.1.2, was seen as a crucial organization. As K(a)1 stated "foreign investors have the ear of the president, there is a council of foreign investors, a quite active organization which meets the president several time per year. And those are the people who are rather free to voice their preferences." Similarly, K(a)12 also argued that foreign investors lobby effectively through the FIC, while a public official even claimed that the interests of foreign investors receive more attention from the government than those of local companies.

For domestic business, the previously mentioned association Atameken was frequently referred to in the interviews. The interviewees had different perspectives on this organization. Even though Atameken was described as a "very pro-government association" (K(a)28), it was acknowledged that it attempts to represent the interests of the private sector through improving laws and regulations and the overall business climate (K(a)1; K(a)4; K(a)14; K(b)6; K(d)5). However, interviewees also noticed shortcomings of this association and argued that its organizational structures are still insufficient (K(a)4; K(a)11). As K(a)11 argued:

> Atameken(. . . .) is just weak... it's not big enough(. . .). Atameken should have ten, at least ten times more employees (. . . .) They just do not have the people. The institutional infrastructure is much too weak. We can discuss about quality but quality is not enough.

Furthermore, it was argued that Atameken only represents the interests of large businesses (K(a)29). According to K(a)29, the Kazakh private sector is characterized by a decisive cleavage between companies: "Small business does not trust large business; large business does not considers the interests of small business; therefore, it is impossible to unite all the employers." Apart from Atameken itself, a notable number of smaller business associations with a more narrowly defined and often industry-specific membership exist in Kazakhstan. These smaller associations are often themselves members of Atameken (K(a)30) and it was argued in the interviews that they are gaining influence (K(b)3). K(a)19 described the structures of associations as follows:

> In Kazakhstan there are more than 120 sectoral associations. The largest ones are the Association of Machine-building Enterprises, the Association of Oil Companies, the Association of Light Industry, the Association of Farmers of Kazakhstan; they are all members of Atameken Association. (. . . .) There are effective associations, there are nominal associations that are there just to be in the list, you know; there are active associations which really work.

While the exchange of information between the private sector and the state apparatus is apparently quite well-institutionalized in Kazakhstan, there were nevertheless several interviewees that expressed doubts over the importance of formal mechanisms in the state-business nexus. On the one hand, this may be due to the varying effectiveness of business associations that was noted in the statement above. On the other hand, it is subject to doubt whether discussions at meetings between state and business really have a decisive influence on decisions taken within the state apparatus (K(a)2, K(a)3; K(a)6; K(a)8; K(a)20; K(a)28). As a consequence, it was argued that personal ties to the government are what matters most. This perspective was summarized by a foreign expert (K(a)3):

> The president likes advisory councils like the foreign investors council (. . .), which is a major gathering of really international top-shots. On a domestic scene it is similar; it goes through Atameken and through these business associations. However, who really—from the private sector—wants to have his things done, has to find his own people in the government or in the administration.

This rather unenthusiastic evaluation of the formal mechanisms constituting the Kazakh state-business nexus is complemented by the interviewee's assessment of the predictability of policy making in Kazakhstan. Experts from focus group (a) were asked to evaluate the predictability of policy making on a scale from one to five (on being the lowest and five the highest grade). While most interviewees did not give a clear evaluation, the answers of those who did included both the highest (K(a)7) and the lowest (K(a)5) possible evaluation. The arithmetic mean of evaluations on this question was slightly above three.[47]

This result does apparently not give much insight into the underlying issues, which may foster or impede the predictability of conditions for businesses in terms of economic policy. However, one may draw some general conclusions from the broader context provided by interviewees in their answers. One influential factor concerning this issue is clearly the personalized political system and decision-making process in Kazakhstan (K(a)3; K(a)5). This issue may explain the different evaluations to a notable degree. As K(a)7) argued, he considers the predictability of Kazakh policy making to be extremely high as long as president Nazarbayev is alive and in power, but might shift to a much lower evaluation whenever this changes. Other interviewees (K(a)2; K(a)26; K(a)28) had a similar perspective. However, there were also interviewees who had the opinion that the decisions of the president himself are not predictable (K(a)3; K(a)16; K(a)22). As K(a)3 argued:

> We do not know how he thinks. If we knew...again. We believe that is the problem, if this is so concentrated, then you can predict with much less probability, especially if that person gets older and the power struggle for the top job has definitively started. So, will there be more defensive maneuvers going forward? I would not say 1 I would say maybe 2, on your scale. Because it all depends on that one person

In spite of these concerns, most interviewees only referred to a limited number of issues when asked about sudden, unexpected shifts in the economic policy of Kazakhstan. The main unexpected changes that were noted by the interviewees were apparently related to the recent economic crisis (K(a)1; K(a)8; K(a)10; K(a)12; K(a)13; K(a)14; K(a)15; K(a)19; K(a)21). However, this crisis was unexpected among most economists and decision makers around the world, and the Kazakh anti-crisis measures were broadly similar to those implemented in other economies. There was also a substantial number of interviewees who argued that the economic policy approach of the Kazakh government is comparatively stable

---

47 Based on explicit evaluations from eight local and eight foreign interviewees. The foreign interviewees gave an average evaluation of 3.3, the locals were slightly more pessimistic with an average of 2.75.

overall (K(a)2; K(a)7; K(a)9; K(a)11; K(a)12; K(a)13; K(a)14; K(a)20; K(a)23). According to K(a)13, "the world economic crisis was not expected, but this government (. . .), they have a pretty consistent vision. They change their policies to adapt to the changing circumstances but they have a very consistent vision."

To summarize, the evaluation of the Kazakh state-business nexus is ambiguous from the perspective of the developmental state concept. In terms of institutions governing the exchange of information, there are structures in place that could foster the cooperation of the private sector and the state apparatus in the field of economic policy. Furthermore, the Kazakh government's role in the economy also shows similarities to the developmental states in other aspects. It was already noted in section 7.3.2.1 that the state-controlled wealth fund Samruk-Kazyna is modeled after similar organizations in Singapore and Malaysia. The interviews left no doubt that the importance of this fund has increased dramatically over the last years. Lastly, it seems that the Kazakh government maintains cooperative and, in some cases, personal ties to selected businessmen. Similar relationships were also present in several East Asian developmental states.

Nevertheless, crucial doubts remain. The focus on industrial upgrading and diversification has certainly been one of the most vital characteristics of the most successful developmental states. In Kazakhstan, these issues have apparently also been the subject of official announcements and presidential speeches. Nevertheless, judging from the interviews it seems that these announcements have been put into practice to a sufficient degree until quite recently. It remains to be seen whether the priorities of the key decision makers have really changed sufficiently to lead to more developmental economic policies. Moreover, it seems that the institutional structures at the intersection off state and business are not always efficient and yet have to be strengthened in order to perform the same functions as similar structures in East Asia.

8.3.1.3 Institutions of the public administration

While the last section dealt with the effectiveness of structures that link the state to the business sector, the state apparatus itself was only discussed to a limited degree. However, the functioning of the public administration and its overall quality are issues that are of essential importance for an assessment of Kazakhstan from the perspective of the developmental state concept. It was already described in section 7.3.1.3 that the Kazakh government has undertaken notable efforts to reform and improve the bureaucracy. In this section, it will be summarized which insights on the success of these reforms can be gained from the interviews carried out in Kazakhstan.

One important matter in this context is the ability of the government to implement its decisions, particularly concerning bureaucratic reforms and economic policies. The interviewees had remarkably diverging perspectives on the issue of implementation. As one might expect from a country governed by an increasingly authoritarian political regime, several informants stated that the hierarchical state apparatus strictly follows orders from the top (K(a)6; K(a)7; K(a)12; K(a)28). The following statement describes the perception of K(a)12 on the role of the president in this process:

> He just has to order. This is how it works: the President makes an order and after that the Government develops a special plan on implementation measures of the Presidents orders. Everything is done in a planned way; it may sound stupid but it will be implemented anyway.

The president as head of the central government has indeed a very strong position in the Kazakh political system. As numerous interviewees confirmed, regional politicians and governments are under strict control from the government in Astana. It was often argued that regional decision makers had only an extremely limited independence in their decision making (K(a)5; K(a)7; K(a)15; K(a)16; K(a)17; K(a)19; K(a)20; K(a)22 K(a)26; K(a)29). Nevertheless, there were also interviewees who asserted that regional decision makers have in practice much more power than it would appear at first sight (K(a)3; K(a)13; K(a)21; K(a)28). In some cases, they may achieve a higher degree of independence due to their personality or the economic strength of their regions (K(a)2; K(a)12). This could have positive consequences for economic development because it may foster the competition between different regions of Kazakhstan. However, it was also argued in the interviews that decision making power of regional politicians is a consequence of their power over implementation. As K(a)8 argued:

> The one thing is when the decisions are made at the level of the government; they make decisions. By the time it reaches the local government, they will carry out those decisions. They can do anything in words but in reality, they will not do anything and will try to justify this with numerous reasons so that you will not be able to pick on it because in reality nothing is done. However, they never refuse to follow orders.

This statement seems to indicate that the hierarchical structure of the Kazakh administration does not necessarily lead to an effective implementation of policies. Indeed, this does not only seem to be an issue in the command structure between the center and regions. It was a very common perspective in the interviews that the effectiveness of policy implementation in the public administration varies substantially and is often lacking altogether (K(a)3; K(a)4; K(a)5;

K(a)8; K(a)10; K(a)16; K(a)25; K(a)27). A Kazakh political analyst (K(a)8) summarized his view as follows:

> There are more words than real policies. Not more than 60 percent of what is being told transform into policy guidelines, concepts. What part of it can reach the legislation process is another issue because by the time it gets there it is either forgotten what it was initially intended for, or it gets so diluted that it doesn't reach the legislation stage. With regard to rule enforcement: mainly, the rules are enforced. We don't have large blocks of unenforced laws. With respect to the unenforced part there is one issue: besides its unevenness along different blocks of state authorities, the quality of bureaucratic apparatus is rather low.

Apart from a general shortcomings in terms of bureaucratic quality, a several interviews argued that cleavages between the decision makers at the top and the lower levels of the state apparatus are an important reason for the lack of implementation (K(a)3; K(a)4; K(a)5; K(a)27). According to a Kazakh expert (K(a)5), the competence of Kazakh public officials decreases drastically from higher to lower levels, which impedes the effectiveness of the highly hierarchical administrative structures:

> The President makes the Prime Minister responsible who will make ministers responsible, who will make people under responsible. The problem is that as you go down, the level of competence in the state administration declines very quickly and very fast. So, that's the big problem—that's the capacity problem they have. (. . . .) It's always been the case there's been more on the table than needs to be implemented than they are able to implement and able to do.

Furthermore, it was noted that the implementation of decisions is insufficiently monitored (K(a)10). Nevertheless, even experts that were generally critical of the effectiveness of implementation acknowledged that it is highly dependent on the subject of policies. As K(a)3 noted, "some things which are critical for the country leadership are get done very quickly and very efficiently. Many other policies, which are not that strategically important many times do not get done although they should have."

Obviously, the issue of implementation and monitoring is closely related to the accountability of actors within the state apparatus. When the interviewees were asked to evaluate the accountability of public servants in Kazakhstan, their answers again varied. An important question when talking about accountability is to whom somebody is accountable. Therefore, several interviewees distinguished between the accountability of bureaucrats toward the general public and accountability within the hierarchy of the state apparatus. During the interview analysis, evaluative coding was used for questions concerning the accountability of public officials. The answers were assigned to the categories rather *accountable*, *rather unaccountable*, and *ambiguous*. Eight interviewees gave an ambiguous answer to this question. Among the interviewees who explicitly referred to the accountability toward the public, four (31%) argued that bureaucrats were rather accountable, whereas nine (69%) argued that they were rather unaccountable. Concerning the relationship to superiors within the state apparatus, twelve interviewees (71%) considered bureaucrats to be rather accountable and five (29%) argued that they were not accountable. However, it should be noted that the answers commonly provided relevant context and were therefore often not comparable in a straightforward manner. The use of evaluative coding and the given numbers therefore represent a considerable simplification of the interviewees' evaluations. Furthermore, the number of available interview transcripts in Kazakhstan where this question was dealt with is limited. As a consequence, the overview in this table can only serve as a starting point of the analysis.

As the answers to the questions on accountability show, both the evaluations of accountability within state structures and toward the public were mixed. The predominant view was that bureaucrats are generally held accountable only within the state structures. It was stressed by public officials themselves and some interviewees of focus group (a) that bureaucrats and regional politicians have to report regularly to higher bodies on their work (K(a)5; K(a)8; K(a)28; K(b)1; K(b)2; K(b)3; K(b)7; K(b)8). However, it was also argued in some interviews that this system has shortcomings and is not sufficiently transparent (K(a)8; K(a)15; K(a)16; K(a)17). As an interviewee from a foreign company K(e)1) stated:

> My personal opinion is that the majority of public officials are not accountable for what they are supposed to be accountable for. We are all well informed about the corruption in the public sector. There are certain indicators by such international organizations as Transparency International where Kazakhstan is almost at the bottom of the list... that's the objective assessment. You can make your own conclusions.

Interestingly, this negative perspective was also shared by interviewees working for the state apparatus. K(b)5 criticized the reporting procedures within the public administration as with the following statement:

> They do exist but they are not formalized. I don't think there is the systematic reporting procedure that would clearly manifest the activity of the agency; some steps are being undertaken in this respect, though. You are aware that the Strategic Planning System exists to ensure each government agency defines its own strategic plan; it's a formal thing though. (. . . .) Do you know what advantage the European Union has? The majority of procedures with respect to public administration are standardized and formalized; they are monitored from the top.

The openness and critical nature of this statement from a person working for the state might be considered surprising for a country whose political regime is generally considered authoritarian. While the interviewee was obviously very critical of the current institutions governing the Kazakh public administration, he also pointed to some improvements that seem to take place currently. In addition, the explicit comparative perspective assumed by the interviewee seems to show that persons within the administration are not only aware of shortcomings but also willing to improve on them by learning from more advanced countries.

Concerning the accountability toward the public, the overall perspective was more negative. While it was acknowledged that regional politicians also have to report to the public and that the Kazakh parliament assumes certain supervisory functions for the bureaucracy, nevertheless it was generally argued that accountability to actors outside the state apparatus is lacking (K(a)1; K(a)3; K(a)11; K(a)20). On the positive side, it was noted that the presence of a relatively free and developed press contributes to more accountability and transparency than in other Central Asian countries (K(a)1).

Even though the perspective that public officials are accountable within the bureaucratic hierarchy but unaccountable to the general public was clearly prevailing in the interviews, it is noticeable that there was no overall consensus on this topic. An issue that is closely related to accountability within bureaucratic structures is the promotion and recruitment system for public officials. Judging from the interviews, both recruiting and promotion processes in the Kazakh bureaucracy are only partly governed by formal institutions. It was stated in several interviews that candidates for the civil service have to pass a formalized examination process that were referred to as quite competitive (K(a)25; K(b)2; K(b)8). K(b)8 summarized his recruitment as follows:

> In order to be hired we had to go through the Agency for Public Service. We had to pass the test; the test on the Constitution, state language, ethics in the public service and the law on education. Then I had an interview where (. . .) he asked questions on professional skills and qualities.

As also mentioned in the statement, the recruitment process is supervised by an agency which is formally called the Agency of Civil Service Affairs of the Republic of Kazakhstan. The agency provides sample test questions on its website (http://www.kyzmet.kz). While these questions are mainly focused on the Kazakh constitution and different laws, candidates also have to answer questions about President Nursultan Nazarbayev. However, there was some doubt in the interviews as to whether the civil service exams are really the key criterion for the selection of candidates. In particular for higher positions on the bureaucratic hierarchy, it was argued that the selection process becomes less transparent. A quite negative assessment was made by a Kazakh expert (K(a)25):

> It is publicly known how much the position of akim of certain oblast costs. Yes, you can go through the exams but the final decision—it is not how much you score there

(. . . .) I would say it depends on the position and the level. If it's kind of low level, it would be quite transparent and you would get most likely. But if it is a higher position—less obvious.

While some interviewees stated that there is a structured and formalized career path for the promotion of civil servants (K(b)2; K(b)7; K(b)8), it was argued by others that such a path is not followed in practice (K(b)3; K(b)5; K(b)6). There was a virtual consensus that the promotion process is not fully meritocratic but based on a number of different criteria. It was argued that promotion depends on clan membership (K(a)9; K(a)12; K(a)16), personal connections within the administration and politics (K(a)5; K(a)6; K(a)8; K(a)13; K(b)7) and the membership in the ruling party, Nur Otan (K(a)25), may play a role in promotion. This does of course not rule out that performance and abilities are also important, the common perspective was that the promotion process is governed by a mixture of institutions that also include some meritocratic elements. As K(a)7 stated: "Actually, if a person is strong enough and strives for it, most likely he will succeed. On the other hand, there are promotion elements that are defined by personal connections, group affiliations etc."

A particularity of the Kazakh bureaucracy seems to be rotation of civil servants at different positions and agencies (K(a)2; K(a)12; K(b)4; K(b)5; K(b)7). One important reason for the rotation of bureaucrats seems to be the generally high level of personnel turnover in the public administration. As was indicated by some interviewees, it is very common that civil servants leave for the private sector after some years of experience, due to the low attractiveness of civil service in terms of workload and payment (K(b)3; K(b)5). This is a sharp difference to the East Asian developmental states, where pursuing a career as a bureaucrat has often been rewarded with compensation comparable to the private sector.[48]

To summarize, one may conclude from the interviews conducted in Kazakhstan that the public administration is still characterized by a significant need for reform. This is especially true when it is evaluated from the perspective of the developmental state concept, as bureaucratic effectiveness is one of its key elements. While formal rules that could lead to a competitive, meritocratic recruitment and promotion process exist, it seems that they are at least partly overshadowed by informal institutions that impede a full-fledged meritocracy. The same is true for formal rules ensuring the accountability of civil servants and the transparency of their actions. Since these mechanisms are only partly enforced,

---

48 This is not true to the same degree for all East Asian developmental states (see section 3.2.2).

the effectiveness seems to vary between different agencies. As K(b)5) summarized: "Each [public agency, M.S.] has its own efficiency. There is no single evaluation mechanism of the performance of public agencies. The one who presents things in a more beautiful manner is considered as being more efficient."

Some of these shortcomings have apparently been recognized, and the reform efforts of the government seem to continue. One of the public officials that were interviewed (K(b)3) summarized some of the reform steps undertaken in 2010 as follows:

> This year the President's decree on the assessment of performance of public agencies was issued (. . . .) Starting from the next year each ministry according to certain criteria will have to pass performance assessment of their activities on an annual basis. There are many performance assessment criteria for that such as: personnel turnover rate, for example, or such criteria as information and how effectively information materials are published on web-pages and portals; whether there is feedback with other public agencies or not – which is considered very important. (. . . .) There will also be the assessment of state procurement and budget allocation. Besides, not only public agencies but also independent experts and NGOs will be entitled to conduct assessment procedures. I think what has been accomplished is a huge progress.

The main objective of this reform is to improve the current evaluation mechanism for the performance of public agencies that was criticized by K(b)5 in the statement above. However, it remains to be seen whether the Kazakh government is willing and able to implement this reform effectively and thoroughly. This would be a first step toward improving the overall bureaucratic quality and the capacity of the public administration to implement the economic policies of the central government.

8.3.2 Uzbekistan

8.3.2.1 The role of the state in the economy: economic policies and objectives

As was described in section 7, the general perception of research on Uzbekistan is that the state has an unusually large role in the economy. The interviews with informants in the region left no doubt that this perception is justified. When interviewees were asked to describe the role of the Uzbek state in the economy, common words they used were "dominant" (U(a)8; U(a)11); U(a)14; U(a)16; U(a)20) and "excessive" (U(a)6; U(a)9). This is of course not a groundbreaking insight, because the Uzbek state is generally considered to have an even more visible role in the economy than the Kazakh state. However, it is interesting to explore the concrete form of the state's interference with economic processes, the effects of this interference on the business sector, the reasons behind state interventions, and the way the state's role changed over time. Furthermore, to assess whether state intervention is seen as facilitating or as impeding economic development it is of crucial importance in the context of the developmental state concept.

As in Kazakhstan, the interviewees from focus groups (a) and (b) were asked whether the Uzbek approach to economic policy is shaped by some kind of reference model. As was mentioned in section 7, the political leadership has officially adopted its own *Uzbek model* consisting of five core principles. While these principles emphasize that the state is the main reformer and that reforms will only take place gradually, they do not define the eventual role that the state is supposed to assume in the economy. Moreover, they do not refer explicitly to an activist industrial policy. Out of 27 respondents that were asked about the reference model the government uses, 12 exclusively mentioned the Uzbek model of reforms and stressed its uniqueness (U(a)5; U(a)7; U(a)8; U(a)10; U(a)11; U(a)12; U(a)16; U(a)18; U(a)19; U(a)20; U(a)21; U(a)25). In contrast, 16 mentioned that the Uzbek government incorporates the experiences of other countries in their economic strategy in some way. Out of the interviewees that mentioned the importance of foreign models for the Uzbek approach, seven (U(a)1; U(a)2; U(a)3; U(a)22; U(a)27; U(b)2; U(b)12) characterized it as fully eclectic in the sense that it takes into account the experience of virtually all countries. In contrast, nine interviewees (U(a)4; U(a)6; U(a)9; U(a)13; U(a)14; U(a)15; U(a)23; U(a)24; U(b)11) stressed the importance of specific countries. Seven of these explicitly referred to the relevance of the East Asian developmental states, particularly South Korea and Japan, for Uzbekistan's approach to economic policy (U(a)4; U(a)9; U(a)13; U(a)15; U(a)23; U(a)24; U(b)11). However, even the latter group emphasized in virtually all cases that crucial differences with any foreign reference models exist.

While it is evident that the state's role in Uzbekistan goes far beyond what is common in Western countries, it is more difficult to evaluate whether its role is comparable to the East Asian developmental states. As was mentioned in section 7, Spechler (2000b) argued that the guiding principle of state action in Uzbekistan is "stability at all cost" (p. 295). Obviously, stability is a broad term that needs further clarification. In the context of Uzbekistan, stability refers above all to the conservation of the current political power structure. As the example of Taiwan, Singapore, or South Korea shows, this objective is not necessarily in conflict with economic development. However, the question from the perspective of the New Institutional Economics is how existing constraints and personal ideologies shape the decisions of current political leaders. Concerning East Asia, it was noted several times in the present study (see Section 3.2.3 and the case studies in Part II) that external threats, as well as scarce resources, are commonly considered to have been essential constraints for the leaders of developmental states. However, it was also argued that these conditions applied mainly to the Northeast Asian developmental states and to Singapore. Concerning the external environment, South Korea, Taiwan, and Meiji Japan all faced military threats from other countries. Singapore had to prove its viability as an independent state surrounded by a comparatively hostile environment, yet there was no evident danger of a foreign invasion. Each of these countries had scarce natural resources. Such constraints were not present to the same degree in the Southeast Asian countries of Malaysia, Thailand, and Indonesia. Still, the political decision makers in these countries (and in Singapore) faced major internal constraints that shaped their decisions. Ethnic diversity was the most obvious of these constraints.

As is the case in Kazakhstan, the conditions in Uzbekistan are clearly different from the three Northeast Asian developmental states, but similar to the emerging economies of Southeast Asia in some respects. Natural resources are more abundant in Uzbekistan than in the Northeast Asian developmental states. As Uzbekistan exports a number or resources, including cotton, natural gas, and gold, it is not easy to quantify how its overall endowment compares to Kazakhstan and the Southeast Asian economies. Its resources in natural gas and oil are clearly lower than those of Kazakhstan (which has a much smaller population) (CIA, 2011). Furthermore, it is evident that the Uzbek regime does face internal challenges to its authority from within the country. While there is no viable, formally recognized opposition, political authority is never fully uncontested. As was described in section 7.3.2, groups related to political Islam seem to be the most apparent internal threat to the current regime.

The perception of the Uzbek political leadership that its political power might be threatened from within the country explains the tight control that the government has retained. In order to prevent any group within Uzbekistan from achieving a position powerful enough to threaten the status quo, the emergence of major private actors in the economy has been effectively impeded. An interviewee (U(a)8) summarized the government's perception of private business as follows:

> The state distrusts our entrepreneurs. Why do you think there are no big companies in the market? It has something to do with the fact that the state does not let them develop, grow. All the large enterprises remain from the Soviet Era. I don't know of a single company which would grow from small into large. Everybody knows about it: either side. For an entrepreneur running a company it is better to open 2–3 smaller companies than grow into one large, you know. The state does not allow them to

grow. (. . . .) Because it is afraid of large enterprises. At the moment when there are no large enterprises it is easier to control, it is easier to impose their own point of view, their policies. It is a different thing with large companies.

Existing private domestic companies above a certain size are checked by the authorities for any affiliation with religious groups or the political opposition (U(a)19). In several of the earlier interviews that were conducted, the private conglomerate Zeromax was named by informants as one of the most important players in the Uzbek economy (U(a)1; U(a)2; U(a)5; U(a)22). This company was involved a variety of Uzbekistan's most important industries, including gold mining, cotton cultivation, textiles, retail, and the oil and gas sector. While it was officially registered in Switzerland and consequently had the status of a foreign investor, it was mainly active in Uzbekistan and was presumably owned by Uzbeks. Press reports (Babadzhanov, Saadi, & Kurbanov, 2010; Institute for War and Peace Research, 2010; Najibullah, 2010; Uznews, 2010) even indicated that the company had close ties to Islam Karimov's eldest daughter. Nevertheless, Uzbek courts shut down Zeromax in May 2010, and its assets were handed over to the government (Institute for War and Peace Research, 2010). As an interviewee (U(a)4) argued, the reason for the company's demise was that the oligarchs who owned Zeromax had decided to be in the opposition. Other sources (Babadzhanov, Saadi, & Kurbanov, 2010; Institute for War and Peace Research, 2010; Najibullah, 2010; Uznews, 2010) speculated about a combination of foreign pressure from Russia and inter-elite cleavages within Uzbekistan.

While the preservation of tight control over all organized interest groups in Uzbekistan is the main tool that the government uses to counter potential threats to its power, it is not the only measure that is undertaken. As was confirmed in virtually all interviews, state intervention in Uzbekistan has an important social component. Prices for basic goods such as staple foods, medicine, and gas are tightly controlled and kept artificially below market levels (U(a)1; U(a)2; U(a)3; U(a)4; U(a)5; U(a)6; U(a)7; U(a)8; U(a)13; U(a)21). According to the perception of interviewees, these policies have the clear objective to avoid societal unrest (U(a)2; U(a)3; U(a)5; U(a)7). Furthermore, the state consciously attempts to shape the industrial structure of the Uzbek economy. However, price controls are not the main mechanism that the state employs for this purpose. Rather, selective trade and foreign exchange policies as well as tax incentives are used to promote strategic industries and selected companies (U(a)1; U(a)4; U(a)5; U(a)13; U(a)21; U(a)22). Companies within these strategic sectors that want to import goods face both explicit import barriers and government-imposed restrictions in their access to foreign currency. A foreign expert (U(a)13) argued that the main objective of the Uzbek government is to promote the localization of production:

Price controls are there for the basic commodities. You know, like bread, vegetable oil and this kind of things. This is regulated strongly by the government. And the rest they control more by curbing imports, not giving conversion for certain imports. They don't interfere so much in the price control but more into what are we going to bring into the country. What is going to be allowed to be brought in the country. We have this policy of import substitution, localization. They want to do everything themselves here. So, that is how they prevent certain imports coming in but there are no so much price mechanisms. It is more localization oriented.

According to the interviews, this import substitution strategy is implemented to achieve several objectives. As in the case of price controls, preserving social stability seems to be one underlying aim of import substitution because several industries are promoted due to the high number of jobs they are expected to create (U(a)1; U(a)8; U(a)16; U(a)17). Moreover, the leadership is aiming for diversification of the Uzbek economy. This relates both to agriculture, which is still dominated by cotton, and to manufacturing (U(a)1; U(a)2; U(a)4; U(a)22). The efforts of the government in this direction are generally seen as genuine by the interviewees, at least when it concerns the president as the key decision maker. Yet, it was also acknowledged that this process is taking place rather slowly. Table 22 shows that the contribution of industry to the Uzbek GDP has increased over the last 15 years, while that of agriculture has declined since 2000. However, similar to Kazakhstan, this increase is due to a rising importance of non-manufacturing industries in the Uzbek economy whereas the contribution of manufacturing industries to the GDP has even decreased slightly. Thus, the World Bank's World Development Indicators do not reflect that the Uzbek government's promotion of manufacturing has had any impact. Nevertheless, a diversification away from agriculture is evident.

Table 22: Distribution of value added in the Uzbek economy, 1995–2010 [as % of GDP]

	1995	**2000**	**2005**	**2010**
Agriculture	32.3	34.4	28.0	19.5
Services	39.9	42.5	48.9	45.1
Industry	27.8	23.1	23.2	35.4
Manufacturing industry	*11.9*	*9.4*	*9.1*	*9.0*
Non-manufacturing industry	*15.9*	*13.7*	*14.1*	*26.4*

Source: World Bank, 2011a for Agriculture, Services, overall Industry and manufacturing industry. Value for non-manufacturing industry calculated as difference between the values for industry and manufacturing industry.

The underlying reason for the state's aspiration for diversification is not easy to identify. This was ascribed by some interviewees to the state's attempt to achieve more economic independence from foreign countries and self-sufficiency in certain sectors (U(a)1; U(a)9). This objective might be conflicting with the pursuit of economic efficiency. However, it cannot be ruled out that diversification is also pursued in order to attain more general developmental goals. Finally, it was argued that increasing government revenue is a key objective of interventions in Uzbekistan (U(a)1;U(a)3; U(a)16). Depending on the time horizon and the constraints the political leadership faces, this goal might not be conflicting, but rather corresponding to the promotion of economic development. As was argued in section 5.3 on the basis of Doner et al. (2005) and others, budget constraints were an underlying reason for the commitment of Chiang Kai-shek and Park Chung-hee to economic growth and diversification.

8.3.2.2 Functioning of the state-business nexus

The preceding section dealt with the general role of the Uzbek state in the economy, its overall approach to economic policy the some of the underlying objectives it seemingly tries to accomplish through interventions. This section is dedicated to explore the concrete forms of interaction between the state apparatus and the business sector.

Even though several interviewees mentioned that the Uzbek leadership considers South Korea and Japan to some degree as possible reference models for its economic policy, the relationship it maintains with business differs considerably from these countries. The governments of both East Asian countries had close, cooperative relationships with the owners of large private business groups. As was described extensively in sections 5.2 and 5.3, the balance of power between the state and these business groups shifted over time, ranging from tight state control over the private companies to an independent stance of business. While the business groups in these two East Asian developmental states often had strong personal ties to the government, their assets were clearly in private hands. Often, several business groups with ties to the government competed in the same markets.

In Uzbekistan, the state exercises a degree of control over the economy that is in several ways even tighter than in Japan and South Korea. As was already noted in the previous section, the Uzbek government has been reluctant to accept the emergence of large private businesses and it is unclear whether any large domestic companies currently in existence should be referred to as truly private. Usually, one state-owned company dominates a specific sector.

When asked about the most important players in the Uzbek economy, the interviewees almost exclusively referred to public enterprises and some joint ventures between these companies and foreign investors. The most commonly mentioned firm was the Navoi Mining and Metallurgy Combinat, a state-owned company that controls mining activities for gold, uranium and other resources. It was followed by UzbekNeftegas, which is also state-owned and controls the oil and gas sector. The third company that was frequently mentioned is Uz-DaewooAvto, a joint venture between the South Korean car company Daewoo (which is a subsidiary of General Motors since 2005) and the Uzbek public enterprise UzAvtosanoat.[49]

It was noted in the interviews that the state's ability to control and influence the economy and, in particular, the private sector has changed over time. As an American expert (U(a)1), who lived for several decades in Uzbekistan, summarized:

> In the early days from 1991 to 1994 we would depict Uzbekistan as Wild West with absolutely no control. It was absolutely no discipline, no economic discipline (...) That's when you have the role of local business mafia or the oligarchs, who pretty much did what they wanted... but then in the mid 1990s you saw again a transition and formation and returning of the state ministries and getting to the point where they got back into control. That was reflected in very dramatic changes in economic structure, the role of the Central Bank, the role of the Ministry of Finance. 1996 was the end of the so-called open conversion mission. Since 1996 we've had again a control, very tightly controlled economic policy.

Apparently, the state apparatus of the newly independent Uzbekistan lost some of the control over the private sector that it had inherited from Soviet times in the early 1990s. However, in contrast to other transition countries, the Uzbek state regained this control quickly and thoroughly, as the statement above indicates. Obviously, the state's role continued to change after 1996. The same interviewee (U(a)1) described the current situation as a "transition period where we are going from complete centralized social structure to a form of a moderate state capitalism." Nevertheless, no class of private businessmen independent of the political elite or even able to challenge the government on political grounds has emerged since the mid-1990s after the early 1990s. As another informant (U(a)4) stated explicitly: "the oligarchs unlike in other countries don't have many choices here other than being in harmony with the government."

Even in sectors that are almost completely privatized, the state retains enormous control. As an example, the agricultural sector is largely in private hands,

---

49   As was noted in Section 8.3.2.1, the now-defunct company Zeromax was named in some of the earlier interviews as an important player.

including the cultivation of cotton, which is one of Uzbekistan's main exports. Yet, the value chain for this product is not liberalized because the state controls the processing plants, which determine the prices that famers obtain for raw cotton (U(a)9). For the telecom business, interviewee U(a)4 summarized:

> Although telecom business with 3–4 large operators looks 100 percent private with pure competition, the government owns part of their business through relatives. There was another case with "Coscom", the telecom company, which was owned by American investors. In 2007 they stopped their operation for the period of 1 month because UzASI (The Uzbek Agency for Information and Communication) simply recalled their license for uncertain reasons. It's still unknown what really happened there.

The state-business nexus takes different forms for domestic private companies and foreign investors. For domestic enterprises, the size of the company has a fundamental impact on its interaction with the state. Above a certain size, the boundary between public sector and state sector in Uzbekistan apparently becomes blurry. Moreover, the government differentiates between companies that are active in strategic sectors, where it takes a bigger interest, and other companies, which are allowed to operate more freely. As a respondent summarized (U(a)3):

> You just can't say private and state. (....) You've got purely private. (....) we talk about a micro-company. And then you reach the next stage you've got a little bigger one who is now looked at [by the State, M.S.] (..) And then you have the beginning of hybrids which are little joint-ventures or either daughter companies of state agencies. (...) So, you say "Oh, there are only a few state companies". No, that's not completely correct. Any time that state is any kind of interest in the joint venture, let's say at the moment there is a legal framework around 25%. We call it "a golden vote". Or it's in a strategic environment, industry. That means that at any time even though the government doesn't have any shareholders in that enterprise, under law it can, its own judgment, come in and block any action. I mean blocking who is a general director, whether it's a salary level and whatever

As a result of the described conditions, the state-business nexus in Uzbekistan is essentially limited to the state's interaction with small domestic enterprises and foreign companies. This interaction takes place in two different ways. As in all economies, the state has a decisive influence because it decides upon formal institutions and enforces them through its agencies. In Uzbekistan, this regulating role is complemented by a direct participation in the business sector through state-owned companies, which assume the key positions in the Uzbek economy and maintain business ties to private enterprises.

The state's interference with the operations of small and medium companies that are not active in strategic sectors is limited in some respects. It seems that the entrepreneurs are able to take many business decisions freely (U(a)6) and can consequently act in accordance with market incentives. Nevertheless, it was argued by several interviewees that the institutional environment in Uzbekistan is generally not to the benefit of small and medium companies. As large companies are the key actors in the leadership's economic strategy, they are not only subject to interventions, but also receive substantial support. Furthermore, there seems to be a tendency of the state to decrease the relative freedom that smaller enterprises had enjoyed before As an Uzbek expert working for an international organization (U(a)20) summarized:

> After the independence there were times when the private business was given enough freedom. But now the tendency is shifting toward constraining the activity of small and medium-sized business. Especially in the recent years the tendency is shifting toward supporting of large private businesses.

He (U(a)20) concluded that "the majority of laws and regulations today are somehow targeted against small and medium-sized businesses." Another interviewee indicated that the state forced private domestic companies to employ labor migrants that returned from other countries due to the crisis (U(a)26), which is obviously a crucial interference in business decisions. A further, and even more important, problem that small and medium domestic companies face is petty corruption at lower levels of the public administration. This is an issue that affects all private companies to some degree. As was argued in the interviews "any business in Uzbekistan without exception has to look at its relative position in the power structure" (U(a)3), meaning that all companies need certain ties to individuals within the state structures to be able to operate (U(a)3; U(a)20). However, foreign investors and larger companies have the advantage of more visibility, better connections to upper levels of the hierarchical state apparatus and their position as government supported enterprises. As a consequence, these companies enjoy better protection from petty corruption and harassment than small and medium domestic businesses (U(a)2; U(a)3; U(a)20).

While one might conclude from this that foreign investors face better conditions in Uzbekistan than domestic private companies, the reality is quite complex and it is not easy to get a clear picture of the situation. In several interviews, the importance of foreign investment for the Uzbek economy was emphasized, and it was stated that the government is very keen to attract FDI (U(a)12; U(a)13). There were also interviewees who noted that certain tax incentives only apply to foreign investors and joint-ventures (U(a)14), or even that foreign companies are generally favored over domestic enterprises by the government (U(a)12). However, the entry to the Uzbek market for international investors is not easy, because the government has been very selective in its stance toward FDI and maintains the economy relatively closed when compared to other countries.

Foreign investors are on the one hand active in industries related to consumer goods. In these sectors, they may cooperate with small and medium Uzbek businesses and face similar conditions. Connections to the upper tiers of the state apparatus are considered a necessity in order to prevent arbitrary interference with the operation of businesses (U(a)3; U(a)20; U(a)21). On the question of whether any large company, be it foreign or domestic, can exist in Uzbekistan without connections, U(a)20 answered:

> No, it cannot. It is 100 percent it cannot exist without connections. They will not manage it even if they try to work in compliance with the existing legislation. They won't be allowed to work freely; hundreds of reasons will be found to impede their activity.

The interviewees were divided on the question of whether foreign ownership has an influence on the security of property rights. While several interviewees argued that foreign ownership of a company leads to a better protection of its property rights (U(a)1; U(a)7); U(a)8; U(a)9; U(a)10; U(a)13; U(a)20), others disagreed (U(a)3; U(a)6; U(a)12; U(a)14; U(a)16; U(a)18; U(a)19). However, it is clear that any benefit that foreign investors might have in this respect is only limited, because some interviewees gave concrete examples where companies with foreign involvement were finally liquidated or expropriated due to the lack of political support (U(a)3; U(a)6; U(a)13). In general, foreign companies have an important role in sectors such as natural resource extraction and manufacturing industries, which are considered strategic by the Uzbek government. In these industries, the Uzbek leadership apparently wants to preserve its control and is therefore cautious to accept foreign influence. However, the apparent need for modern technology makes the involvement of foreign investors a necessity that the decision makers within the state apparatus acknowledge (U(a)2).

A successful and efficient exploitation of the country's natural resources in terms of oil and gas would be difficult without the involvement of foreign companies. The same is true for automobile production and chemical industry. In these strategic industries, foreign investments have to be approved through a presidential decree and are usually required take place in the form of joint-ventures with public enterprises (U(a)1; U(a)13). Foreign actors that receive such a decree enjoy a high status that provides them with more protection from interference of the lower levels of the state apparatus with their operations. However, the Uzbek state's influence in these joint ventures is profound because the state-owned companies are tightly controlled and essentially act as representatives of the government. As one interviewee stated about UzbekNeftegas, the state-owned company assuming the key position in the oil and gas sector: "Uz-bekNeftegas is practically the Ministry of Oil and Gas" (U(a)4).

On the Uzbek side, there seems to be a perception that foreign investors are commonly only interested in short-term profits and not in the long-term development of industries within the country, which state actors see as a justification for intervention (U(a)8). There was widespread evidence in the interviews that the promotion of long-term investments is a major objective of Uzbek economic policy. Benefits that investors receive include tax exemptions, public loans and protection from international competition on the Uzbek market (U(a)1; U(a)2; U(a) 3); U(a)4; U(a) 7; U(a)10; U(a)11; U(a)16). These measures are aimed at foreign companies involved in import substitution and exporting in particular (U(a)6; U(a)8; U(a)9; U(a)12; U(a)14; U(a)18), even though some tax incentives are also available to specific investments by domestic companies (U(a)13).

Despite the Uzbek state's efforts to promote long-term investment projects and the stable political conditions, several interviewees stressed that the conditions for investments remain unpredictable overall (U(a)4; U(a)10; U(a)14; U(a)16). As U(a)16 summarized:

> It is absolutely predictable on the one hand; on the other hand it absolutely depends on the most unexpected circumstances, you know. It depends on the sectors of economy we are talking about here, about sympathies and antipathies with respect to some companies or some group of companies or some people who are involved in a particular field, you know.

This is obviously a major impediment for any long-term commitment. Difficulties in the implementation process of supportive policies and frequent changes in the legislation cause problems. As one interviewee summarized: "the direction of the government management is not foreseen by businesses" (U(a)10). While it is well known that certain strategic industries receive government support, the publicly available information on the sectors which are promoted is not comprehensive (U(a)11). Several interviewees stated that they are unaware whether existing benefits for investments will be maintained in the future (U(a)3; U(a)4). It was also argued in the interviews that the policies and regulations underlying these benefits are often not devised in a expedient way and are therefore more than counterbalanced by a generally unsatisfactory business climate characterized by high taxes and customs duties (U(a)6). While the tax benefits granted to specific projects are high, they are commonly only granted for a defined period of three to five years (U(a)6; U(a)11). However, these tax breaks have also been prolonged because of discretionary decisions of the relevant political decision makers (U(a)6). The government's future policies concerning other benefits, such as the protection of local producers through trade barriers, are even less clear. Judging from the interviews, there is no publicly known plan for the removal of these protectionist measures, even though one informant expected a gradual liberalization (U(a)12).

Another informant argued that the granting of subsidies depends more than anything on the budget available to the government and not on any specified approach to economic policy (U(a)3). Major shortcomings concerning the implementation of supportive measures for specific industries were noted by U(a)9:

> Generally speaking, in our country there is no plan for them to be lifted; no certain long-term programs, you know. For example, a particular program comes in effect which means that certain goals for defined industries will be set in terms of tax exemptions etc. (....) There are no further standards which would check the efficiency of these very measures – how much is produced, how much remains; why they failed to produce that much etc. This is because, in the end, the speech of the President is more important. What I mean is at the beginning of the year large-scale project starts where objectives and plans for a certain period are defined and then, at the end of the year the President gives speech which allegedly completes the projects in process. Of course, then the given process fades little by little and bears less popularity in the years to come. Of course, the job is done within the ministries and they are well informed about it but the people who have to be informed in the first place are not informed at all.

This is a major difference to the economic policies of developmental states in East Asia, where state support for nascent industries was generally granted for a defined time-frame. This difference and its negative consequences were explicitly noticed by the interviewee who made the statement above (U(a)9):

> It is also important to note that the situation with open-ended subsidies to some extent undermines the will of the managers to become competitive. At the times when companies in Korea were finding their feet, subsidies were 100 percent. Gradually, the state lifted subsidies and in 10-years time companies were left with 0 percent of subsidies but they were stable and produced competitive goods. They knew perfectly that if they don't make profit, in 10 years they would have nothing. The situation is totally different here. The people at the top have become obese. They live in clover and don't have anything to worry about since the state will take care of them for the taxes we pay. This is the difference.

There is some evidence that the country of origin of investors has a decisive influence on their ability to adapt to the local conditions in Uzbekistan. Judging from some interviews, it is easier for investors from emerging economies to adapt to local conditions. This refers in particular to companies from South Korea, but also to investors from Turkey, the People's Republic of China or Russia. South Korean companies do not benefit only from good diplomatic relationships between the two countries (U(a)4), but also from direct support of the South Korean government for their activities in Uzbekistan (U(a)3). Furthermore, the presence of a notable Korean minority that has been living in Uzbekistan since the rule of Stalin is an additional advantage. A Korean businessman who is involved in a joint-venture argued that Koreans and Uzbeks have generally a similar mentality (U(e)19). Concerning the obstacles for doing business in Uzbekistan, a South Korean investor (U(e)19) noted that the environment in South Korea was very similar 20 or 30 years ago in terms of corruption in the public administration and other conditions. He acknowledged that deals with this problem by focusing exclusively on business issues while leaving any interaction with Uzbek authorities to his local partner. In contrast, the representative of an American partner in an Uzbek-American joint-venture (U(e)6) stated that his company is considering leaving Uzbekistan owing to concerns about the compliance of the joint activities with American laws and regulations. He also admitted that the decision makers in the headquarters of his company Uzbek subsidiary have limited knowledge of the local conditions and are mainly interested in short-term profits.

When the interviewees of focus group (a) were asked to evaluate the predictability of policy making in Uzbekistan on a scale from 1 (very unpredictable) to 5 (very predictable), their answers varied widely. The interviewees gave both the lowest and the highest grade; the average evaluation was 3.6.[50] Without context, it is hardly possible to draw conclusions from this ambiguous result. However, the explanations that interviewees gave for their answers do provide some insights. Several interviewees did not want to give a single evaluation for the overall predictability and distinguished between several dimensions. U(a)20 distinguished between the predictability of conditions for small and medium domestic enterprises, which he estimated at 1, and for larger companies which he estimated at 4. As he (U(a)20) summarized:

> For smaller players in the market, the economic policy is absolutely unpredictable. When it comes to larger companies that make decisions in top circles at the government level, for them the economic policy is transparent and predictable. For small and medium-sized businesses there are moments that are predictable and unpredictable. Let's take markets and bazaars; for small players the policy is absolutely unpredictable.

Interviewee U(a)3 argued that predictability is quite high, at 4, for companies that have an understanding of Uzbekistan, but much lower for foreign companies if they "don't understand the system." The American expert U(a)4 argued that the overall predictability of the conditions in Uzbekistan is quite high (evaluation 4), but that the predictability of regulations and their implementation is low (evaluation 2). He explained this by stating that the economic policy is

---

50 This question was not asked to other focus groups.

very stable in the sense that a gradual transition strategy with major barriers for foreign trade is pursued. No changes to this overall strategy are expected. Yet, the implementation of specific rules seems to be hardly predictable. This unequal implementation and of rules, which relates to a selective enforcement, is also confirmed in the following statement by an Uzbek interviewee (U(a)6):

> There are laws the observance and application of which will be so much observed making the earth tremble; the enforcement organs will be ready to overthrow everything to observe these laws. There are laws that have been adopted 10 times but never applied or executed for various reasons. Either it doesn't pay or impossible to implement. There is no definite answer for that even on a 5-point scale. You see, there is so much contradiction within the legislation which makes execution of laws impossible. There are provisions related to the business which are almost impossible to implement but are strictly observed.

The lack of predictability concerning the enforcement of rules and regulations is certainly a serious impediment for the economic development of Uzbekistan. This leads to the question as to whether relevant actors at the upper levels of the state apparatus are aware of this issue. In East Asia, one of the essential functions of the state-business nexus was the effective exchange of information between companies and important political as well as bureaucratic decision makers. In Uzbekistan, the unfavorable conditions, faced in particular by small and medium domestic companies, may either be a sign that this exchange of information does not work effectively or that the critical actors within the Uzbek state have been unwilling (or unable) to improve the situation.

When asked about organizations that play a role for the communication between smaller companies and the state, interviewees often referred to the Chamber of Commerce and Industry (CCI) (U(a)3; U(a)5; U(a)6; U(a)8; U(a)11; U(a)19; U(a)20; U(a)26). As was mentioned in section 7.3.2.2 of the present study, this chamber declared the representation of the interests of Uzbek entrepreneurs as part of its mission. It has to be noted that even though the CCI is officially declared as a non-governmental organization, it was established through a presidential decree and "receives orders as any other government organ," according to an Uzbek expert (U(a)6). Nevertheless, it was argued in several interviews that it plays a positive role. It serves as a general lobbyist for small and medium businesses, provides support in legal disputes, and organizes meetings between the private sector and government organs (U(a)3); U(a)6; U(a)8; U(a)19). Another organization that serves as a representative body for business and attempts to improve the exchange of information with the state organs is the American Chamber of Commerce. This organization does not only represent American companies but also foreign investors from Europe, East Asia, and India. It even has some domestic Uzbek companies among its members. However, it has only 90 members, which are all headquartered in Tashkent (U(a)1). Its membership is therefore much smaller and less diverse than that of the Uzbek CCI (U(a)1.

While the objectives of the CCI were generally seen as positive in the interviews, there were some interviewees who argued that the Chamber had only limited effectiveness in achieving those objectives. In particular, this referred to the meetings between the business sector and government representatives. As U(a)16 noted concerning the information exchange initiated by the CCI: "there are issues you are allowed to discuss, there are issues you are not allowed to discuss." Other interviewees (U(a)6; U(a)8); U(a)20; U(a)21) had similar perceptions and argued that the impact of regular meetings between business and public officials is quite low. Reasons given were the lack of a fully open dialogue and the limited effect of the meetings on the actions of actors within the state apparatus. For meetings organized by the American Chamber of Commerce, it was noted that only government representatives at a very low level of the hierarchy commonly take part in them (U(a)1). A genuine information exchange between the business community and the crucial decision makers within the state structures thus hardly seems to take place, at least not in a formalized and organized way. The conditions for large foreign investors and joint-ventures may of course differ due to their importance for the Uzbek economy and resulting ties to the upper levels of the state apparatus.

8.3.2.3 Institutions of the public administration

Several issues that were raised in the two preceding sections are related to the coherence of state action. There is no doubt that the state apparatus has a dominating role in the Uzbek economy. It is less clear whether state agencies act according to an overall strategy defined by decision makers at the top or whether their actions are rather inconsistent and arbitrary. The analysis of the state-business nexus and corresponding quotes from the expert interviews indeed provide some indication that the internal coherence of state action is not particularly high. This issue will be analyzed in more detail here.

Incoherence within the Uzbek state apparatus would be in some ways surprising, because its functions along highly hierarchical lines. The Uzbek state apparatus is highly centralized and able to exercise an unusual amount of influence over agencies. The central government controls the economy down to the regional level through appointing all regional hokims and local authorities (U(a)1; see also Perlman & Gleason, 2007, p. 1338). When the interviewees were asked whether regional politicians and lower-ranking public officials have some independence in their decisions, several plainly answered with "no" (U(a)3; U(a)6); U(a)9; U(a)11; U(a)20). Others essentially agreed that the state apparatus is very hierarchical and centralized, but conceded that there may be limited decision-making power in specific cases. This mainly refers to decisions where the upper levels of the state apparatus do not take an immediate interest (U(a)4; U(a)13; U(a)17). As argued by U(a)4: "If the output of certain decision is not interesting for the state, then the state does not interfere."

Other questions within the interviews led to a similar picture. When interviewees were asked to assess the accountability of public servants, they mostly distinguished between their accountability within state structures, i.e. toward their superiors, and their accountability toward the general public. During the interview analysis, evaluative coding was used. The answers were assigned to the categories rather *accountable, rather unaccountable,* and *ambiguous,* and the results are summarized in Table 23. As the table shows, there was general agreement among the interviewees that bureaucrats are accountable to higher levels within the structure of the public administration. However, it should be noted that the answers commonly provided relevant context and were often not comparable in a straightforward manner. The use of evaluative coding and the presentation of the results in Table 23 therefore represent a considerable simplification of the interviewees' evaluations and can only serve as a starting point of the analysis, as was already noted in the preceding section on Kazakhstan.

Table 23: Accountability of Uzbek public officials

	Accountability to-ward superiors	Accountability to-ward the public	Ambiguous answer	No answer
Focus group a				
Rather Yes	18 (95%)	2 (22%)	3	1
Rather No	1 (5%)	7 (78%)		
Focus group d				
Rather Yes	5 (100%)	6 (60%)	11	1
Rather No	0 (0%)	4 (40%		
Focus group e				
Rather Yes	7 (86%)	6 (50%)	2	5
Rather No	1 (14%)	6 (50%)		
Total				
Rather Yes	30 (94%)	14 (45%)	15	7
Rather No	2 (6%)	17 (55%)		

Source: *23 interviews with focus group (a), 22 interviews with focus group (d), and 19 interviews with focus group (e).*
Note: *Several interviews only referred to either accountability toward superiors or accountability toward the public in their answers.*

As Table 23 shows, there was hardly any doubt for the interviewees that public officials are accountable for their actions within the state structures. With the exception of only two respondents, there was a consensus on this question. The picture is less clear concerning the accountability toward the general public. While the interviewees as a whole were almost equally divided over this issue, there were remarkable differences between the different focus groups. Among the representatives of international organizations and other experts in focus group (a), there were notably more interviewees that had a negative opinion on the bureaucrats' accountability toward the public. The two other focus groups, which both comprise the representatives of companies, had a more balanced perception. This may be due to the fact that these interviewees referred more to their personal experience than to a generalized perception. These personal experiences varied significantly, as is evidenced by two selected statements from representatives of foreign companies:

> Firstly, again, it all depends. At least, I work with people who are accountable for their words they say even; let alone for the papers they sign. That's certain for the signed papers. Even for the words they say, you know; for instance, we agree on something; we decide on something, we define the strategy but we don't put it in writing. Nevertheless, the agreements are fully implemented. Again, a great deal depends on the superior bodies. (U(e)13)

> You know, here what I've seen is nobody is accountable for anything. (. . .) the problem is, you know, accountability has to start from the top. Only when there is the problem does the question of accountability come up. Otherwise nobody checks anyone on a daily basis. I mean on a weekly basis or monthly. When the problem does happen then something, they say who's responsible? (. . .) I deal with a lot of government organizations. And when we go to talk to them, nobody seems to know who is in charge of what or the case has been passed onto somebody else. Why? (. . .) Whoever can do what they want will do it. It's as simple as that. (U(e)9)

Yet, even in from these comparatively clear statements, it is apparent that any general evaluation of the accountability of Uzbek public servants must remain utterly superficial. The degree of accountability that a private company experiences may depend on the public agency it interacts with as well as on the specific public servant involved in the interaction. There seems to be a considerable heterogeneity in the quality of the Uzbek bureaucracy. The statement of U(e)9 relates the accountability of public officials toward the public to the internal structures of the bureaucracy. This is an important point, because under normal circumstances public officials can only be held accountable by private actors if they are also accountable within the hierarchy of the state apparatus. Overall, the interviews provided notable evidence that individual bureaucrats are accountable to their superiors (see Table 23). However, it was also noted earlier that actors on the upper levels of the state apparatus may give lower ranking officials notable freedom in decisions that are not of immediate interest to them. Indeed, the limited accountability of public servants toward at least some private actors may be a result of cleavages within state structures, particularly between higher and lower tiers of the hierarchy. Another representative of a foreign company (U(e)12) noted:

> I think public officials are mostly puppets. I had face to face meetings with Shaykhov and Ganiev and they told me honestly whether they can help us or not in a particular situation. The people, who are at the steering wheel, so to speak, they are honest with you. The people who are at a lower level, who are afraid to be held accountable, may let you down and may not even fulfil their responsibilities. It's better not to talk to this kind of people. If you need something, you need go and talk to the upper level.[51]

Judging from this statement, one may conclude that the hierarchical structure itself contributes to the lack of accountability of the lower levels of the Uzbek public administration. As it seems, lower-ranking officials do not necessarily perceive that they would be rewarded for fulfilling their formally defined obligations. Rather, they apparently face incentives to keep a low profile within the state apparatus in order to avoid the interference of superiors with their activities. This can lead to a lack of communication between different tiers, which would affect the overall bureaucratic effectiveness. Such a cleavage between the lower tiers of the bureaucracy and the upper tiers could be one of several underlying reasons for the utmost importance that personal ties to individuals have for private companies (see preceding section).

The issue of interaction between different levels of the bureaucratic hierarchy is directly related to the recruitment and promotion process of the public administration. As was described in detail in Part II of the present study, meritocratic recruitment and promotion processes have generally been considered vital for the success of the East Asian developmental states. In the most successful East Asian economies, meritocracy was ensured through formal institutions that governed recruitment and promotion. In Uzbekistan, the institutions governing these processes seem to be much less formalized than in East Asia. When asked about their recruitment process to become public official, the interviewees of focus group (b) mostly referred to job interviews they had to pass (U(b)4; U(b)5; U(b)7; U(b)8; U(b)9; U(b)11; U(b)13). U(b)7 summarized the process he had to go through and the subsequent changes as follows:

---

51 Alisher Shaykhov is chairman of the Chamber of Commerce and Industry (CCI), Elyor Ganiev is currently Minister of Foreign Affairs and Deputy Prime Minister (he was Minister of Foreign Economic Relations before).

> I submitted my documents. They reviewed my documents. Seems like everything went ok and I was invited for a job interview. The questions were mainly economic related because I intended to work at the department for economy at hokimiyat. So, I was hired based on the results of the interview. (. . . .) Today there are lots of specialists out there and the selection process is stricter and more thorough. The process itself hasn't changed but the requirements have.

Other interviewees also argued that the recruitment process has become more selective and strict over the last decades. However, there seem to be some differences between agencies. While one interviewee stated that candidates at his agency have to pass both psychological and general knowledge tests (U(b)13), others explicitly stated that the recruitment process exclusively consists of an interview (U(b)9). Another interviewee said that the human resources department also attends diploma defense sessions at universities to pre-select suitable candidates for job interviews (U(b)11).

The heavy reliance on job interviews and relative diversity of recruitment procedures at different agencies does apparently not mean that the recruitment process in Uzbekistan is not meritocratic. However, there is a lack of formalization when compared to East Asia. While job interviews can lead to meritocratic recruitment, they are apparently less transparent as a recruitment tool than entry examinations with published results. Thus, it cannot be ruled out that personal connections at least in some cases continue to play an important role in the recruitment process of the Uzbek public administration. It was also noted in the interviews that the career path for public servants is not clearly defined in most cases. This is in contrast to the South Korean and Japanese bureaucracies where public officials were promoted according to transparent rules and faced a quite predictable career. This lack of formalization may contribute to the cleavages between different bureaucratic tiers that were noted earlier, because they lead to an intransparent institutional environment within the bureaucracy.

While cleavages between different ties of the state apparatus are an important issue, it is another question to which degree the activities of different agencies and different ministries are coordinated. In this respect, there were statements within the interviews which seem to be at least slightly contradictory. As an example, interviewee U(a)9 stressed the unusually hierarchical and authoritarian character of the Uzbek state apparatus:

> Our system is bottom-up. I will explain what I mean. Since it is total mistrust in the ministries in our country, the President is trying to control and monitor absolutely everybody and everything. For example, if a particular document is to be signed, it is not signed by the respective minister, it is signed by the President. He gives instructions what to do and how to do. In the end, the ministers are relieved of all authorities although the entire job should be done by the minister. Therefore, it hap-

pens that the minister in its turn takes away authorities from his subordinates. All the major decisions are made by the President himself, not the ministers.

One may conclude from this statement that President Karimov takes essentially all important decisions, keeps ministers in a subservient position and thus coordinates all activities of the state apparatus. In contrast, U(a)1 argued:

> The state is not one. You know, the President wants to develop all sectors of the economy. But then if you look (. . .) at the Ministry of Economy, Ministry of Finance, their focus is on big projects. If you look at the Ministry of Agriculture and Water Resources it's different. If you look at other ministries it's different. So, (. . .) the state speaks from several different positions.

It might be possible to solve this ostensible contraction by taking into account the difference between formal control over decisions and the actual involvement in their implementation. As it was argued in the preceding sections, political stability has been the key objective of the Uzbek leadership over the last two decades. From the perspective of the president, this objective may require that all authority over major decisions rests eventually in his hands. However, it may not require that he actually controls the implementation of decisions and the coordination of state activities on a daily basis—at least not in fields that do not directly affect political stability from his perspective. There is hardly any doubt that the Uzbek state follows has a clearly defined approach to economic transition in terms of gradualism, a tightly controlled economy, and import substitution. Yet, it seems that the involvement of the Uzbek state in the economy follows a less coherent strategy than one might assume. This may explain the low degree of predictability that private economic actors without close ties to the state apparatus seem to face in Uzbekistan. Both horizontal cleavages between different tiers of the administrative hierarchy and vertical cleavages between different agencies that follow diverging policy approaches may decrease the coherence of state action significantly.

9 Implications from the empirical study: a discussion

9.1 Kazakhstan and Uzbekistan: developmental, predatory, or intermediate states?

As the two largest countries and economies of Central Asia, Kazakhstan and Uzbekistan have received considerable attention in the economic literature on the region. Apparently, both countries' economies continue to differ significantly from the advanced Western economies in terms of the institutional environment. Comparative studies of Kazakhstan and Uzbekistan have generally stressed the more reformist stance of Kazakhstan relative to its southern neighbor (Blackmon, 2005; 2007; Perlman & Gleason, 2005; 2007). The interviews that served as a basis for Section 8 do not cast doubt on this basic insight. However, the developmental state concept offers a new perspective on the developments in both countries.

In order to evaluate Kazakhstan and Uzbekistan in the light of the developmental state concept, it makes sense to recall some of the key insights of the earlier sections of this study. As a conclusion to the literature review in Part I, a synthesis of a variety of definitions of the developmental state was developed. As a result of this synthesis, the three key elements of developmental states according to the literature were presented in Section 4.2:

(1) Developmental states are committed to the economic development of their country's societies;

(2) they pursue activist policies that involve the mid- to long-term planning of economic development;

(3) they have the capability of choosing and implementing economic policies that are overall adequate for achieving their objectives. This capability rests mainly on a capable (economic) bureaucracy and an effective interaction between state and business.

It was also noted in Section 4.2 that another type of state that is commonly identified in economic research on developing and emerging economies, namely the predatory state, is characterized by a much lower state capacity and an extremely low—or even non-existing—commitment to economic growth. Furthermore, it was argued that most developing and emerging countries do not fit into either of these categories. Rather, they represent examples of intermediate states, which deviate from the extremes of developmental and predatory states in a variety of ways. However, it should be noted that this typology of states is very cursory. Obviously, it is not possible to measure the commitment to economic development of a government or political leader in an unambiguous, objective way. The same is true for a state apparatus' capacity to implement policies, even though the indicators for government effectiveness or bureaucratic quality that are published by international organizations may serve as an approximation. Finally, it is often a matter of definition whether a specific country represents an example of the large group of intermediate states or whether it should be considered one of the two antipodes. This is exemplified by Malaysia, Thailand, and Indonesia, which were considered to be intermediate states by Doner et al (2005), but developmental states by other scholars (see Section 4.1).

Through the case studies in Part II, the characteristics of developmental states were explored further. In particular, it was argued that the relationship of the East Asian developmental states with foreign countries is of crucial importance for understanding their successful economic development. Foreign countries were not only important because they represented military threats that committed East Asian governments to economic growth; they also served as partners and reference models that had a decisive impact on economic policy and the path of institutional development. Moreover, it was noted that the state-business relations in developmental states shifted notably over time. As the East Asian countries caught up with the advanced economies in Western Europe and North America, their business sectors increased in importance and developed business ties with international companies. In this way, businesses became gradually more influential in the East Asian developmental states.

Section 7, and even more so the analysis of interviews in Section 8, provided important insights for the evaluation of Kazakhstan and Uzbekistan from the perspective of the developmental state concept. Some of these are summarized in Table 24, which also includes some of the key quotes from interviews that were already presented in Section 8. While both countries share important similarities, there are also crucial differences. These are particularly apparent in the state-business nexus. State-business interaction took place in a variety of ways in the East Asian developmental states. These differences were noted in Part II. However, it has generally been considered a key characteristic of developmental states that they maintained cooperative relations with the business sector. They were commonly governed by formal mechanisms, which ensured the effective exchange of information. This differs significantly from the state-business nexus found in Uzbekistan. The common perception among interviewees was that the Uzbek government holds an essentially hostile stance toward private business. Some exceptions are made for foreign investors which operate in specific sectors under the auspices of the central government. Formal mechanisms to exchange information between the state apparatus and business are lacking almost completely. Some changes in the state-business nexus were noted in the interviews. Even though it is part of the state apparatus, several interviewees perceived the Chamber of Commerce and Industries as an organization that represents business interests and facilitates the exchange of information between smaller companies and the government. Furthermore, meetings between representatives of the state and businessmen take place, even though it was stated that only low-level representatives of the state apparatus take place. The effectiveness of these meetings is highly doubtful. The key companies in Uzbekistan are state-owned enterprises and the joint ventures these enterprises form with a small number of foreign investors. As a result of the political conditions in Uzbekistan and an overall non-transparent environment, the functioning of these entities is hardly observable.

The state-business nexus in Kazakhstan is notably different from Uzbekistan. While there is no doubt that the Kazakh state plays a significant, or even dominating, role in the economy, the environment is—at least superficially— much more transparent than in Uzbekistan. It is known which companies are entirely controlled by the state through the holding Samruk-Kazyna. Furthermore, the ownership structure of major private companies such as ENRC and Kazakhmys is published. Thus, it is known which share the Kazakh state owns and which share is held by private businessmen. Of course, this does not mean that internal distribution of power and the real degree of state influence in these private companies is observable. Nevertheless, the fact that the state shares the ownership of companies that have a crucial role for the Kazakh economy with private entrepreneurs seems to evidence that cooperative relations between government and these selected businessmen exist. Moreover, formal and well-known mechanisms for the exchange between the state apparatus and the overall private sector exist in Kazakhstan. It was noted in the interviews that regular and frequent meetings between high-level government representatives and the private sector are well-institutionalized. While it is hard to evaluate whether this interaction has a decisive influence on the decisions of the Kazakh government, this frequent interaction represents a clear difference to Uzbekistan. Therefore, the state-business relations in Kazakhstan show notably more similarities to the East Asian developmental states than those in Uzbekistan.

Comparable differences and similarities between Kazakhstan and Uzbekistan exist in the area of the public administration. Judging from the interviews, the institutions governing the state bureaucracy have been left basically unchanged from Soviet times in Uzbekistan. The recruitment process seems to vary between agencies and is mostly limited to job interviews. While the process itself does not seem to have undergone profound changes since Soviet times, it was argued in interviews with public officials that it has become more selective. It was also argued that the higher levels of the state apparatus have the ability to enforce their decisions through the bureaucracy. However, there was also doubt as to whether the implementation of policies decided at the top always takes place. It was stated that different decisions taken at the higher levels of the state apparatus actually contradict each other, which makes the full implementation of the resulting rules impossible. While not mentioned explicitly in the interviews, it seems highly probable that the top level's commitment to some of the adopted decisions is only superficial.

The rules and mechanisms governing recruitment and promotion represent a clear difference between the public administrations of Kazakhstan and Uzbekistan. As was noted in Sections 7 and 8, the Kazakh government has undertaken major steps toward a reform of the formal institutions of the bureaucracy. A transparent mechanism based on entry examinations governs the recruitment process in the Kazakh civil service. However, both the literature on Kazakhstan and the interviews analyzed in Section 8 cast doubt on the full enforcement of formal institutions in the recruitment and promotion process. Formal, meritocratic mechanisms are often bypassed in the reality. As in Uzbekistan, issues concerning the implementation of policies by the public administration were noted in the interviews carried out in Kazakhstan. This is evidenced by such quotes: "There are more words than real policies. Not more than 60 percent of what is being told transform into policy guidelines" (K(a)8).

It was also argued that regional politicians and lower-ranking public officials may not carry out what is decided at the center, either due to unwillingness (and lack of enforcement) or due to a lack of capability. However, there were also statements arguing that policies which are critical for the highest level of the state apparatus get implemented quickly and efficiently. This is a crucial similarity between Kazakhstan and Uzbekistan. Judging from the perceptions of interviewees, the key decision makers at the central governments of both countries have the ability to enforce the full implementation of decisions in specific cases. Yet, in reality the implementation of policies is often lacking.

Table 24: Summary of interview results for the public administration and the state-business nexus

	Kazakhstan	Uzbekistan
Bureaucratic Recruitment and promotion	**Formal mechanism based on entry examinations, however complemented with other, intransparent mechanisms.** In order to be hired we had to go through the Agency for Public Service. We had to pass the test; the test on the Constitution, state language, ethics in the public service and the law on education. K(b)8 Yes, you can go through the exams but the final decision—it is not how much you score there. (K(a)25)	**Recruitment based on interviews. Importance of meritocratic elements hard to evaluate.** I was hired based on the results of the interview. (. . . .) Today there are lots of specialists out there and the selection process is stricter and more thorough. The process itself hasn't changed but the requirements have. (U(b)7)
Capacity to implement	**Effectiveness of implementation varies** There are more words than real policies. Not more than 60 percent of what is being told transform into policy guidelines, concepts. (K(a)8) Some things which are critical for the country leadership are get done very quickly and very efficiently. Many other policies, which are not that strategically important many times do not get done although they should have. (K(a)3)	**Effectiveness of implementation varies** There are laws the observance and application of which will be so much observed making the earth tremble; the enforcement organs will be ready to overthrow everything to observe these laws. There are laws that have been adopted 10 times but never applied or executed for various reasons. (. . . .) there is so much contradiction within the legislation which makes execution of laws impossible. (U(a)6)
State-business interaction	**Frequent and formalized interaction involving high-level representatives, effectiveness cast into doubt by some** There are forums that the government conducts on a regular basis (. . .). The government is actually trying to keep contact with the businesses. (. . .) the Ministry of Industry and Trade can come or Deputy Minister can come to such meetings and they can even put him on a spot and ask questions directly to him, give examples, and they answer it. (K(a)2)	**Some meetings take place, however it seems they don't involve high-level representatives. The effectiveness is subject to severe doubts** There are issues you are allowed to discuss, there are issues you are not allowed to discuss. (U(a)16) Government is not necessarily afraid but doesn't want to have an open dialogue because first of all that puts them in the position where they have to respond to that dialogue. And if they can't respond to it, you know, why be embarrassed by not being able to answer the questions. (U(a)3)
Rule enforcement and predictability of conditions	**Personalized political system leads to certain unpredictability, rule enforcement seems to be more predictable than in Uzbekistan** We do not know how he [Nazarbayev; M.S.] thinks. (. . . .) We believe that is the problem, if this is so concentrated, then you can predict with much less probability, especially if that person gets older and the power struggle for the top job has definitively started. (K(a)3) With regard to rule enforcement: mainly, the rules are enforced. We don't have large blocks of unenforced laws. (K(a)8)	**Personalized political system leads to certain unpredictability, which also includes the enforcement of rules** When it comes to larger companies that make decisions in top circles at the government level, for them the economic policy is transparent and predictable. For small and medium-sized businesses there are moments that are predictable and unpredictable. (U(a)20) It is absolutely predictable on the one hand; on the other hand it absolutely depends on the most unexpected circumstances, you know. It depends on the sectors of economy we are talking about here, about sympathies and antipathies. (U(a)16)

What do these institutional differences and similarities between Kazakhstan and Uzbekistan mean from the perspective of the developmental state concept? Focusing on formal institutions, Kazakhstan shares more characteristics with the East Asian developmental states than Uzbekistan. Concerning the public administration and the state-business nexus, the Kazakh leadership has established formal rules that bear notable similarities to East Asian countries. These formal rules are apparently bypassed in some instances, which casts doubt on a characterization of Kazakhstan as a developmental state. This doubt is further exacerbated by the fact that the economy continues to be highly reliant on extractive industries. Data on value added to GDP does not yet evidence any noteworthy diversification toward manufacturing (see Table 21 in Section 8.3.1.1).

Nevertheless, significant positive aspects remain. Even though the formal institutions in the bureaucratic recruitment and promotion process may be bypassed in some instances, they represent a foundation for system that is not only meritocratic, but also transparent. In this context, it is remarkable that harsh criticism on the current implementation of formal rules for recruitment and promotion also comes from *within* the state apparatus. The Agency of Civil Service Affairs of the Republic of Kazakhstan itself has publicly criticized the continued prevalence of corruption, including bypassing the competitive recruitment process, abusing power while in office, and unlawfully dismissing bureaucrats who lack personal ties to newly appointed superiors in its reports (Emrich-Bakenova, pp. 727–730). One the one hand, the fact that the agency that is supposed to be at the forefront of bureaucratic reform has not been able to eradicate these problems successfully casts doubt on the civil service reforms in Kazakhstan. On the other hand, it is apparent that parts of the administration are committed to reforms and that the political conditions are sufficiently liberal to permit open criticism and conflict within the state apparatus.

Further positive aspects of the Kazakh institutional environment are obvious in the state-business nexus. Similar to the East Asian developmental states, the government has established mechanisms that ensure a frequent and, as it seems, open interaction between the private sector and the administration. Of course, the mere existence of such mechanisms does not necessarily mean that they have a substantial impact on the Kazakh economic policy and the path of institutional change. However, it seems highly probable that the interaction has at least some positive effects for the business climate in Kazakhstan, because it enables the private sector to voice its preferences effectively and broadens the basis of information for key decision makers in the government and the bureaucracy.

An underlying issue in this context has been attitude of the Kazakh leadership toward other countries. As was argued in the conclusions to Part II of this study, learning from the experience of foreign reference economies has been of utmost importance for the East Asian developmental states. This does not mean that they merely copied foreign policies and institutions. Rather, the path of institutional change in the developmental states was characterized by a peculiar blend of the national heritage and lessons from the experience of more advanced economies. As it seems, the Kazakh government is also attempting to learn from the development of other countries. This is not only reflected in official statements. As was noted previously, the holding company Samruk-Kazyna was modeled after similar organizations in Singapore and Malaysia. This holding has drastically increased in importance over the last few years and has become the state's key tool to influence the path of economic development. In this way, the holding might play a role similar to the economic pilot agencies in the successful East Asian developmental states. In addition, the interviews analyzed in Section 8 strongly support the perception that the experiences of advanced economies are taken into account by the Kazakh leadership. As the importance of foreign reference models was also noted in interviews with Kazakh public officials, one might conclude that the foreign influence was not limited to the adoption of policies and institutions, but that it also shaped the ideologies of actors within the state apparatus.

While Kazakhstan has established formal institutions that bear notable similarities to the East Asian developmental states in some key areas, such institutions are much harder to find in Uzbekistan. As has been noted throughout this study, the Uzbek leadership has only implemented limited reforms, which resulted in a gradual change of the formal institutions inherited from Soviet times. As was summarized, the formal rules governing the bureaucratic recruitment process have not changed in recent years. In the state-business nexus, formal mechanisms for the interaction of state and business are merely emerging. It was already argued in the introduction to this study that the conditions faced by Uzbekistan after the dissolution of the Soviet Union resembled the conditions faced by South Korea and Taiwan after their independence from Japan in some ways. Judging on the basis of formal institutional development concerning the bureaucracy and the state-business nexus, it does not seem as if the similarities between Uzbekistan and the East Asian developmental states have increased much over the last two decades.

It is possible that this evaluation underestimates the changes that have taken place. It was noted in the interviews that the bureaucratic recruitment process itself has not changed much, yet it was stated that the process became more selective. In this way, Uzbekistan's civil service may have become more meritocratic. In addition, the absence of formal mechanisms of interaction in the Uzbek state-business nexus may not be as important because informal ties may serve as a substitute. However, the experience of countries such as Indonesia and Thailand suggests that informal ties are not a sufficient substitute for formal cooperative mechanisms because of their intransparency. Thailand's economic take-off essentially began after state-business relations became more formalized in the 1980s whereas the continuing importance of informal ties in Indonesia has probably contributed to its comparatively lackluster economic performance.

As in the case of Kazakhstan, the attitude of the Uzbek leadership toward foreign countries can be seen as an underlying factor when analyzing the path of institutional change that it pursued since the early 1990s. Since the dissolution of the Soviet Union, the government stressed the independence of Uzbekistan. As was noted, foreign countries, such as Turkey and the East Asian developmental states, were mentioned by the president as possible reference models in the first years of independence (see Section 7.3.2.1). However, the uniqueness of Uzbekistan and the *Uzbek model* of development have since been stressed. This was also reflected in the interviews: in sharp contrast to Kazakhstan, a notable share of interviewees in Uzbekistan did not mention any foreign influence on the government's approach to reforms and economic policy.

What is the overall evaluation of Kazakhstan and Uzbekistan from the perspective of the developmental state concept? There is not much evidence that would suggest that Uzbekistan is a developmental state. While the government preserved state structures from disintegrating and achieved a remarkable economic stability, it does not seem as if economic development has been its key priority over the last two decades. This does not mean that Uzbekistan is a predatory state, as Perlman and Gleason (2005, p. 101) seem to suggest. Rather, Uzbekistan should be characterized as an intermediate state where the leadership combines the pursuit of economic development with other, non-developmental objectives.

Economic development seems to have been a higher priority for the Kazakh leadership over the last few decades. This is evidenced by the more ambitious reform efforts and by the willingness to learn from other countries. In this way, Kazakhstan bears more resemblance to a developmental state than Uzbekistan. However, crucial differences remain. The implementation of civil service reforms has not been fully successful and non-transparent, non-meritocratic elements remain. Furthermore, there is no evidence of a diversification of the economy that would resemble the continuous industrial upgrading of the East Asian developmental states. As argued in the interviews, the government has been announcing for some time that diversification was important. Yet, its commitment to this objective seems to have been lacking. It was suggested in some interviews that this has changed in recent years, but it remains to be seen whether a credible commitment to diversification will be sustained after the direct impact of the economic crisis has vanished. To conclude, there are crucial differences between Kazakhstan and the Northeast Asian developmental states, which make it unlikely that it will achieve a similarly successful economic development. However, some lessons from East Asia have been adopted. Kazakhstan does show more resemblance to the resource-rich, but economically relatively less successful, Southeast Asian developmental states such as Thailand and Indonesia. As was argued in previous sections, it is also a matter of definition whether a state constitutes a developmental or an intermediate state. Arguably, Kazakhstan should still be considered an intermediate state for now, but it has been notably more developmental than Uzbekistan.

9.2 Theoretical considerations on the prospects for the emergence of developmental states in Central Asia

The last section has essentially been a synopsis of the insights derived from interviews and desk research. It represented an overview over the similarities and differences between the current institutional environment in Kazakhstan and Uzbekistan and the institutions that characterized the East Asian developmental states in earlier decades. It did not involve any theorizing on the emergence of developmental states and did not attempt to explain why the political decision makers in Kazakhstan and Uzbekistan have been following different transition approaches. It was not attempted to answer the question whether developmental states could emerge in these countries in the future.

This section is aimed at analyzing the past development of Kazakhstan and Uzbekistan as well as some future prospects from a theoretical perspective. Scholars have given different explanations for the diverging development of the two largest Central Asian republics. According to Blackmon (2005), differences in the initial conditions inherited from the Soviet period as well as the personal ideologies of Karimov and Nazarbayev played a fundamental role. Concerning the initial conditions, she emphasizes Kazakhstan's thorough integration of its infrastructure with Russia and the relative independence of the geographically more distant Uzbekistan (Blackmon, 2005, pp. 394–400). In contrast, Perlman and Gleason (2007) stress the similarity of the initial conditions faced by both countries after the dissolution of the Soviet Union. They argue that both countries were similar in terms of cultural heritage, formal institutions and situational factors at independence. Based on this notion, Perlman and Gleason (2007) argue that the diverging paths of development and the stronger reform efforts in Kazakhstan were the result of different policy choices and reject cultural explanations for development. They suggest that analyzing the interaction between culture and formal institutions would be a productive line of thought for future research (Perlman & Gleason, 2007, pp. 1339–1340).

It was already mentioned in Section 3.2.3 that scientific research on East Asia has also generally rejected explanations based on culture. Indeed, it is apparent from manifold historical examples that culture alone is not sufficient to explain economic success or failure. However, this does not mean that culture does not matter at all. From the theoretical perspective adopted in this study, culture matters it two different but interrelated ways: it is the source of informal institutions and shapes the ideology of actors (see Section 2.3.2). This not only refers to the ideology of key actors, such as Nazarbayev and Karimov, but to the ideology of any individual that may have the most minuscule influence on institutional change. Apart from culture, ideologies are also shaped by the knowledge and current experiences of actors. This theoretical perspective offers further insights on the underlying reasons for the diverging development of Kazakhstan and Uzbekistan.

Arguably, staying in power is one of the key objectives of any political leader. A further, closely related objective of a political leader is to maintain the independence and territorial integrity of his country. As was noted throughout this study, it is commonly argued that the governments of the East Asian developmental states were committed to economic growth because they faced various threats to their power, including but not limited to external military threats to the independence of their countries. From this perspective, economic development was only a secondary objective that was pursued as a means to the underlying objective of preserving the political status quo.

What does this mean for Central Asia? The notion of Perlman and Gleason (2007, p. 1339) that the leaders of Kazakhstan and Uzbekistan encountered similar conditions after independence is only partly true. The key question is what imperatives the presidents of the newly countries faced in order to preserve their power. In this context, one may reflect on the ideologies of the people that have been governed by Nazarbayev and Karimov over the last two decades. The experience of neighboring countries may be an important influence on the knowledge and current experiences of these individuals. Uzbekistan is bordered by five countries: Kazakhstan, Kyrgyzstan, Tajikistan, Turkmenistan, and Afghanistan. Tajikistan and Afghanistan both experienced civil wars involving Islamist groups in the 1990s. Kyrgyzstan has been relatively stable in the first decade of independence, but has been characterized by political uprisings more recently. Turkmenistan has been ruled by a regime that is more authoritarian and isolationist than that of Uzbekistan. From this perspective, the relative economic stability and domestic peace their country may rightfully appear as a major achievement to Uzbek people.

In contrast to Uzbekistan, Kazakhstan does not border Tajikistan or Afghanistan, but it borders China and Russia. Moreover, it was noted in Section 7.3.1 that Russians made up about 40% of Kazakhstan's population in 1989 and outnumbered Kazakhs in northern regions. This was not only a threat to Kazakhstan's territorial integrity in the early years of independence, but it presumably also shaped the ideologies of the inhabitants of the country. Throughout the two decades of independence, the economic policies and reforms showed notable parallels to Russia, assuming a reformist stance in the early 1990s and returning to a stronger role of the state in more recent years. Moreover, the economic development of both countries has been similar: a pronounced transition recession in the first years of independence followed by robust growth rates based on the export of natural resources. It seems at least possible that the political conditions in Kazakhstan would have been less stable if the Kazakh economy had performed significantly worse than the Russian economy in the last decades. In addition, Kazakhstan's territorial integrity might have been cast into doubt. From this perspective, economic development was presumably a more important objective for Nazarbayev than for Karimov. This line of argument does not rule out that policy choices based on the personal ideologies of the respective presidents were important for the path of transition.

What is the implication of these theory-based considerations for the future prospects on Central Asia? It was argued several times in the sections on East Asia that individuals' ideologies as well as a sense of competition between different economies may have been decisive for the regional dynamics that evolved in Northeast and Southeast Asia. Concerning Central Asia, it was noted that Uzbekistan and Kazakhstan have competed for the status of the regional leader over the last two decades. The economic success of both countries has been fundamental to this rivalry. If the economic competition between Kazakhstan and Uzbekistan continues or even increases, it may be possible that a regional dynamic emerges that benefits both countries.

10 Conclusions: Findings and limitations of the study

This study had the objective to answer two main research questions:

(1) What are the characteristic institutions of developmental states and under which circumstances did they emerge in East Asia?

(2) Are institutions that were characteristic for developmental states in East Asia present or emerging in Central Asia?

In order to set the basis for answering these questions, a model of institutional change based on the Northian New Institutional Economics (NIE) was drafted in Section 2. Furthermore, the developmental state literature was summarized. Some key elements of the developmental state according to the literature were identified. This includes the influential role of an autonomous, meritocratic bureaucracy, a cooperative relationship between the state apparatus and the business sector and the implementation of activist industrial policies. Furthermore, it is commonly argued that the political leadership and the bureaucracy in developmental states were highly committed to the objective of economic development. According to the literature, this commitment was the result of specific constraints faced by the developmental states: scarce natural resources, foreign military threats, and the persistence of broad political coalitions (Doner et al., 2005). Furthermore, it is argued that activist industrial policies contributed to economic development because they helped to overcome backwardness by initiating "a simultaneous move from a low-equilibrium to a high-equilibrium" (Chang, 1999, pp. 193–194), which would otherwise not have occurred due to market failures. In the conclusions to Part I (Section 4), it was noted that one of the key shortcomings of the literature on East Asia is the lack of an overarching theoretical framework that helps to explain the emergence of the specific institutional environment of developmental states. In addition, the underlying reasons for the apparent ability of East Asian governments and bureaucracies to overcome some of the pitfalls associated with industrial policy deserve more theoretical scrutiny.

The case studies in Part II led to several insights on these issues, which are summarized in Section 6. In contrast to other developing economies characterized by state intervention, the developmental states not only achieved a rapid factor accumulation, but also realized a sufficiently efficient factor allocation. Among other factors, a key explanation for the latter achievement is the leadership's commitment the objective of sustained economic growth. While the importance of scarce resources, external threats, and broad political conditions for this commitment was not disputed, it was argued that the presence of these conditions is not sufficient to explain the emergence of developmental states. Instead of focusing purely on constraints, the ideologies of both the key decision makers and the general public as embodied in their mental models of the world should be taken into account. Crucial influences on the mental models of economic actors in the developmental states included:

(1) A regional dynamic of economic growth, which compelled political leaders to prove their legitimacy by supporting the economic development of their countries.

(2) The knowledge that other countries had achieved sustained economic growth through activist economic policies.

(3) Ties to advanced economies, which had, in some cases, a direct impact on the institutional development.

The relationship of the developmental states to foreign countries is of particular importance in this context. The existing literature on the developmental states has stressed the international environment of developmental states primarily as the source of military threats. However, foreign countries also represented reference models for a viable path to economic prosperity. Through consciously and often explicitly adopting the institutions and policies of other, economically more advanced countries, the developmental states also avoided some of the general pitfalls associated with activist economic policies. Furthermore, it was argued that the existence of various centers of power governed by diverging ideologies served to limit the power of individual bureaucratic agencies. The competition of these centers of power contributed to the gradual liberalization of the East Asian economies as their economic backwardness and the necessity for state interventions decreased. Table 25 represents a brief synopsis of some key findings on the developmental state from a theoretical perspective.

While the developmental states show significant variations in their concrete set of formal institutions, a stylized model of the developmental state based on the interrelationships between different organizations, institutions, and exogenous factors was presented in Section 6.5. In Part III, the economies of Central Asia were analyzed by applying the framework developed in Parts I and II. The key findings of this part are summarized in Section 9. It was found that none of the five Central Asian countries currently represents a clear-cut example of a developmental state. However, it was argued that particularly Kazakhstan has attempted to learn from the successful East Asian economies and that it shows characteristics of a developmental state in some key areas. If a Central Asian regional dynamic based on the economic competition between Kazakhstan and Uzbekistan unfolds in the near future, the political leaders might adopt even more lessons from the successful East Asian developmental states.

Table 25: Synopsis of conclusions on the developmental state from a theoretical perspective

Theoretical Aspect	Past literature	Insights from this study
External environment	Foreign countries primarily seen as the origin of military threats that constrained political decision makers.	Crucial importance of ties to advanced economies that served as reference economies in terms of industrial structure, formal institutions, and economic policy.
Economic backwardness	Underlying reason for the necessity of state interventions because of coordination failures. Focus on learning in terms of technological and managerial capabilities.	Underlying reason for the necessity of state interventions because of coordination failures and prohibitively high information costs. Learning from advanced economies not only focused on technology and management, but also on institutions, policy and viable paths to economic catch-up.
Role of the developmental state in the economy	Promoting economic development in a plan-rational way through interventions.	Promoting economic development through interventions at the beginning of economic take-off and gradually retreating from an activist role as economic backwardness decreases.
Culture	In scholarly literature commonly rejected from the list of decisive factors for East Asian growth.	Seen as the source of informal constraints and a fundamental influence on ideologies (together with knowledge and current experiences). Ideologies considered influential for the emergence of developmental states.
Commitment to economic growth	Either seen as driven exclusively by exogenous constraints or as inherent to leaders' mindset.	Based on both exogenous constraints and the ideologies of key actors and the general public. Ideologies subject to change because of changes in knowledge and current experiences (including the experience of regional economic dynamism).
Structure of the bureaucracy	Strong role of a pilot agency that exercises control over other parts of the bureaucracy.	Several competing centers of power within the administration mitigate the role of the pilot agency and hinder the abuse of power.

Clearly, the analysis within this study has some limitations. In order to account for the complexity of the issues, a qualitative research approach based on process tracing and an explicit theoretical framework was pursued. This approach has led to valuable insights on the theoretical concept of the developmental state and the economic policies pursued by the governments in East and Central Asia. However, there is still a lot of ground to be explored in future research. As already mentioned in the introduction to this study, the interview-based empirical study on Kazakhstan and Uzbekistan had an overall exploratory character. Interviewees with different personal and professional backgrounds were asked to share their knowledge on a variety of different issues and both interviewers and informants were given a substantial amount of freedom concerning the topics to be discussed. It would make sense to conduct further research based on survey or structured interviews in order to confirm some of the conclusions that were drawn in Section 9.

Furthermore, the country focus of this study could be extended in future research. Part II focused on the East Asian countries that have been commonly referred to as developmental states in order to get a clear understanding of their development and their institutional characteristics. All countries analyzed in Part II have experienced periods of remarkable economic growth, even though there were significant differences in the sustainability of this success. However, the most successful East Asian economy of recent years, the People's Republic of China, has been excluded from this analysis. China is much larger than any of the other East Asian economies and faced an institutional heritage and a set of constraints that distinguishes it from the developmental states analyzed here. An analysis of its path of institutional change along the lines applied here could lead to further insights that could also prove valuable for understanding the transition process in Central Asia.

References

Abazov, R. (1999). Economic migration in post-Soviet Central Asia: The case of Kyrgyzstan. *Post-Communist Economies, 11*(2), 237–252.

Abazov, R. (2006, October). Kazakhstan's bolashak program: Short term fix or long term program. *Central Asia-Caucasus Analyst, 8*(19), 5–7. Retrieved from http://www. cacianalyst.org/?q=issueachive

Abbott, J. (2004). 'Not like the rest' differential development in Malaysia and Thailand. In L. Low (Ed.): *Developmental states: Relevancy, redundancy or reconfiguration?* (pp. 179–200). Hauppauge, NY: Nova Science Publishers.

Ahrens, J. (1994). *Der russische Systemwandel. Reform und Transformation des (post)sowjetischen Wirtschaftssystems.* Frankfurt am Main, Germany: Peter Lang.

Ahrens, J. (2002). *Governance and economic development: A comparative institutional approach. New thinking in political economy.* Cheltenham, UK: Elgar.

Aichi, K. (1969). Japan's legacy and destiny of change. *Foreign Affairs, 48*(1), 21–38.

Akyüz, Y., & Gore, C. (1996). The investment-profits nexus in East Asian industrialization. *World Development, 24*(3), 461–470.

Akyüz, Y., Chang, H.-J., & Kozul-Wright, R. (1998). New perspectives on East Asian development. *Journal of Development Studies, 34*(6), 4–36.

Alesina, A. (2007, August). *The choice of institutions.* Paper presented at Munich Lectures 2006 November 14th, revised August 2007. Retrieved from http:// www.economics. harvard.edu/faculty/alesina/unpublished_papers_alesina

Allen, G. C. (1968). The public and co-operative sectors in Japan. *Annals of Public & Co-operative Economy, 39*(2), 133–156.

Amsden, A. H. (1989). *Asia's next giant: South Korea and late industrialization* (1. issue as an Oxford Univ. Press paperback.). New York, NY: Oxford Univ. Press.

Amsden, A. H. (1991). Diffusion of development: The late-industrializing model and greater East Asia. *American Economic Review, Papers and Proceedings, 81*(2), 282–286.

302

Amsden, A. H. (1995). Like the rest: South-East Asia's 'late' industrialization. *Journal of International Development, 7*(5), 791–799.

Amsden, A. H. (2001). *The rise of "the rest": Challenges to the West from late-industrializing economies.* New York, NY: Oxford University Press.

Aoki, M. (1997a). Unintended fit: Organizational evolution and government design of institutions in Japan. In M. Aoki, H.-K. Kim and M. Okuno-Fujiwara (Eds.), *The role of government in East Asian economic development: Comparative institutional analysis* (1st ed., pp. 233–253). Oxford, UK: Oxford University Press.

Aoki, M., Kim, H.-K., & Okuno-Fujiwara, M. (Eds.) (1997b). *The role of government in East Asian economic development: Comparative institutional analysis* (1st ed., pp. 233–253). Oxford: Oxford University Press.

Aoki, M., Murdock, K., & Okuno-Fujiwara, M. (1997). Beyond the East Asian miracle: Introducing the market-enhancing view. In M. Aoki, H.-K. Kim and M. Okuno-Fujiwara (Eds.), *The role of government in East Asian economic development: Comparative institutional analysis* (1st ed., pp. 1–37). Oxford: Oxford University Press.

Ayal, E. B. (1963). Value systems and economic development in Japan and Thailand. *Journal of Social Issues, 19*, 35–51.

Babadzhanov, U., Saadi, S., & Kurbanov, T. (2010, June 23). Zeromax scandal raises questions about ownership: Bankrupt firm operates in face of court proceedings. *Central Asia Online.* Retrieved from http://centralasiaonline.com

Bates, R. H. (1999). *Institutions and economic performance,* paper prepared for delivery at the IMF Conference on Second Generation Reforms. Retrieved from:http://www.imf.org/external/pubs/ft/seminar/1999/reforms/bates.htm

Batson, B. A. (1980). Siam and Japan: The perils of independence. In A. W. McCoy (Ed.), *Southeast Asia under Japanese occupation* (pp. 267–302). New Haven, CT: Yale Southeast Asia Studies Monograph No. 22.

Bennett, A. (2008). Building communities, bridging gaps: Alexander George's contributions to research methods. *Political Psychology, 29*(4), 489–507. doi: 10.1111/j.1467-9221.20 08.00646.x

Bertelsmann Foundation (2009a). *BTI 2010: Kazakhstan country report.* Gütersloh: Bertelsmann Stiftung.

Bertelsmann Foundation (2009b). *BTI 2010: Uzbekistan country report.* Gütersloh: Bertelsmann Stiftung.

Besley, T. (2007). The New Political Economy. *The Economic Journal, 117*(524), 570–587. doi: 10.1111/j.1468-0297.2007.02097.x

Bhagwati, J. N. (1988). Export-promoting trade strategy: Issues and evidence. *World Bank Research Observer, 3*(1), 27–57.

Bidder, B. (2011, November 1). Kirgisiens neuer Präsident will die Air Force rauswerfen. *Spiegel Online.* Retrieved from http://www.spiegel.de

Blackmon, P. (2005). Back to the USSR: why the past does matter in explaining differences in the economic reform processes of Kazakhstan and Uzbekistan. *Central Asian Survey, 24*(4), 391–404. doi: 10.1080=02634930500453285

Blackmon, P. (2007). Divergent paths, divergent outcomes: linking differences in economic reform to levels of US foreign direct investment and business in Kazakhstan and Uzbekistan. *Central Asian Survey, 26*(3), 355–372. doi: 10.1080/ 02634930701702563

Booth, A. (2003). Education and economic development in Southeast Asia: myths and realities. In: K. S. Jomo, (Ed.), *Southeast Asian Paper Tigers: From miracle to debacle and beyond* (pp. 173–195). London: RoutledgeCurzon.

Bowyer, A. C. (2008). *Parliament and political parties in Kazakhstan* (Silk Road Paper May 2008). Washington, D.C.: Johns Hopkins University-SAIS. Retrieved from http:// www.isdp.eu/publications/silk-road-papers.html

Buchanan, J. M. (1989). The public-choice perspective. In: *Essays on the Political Economy*, Honolulu, HI: University of Hawaii Press.

Campos, J. E., Root, H. (1996). *The key to the Asian miracle: Making shared growth credible.* Washington, D.C.: Brookings Institution.

Case, W. F. (2000). The new Malaysian nationalism: Infirm beginnings, crashing finale. *Asian Ethnicity, 1*(2), 131–147.

Case, W. F. (2005). Malaysia: New reforms, old continuities, tense ambiguities. *The Journal of Development Studies, 41*(2), 284–309. doi: 0.1080/ 0022038042000 309 250

Castells, M. (1992). Four Asian Tigers with a dragon head: A comparative analysis of the state, economy, and society in the Asian pacific rim. In:

Richard P. Appelbaum & Jeffrey Henderson, (Eds.), *States and development in the Asian pacific rim* (pp. 33–70). Newbury Park, CA: Sage Publications.

Center for International Programs (2011). *Bolashak at a glance: "Bolashak" means "future".* Retrieved November 15, 2011, from http://www.educip.kz/grantMenu-en-US/

Chamber of Commerce and Industry of Uzbekistan (2011). *Goals and mission.* Retrieved from http://chamber.uz/index.php?id=229&L=3

Chang, H.-J. (1993). The political economy of industrial policy in Korea. *Cambridge Journal of Economics, 17,* 131–157.

Chang, H.-J. (1999). The economic theory of the developmental state. In M. Woo-Cumings (Ed.), *Cornell studies in political economy: The developmental state* (1st ed., pp. 182–199). Ithaca: Cornell Univ. Press.

Chang, H.-J. (2003). Kicking away the ladder: Infant industry promotion in historical perspective. *Oxford Development Studies, 31*(1), 21–32.

Chen, E. K. Y. (1979). *Hypergrowth in Asian economies: A comparative survey of Hong Kong, Japan, Korea, Singapore and Taiwan.* London: Macmillan.

Cheng, T.-J., Haggard, S., & Kang, D. C. (1998). Institutions and growth in Korea and Taiwan: The bureaucracy. *Journal of Development Studies, 34*(6), 87–111.

CIA (2011). *The world factbook.* Retrieved January 11, 2012, from https://www.cia.gov/library/publications/the-world-factbook/index.html

Clem, R. S. (1992). The frontier and colonialism in Russian and Soviet Central Asia. In R. R. Churchill, R. A. Lewis, & A. Tate (Eds.), *Studies of the Harriman Institute: Geographic perspectives on Soviet Central Asia* (pp. 19–35). New York: Routledge.

Coase, R. H. (1937). The nature of the firm. *Economica, 4,* 386–405.

Coase, R. H. (1998). The New Institutional Economics. *American Economic Review, Papers and Proceedings, 88*(2), 72–74.

Cumings, B. (1984). The origins and development of the Northeast Asian political economy: industrial sectors, product cycles, and political consequences. *International Organization, 38*(1), 1–40.

Cumings, B. (1999). Webs with no spiders, spiders with no webs: The genealogy of the developmental state. In M. Woo-Cumings (Ed.), (1st ed., pp. 61–92). Ithaca: Cornell Univ. Press.

Cummings, S. (2002). *Understanding politics in kazakhstan* (DEMSTAR Research Report No. 10). Retrieved from http://www.demstar.dk/papers/Understanding Kazakhstan.pdf

Davé, B. (2009). *Nations in Transit 2009: Kazakhstan*. Freedom House: Nations in Transit. Retrieved from http://www.freedomhouse.org/template.cfm?page=485

Davis, L., & North, D. C. (1971). *Institutional change and American economic growth*. New York: Cambridge University Press.

Demange, J.-M. (2009). Sovereign wealth funds in South-East Asia. *Revue d'Économie Financière, Special Issue 2009*, 83–96.

Denzau, A. T., & North, D. C. (1994). Shared mental models: Ideologies and institutions. *Kyklos, 47*(1), 3–31.

Dethier, J.-J. (1999). *Governance and economic performance: A Survey* (ZEF Discussion Paper on Development Policy 5). Bonn: Zentrum für Entwicklungsforschung.

Deyo, F. C. (Ed.) (1987). *The political economy of the new Asian industrialism*. Ithaca and London: Cornell University Press.

Dietl, H. (1993). *Institutionen und Zeit,* Tübingen: J.C.B. Mohr.

DiMaggio, P. (1998). The new institutionalisms: Avenues of collaboration. *Journal of Institutional and Theoretical Economics, 154*, 696–705.

Doner, R. F., Ritchie, B. K., & Slater, D. (2005). Systemic vulnerability and the origins of developmental states: Northeast and Southeast Asia in comparative perspective. *International Organization, 59*, 327–361. doi: 10.1017/S0020818305050113

Dowling, J. M. (1994). Is there an Asian industrial growth paradigm? *Journal of Asian Economics, 5*(4), 525–535.

EBRD (2011). *Transition indicators by country*. Retrieved September 26, 2011, from http://www.ebrd.com/pages/research/economics/data/macro.shtml

Eckert, C. J. (1991). *Offspring of empire: The koch 'ang kim and the colonial origins of Korean Capitalism, 1876–1945*. Seattle: University of Washington Press.

Economist (1997, July 7). Aaarghmola. *Economist, 344*(8027). Retrieved November 12, 2011, from http://www.economist.com/node/152269

Economist (2004, July 15). An embarrassing friend: The United States is suspending aid to the government of Uzbekistan. *Economist, _372*(8384). Retrieved November 12, 2011, from http://www.economist.com/node/2926154

Economist (2005, August 4) Uzbekistan and America: Evicted. *Economist, 376*(8438). Retrieved October 14, 2011, from http://www.economist.com/node/4257097

Economist (2011a, August 11): Kyrgyzstan's Uzbeks: Weak fences, bad neighbours. *Economist, 399*(8746). Retrieved November 12, 2011, from http://www.economist .com/node/21525965

Economist (2011b, October 20). An election in Kyrgyzstan: Bridging the divide. *Economist, 400*(8756) Retrieved November 12, 2011, from http://www.economist .com/node/21533455

Eden, L., Herman, C. F., & Li, D. (2005, March). *Bringing case studies back in: qualitative research in international business.* Presentation at the 46th Annual International Studies Association Convention.

Edwards, M. (2003). The new Great Game and the new great gamers: disciples of Kipling and Mackinder. *Central Asian Survey, 22*(1), 83–102. doi: 10.1080/0263493032000108644

Eggertsson, T. (1990). *Economic behavior and institutions.* Cambridge: Cambridge University Press.

Eggertsson, T. (1997). The old theory of economic policy and the new institutionalism. *World Development, 25*(8), 1187–1203.

Emrich-Bakenova, S. (2009). Trajectory of civil service development in Kazakhstan: Nexus of politics and administration. *Governance: An International Journal of Policy, Administration, and Institutions, 22*(4), 717–745.

Encarnation, D. J. & Mason, M. (1990). Neither MITI nor America: the political economy of capital liberalization in Japan. *International Organization, 44*(1), 25–54.

ENRC (2011). *Major shareholders.* Retrieved December 28, 2011, from http://www.enrc. com/en-GB/Investors/Major-Shareholders/

Ergashev, B., Iusupov, I., Pogrebniak, A., Korenev, I., Allaev, B., & Gaibullaev, O., et al. (2006). Public administration reform in Uzbekistan. *Problems of Economic Transition, 48*(12), 32–82.

Eucken, W. (1952/1990). *Grundsätze der Wirtschaftspolitik.* (6th edition), Tübingen: J.C.B. Mohr.

Evans, P. (1989). Predatory, developmental, and other apparatuses: A comparative political economy perspective on the third world state. *Sociological Forum, 4*(4), 561–587.

Evans, P. (1995). *Embedded autonomy: States and industrial transformation. Princeton paperbacks.* Princeton, NJ: Princeton Univ. Press.

Evans, P. (1998). Transferable lessons? Re-examining the institutional prerequisites of East Asian economic policies. *Journal of Development Studies, 34*(6), 66–86.

Feeny, D. (1998). Thailand versus Japan: Why was Japan first? In: Y. Hayami & M. Aoki (Eds.), *The Institutional Foundations of East Asian Economic Development: Proceedings of the Iea Conference Held in Tokyo, Japan (Iea Conference Volume)* (pp. 413–442). Basingstoke: Palgrave Macmillan.

Felker, G.(2003). Technology policies and innovation systems in Southeast Asia. In: K. S. Jomo, (Ed.), *Southeast Asian Paper Tigers: From miracle to debacle and beyond* (pp. 136–172). London: RoutledgeCurzon.

FIC (2011). *Mission.* Retrieved December 14, 2011, from http://www. fic.kz/content.asp ?parent=1&lng=en&mid=10

Flick, U. (2009). *An introduction to qualitative research* (4th ed.). London: Sage Publications.

Foltz, R. (1996). The Tajiks of Uzbekistan. *Central Asian Survey, 15*(2), 213–216. doi: 10.1080/02634939608400946

Forbes (2011). *The world's billionaires.* Retrieved November 17, 2011, from http://www. forbes.com/wealth/billionaires

Fredholm, M. (2003). *Uzbekistan & the threat from Islamic Extremism.* Shrivenham: Conflict Studies Research Centre. Retrieved from http://www.da.mod.uk/colleges/arag/document-listings/ca/K39-MP.pdf/ view

Freedom House (2011). *Country ratings and status, FIW 1973–2011.* Retrieved August 1, 2011, from http://www.freedomhouse.org/template.cfm?page= 439

Frey, B. (1988). Political economy and institutional choice. *European Journal of Political Economy, 4*(3), 349–366.

Fulcher, J. (1988). The bureaucratization of the state and the rise of Japan. *The British Journal of Sociology, 39*(2), 228–254.

George, A. L. (1979a). Case studies and theory development: The method of structured, focused comparison. In G. Lauren (Ed.), *Diplomacy: New approaches in history, theory and policy* (pp. 43–68). New York: The Free Press.

George, A. L., & Bennett, A. (2005). *Case studies and theory development in the social sciences.* Cambridge, MA: MIT Press.

Gerschenkron, Alexander (1962). *Economic backwardness in historical perspective: A book of essays.* Cambridge, MA: The Belknap Press of Harvard University Press.

Gläser, J., & Laudel, G. (2009). *Experteninterviews und qualitative Inhaltsanalyse* (4th ed.). Wiesbaden: VS Verlag für Sozialwissenschaften.

Gleason, G. (2006). The Uzbek expulsion of U.S. forces and realignment in Central Asia. *Problems of post-communism, 53*(2), 49–60.

Goldstone, J. A. (1991). Ideology, cultural frameworks, and the process of revolution. *Theory and Society, 20,* 405–453.

Grabowski, R. (1994). The successful developmental state: Where does it come from? *World Development, 22*(3), 413–422.

Grabowski, R. (2007). Political development and growth: Japan until World War II. *Journal of the Asia Pacific Economy, 12*(4), 522–547. doi: 10.1080/1354786070 1594186

Greif, A. (1998). Historical and comparative institutional analysis. *American Economic Review, Papers and Proceedings, 88*(2), 80–84.

Grindle, M. S., & Thomas, J.W. (1989). Policy makers, policy choices, and policy outcomes: The political economy of reform in developing countries, *Policy Sciences, 22,* 213–248.

Gronewegen, J., Kersthold, F., & Nagelkerke, A. (1995). On integrating new and old institutionalism: Douglass North building bridges, *Journal of Economic Issues, 29*(2), 467–475.

Gulyamov, R. (2011). Further deepening and liberalization of economy in conditions of modernization. In: Institute for Forecasting and Macroeconomic Research (Ed.), *Conceptual directions of further deepening democratic reforms and development of civil society* (pp. 374–377). Tashkent: Uzbekiston.

Haggard, S. & Cheng, T.-J. (1987). State and foreign capital in the East Asian NICs. In: Deyo, F. C. (Ed.) (1987). *The political economy of the new Asian industrialism* (pp. 84–135). Ithaca and London: Cornell University Press.

Haggard, S. (1990). *Pathways from the periphery: The politics of growth in the newly industrializing countries*. Ithaca and London: Cornell University Press.

Haggard, S. (2004). Institutions and growth in East Asia. *Studies in Comparative International Development, 38*(4), 53–81.

Hall, P. A. & Taylor, R. C. R.(1996). Political science and the three new institutionalisms. *Political Studies*, 44, 936–957.

Hall, P. A. (2003). Aligning ontology and methodology in comparative research. In J. Mahoney & D. Rueschemeyer (Eds.), *Comparative historical analysis in the social sciences* (pp. 373–404). Cambridge: Cambridge University Press.

Hall, P. A., & Soskice, D. (2001). *Varieties of capitalism: The institutional foundations of comparative advantage*. Oxford: Oxford University Press.

Hayami, Y. & Aoki, M. (Eds.) (1998). *The institutional foundations of East Asian economic development: Proceedings of the IEA Conference held in Tokyo, Japan (IEA Conference Volume)*. Basingstoke: Palgrave Macmillan.

Hayek, F. A. von (1969). *Freiburger Studien.*Tübingen, Germany: J.C.B. Mohr (Paul Siebeck).

Hechter, M., Matesan, I. E., & Hale, C. (2009). Resistance to alien rule in Taiwan and Korea. *Nations and Nationalism, 15*(1), 36–59. doi: 10.1111/j.1469-8129.2009.00378.x

Heinrich, A. (2010). *The formal political system in Azerbaijan and Kazakhstan: A background study* (Arbeitspapiere und Materialien – No. 107). Bremen: Forschungsstelle Osteuropa.

Herring, R. J. (1999). Embedded particularism: India's failed developmental state. In M. Woo-Cumings (Ed.), *Cornell studies in political economy:*

The developmental state (1st ed., pp. 306–334). Ithaca: Cornell Univ. Press.

Hewison, K. (2002). Thailand: Boom, bust, and recovery. *Perspectives on Global Development & Technolog, 1*(3/4), 225–250.

Hewison, K. (2005). Neo-liberalism and domestic capital: The political outcomes of the economic crisis in Thailand. *The Journal of Development Studies,.41*(2), 310–330. doi: 10.1080/0022038042000309269

Hiro, D. (2009). *Inside Central Asia: A political and cultural history of Uzbekistan, Turkmenistan, Kazakhstan, Kyrgyzstan, Tajikistan, Turkey, and Iran.* New York & London: Overlook Duckworth, Peter Mayer Publishers, Inc.

Hopf, C. (1979). Soziologie und qualitative Sozialforschung. In: C. Hopf & E. Weingarten (Eds.), *Qualitative Sozialforschung* (pp. 11–37). Stuttgart: Klett-Cotta.

Huff, W. G. (1995). The developmental state, government, and Singapore's economic development since 1960. *World Development, Vol. 23*(8), 1421–1438.

Huff, W. G. (1999). Singapore's economic development: Four lessons and some doubts. *Oxford Development Studies, 27*(1), 33–55

Huff, W. G. (2001). Entitlements, destitution, and emigration in the 1930s Singapore great depression. *Economic History Review, 54*(2), 290–323.

Hussy, W., Schreier, M., & Echterhof, G. (2010). *Forschungsmethoden in Psychologie und Sozialwissenschaften.* Berlin: Springer-Verlag.

IMF (2011). *World Economic Outlook Database.* Retrieved October 28, 2011, from http://www.imf.org/external/pubs/ft/weo/2011/02/weodata/index.aspx

Institute for War and Peace Research (2010, June 2). Uzbekistan: Mystery surrounds Zeromax collapse. *Institute for War and Peace Research Reporting.* Retrieved from http://iwpr.net/report-news/uzbekistan-mystery-surrounds-zeromax-collapse

Interfax. (2010, December 3). Kazakhstan has achieved purposes of OSCE presidency. *Central Asia Business News.*

Interfax. (2011a, April 13). Nazarbayev's son-in-law strengthening positions. *Central Asia Business News.*

Interfax. (2011b, April 11). Atameken Union stands a good chance to make a political party. *Central Asia Business News*.

Itoh, M. & Urata, S. (1998). Upgrading technological capabilities of small and medium size enterprises : public and private support in the Japanese and Korean auto parts industries. In: Y. Hayami & M. Aoki (Eds.), *The institutional foundations of East Asian economic development: Proceedings of the IEA Conference held in Tokyo, Japan (IEA Conference Volume)* (pp. 318–346). Basingstoke: Palgrave Macmillan.

Jackson, G. (2001). The origins of nonliberal corporate governance in Germany and Japan. In W. Streeck & K. Yamamura (Eds.): *The origins of nonliberal capitalism: Germany and Japan in comparison* (pp.121–170). Ithaca and London: Cornell University Press.

Johnson, C. (1982). *MITI and the Japanese miracle: The growth of industrial policy, 1925 – 1975*. Stanford, Calif.: Stanford Univ. Press.

Johnson, C. (1983). The "internationalization" of the Japanese Economy. *California Management Review, 15*(3), 5–26.

Johnson, C. (1985). The institutional foundations of Japanese industrial policy. *California Management Review, 27*(4), 59–69.

Johnson, C. (1986). The nonsocialist NICs: East Asia. *International Organization, 40*(2), 557–565.

Johnson, C. (1987). Political institutions and economic performance: The government-business relationship in Japan, South Korea, and Taiwan. In: F. C. Deyo (Ed.), *The Political Economy of the New Asian Industrialism* (pp. 136–164). Ithaca and London: Cornell University Press.

Johnson, C. (1993). Comparative capitalism: The Japanese difference. *California Management Review, 35*(4), 51–67.

Johnson, C. (1999). The developmental state: Odyssey of a concept. In M. Woo-Cumings (Ed.), *Cornell studies in political economy: The developmental state* (1st ed., pp. 32–60). Ithaca: Cornell Univ. Press Jomo, K. S. (Ed.) (2003a). *Southeast Asian Paper Tigers: From miracle to debacle and beyond*. London: RoutledgeCurzon.

Jomo, K. S. & Gomez, E. T. (1997). Rents and development in multiethnic Malaysia. In M. Aoki, H.-K. Kim and M. Okuno-Fujiwara (Eds.), *The Role of Government in East Asian Economic Development: Comparative Institutional Analysis* (1st ed., pp. 342–372). Oxford: Oxford University Press.

Jomo, K. S. & Wee, C. H. (2003). The political economy of Malaysian federalism: Economic development, public policy and conflict containment. *Journal of International Development, 15*, 441–456. doi: 10.1002/jid.995

Jomo, K. S. (2004). Southeast Asian developmental states in comparative perspective. In L. Low (Ed.): *Developmental States: Relevancy, Redundancy or Reconfiguration?* (pp. 57–77). Hauppauge, NY: Nova Science Publishers.

Jomo, K. S. (2006). Pathways through financial crisis: Malaysia. *Global Governance, 12*, 489–505.

Jomo, K. S. and Wee, C.-H. (2003). The political economy of Malaysian federalism: Economic development, public policy and conflict containment. *Journal of International Development, 15*, 441–456. doi: 10.1002/jid.995

Kang, D. C. (1995). South Korean and Taiwanese development and the new institutional economics. *International Organization, 49*(3), 555–587.

Karimov, I. A. (1992). *Uzbekistan: svoi put' obnovleniia I progress [Uzbekistan: Its Own Way of Renovation and Progress]*. Tashkent: Uzbekiston.

Karimov, I. A. (2010, May). *Address by the President of the Republic of Uzbekistan H.E. Mr. Islam Karimov*. Opening Session of the 43rd Annual Meeting of the Board of Governors of the Asian Development Bank.

Kaufmann, D., Kraay, A., & Zoido-Lobatón, P. (1999). Governance matters (World Bank Policy Research Working Paper No. 2196). Washington, D.C.: World Bank.

Kazakhmys (2011). *Governance: Serving the interests of our stakeholders.* Retrieved December 13, 2011, from http://www.kazakhmys.com/en/investors_media/gover nance

Kim, C. N. (2007). *The Korean Presidents: Leadership for nation building.* Norwalk, CT: Eastbridge.

Kim, H.-K. & Ma, J. (1997). The role of government in acquiring technological capability: The case of the petrochemical industry in East Asia. In M. Aoki, H.-K. Kim and M. Okuno-Fujiwara (Eds.), *The role of government in East Asian economic development: Comparative institutional analysis* (1st ed., pp. 101–133). Oxford: Oxford University Press.

Kim, H.-K. (1995). The Japanese civil service and economic development: Lessons for policy makers from other countries. In: H.-K. Kim, M. Muramatsu, T. J. Pempel, & K. Yamamura (eds.), *The Japanese civil service and economic development: Catalysts of change* (pp. 506–539). Oxford: Oxford University Press.

Klevemann, L. (2003). *The new Great Game: Blood and oil in Central Asia.* New York, NY: Grove Press.

Kohli, A. (1994). Where do high-growth political economies come from? The Japanese lineage of Korea's "developmental state". *World Development, 22*(9), 1269–1 293.

Kohli, A. (1999). Where do high-growth political economies come from? The Japanese lineage of Korea's "developmental state". In M. Woo-Cumings (Ed.), *The developmental state* (1st ed., pp. 93–136). Ithaca: Cornell Univ. Press.

Kojima, K. (2000). The "flying geese" model of Asian economic development: origin, theoretical extensions, and regional policy implications. *Journal of Asian Economics, 11*, 375–401.

Koo, H. (1987). The interplay of state, social class, and world system in East Asian development: The cases of South Korea and Taiwan. In: F. C. Deyo (Ed.), *The political economy of the new Asian industrialism* (pp. 165–181). Ithaca and London: Cornell University Press.

Kosai, Y. (1987). The politics of economic management. In: K. Yamamura & Y. Yasuba, *The political economy of Japan: Volume 1 The domestic transformation.* Stanford, CA: Stanford University Press.

Kosai, Y., & Takeuchi, F. (1998). Japan's influence on the East Asian economies. In H. S. Rowen (Ed.), *Behind East Asian growth: the political and social foundations of prosperity* (pp. 297–318). London and New York: Routledge.

Krueger, A. O. (1990). Asian trade and growth lessons. *American Economic Review, Papers and Proceedings, 80*(2), 108–112.

Krueger, A. O. (1993). *Political economy of policy reform in developing countries.* Cambridge, MA and London: The MIT Press.

Krugman, P. (1994). The myth of Asia's miracle. *Foreign Affairs,* 73(6), 62–78.

Kuckartz, U. (2010). *Einführung in die computergestützte Analyse qualitativer Daten* (3rd ed.). Wiesbaden, Germany: VS Verlag für Sozialwissenschaften.

314

Laruelle, M., Huchet, J.-F., Peyrouse, S. & Balci, B. (eds.) (2010). *China and India in Central Asia: A new "Great Game"?* New York, NY: Palgrave Macmillan.

Leftwich, A. (1995). Bringing politics back in: Toward a model of the developmental state. *The Journal of Development Studies, 31*(3), 400–427.

Lehmbruch, G. (2001). The institutional embedding of market economies: The German "model" and its impact on Japan. In W. Streeck & K. Yamamura (Eds.), *The origins of nonliberal capitalism. Germany and Japan in comparison* (pp. 39–93). Ithaca and London: Cornell Univ. Press.

Leitch LePoer, B. (Ed.) (1991). *Singapore: A country study.* Washington, D.C.: Library of Congress.

Libman, A. (2008). *Economic role of public administration in Central Asia: Decentralization and hybrid political regime* (MPRA Paper No. 10940). Retrieved from: http://mpra.ub.uni-muenchen.de/10940/

Libman, A. (2010). Governments and companies in the post-Soviet world: Power, intentions, and institutional consistency. *Eurasian Review, 3*, 41–66.

Low, L. (2004) Singapore's development between a rock and a hard place. In: L. Low (Ed.), *Developmental states: Relevancy, redundancy or reconfiguration?* Hauppauge, NY: Nova Science Publishers.

Luedde-Neurath, R. (1988). State intervention and export-oriented development in South Korea. In G. White (Ed.), *Developmental states in East Asia* (pp. 1–29). New York, NY: St. Martin's Press.

Maddison, A. (2005). Asia in the world economy 1500–2030 AD. *Asian-Pacific Economic Literature, 20*(2), 1–37.

Maddison, A. (2010). *Statistics on world population, GDP and per capita GDP, 1–2008 AD.* Retrieved July 19, 2011, from http://www.ggdc.net/MADDISON/oriindex.htm

Malashenko, A. (2005). Islam, politics, and the security of Central Asia. *Russian Social Science Review, 46*(1), 4–18.

Maratov, A. (2011, May 4). Kazakh presidential advisor calls for dividing power and business. *Trend News Agency.* Retrieved December 15, 2011, from http://en.trend.az /news/politics/1871000.html

Menon, R. (2003). The new Great Game in Central Asia. *Survival, 45*(2), 187–204.

Minns, J. (2001). Of miracles and models: the rise and decline of the developmental state in South Korea. *Third World Quarterly, 22*(6), 1025–1043. doi: 10.1080/014365901200997 77

Muramatsu, M., & Krauss, E. S. (1987). The conservative policy line and the development of patterned pluralism. In: K. Yamamura & Y. Yasuba, *The political economy of Japan: Volume 1 The domestic transformation*. Stanford, CA: Stanford University Press.

Najibullah, F. (2010, June 16). The demise of Uzbekistan's cash cow Zeromax. *Radio Free Europe/Radio Liberty*. Retrieved from http://www.rferl.org/ content/Zeroing_In_On_The_Demise_Of_Uzbekistans_Cash_Cow/ 2073867.html

Nazarbaev, N. A. (1997). Strategy 2030: Prosperity, security and ever growing welfare of all the Kazakhstanis. Message of the President of the country to the people of Kazakhstan. Retrieved July 30, 2011 from http://www.akorda.kz/en/kazakhstan /kazakhstan2030 /strategy_2030

Nazarbayev, N. A. (2008, February). *Growth of welfare of Kazakhstan's citizens is the primary goal of state policy*. Address by the President of the Republic of Kazakhstan H.E. Mr. Nursultan Nazarbayev to the people of Kazakhstan. Retrieved October 15, 2011, from http://www.akorda.kz/en/speeches/addresses_of_the_president_of_ kazakhstan

Neef, C. (2011, April 2). Nervöser Nasarbajew verordnet seinem Volk eine Blitzwahl. *Spiegel Online*. Retrieved from http://www.spiegel.de

Ng, C. V., Sudo, S., & Crone, D. (1992). The strategic dimension of the "East Asian developmental states". *ASEAN Economic Bulletin, 9* (2), 219–233.

Niskanen, W. A. (1968). Nonmarket decision making: The peculiar economics of bureaucracy. *The American Economic Review, Papers and Proceedings, 58*(2), 293–305.

North, D. C. (1990). *Institutions, institutional change and economic performance* (27. print.). *Political economy of institutions and decisions*. New York: Cambridge University Press.

North, D.C. (1991). Institutions. *Journal of Economic Perspectives, 5*(1), 97–112.

316

North, D.C. (1992). Institutions, ideology, and economic performance. *Cato Journal, 11*(3), 477–496.

North, D.C. (1994). Economic performance through time. *American Economic Review, 84*(3), 359–386.

North, D.C.,& Weingast, B. R. (1989). Constitutions and commitment: The evolution of institutions governing public choice in seventeenth-century England. *Journal of Economic History, 49*(4), 803–832.

Olcott, M. B.l (1992). Central Asia's catapult to independence. *Foreign Affairs, 71*(3), 108–130.

Olson, M. L. (1964). *The logic of collective action: Public goods and the theory of groups.* Cambridge, MA: Harvard University Press.

Olson, M. L. (1982). *The rise and decline of nations: Economic growth, stagflation, and social rigidities.* New Haven: Yale Univ. Press.

OSCE (2011). *Republic of Kazakhstan early Presidential election 3 April 2011* (OSCE/ ODIHR Election Observation Mission Final Report). Warsaw: OSCE.

Ostapenko, E. (2011, July 5). Renewed "Akjol" party capable of joining Kazakh parliament. *Trend News Agency.* Retrieved December 15, 2011, from http://pda.trend.az /en/1900662.html

Pannier, B. (2009). *Nations in transit 2009: Uzbekistan.* Freedom House: Nations in Transit. Retrieved from http://www.freedomhouse.org/ template.cfm?page=485

Pannier, B. (2011). *Nations in Transit 2011: Uzbekistan* (pp 605–623). Freedom House: Nations in Transit. Retrieved from http://www.freedomhouse.org /images/File/nit /2011/NIT-2011-Uzbekistan.pdf

Patrick, H. (1977). The future of the Japanese economy: Output and labor productivity, *Journal of Japanese Studies, 3*(2), 219–249.

Pempel, T. J. (1999). The developmental regime in a changing world economy. In: M. Woo-Cumings (Ed.), *The developmental state* (1st ed., pp. 137–181). Ithaca: Cornell Univ. Press.

Pereira, A. A., & Tong, C. K. (2005). Power and developmental regimes in Singapore, China and Malaysia. *Global Economic Review, 34*(1), 129–144. doi: 10.1080/122650804200032 8980

Perkins, D. H. (1994). There are at least three models of Asian development. *World Development, 22*(4), 655–661.

Perlman, B. J., & Gleason, G. (2005). Comparative perspectives on third generation reform: Realignment and misalignment in Central Asian reform programs. *International Public Management Review*, 6(1), 100–116. Retrieved from: http://www.ipmr.net

Perlman, B. J., & Gleason, G. (2007). Cultural determinism versus administrative logic: Asian values and administrative reform in Kazakhstan and Uzbekistan. *International Journal of Public Administration, 30*, 1327–1342.

Pirie, I. (2008). *The Korean developmental state: From dirigisme to neoliberalism* (Vol. 73). *Routledge studies in the growth economies of Asia, 73.* London: Routledge.

Pomfret, R. (1995). *The economies of Central Asia.* Princeton, NJ: Princeton University Press.

Pomfret, R. (2000). The Uzbek model of economic development, 1991–1999. *Economics of Transition, 8*(3), 733–748.

Pomfret, R. (2003). *Central Asia since 1991: The experience of the new independent states* (OECD Development Centre Working Paper No. 212). Paris: OECD.

Pomfret, R. (2005). Kazakhstan's economy since independence: Does the oil boom offer a second chance for sustainable development? *Europe-Asia Studies, 57*(6), 859–876. doi: 10.1080/09668130500199467

Pomfret, R. (2006). *The Central Asian economies since independence.* Princeton and Oxford: Princeton University Press.

Pomfret, R. (2007). Central Asia since the dissolution of the Soviet Union: Economic reforms and their impact on state-society relations. *Perspectives on Global Development and Technology, 6*, 313–343. doi: 10.1163/156914907X207775

Pomfret, R. (2010a). Constructing market-based economies in central Asia: A natural experiment? *The European Journal of Comparative Economics, 7*(2), 449–467.

Pomfret, R. (2010b). *Central Asia after two decades of independence* (UNU-Wider Working Paper No. 2010/53). Helsinki: United Nations University World Institute for Development Economics Research.

Quian, Y. & Weingast, B. R. (1997). Institutions, state activism, and economic development: A comparison of state-owned and township-village enterprises in China. In M. Aoki, H.-K. Kim and M. Okuno-Fujiwara

318

(Eds.), *The role of government in East Asian economic development: Comparative institutional analysis* (1st ed., pp. 254–275). Oxford, UK: Oxford University Press.

Raphael, J. H., & Rohlen, T. P. (1998). How many models of Japanese growth do we want or need? In H. S. Rowen (Ed.), *Behind east asian growth: the political and social foundations of prosperity* (pp. 265–296). London and New York: Routledge.

Rasiah, R. (2003). Manufacturing export growth in Indonesia, Malaysia and Thailand. In: K. S. Jomo (Ed.), *Southeast Asian Paper Tigers: From miracle to debacle and beyond* (pp. 19–80). London: RoutledgeCurzon.

Reppegather, A. & Troschke, M. (2006). *Graduelle Transformation von Wirtschaftsordnungen: Ein Vergleich der Reformstrategien Chinas und Usbekistans* (Working Paper Nr. 260). München: Osteuropa-Institut.

Rock, M. T. (1995). Thai industrial policy: How irrelevant was it to export success? *Journal of International Development, 7*(5), 745–757.

Rodrik, D. (1995). Getting interventions right: how South Korea and Taiwan grew rich. *Economic Policy, 10*(20), 53–107.

Rodrik, D. (1996). Understanding economic policy reform. *Journal of Economic Literature, 34,* 9–41.

Roland, G. (2004). Understanding institutional change: Fast-moving and slow-moving institutions, *Studies in Comparative International Development, 38*(4), 109–131.

Root, H. L. & Weingast, B. R. (1996). The state's role in East Asian development. In H. L. Root (1996), *Small countries, big lessons: Governance and the rise of East Asia* (pp. 139–144). Hong Kong: Oxford Univ. Press.

Root, H. L. (1996). *Small countries, big lessons: Governance and the rise of East Asia.* Hong Kong: Oxford University Press.

Root, H. L. (1998). Distinctive institutions in the rise of industrial Asia. In H. S. Rowen (Ed.), *Behind East Asian growth: the political and social foundations of prosperity* (pp. 60–77). London and New York: Routledge.

Rowen, H. S. (1998). The political and social foundations of the rise of East Asia: an overview. In H. S. Rowen (Ed.), *Behind East Asian growth: the political and social foundations of prosperity* (pp. 1–36). London and New York: Routledge.

Saidova (2010, June). *The Uzbek economy during the global financial crisis and post-crisis period*. Presentation at the 7th Economic and Social Reform Policy Dialogue Forum, Tashkent.

Sam, C.-Y. (2008). Partial privatization, corporate governance, and the role of state-owned holding companies. *Journal of the Asia Pacific Economy, 13*(1), 58–81. doi: 10.1080 /13547860701731895

Samruk-Kazyna (2011). *Subsidiary companies*. Retrieved December 13, 2011, from http:// www.sk.kz/company/indicators

Scharff, R. (2010). Kasachstan: Aktuelle Wirtschaftslage und wirtschaftspolitische Strategie. *Zentralasienanalysen, 26*, 2–12. Retrieved from http://www.laender-analysen.de/zentral asien/archiv.html

Schatz, E. (2004). Modern clan politics: The power of "blood" in Kazakhstan and beyond. Seattle, WA: University of Washington Press.

Schiek, S. & Hensell, S. (forthcoming February 2012). Seeing like a President: The Dilemma of Inclusion in Kazakhstan. In S. Stewart, M. Klein, A. Schmitz, & H.-H- Schröder (Eds.), Presidents, Oligarchs and Bureaucrats: Forms of Rule in the Post-Soviet Space. Farnham: Ashgate.

Schmitz, A. (2009). *Kasachstan: Neue Führungsmacht im postsowjetischen Raum?* (SWP-Studie). Berlin.

Schreier, M. (forthcoming February 2012). *Qualitative content analysis in practice*. London: Sage Publications.

Schumpeter, J.A. (1938). *The theory of economic development*. Cambridge, Mass.: Harvard University Press.

Shin, J.-S. (2005). Globalization and challenges to the developmental state: A comparison between South Korea and Singapore. *Global Economic Review, 34(4)*, 379–395.

Shirk, S. L. (1993). *The political logic of economic reform in China*. Berkeley, CA: University of California Press.

Silberman, B. S. (1966). Criteria for recruitment and success in the Japanese bureaucracy, 1868–1900: "Traditional" and "modern" criteria in bureaucratic development. *Economic Development and Cultural Change, 14*(2), 158–173.

Silberman, B. S. (1967). Bureaucratic development and the structure of decision-making in the Meiji period: The case of the genrō. *Journal of Asian Studies, 27*(1), 81–94.

Silberman, B. S. (1970). Bureaucratic development and the structure of decision-making in Japan: 1868–1925. *Journal of Asian Studies, 29*(2), 347–362.

Silberman, B. S. (1995). The structure of bureaucratic rationality and economic development in Japan. In: H.-K. Kim, M. Muramatsu, T. J. Pempel, & K. Yamamura (eds.), *The Japanese civil service and economic development: Catalysts of change* (pp. 135–173). Oxford: Oxford University Press.

Simon, G. (2009). Market reforms and "economic miracle" in Kazakhstan. *Economic Annals, 54*(182). doi: 10.2298/EKA0982067S

Spechler, D. R. & Spechler, M. C. (2010). The foreign policy of Uzbekistan: sources, objectives and outcomes: 1991–2009. *Central Asian Survey, 29*(2), 159–170. doi: 10.1080/02634937.2010.490679

Spechler, M. C. (2000a). Hunting for the Central Asian tiger. *Comparative Economic Studies, 42*(3), 101–102.

Spechler, M. C. (2000b). Uzbekistan: The silk road to nowhere? *Contemporary Economic Policy,18*(3), 295–303.

Spechler, M. C. (2003). Returning to convertibility in Uzbekistan? *Policy Reform, 6*(1), 51–56. doi: 10.1080/1384128032000101420

Spechler, M. C. (2004). Central Asia on the edge of globalization. *Challenge, 47*(3), 62–77.

Spechler, M. C. (2008a). The economies of Central Asia: A survey. *Comparative Economic Studies, 50*, 30–52.

Spechler, M. C. (2008b). *The political economy of reform in Central Asia: Uzbekistan under authoritarianism,* Oxford and New York: Routledge.

Stevens, D. (2007). Political society and civil society in Uzbekistan—never the twain shall meet? *Central Asian Survey, 26* (1), 49–64. doi: 10.1080/02634930701423467

Stiglitz, J. E. & Uy, M. (1996). Financial markets, public policy, and the East Asian miracle. *The World Bank Research Observer, 11*(2), 249–276.

Stiglitz, J. E. (1996). Some lessons from the East Asian miracle. *The World Bank Research Observer, 11*(2), 151–177.

Streeck, W., & Yamamura, K. (2003). Introduction: Convergence or diversity? Stability and Change in German and Japanese Capitalism. In: K. Yamamura & W. Streeck (Eds.) (2003), *The end of diversity? Prospects for German and Japanese capitalism*. Ithaca and London: Cornell Univ. Press.

Streeck, W., & Yamamura, K. (Eds.) (2001). *The origins of nonliberal capitalism: Germany and Japan in comparison*. Ithaca and London: Cornell Univ. Press.

Tan, J. (2009). Can the East Asian Developmental State be Replicated? The Case of Malaysia. In: R. Springborg (Ed.), *Development models in Muslim contexts: Chinese, 'islamic' and neo-liberal alternatives*. Edinburgh: Edinburgh University Press.

Thelen, K. (1999). Historical institutionalism in comparative politics. *Annual Review of Political Science, 2*, 369–404. doi: 10.1146/annurev.polisci.2.1.369

Thompson, M. R. (1996). Late industrialisers, late democratisers: developmental states in the Asia-Pacific. *Third World Quarterly 17*(4), 625–647.

Thomson, C. N. (1993). Political identity among Chinese in Thailand. *Geographical Review, 83*(4), 397–409.

Uznews (2010, May 14). Court shuts presidential daughter-owned Zeromax's operations in Uzbekistan. Retrieved from Uznews.net

Vartiainen, J. (1999). The economics of successful state intervention in industrial transformation. In: M. Woo-Cumings (Ed.), *The developmental state* (1st ed., pp. 200–234). Ithaca: Cornell Univ. Press.

Voigt, S., & Kiwit, D. (1995). *Black markets, Mafiosi and the prospects for economic development in Russia: analyzing the interplay of external and internal institutions* (Diskussionsbeitrag Band 5). Jena: Max-Planck-Institut zur Erforschung von Wirtschaftssystemen.

Vu, T. (2007). State formation and the origins of developmental states in South Korea and Indonesia. *Studies in Comparative International Development, 41*(4), 27–56.

Wade, R. H. (1988). State intervention in 'outward-looking' development: Neoclassical theory and Taiwanese practice. In G. White (Ed.), *Developmental states in East Asia* (pp. 1–29). New York, NY: St. Martin's Press.

Wade, R. H. (1990/2004). *Governing the market: Economic theory and the role of government in East Asian industrialization; with a new introduction by the author* (2. pbk. ed. with a new introduction from the author, 2004). Princeton, NJ: Princeton Univ. Press.

Wade, R. H. (2008). How can middle-income countries escape 'gravity' and catch up with high-income countries? The case for open economy industrial policy. *Halduskultuur*, *9*, 12–29.

Weber, M. (1922/1985). *Wirtschaft und Gesellschaft: Grundriss der verstehenden Soziologie*. 5th, revised edition (Studienausgabe). Tübingen, Germany: J.C.B. Mohr (Paul Siebeck).

White, G., & Wade, R. (1988). Developmental states and markets in East Asia: an introduction. In G. White (Ed.), *Developmental States in East Asia* (pp. 1–29). New York, NY: St. Martin's Press.

Williamson, J. (1990). What Washington means by policy reform. In: J. Williamson (ed.), *Latin American adjustment: How much has happened?* (pp. 5–20). Washington, D.C.: Institute for International Economics.

Williamson, O. E. (1971). The vertical integration of production: Market failure considerations. *American Economic Review, Papers and Proceedings, 61*, 112–123.

Williamson, O. E. (1975). *Markets and hierarchies: Analysis and antitrust implications*. New York, NY: The Free Press.

Williamson, O. E. (1985). *The economic institutions of capitalism: Firms, markets, Relational contracting*. New York, NY: The Free Press.

Williamson, O. E. (2000). The New Institutional Economics: Taking stock, looking ahead. *Journal of Economic Literature, 38*, 595–613.

Wolfel, R. L. (2002). North to Astana: Nationalistic motives for the movement of the Kazakh(stani) capital. *Nationalities Papers, Vol. 30*(3), 485–506. doi: 10.1080/00 90599022000011723

Woo-Cumings, M. (1995). Developmental bureaucracy in comparative perspective: The evolution of the Korean civil service. In: H.-K. Kim, M. Muramatsu, T. J. Pempel, & K. Yamamura (eds.), *The Japanese civil service and economic development: Catalysts of change* (pp. 431–458). Oxford: Clarendon Press.

Woo-Cumings, M. (1998). National security and the rise of the developmental state in South Korea and Taiwan. In H. S. Rowen (Ed.), *Behind East Asian growth: the political and social foundations of prosperity* (pp. 319–337). London and New York: Routledge.

Woo-Cumings, M. (1999). Introduction: Chalmers Johnson and the politics of nationalism and development. In M. Woo-Cumings (Ed.), *Cornell studies in political economy: The developmental state* (1st ed., pp. 1–31). Ithaca: Cornell Univ. Press.

World Bank (1991). *World development report 1991: The challenge of development.* Oxford: Oxford University Press. Retrieved from: http://www.worldbank.org/ reference/

World Bank (1993). *The East Asian miracle: Economic growth and public policy. A world bank policy research report.* Oxford: Oxford Univ. Press.

World Bank (1997). *Kazakstan: Transition of the state* (World Bank country study 16388). Washington, D.C.: World Bank.

World Bank (2005). *Kazakhstan: Reforming the public sector wage system* (Report No. 31707-KZ). Washington, D.C.: World Bank.

World Bank (2011a). *World development indicators.* Retrieved August 30, 2011, from http:// data.worldbank.org/data-catalog/world-development-indicators

World Bank (2011b) *Worldwide governance indicators.* Retrieved October 14, 2011, from http://info.worldbank.org/governance/wgi/index.asp

Yamamura, K. (1995). The role of government in Japan's 'catch-up' industrialization: A neoinstitutionalist perspective. In: H.-K. Kim, M. Muramatsu, T. J. Pempel, & K. Yamamura (Eds.), *The Japanese civil service and economic development: Catalysts of change* (pp. 102–132). Oxford: Clarendon Press.

Yamamura, K., & Streeck, W. (Eds.) (2003). *The end of diversity? Prospects for German and Japanese capitalism.* Ithaca and London: Cornell Univ. Press.

Yasuba, Y. and L. Dhiravegin (1985) Initial conditions, institutional changes, policy, and their consequences: Siam and Japan, 1850–1914. In: K. Ohkawa and G. Ranis (eds), *Japan and the developing countries: A comparative analysis* (pp. 19–34). Oxford: Basil Blackwell.

Young, A. (1995). The tyranny of numbers: Confronting the statistical realities of the East Asian growth experience. *The Quarterly Journal of Economics, 110*(3), 641–680.

Zardykhan, Z. (2004). Russians in Kazakhstan and demographic change: Imperial legacy and the Kazakh way of nation building. *Asian Ethnicity, 5*(1), 61–79. doi: 10.1080/14631360 32000168907

Zelditch, M. Jr. (1979). Methodologische Probleme in der Feldforschung. In: C. Hopf & E. Weingarten (Eds.), *Qualitative Sozialforschung* (pp. 119–137). Stuttgart: Klett-Cotta.

Appendix A: Code system research project *Emerging Market Economies*

Actors
        International Organizations
        Major players in the economy
        Political decision makers
Background information
        Information on activities of company/organization of interviewee
        Information on interviewee
Economic Outlook
Functioning of state-owned companies
Functioning of the market economy
        Ease of doing business
        Accountability of private actors
        Corporate Governance
            Relationship with owners/shareholders
            Financing of companies
        Education and vocational training
        Industrial Relations
            Wage-setting process
            Employer Associations
            Unions
        Inter-Firm Relations
            Relationship with clients
            Relationship with suppliers
            Relationship with competitors
        Intra-Firm relations
        Openness of markets
            Possibility of foreign take-over
            Competition
            Openness of markets for new domestic competitors
            Openness to cross border trade
            Openness to FDI
                Welcomed in all sectors
                    No
                    Yes
Industry-specific information
        Other
        Services
        Natural Resources
        Financial Sector
Kazakhstan
Participation
        State-business nexus
            Information exchange
            Organizations
        Decision making power of bureaucrats/lower ranking politicians
            Absolutely no independence
            Limited independence
Path Dependency
        Cultural Legacy
        Soviet legacy

Role of the state
    Reference Model
        Foreign reference
            China
            India
            Mercantilist
            Fully eclectic
            East Asia in general
                Taiwan
                Malaysia
                Singapore
                Japan
                South Korea
            Western Countries
            Turkey
            Russia
        No similarities to other countries
    Objectives of state intervention
    Consistency of economic policy
    Constraints for political decision makers
    Institutions and Organizations of the public administration
        Accountability of Government/ Bureaucratic actors
            No answer
            Ambiguous answer
            Accountable toward the public
                Rather No
                Rather Yes
            Accountable toward superiors
                Rather No
                Rather Yes
        Transparency of state action
            Promotion Process
            Recruitment Process
        Predictability of state action
    Macroeconomic steering and industrial policy
        Price controls
        Promotion of long-term commitment
        Promotion of specific sectors
        Diversification
    Macroeconomic steering capability
    Monetary policy and stability
    Rule of law and enforcement of rules
        Mechanisms for rule enforcement
            Informal mechanisms
            Formal mechanisms
        Security of property rights
            Positive influence of foreign ownership
                Ambiguous
                Rather no
                Rather yes
            Evaluation Property Rights
            Examples of expropriations
        General enforcement of rules
Social security system

Appendix B: Information on interviewees from focus groups (a) and (b)

Kazakhstan

Interviewee	Date of Interview	Background of Interviewee	Origin of Interviewee
K(a)1	September 2009	International Organizations	Kazakhstan
K(a)2	October 2009	International Organizations	Kazakhstan
K(a)3	October 2009	International Organizations	Western country
K(a)4	October 2009	International Organizations	Western country
K(a)5	October 2009	Political/Economic Analysis	Kazakhstan
K(a)6	October 2009	Other	Western country
K(a)7	November 2009	Other	Western country
K(a)8	November 2009	Political/Economic Analysis	Kazakhstan
K(a)9	November 2009	Academia	Kazakhstan
K(a)10	November 2009	Political/Economic Analysis	Kazakhstan
K(a)11	November 2009	International Organizations	Western country
K(a)12	November 2009	Political/Economic Analysis	Kazakhstan
K(a)13	November 2009	International Organizations	Western country
K(a)14	March 2010	International Organizations	Western country
K(a)15	April 2010	Other	Kazakhstan
K(a)16	April 2010	Political/Economic Analysis	Kazakhstan
K(a)17	April 2010	Other	Kazakhstan
K(a)18	May 2010	Other	Other
K(a)19	May 2010	Other	Kazakhstan
K(a)20	May 2010	Other	Western country
K(a)21	May 2010	Other	Western country
K(a)22	May 2010	Academia	Western country
K(a)23	June 2010	Other	Kazakhstan
K(a)24	June 2010	Other	Western country
K(a)25	June 2010	International Organizations	Kazakhstan
K(a)26	July 2010	Other	Western country
K(a)27	September 2010	Other	Kazakhstan
K(a)28	May 2010	International Organizations	Kazakhstan
K(a)29	October 2009	Other	Kazakhstan
K(a)30	March 2010	Other	Kazakhstan
K(b)1	April 2010	Public Official	Kazakhstan
K(b)2	April 2010	Public Official	Kazakhstan
K(b)3	April 2010	Public Official	Kazakhstan
K(b)4	May 2010	Public Official	Kazakhstan
K(b)5	October 2010	Public Official	Kazakhstan
K(b)6	October 2010	Public Official	Kazakhstan
K(b)7	June 2010	Public Official	Kazakhstan
K(b)8	May 2010	Public Official	Kazakhstan

Uzbekistan

Interviewee	Date of Interview	Background of Interviewee	Origin of Interviewee
U(a)1	October 2009	International Organizations	Western country
U(a)2	November 2009	International Organizations	Other
U(a)3	December 2009	Other	Western country
U(a)4	May 2010	Foreign Relations	Western country
U(a)5	April 2010	Other	Uzbekistan
U(a)6	April 2010	Political/Economic Analysis	Uzbekistan
U(a)7	April 2010	Academia	Uzbekistan
U(a)8	April 2010	International Organizations	Uzbekistan
U(a)9	May 2010	International Organizations	Uzbekistan
U(a)10	May 2010	International Organizations	Uzbekistan
U(a)11	June 2010	Academia	Uzbekistan
U(a)12	June 2010	Other	Uzbekistan
U(a)13	July 2010	Foreign Relations	Western country
U(a)14	July 2010	Other	Uzbekistan
U(a)15	July 2010	Foreign Relations	Western country
U(a)16	July 2010	Other	Uzbekistan
U(a)17	November 2010	Other	Uzbekistan
U(a)18	November 2010	Other	Uzbekistan
U(a)19	November 2010	Other	Uzbekistan
U(a)20	November 2010	International Organizations	Uzbekistan
U(a)21	October 2009	International Organizations	East Asia
U(a)22	January 2010	Other	Uzbekistan
U(a)23	May 2010	Foreign Relations	Other
U(a)24	May 2010	Foreign Relations	Western country
U(a)25	June 2010	International Organizations	Western country
U(a)26	March 2011	Other	Uzbekistan
U(a)27	November 2009	International Organization	East Asia
U(b)1	November 2010	Public Official	Uzbekistan
U(b)2	November 2010	Public Official	Uzbekistan
U(b)3	November 2010	Public Official	Uzbekistan
U(b)4	November 2010	Public Official	Uzbekistan
U(b)5	December 2010	Public Official	Uzbekistan
U(b)6	December 2010	Public Official	Uzbekistan
U(b)7	December 2010	Public Official	Uzbekistan
U(b)8	December 2010	Public Official	Uzbekistan
U(b)9	December 2010	Public Official	Uzbekistan
U(b)10	December 2010	Public Official	Uzbekistan
U(b)11	February 2011	Public Official	Uzbekistan
U(b)12	March 2011	Public Official	Uzbekistan
U(b)13	March 2011	Public Official	Uzbekistan
U(b)14	March 2011	Public Official	Uzbekistan

Emerging Markets Studies

Edited by Joachim Ahrens, Alexander Ebner, Herman W. Hoen, Bernhard Seliger and Ralph Michael Wrobel

The Peter Lang series *Emerging Markets Studies* includes works which address opportunities, problems, and challenges of socio-economic development and reform in so-called emerging markets. These comprise middle-income developing and transition economies which are relevant for the world economy due to a large market potential, a favorable or improving investment climate, or due to the availability of important natural resources. Emerging markets have realized or show the potential to generate sustained socio-economic development and growth processes over time.

The volumes in this series seek to address three key questions: What are the determinants of successful socio-economic development, What are appropriate reform strategies to overcome impediments to catching-up processes, and How do politico-institutional factors affect the performance of an emerging economy?

The scope of the series is comparative, institutionalist, and international. The overall focus of all titles is to enhance the understanding of socio-economic catching-up processes and their institutional foundations from a political-economy perspective. Due to the complexity of development processes and policy reform, various methodological tools and academic approaches may prove to be appropriate. Hence the series includes contributions from various disciplines such as economics, political science, or sociology.

www.peterlang.de